Baseball's
GREATEST SERIES

Baseball's
GREATEST SERIES

Yankees, Mariners,

and the

1995 Matchup

That Changed History

CHRIS DONNELLY

RIVERGATE BOOKS
An Imprint of Rutgers University Press
NEW BRUNSWICK, NEW JERSEY, AND LONDON

Second printing, 2010

Library of Congress Cataloging-in-Publication Data

Donnelly, Chris
Baseball's greatest series : Yankees, Mariners, and the 1995 matchup that changed history / Chris Donnelly.
p. cm.
Includes bibliographical references and index.
ISBN 978-0-8135-4662-9 (hardcover : alk. paper)
1. New York Yankees (Baseball team)—History—Sources. 2. Seattle Mariners (Baseball team)—History—
Sources. 3. Sports rivalries—United States—History—Sources. I. Title.
GV875.N4D66 2010
796.357'640973—dc22
2009016195
A British Cataloging-in-Publication record for this book is available from the British Library.

Visit our Web site: http://rutgerspress.rutgers.edu

To Jamie,
without whom this book would never have been written.
You are the best.

In loving memory of Christopher Martin Singer.
"Big" would have really enjoyed this book.

CONTENTS

PREFACE

Of all the places to be on Sunday, October 8, 1995, I, a lifelong Yankee fan, was in Boston. It was Columbus Day weekend, and I spent it visiting my aunt in New England. For the first time since I began following baseball, the Yankees were in the playoffs, going up against the Seattle Mariners in the Division Series. The first four games had been beyond anything I expected. Game 2 lasted until 1:15 in the morning, and even though I had school the next day, I stayed up to watch every minute. Jim Leyritz's game-winning home run seemed like the greatest moment I had ever witnessed in sports. But the Yankees blew a two-games-to-none lead and now a decisive Game 5 was being played this Sunday night. After a day of visiting tourist attractions in Beantown, I settled into my aunt's living room and forced her, my uncle, and father (all Mets fans) to watch the Yankees. Game 5 was excruciating. Up by two runs in the eighth inning, the Yankees lost the lead, and the game went into extra innings. When the Yankees went ahead in the eleventh inning, I was already figuring out who would pitch Game 1 of the ALCS for New York. But in the bottom of the inning, the Mariners, as they had all season, battled back. A bunt base hit and a seeing-eye single brought Edgar Martinez to the plate with the series-winning run on first base. It was a nightmare. Martinez had a history of killing the Yankees. Admittedly I am a pessimist, but certainly I wasn't alone in thinking this could only end one way for the Yankees: badly. On an 0–1 splitter, Martinez lined a double down the left-field line, easily tying the game. While some may have hoped the Yankees could throw out Ken Griffey Jr. at the plate and keep the series alive, I was not one of them. I knew he would score. He had to. Griffey killed the Yankees even more than Martinez did, so why wouldn't he do this to us again? As Griffey slid into home plate to win the game, I slowly got up, walked into the room where I was staying, and lay down on the guest bed. Before I knew it, I was crying my eyes out. Uncontrollably sobbing like I never had before. In an era before the Yankees seemingly made the playoffs every year, it felt as though their only chance to ever win another World Series had just vanished in mere seconds. That night was the last time I cried over sports.

The 1995 Division Series between the Yankees and Mariners was the best baseball I have ever witnessed. The drama on the field was matched by the drama off. George Steinbrenner spent the week lashing out at anyone whom he felt was shortchanging the Yankees, from players to umpires to team owners. Meanwhile, the Mariners were fighting for their very existence, as their owners had threatened to move the team if a new stadium was not built. For years I had reminisced fondly on that series, even though the Yankees had lost. The success of both teams in the years since then, however, seemingly erased the memory of that series in the minds of many baseball fans. In the fall of 2006, I finally decided (with a little prodding from my wife) that it was time to remind people just how exciting the 1995 series was and that its impact was still being felt over a decade later. As I began to interview those who had actually played a role in the series, I learned I was not alone in my way of thinking. Many members of the '95 Mariners could not stop talking about their fond memories of that season. Additionally, many of the '95 Yankees had equally fond memories, particularly of their teammates, many of whom they never played with again after Edgar Martinez doubled down the left-field line. I hope they and baseball fans across the country enjoy reading this book as much as I did writing it, for the story of this series is truly one of heartbreak, comebacks, rebirth, and redemption.

ACKNOWLEDGMENTS

This book would not have been possible without the help and support of many people: my mother, Sandy, who took me to my first World Series victory parade; my father, Tim, who took me to Cooperstown every summer for Hall of Fame weekend; my brothers, Tim and Mike; my brother-in-law, Glenn; my sisters-in-law, Jen, Julie, and Taylor; my mother- and father-in-law, Karen and Roy; my second parents, Marty and Donna; and the Donnellys, Kassabs, Praschils, Leahys, Dudases, Salzanos, Kennedys, and O'Connors. For their nonstop support, my thanks to all of my friends, from the people I knew back at Lincoln School to those I have come to know through college and work.

The cooperation of the following people, who put up with constant phone calls and emails, is deeply appreciated: Jay Horwitz, Lauren Moran, Mike McNally, Terry Galbraith Brown, Kate Manchester, Ray Schulte, Martin Coco, Martin McNeal, Lilly Walters Schermerhorn, Jamie Ramsey, Joe Bick, Amy Summers, JoAnn Poysky, Melissa Geraghty, Steven Fehr, Jeff at Branded Solutions, Alan Nero, Bart Swain, Kevin McLaughlin, Ben VanHouten, Gordon Engelhardt, Russ Spielman, Pat O'Connell, Dan O'Connor, and Ben at the Hall of Fame.

I would especially like to thank four people. My editor, Beth Kressel, guided me through this process. Writing a book was a bit harder than I thought. At first, I wanted to include every single piece of information I could. Fortunately, Beth taught me how to streamline. She could not have been easier to work with. Molan Goldstein, who went through hundreds of pages of text to fine-tune the manuscript, also deserves my appreciation. Lastly, Tim Hevly and Kelly Munroe of the Seattle Mariners were incredibly helpful and cooperative in setting up interviews with various current and former Seattle Mariners. Tim and Kelly are complete professionals, and the hospitality they, as well as various other members of the Mariners, showed me was appreciated more than they will ever know.

Baseball's
GREATEST SERIES

1

Don-nie Base-ball

"There are certain people you cheer for, and Mattingly was one of them. He is the Yankees."   Jay Buhner

The crowd was still in a frenzy as Donald Arthur Mattingly strode to the plate moments after his teammate, Ruben Sierra, homered into the right-center-field bleachers. It was the second game of the 1995 Division Series between the Yankees and the Mariners, and it was now tied at 2. Sierra's shot, a high drive off a breaking ball, had incited an already-overcharged crowd of 57,126 at Yankee Stadium.

For any team—for its players, its owners, and, of course, its fans—postseason play is an especially exciting and urgent time of year. But for these two teams in this particular year, the games took on special significance. After years of mediocrity and downright failure, the Yankees and the Mariners were each hoping for redemption in 1995. And more was at stake than each team's baseball honor. There were players' and coaches' contracts on the line, and the Mariners found themselves fighting for their very home in the heart of Washington State. Franchise and individual interests aside, on a national level, fans' feelings about baseball had reached an all-time low, so playing heart-stopping, drama-filled baseball became important from a business perspective that transcended the interests of each team and was urgent for the very salvation of Major League Baseball.

No player or person was more representative of what these post-season games meant to New York, and arguably to all lovers of baseball in its purist form, than Don Mattingly. Nicknamed "Donnie Baseball" by the Minnesota Twins' Kirby Puckett, Mattingly was born and raised in Evansville, Indiana, a town of over 100,000 located on the Ohio River. Growing up, he'd shown an affinity for both baseball and basketball. Ultimately, baseball won out as he was selected nineteenth overall in the 1979 draft by the Yankees. He made his Major League debut as a left fielder on September 8, 1982, a year after New York lost the World Series to the Dodgers. Gradually, Mattingly saw more playing time, particularly at first base. In 1984, he emerged as one of the game's best hitters. That year he batted .343, besting teammate Dave Winfield on the final day of the season for the American League batting title. In 1985, Mattingly drove in 145 runs, hit thirty-five home runs, batted .324, and won the first of nine Gold Gloves he would earn at first base. He also captured the American League's Most Valuable Player award, the first Yankee to win it since 1976. Personal success, however, was overcome by the Yankees' inability to reach the playoffs for a fourth straight season. Despite ninety-seven victories, New York finished two games behind the Toronto Blue Jays for the American League East division title. It was the closest Mattingly came to the postseason for nearly a decade.

In 1986, Mattingly set a Yankees record with 238 hits, batted .352, won another Gold Glove, and finished second in the MVP voting. The Yankees also finished second that year, losing the division to the Red Sox. In 1987, Mattingly tied a Major League record by hitting a home run in eight consecutive games. He also set a Major League record by hitting six grand slams in a season. During the 1989 season, he drove in 113 runs and made the last of his six All-Star Game appearances. That season marked the end of Mattingly's six-year stretch as the greatest hitter in baseball. Yet, during that time, despite all the personal accolades and achievements, the Yankees never made the postseason. Instead, the team got progressively worse as the decade went along. By 1990, the Yankees were in complete disarray, finishing an American League worst 67–95. Not only was the team awful, but Mattingly, their only legitimate star, finally succumbed to a back injury he had first experienced in 1987. His back had been problematic ever since, and by 1990 it was so bad that he was forced to miss sixty games. He finished the season with a career-worst .256 batting average and only five home runs. Mattingly's back would trouble him throughout the rest of his career.

In 1991, Mattingly was named captain of the Yankees but returned to another subpar team. They finished in fifth place, twenty games behind the Blue Jays. Mattingly batted .288 and won another Gold Glove, but he hit only nine home runs. In 1992, he hit just fourteen homers as the Yankees finished in fourth place. The back problem had sapped Mattingly of the power he had displayed throughout the 1980s. Yet even with a drop in offensive numbers, he remained the best-fielding first baseman in baseball, and his all-out hustle and style of play deeply endeared him to Yankee fans. To them, Mattingly represented the only shining light of a despondent ballclub throughout most of the eighties and early nineties. Even if fans could not count on the team, they could always count on a great performance from Mattingly, regardless of his back. And as the team perennially fell out of postseason contention, Mattingly's struggle to make the postseason became their struggle.

Mattingly also earned a reputation among his teammates and opponents as the ultimate professional. "[Mattingly] was an inspiration to me. Just a class individual. Everything you want in a superstar, he was," said Randy Velarde. Jim Abbott referred to Mattingly as the best teammate he ever had, as did Jim Leyritz. "Donnie was a class act all the way. His intuitiveness for the game was amazing. I'd rather have him at first [base] than anyone else. He knew what guys were thinking. He was aware of everything going on, and he was never braggadocios. He went about his business," recalled Lee Guetterman, who played with and against Mattingly. Manager Buck Showalter was so confident in his captain that he delegated certain responsibilities to Mattingly, essentially letting him police situations in the clubhouse. Years after playing with him, nearly all of Mattingly's teammates still affectionately referred to him as "Cappie."[1]

• • • • • • • •

By 1993, Mattingly was starting to get mentioned in the same breath as Ernie Banks, another great player who never made the playoffs. The year 1993, however, became a turning point for the Yankees. Led by Buck Showalter and a resurgent Mattingly, who batted .291

and drove in eighty-six runs, the team made a run for the division title. They fell short but finished in second place for the first time in seven years. In 1994, the Yankees were the best team in the American League. Mattingly was hitting .306 on August 12, but on that day, the players went on strike. The players' strike was heartbreaking for a variety of reasons, not the least of which was that it possibly robbed Mattingly of his chance to finally make the playoffs. His contract expired after 1995, and there was no guarantee that the strike would end before then or that Mattingly would return once it did. His back was progressively becoming more of an issue, as was his desire to spend more time with his family. With the strike continuing into the winter and spring of 1995, fans were left to wonder whether they might ever see Mattingly in uniform again. It seemed as if the captain was destined never to reach the postseason and would end up as the greatest Yankee never to play meaningful October baseball.

When an injunction against the owners ended the strike in April 1995, hope sprang anew for the Captain. The Yankees made several key off-season acquisitions, leading many to predict that they would run away with the American League East. Throughout the spring, there was talk that it might be Mattingly's last season, and teammates expressed a desire to get their captain to the playoffs at least once. By then, no active player had been in more games and not made the postseason than Mattingly.

As the regular season progressed, however, the Yankees' playoff hopes quickly faded. Injuries crippled the team, particularly the pitching staff, which lost three of their five starters within the first month of the season. The Yankees stumbled and by June were in last place. Mattingly was one of those felled by injuries. An infection in his right eye left him unable to differentiate between pitches. As a result, his power numbers collapsed, and he hit only one home run in the first half of the season. It was unfortunate because Mattingly had felt especially healthy once the season began and may have been on track for his best season in years.[2] He hit .313 in May and only struck out once. But then the infection took its course, and Mattingly hit only .247 in June. His drop in offensive performance led the *New York Daily News* to write "Done Don?" on the back page of their June 27 newspaper. WFAN's Mike and the Mad Dog, hosts of the most popular radio sports show in New York, were calling daily for Mattingly to be removed from the lineup. In fact, their comments sparked an intermedia war between those defending Mattingly and those who felt he shouldn't be playing. The Yankees' radio announcer, Michael Kay, was the Captain's main defender, claiming the people who attacked Mattingly didn't even witness Yankee games in person.[3] The conflict among the media only drew more attention to Mattingly's struggles. Shortly thereafter, the Captain approached Showalter and requested he be dropped lower in the lineup to help ease the pressure on his manager. "I told him to shut up," recalled Showalter. "Mattingly's presence was important by itself. I was willing to lose my job over this."[4] Then in September, the Yankees caught fire, going on a historic run. Mattingly played a huge role in the late season surge by hitting .321 after September 1.[5] The Yankees won the first-ever American League wild-card berth on the season's last day. As the final out of the game was made, all eyes turned to Mattingly, who knelt down and pounded the ground with his fist. Finally, he was going to the playoffs.

Mattingly went 2–4 in the Yankees' Game 1 victory. It was an exciting atmosphere, as the home crowd applauded any time Mattingly so much as showed his face. He already had a hit in Game 2 when he came to bat in the sixth inning. Still giddy over Sierra's game-tying home run, the crowd looked for something special from Mattingly. After a first-pitch ball, Yankee Stadium organist Eddie Layton began playing "Charge" over the public-address system, to which the crowd enthusiastically replied. In the Mariners' bullpen, Bill Risley warmed up. Staring from the mound at Mattingly was Andy Benes. Benes, whom the Mariners had acquired midseason, had grown up in Evansville, too. He was six years younger than Mattingly, so he had watched the Captain along with the other residents of Evansville with great pride and reverence during the eighties. But that was then. Now, Benes wanted to get his fellow Indianan out without sustaining further damage. Benes threw a 1–0 changeup but missed his spot. Instead of dipping down, the ball stayed over the plate long enough for Mattingly to turn on it. Using a leg kick he had developed midseason to generate power, the Captain crushed Benes's pitch, drilling it high and deep to right-center field. In the Yankees' dugout, his teammates immediately jumped up from the bench to watch the flight of the ball. Jay Buhner, the Mariners' right fielder and a former teammate of Mattingly's, chased the ball in vain. It landed in the first row of the right-field bleachers where several fans scrambled for possession of the cherished souvenir. Mattingly rounded first base and, having watched the ball land over the fence, allowed himself a minuscule fist pump. His teammates raised their arms in triumph. Bernie Williams led the celebration, enthusiastically waving his fists and high-fiving teammate Jorge Posada. Mattingly continued around the bases, finally reaching home plate where he high-fived teammate Dion James and then the batboy. As he returned to the dugout to receive further congratulations, pandemonium ensued all around him. Full cups of beer fell from the upper deck, showering fans in the lower level. Vince Coleman, Ken Griffey Jr., and Buhner all took cover in the outfield as liquor bottles, coins, and other objects began littering the field. "It was the only time I ever felt unsafe. The dugout was shaking," said Showalter. It was a terribly misguided yet touching display of emotion for their long-suffering captain. Mariners manager Lou Piniella, trying to protect his players and perhaps attempting to stem the Yankees' momentum, pulled his team off the field. As he did so, a program struck him directly in the stomach. Eventually, the crowd settled as the grounds crew cleaned off the field. Chants of "Don-nie Base-ball" sprang up across Yankee Stadium. It was an outpouring of affection not seen at the stadium in years, perhaps decades. "You enjoy it. When it's that loud, it becomes almost funny," recalled Paul O'Neill of the moment. Though he had just given up the go-ahead run, Andy Benes still thought the reaction of love and support by the fans for their captain was one of the "coolest things" he had ever seen.[6] In the middle of it all, calmly standing in the dugout awaiting resumption of play as if none of this was occurring, was Donald Arthur Mattingly. Mattingly's home run, the last of his career, nearly started a riot and could have potentially caused the Yankees to forfeit the game. Programs, bottles, coins, and who knows what else littered the field. People were running for cover, and players were high-fiving one another like they were still in Little League. It was the surreal atmosphere that was the 1995 Division Series between the Yankees and the Mariners. Yet Game 2, already in the sixth inning, was only just beginning to get crazy. And, for both teams, which had been waiting for years for this kind of drama to revive their ball clubs, the series hadn't even come close to its most dramatic moments.

2

Winless in Seattle

"I also don't think this is a town that will ever draw 25 or 30,000 regularly. It's a town that's much more concerned with culture than athletics." —Jim Bouton, referring to Seattle in *Ball Four*

I n 1969, there was scant evidence of the skyscrapers that would dot the city streets of Seattle in the years to come. From Puget Sound, one could see the world-famous Space Needle hovering above the city's northern side. To the southeast, with Mount Rainier towering behind it, lay Sick's Stadium. At Sick's, minor-league baseball had thrived in Seattle for decades. The Rainiers of the Pacific Coast League played there since 1938 under the management of such baseball superstars as Rogers Hornsby, the Hall of Fame second baseman, and Lefty O'Doul, who once collected 254 hits in a season for the Philadelphia Phillies.[1] Throughout the years, the Rainiers had been affiliated with several Major League teams, including the Tigers, the Reds, the Red Sox and the Angels. Because of this affiliation, the Seattle community saw its share of future major leaguers. But decades of local minor-league baseball had left a yearning in the "Emerald City" for a Major League team. When Major League Baseball announced that it would be expanding, Seattle, led by King County officials and Washington senator Warren Magnuson, decided to take a shot at receiving Major League affiliation. As would occur so many

7

times throughout the next thirty years, politics played a crucial role in Seattle baseball.[2]

In 1967, the Athletics moved from Kansas City to Oakland, infuriating Missouri senator Stuart Symington. He threatened the American League with a lawsuit, and the owners decided to quickly appease the senator by agreeing to add two teams to the American League.[3] One would be located in Kansas City, while the other would be placed in another not-yet-determined city. Hoping to snare the other team, Seattle sent a delegation led by Senator Magnuson to the 1967 winter meetings of the AL team owners to plead the city's case. Convinced of the viability of baseball in the Pacific Northwest, the owners agreed to award the other team to Seattle based on two conditions. First, Sick's Stadium, which had been simply a minor-league park, had to be renovated and enlarged from 11,000 seats to 30,000 seats. Sick's would serve as a temporary home to the new team. Second, the owners demanded that a new stadium be built. A $40 million bond issue to build a domed stadium, with construction beginning no later than December 31, 1970, had to be voted on and passed by residents of Seattle. Dewey and Max Soriano would be the owners of this new team, spawning the birth of Major League baseball in Seattle.[4]

In February 1968, due largely to a local media blitz and visits to Seattle by baseball players like Mickey Mantle, Carl Yastrzemski, Ron Santo, and Joe DiMaggio, voters approved the bond referendum for what would eventually become the Kingdome.[5] Renovation of Sick's Stadium began and the ball club, named the Pilots, set about building a team for the 1969 season. During the expansion draft, the club acquired such players as Tommy Davis, Diego Segui, Tommy Harper, Don Mincher, Jim Bouton, and rookie Lou Piniella. Expectations for the Pilots were not great, but still, as the 1969 season approached, there was a high level of anticipation from the Seattle community. Once the season began, the ambience surrounding the Pilots disappeared nearly as fast as it had been created.

· · · · · · · · ·

The Pilots won their first game on April 8, defeating the California Angels in Anaheim, and three days later they would even win their home opener in Seattle. These victories, however, represented the few successes of the franchise. The Pilots were 4–4 after eight games and never reached .500 again. The team suffered from a multitude of problems, not the least of which was a simple lack of talent. The roster featured an assortment of has-beens and never-would-be's. Former All-Stars like Tommy Davis and Tommy Harper dotted the lineup, but their best years were far behind them. The team's manager, "a short, portly, bald, ruddy-faced, twinkly eyed man" named Joe Schultz,[6] had little to work with and he knew it. As the season went along, the team's record and performance gradually worsened.

The Pilots' home facility added to their inaugural-season woes. Opened in 1938, Sick's originally seated only 11,000—adequate for a minor-league facility but paltry for a Major League park.[7] It consisted of only a single level of seating and was a colorless, unpleasing structure, lacking any of the frills or aesthetic pleasures of a Fenway Park, Yankee Stadium, or Wrigley Field. Charlie Finley, owner of the Athletics, once referred to Sick's Stadium as a "pigsty."[8] Perhaps the only benefit of its small size was the intimacy it created for the fans, who had a superb view of every play. Once Seattle was forced to expand seating capacity after being awarded the Pilots, construction crews set upon Sick's to add another 14,000 seats. A problem arose, however, when the expansion was not completed in time for the start of the 1969 season. On opening day in Seattle, construction workers took breaks to enjoy the action on the field, and those without tickets could leer through holes in the left-field fence where seats were planned but not yet added.[9] Even worse, Sick's water pressure was so poor that opposing players preferred to shower at their hotels, and when crowds exceeded 10,000, the toilets stopped flushing.[10]

Adding insult to injury, the Pilots sported the oddest and least attractive uniforms in baseball. Modeled after maritime and aviation uniforms, the team's logo was a ship's wheel surrounding a baseball from which gold wings extended. This logo was sewn onto the chest of both the home and away uniforms. But the most interesting aspect of the uniform was the hat, which featured a single gold S. Underneath the S was a gold braid and "scrambled eggs," military parlance that refers to leaf-shaped emblems. In essence, the hat mimicked those worn by pilots in the armed forces. "They're so gaudy," wrote Jim Bouton in *Ball Four*. "We look like goddamn clowns."[11]

Poor performance on the field, a deficient stadium, and ridiculous uniforms were more than enough to keep the fans away. Despite a large ceremony downtown before the Pilots' home opener, which included receiving ceremonial keys to the city, public interest in the team sharply declined within weeks. The Pilots had no TV contract and were barely heard on the radio, so unless fans were attending games, there were few ways to follow the team.[12] The poor attendance and lack of a TV deal meant the team was losing revenue and could not pay its bills. It was evident as the initial season came to a close that the Pilots were in financial trouble. They needed to draw 850,000 during the 1969 season to break even but only attracted 677,944 spectators.[13] Rumors spread that baseball would not survive in Seattle, but 1970 began without any indication that the Pilots would be playing anywhere else. The team reported to spring training that year. The new manager, Dave Bristol, and his players even posed for their Topps trading cards.[14] As late as March 1, the *Seattle Post-Intelligencer* was still holding a contest to become a Pilots batboy for the summer.[15] Then, everything changed.

Unbeknownst to many, Major League Baseball owners had been expressing their disappointment with the situation in Seattle. The Pilots' poor attendance numbers and financial troubles convinced them that baseball would not thrive there. In the middle of spring training, American League officials announced they would have to take a "serious second look" at whether to keep the Pilots in Seattle. On March 31, merely six days before the 1970 season was to start, the Pilots were officially sold and moved to Milwaukee, where they became the Brewers.[16] After just one year, Major League Baseball was officially dead in Seattle. But some Seattleites refused to let baseball leave without a fight.

· · · · · · · · ·

For the first of many times, Slade Gorton stepped in to save baseball in the city. As Washington State's attorney general in 1970, Gorton was livid over the Pilots' departure and moved to sue the American League for breach of contract, claiming they had welshed on several agreements with Seattle by letting the team move to Milwaukee. Gorton, who argued the case with lawyer Bill Dwyer, sought to collect $32.5 million from the league, specifically for funds that

Seattle had expended to fix Sick's Stadium and to begin construction on the Kingdome.[17] The lawsuit was not originally intended to bring a Major League team back to the region. When the issue finally went to trial in 1976, a seemingly flabby case against the American League instead backed the owners into a corner. The trial revealed various types of deceit on the owners' behalf, shining a particularly negative light on Oakland A's owner Charlie Finley and former Washington Senators owner Bob Short.[18] Realizing they were on the losing side of the argument, the owners agreed to expand yet again, adding two teams to the American League. One would be located in Toronto and the other in Seattle. In response, Gorton dropped the lawsuit.[19]

Baseball was back in Seattle. Four local businessmen—Stan Golub, Walter Schoefeld, Jim Walsh, and Jim Stillwell—joined with recording executive Lester Smith and entertainer Danny Kaye as the owners of the new franchise. Housed in a new state-of-the-art facility, the team, called the Mariners, began play before 57,762 at the Kingdome on April 6, 1977.[20] Despite the team's shutout that day by the California Angels, the crowd and the city were elated to have baseball back. The elation, much as it had been for the Pilots, was short lived. The new baseball team in Seattle would be no different from the old one. Poor upper management, marginal talent, and a subpar playing facility handicapped the Seattle Mariners for years to come.

The 1977 Mariners were shut out in their first two games before winning their third game, one bright spot during a season that saw them lose ninety-eight games. The poor performance could be easily written off as the jitters of an expansion team in its first year. Seattle's problems, however, were more complex than that. In an effort to assemble a team that would win fast and keep fans coming to the ballpark, the ownership had selected the best proven players available during the expansion draft, instead of opting for younger players whose full potential wouldn't blossom for a few years. "They [the other teams] froze all the good players," recalled then-owner Lester Smith. "What were we going to do?"[21] The Mariners ended up with an abundance of players whose best years were long since gone, or who would never muster stellar careers. In their initial season, Seattle used an astounding seventeen different starting pitchers, only one of whom won more than eight games.[22] Their top five starters that year—Glenn Abbott, Dick Pole, Gary Wheelock, John Montage, and Tom House—won a combined total of just 146 games in their

Major League careers. Frank MacCormick, who began the season in the Mariners' starting rotation, lasted only three starts and was back in single-A ball before the year was over.[23] The Mariners' inability to draft a substantial amount of young talent, particularly pitchers, would cripple the franchise for years. Instead of progressing through the early years, even by just baby steps, the Mariners were as bad or worse in the seasons after 1977. They lost 98 games in 1977, 104 in 1978, 95 in 1979, and 103 in 1980. Excluding the truncated schedule of October, the Mariners did not have a month in which they posted a winning record until June 1979.[24] The failure to show even a hint of improvement pushed the fan base away in droves. After drawing over 1.3 million to the Kingdome during the initial season, attendance fell to just 836,000 in 1980, a disastrous 36 percent drop in just four seasons.[25] The lethargy extended to the media. In the late 1970s, *Seattle Times* sports editor Georg Myers informed Mariners public relations director Randy Adamack that he had "no interest in baseball" and that Adamack would not see him at any games.[26] Who could blame Myers? Editors, writers, and fans had little reason to show up, outside of witnessing the purely entertaining ways the Mariners found to lose.

During a July 10 game against the Twins in 1977, Mariners starting pitcher Stan Thomas attempted to hit the Twins' Mike Cubbage due to a long-standing feud between the two. Thomas threw at Cubbage four times with the intention of hitting him and missed each time. The Mariners lost that game 15–0 and Mariners manager Darrell Johnson hit Thomas with the highest fine he gave a player in his managerial career.[27]

In September 1979, the Mariners started a rookie pitcher named Roy Branch against the Texas Rangers. The first pitch Branch threw in the Major Leagues was hit for a home run by Mickey Rivers, making Branch the first pitcher in seven years to have accomplished such a feat.[28] The Mariners lost the game 5–2, and Branch made only one more start in the Major Leagues.

Byron McLaughlin, who pitched for the Mariners from 1977 to 1980, once missed a start because he mistakenly thought the game, which began in the afternoon, was scheduled to start at night. In 1980, pitcher Rick Honeycutt was ejected from a game and eventually suspended for using a thumbtack bandaged to his finger to scuff the ball.[29]

There was also Mario Mendoza, a light-hitting shortstop whom the Mariners acquired from the Pittsburgh Pirates in 1979. During his first season in Seattle, Mendoza mustered only a .198 batting average. It was one of the worst single-season averages in baseball history for a full-time player.[30] Eventually, the Kansas City Royals' George Brett was glancing at player's batting averages in the newspaper and quipped, "I knew I was off to a bad start when I saw my average listed below the Mendoza Line."[31] The expression stuck and from that point on, any player who failed to hit higher than .200 was said to be below the "Mendoza Line."

It was all part of the Seattle legacy of embarrassment, and by 1981, the original owners had had it. The team was no better than the expansion team of 1977 and had not drawn more than a million fans in any season since then. Facing extreme financial hardships, the owners decided to sell the team to George Argyros. Argyros was born in Detroit to second-generation Greek Americans and moved to Pasadena when he was ten. He attended Michigan State University and graduated from Chapman College, where he majored in business and economics.[32] By 1981, he was a wealthy real estate developer who had purchased the former San Clemente home of President Richard Nixon.[33] The opportunity to buy the Mariners came his way thanks to Hall of Famer Harmon Killebrew, who notified him of the team owners' intent to sell.[34] He made an offer to buy the team and the owners accepted. Argyros paid $10.4 million for an 80 percent share of the team. Original owners Golub, Smith, Schoenfeld, and Kaye each maintained a meager 5 percent share. When asked why the American League would allow someone outside of Seattle to purchase the club, league president Lee MacPhail's response was telling of the type of future the team had in store. "There was nobody around willing to purchase the club locally," said MacPhail.[35]

Argyros was originally received as a savior in Seattle. He would keep the team in the city and as a wealthy business owner it was believed he could run the club with more structure and acquire better talent than the previous ownership. The honeymoon was short lived. Though acquaintances would refer to Argyros's big heart and point to his various acts of small kindness and courtesies—including contributions to the Boy Scouts, programs for abused children, and cultural activities[36]—his legacy in Seattle would be that of a penny-pinching owner who presided over the worst trades in club history, allowed some of the best players to sign with other teams, hired and fired managers on impulse, and generally ran the club with little knowledge of the actual game itself. It all went downhill from the beginning.

In fairness to Argyros, he walked into an extremely difficult situation. As the *New York Times* wrote in a 1981 team preview, "People who have watched the Mariners in spring training suspect they could be a disaster."[37] "We needed to start from scratch," said Argyros. "The Mariners had gotten short-changed in the expansion draft. We had to expand the farm system, develop players, and it wasn't easy."[38] In a strike-shortened season, the team finished 44–65 and placed next to last in league attendance.[39] Part of the reason for the disaster was the team's manager at the beginning of the year, Maury Wills. Wills had been hired in 1980 to replace Darrell Johnson, but unbeknownst to Seattle management, Wills was battling a serious drug problem. The result was a series of strange and erratic decisions that drew further ridicule to a team already on pace to be perennial losers. Asked before the start of the 1981 season who his center fielder would be, Wills replied, "I wouldn't be surprised if it was Leon Roberts." Apparently Wills didn't know or didn't remember that Roberts had been traded from Seattle weeks earlier.[40] During a spring training game in 1981, Wills went to the mound and signaled for a right-handed pitcher, but there was no right-hander warming up.[41]

The biggest gaffe Wills committed, however, couldn't be blamed on a simple verbal mistake or inattention. It was just downright cheating. Before an April 25 game against the A's at the Kingdome, Wills instructed the Mariners' grounds crew to make the batter's box six inches longer in front than normal. The purpose was to allow Tom Paciorek, a Mariner outfielder who liked to stand near the front of the box, a little more room. Paciorek had recently been called out for stepping outside the box on a swing and Wills thought the box extension would give him an advantage.[42] Inexplicably, Wills did not think that either the umpires or the opposing players would notice the extra length. Sure enough, before the game even started, A's manager Billy Martin noticed and brought it to umpire Bill Kunkel's attention. Kunkel measured the box and saw it was too long.[43] Wills was fined $500 and suspended two games for the stunt.[44] In his autobiography, Wills would shirk responsibility and blamed the entire incident on his grounds crew for informing Billy Martin of the extra distance.[45] The Mariners got off to a 6–18 start under Wills in 1981, and he was finally fired.

Wills had not been George Argyros's hire, so there was no blood on his hands for Wills's actions. The firing allowed Argyros to make his first managerial decision, and he did—sort of. On the advice of a beat writer from the *Seattle Post-Intelligencer* named Tracy Ringolsby, Argyros hired Rene Lachemann.[46] The move appeared to pay off. Although the Mariners floundered through the rest of the 1981 season, they played well throughout the early part of 1982. Finally armed with a capable starting rotation—featuring pitchers such as Floyd Bannister, Gaylord Perry, and Jim Beattie—the Mariners were three games over .500 on July 28 and only five games out of first. The team then fell apart, going 25–38 the rest of the year and finishing seventeen games out of first place. The Mariners played their final home game of the year before only 6,742 people.[47] In fact, despite drawing over one million fans for the first time in five years, the Mariners attendance had been a particular source of embarrassment for them in 1982, thanks to a bizarre promotional giveaway. In 1981, Tom Paciorek had filmed a commercial for the Mariners falsely claiming there would be a Funny Nose Glasses Night at the Kingdome, when it was actually Mariners Jacket Night. As a result of the commercial, however, the Mariners decided to have Funny Nose Glasses Night on May 8, 1982 during a Saturday night game against the Yankees. Players, fans, and even Argyros sported a pair as nearly 37,000 people filled the Kingdome that night for the kooky promotion. Two nights earlier against the Yankees, with Gaylord Perry on the mound looking for his 300th career victory, the Mariners drew only 27,000 fans. A player making baseball history attracted 10,000 fewer fans than the plastic-nose giveaway.[48]

By 1983, the relationship between George Argyros and his manager was crumbling. Some owners took a hands-off approach to their team, but Argyros was a constant second guesser, and it was common for him to call down to the dugout during a game. The behavior wore on Lachemann, who didn't hide his displeasure with his boss. Of Argyros, Lachemann once remarked, "He was just a fan, one who didn't know the game."[49] During an eight-game losing streak in the middle of 1983, Lachemann was let go with the team's record at 26–47. The firing did not endear Argyros in the Mariners' clubhouse, where

Lachemann was known as a players' manager. "There were a lot guys with tears in their eyes," said Mariners relief pitcher Bill Caudill after the announcement. "This is like losing a best friend . . . it was heaven playing for Lach."[50]

Lachemann would be the first in a series of Seattle managers to come and go under Argyros. All told, eight men would serve in that position during the eight years Argyros owned the team. None would last more than two full seasons, and none would leave with a winning record. "We had one-day managers, one-month managers, one-week managers," said Julio Cruz, who played second base for Seattle for six seasons.[51] Replacing Lachemann was Del Crandall, a former manager of the Brewers whose most recent managerial job had been with the Albuquerque Dukes of the Pacific Coast League. "We are a young franchise and a young franchise needs careful handling. I believe Del Crandall is a winner and a leader," said George Argyros after the hiring.[52] But Crandall was unable to guide the Mariners toward success. They went 34–55 the rest of the 1983 season, finishing in last place in the American League West. They were no better in 1984, posting a 59–76 record before Crandall was let go.

Argyros made an internal hire next when he replaced Crandall with Chuck Cottier, the Mariners' third base coach at the time. Under Cottier, the Mariners went 15–12 to finish the season, offering a possible glimmer of hope for 1985. The hope faded as the Mariners went 74–88 in 1985 and finished in sixth place. When the team started the 1986 season slowly, Cottier was fired. Cottier had the highest winning percentage of any manager in team history at .452, but the Mariners had not gotten any better in the season and a half he was at the helm.[53] Cottier also had the unfortunate distinction of having to watch two of the more embarrassing moments in Mariner history. The first came on July 10, 1985, when the Mariners had two runners thrown out at home plate on the same play. Playing at the Kingdome against the Blue Jays, Phil Bradley tried to score from second base on a single to right field and collided with catcher Buck Martinez at home. Bradley was called out, but in the process he dislocated Martinez's ankle. Martinez, still on his back, threw to third base, trying to nail an advancing Gorman Thomas. The throw went wild and Thomas headed home, but the Blue Jays quickly recovered and threw to Martinez who, still lying on the ground, scooped the ball and tagged Thomas out on the leg for an unconventional 9–2–6–2 double play.[54]

The second embarrassment came on April 29, 1986, when Boston Red Sox pitcher Roger Clemens set a Major League record by striking out twenty Mariners in a nine-inning game. It was not long after Clemens's performance that Cottier was let go. Before a permanent replacement for Cottier was found, Mariners third-base coach Marty Martinez was named acting manager for one game. The Mariners lost that game, 4–2. Even a one-day manager had a losing record for Seattle. "Now I know what Chuck went through," said Martinez after the loss.[55]

The day after that loss, the Mariners hired Dick Williams, a well-established and successful manager. Williams, who previously led three different teams to the World Series, was an old-school hard-core manager. Unlike Crandall or Lachemann, he was not regarded as a player's manager.[56] "I'm demanding," said Williams at his initial press conference. "I'm not hired to be a nice guy."[57] As with previous managers before him, Williams received praise from his new boss. "In Dick Williams, the Seattle Mariners will have an experienced manager who is an established winner," said Argyros. "He is a World Series championship manager." But the Mariners were not a World Series team, and they finished last in 1986—their fourth last-place finish in ten seasons. They improved in 1987, as Williams led them to their best finish in history. But for the Mariners, best finish was a relative term, as they still lost eighty-four games and finished in fourth place. In 1988, they got off to another sluggish start and rumors swirled that Williams would be let go. With the team at 16–22, Argyros tried to downplay any such talk. "Dick is an experienced manager and if anyone can turn this team around, he can," the Mariners owner told the Associated Press.[58] Apparently, then, no one could turn the team around, because after that statement, the Mariners went 7–11. By that time, it was a badly kept secret that many players were unhappy with Williams's management style. Pitcher Mark Langston had been critical of Williams, telling the media that "leadership starts with the manager and if it's not working, then something has to be done. This team is going in the wrong direction and we've worked too hard for that."[59] The day after Langston's comment, Williams was let go, though all involved said Langston's remarks had nothing to do with the move. "I think Dick had lost control of the club," remarked Mariners general manager Dick Balderson on the day of the firing.[60] Though he offered nothing but praise for his newly departed manager, Argyros was blunt about the state of the team. "I'm disappointed and I'm tired, tired of this losing."[61] The losing would continue under interim manager Jim Snyder, as the Mariners finished the season last in the division, thirty-five games behind first-place Oakland.

During the off-season, Argyros hired Jim Lefebvre, the last of eight men to serve under him as manager. Lefebvre "was our No. 1 choice because he's a winner," declared Mariners executive Woody Woodward the day Lefebvre was hired.[62] For Mariners fans, it was an all-too-familiar declaration. For all the talk about hiring managers who were proven winners, Seattle had nothing to show for it. By 1989, the Mariners had been in the American League for twelve seasons without once finishing .500 or better. Their best season had only resulted in a fourth place finish. By contrast, the Toronto Blue Jays, who had entered the American League with Seattle in 1977, had finished higher than .500 six times, made the playoffs in 1985, had only four managers in their history, and were perennial contenders in the American League East.

• • • • • • • • •

Under Argyros's management, Seattle also became infamous for constantly trading away its best players or allowing them to walk via free agency. Argyros was notoriously tightfisted and did not believe in signing players to long-term contracts.[63] "Costs were so high, and we had a poor lease with the stadium. There just wasn't enough revenue to support baseball," said Argyros.[64] The result was a series of teams that played below-average baseball, a fan base that had no desire to witness it in person, and a feeling around the league that flourishing as a player in Seattle wasn't possible because you'd simply be traded away. "If you were a good player with a rising salary, they said, 'We're going to lose [him] anyway; let's get rid of him,'" said Dave Henderson, who would himself be a victim of Seattle's purging of talented players.[65]

"Ownership was unstable," recalled Ken Phelps, who played with the Mariners from 1983 to 1988. "You wondered who would be around for the next season. There were never any three- or four-year contracts. Most contracts were year-to-year."[66]

"In my heart, I truly believe we could have been as good as Oakland was in their heyday," said Chuck Cottier, referring to the loss of quality player after quality player. "You saw what happened to them when they went to other organizations. They had nice careers and wound up as millionaires with other teams."[67]

"We'd start to make progress, but then we wouldn't make it all the way and changes would happen," recalled Phil Bradley, a Mariners outfielder for four seasons who was eventually traded away to the Phillies. "The Angels would start the year with twenty veterans and five rookies, but we'd start with twenty rookies and five veterans because of the trades. I can't recall a person actually becoming a free agent. They'd always be traded first once they became too expensive."[68]

The legacy of failed transactions and of inability to retain players began on October 23, 1981, when the Mariners traded away a player to be named later to the Kansas City Royals for Manny Castillo. Castillo played one full season with Seattle in 1982, batting just .257 with three home runs. Perhaps his greatest notoriety came when the Mariners had him pitch in a game against the Blue Jays. Castillo gave up seven earned runs in less than three innings.[69] After 1983, he never played another game in the majors. The player to be named later in the deal turned out to be pitcher Bud Black. Black would have a respectable career, winning 121 games and helping the Royals to their first world championship in 1985.

Floyd Bannister was the Mariners' most consistent pitcher from 1979 to 1982, averaging ten wins a year and striking out 209 hitters during the 1982 season. A free agent at the end of that season, Bannister left Seattle and signed with the White Sox, where he won seventeen games and led them to the postseason. He went on to win ten or more games during each of the next six seasons after he left Seattle.

Before the start of the 1986 season, the Mariners traded Darnell Coles to the Tigers for relief pitcher Rich Monteleone. Coles hit twenty home runs and drove in eighty-six runs for Detroit that year, while Monteleone pitched only three games for the Mariners before being released. The Coles trade was merely a preview of the fire sale that would occur in Seattle during 1986. On June 26, Seattle sent a player to be named later to the White Sox for Scott Bradley. Bradley was a light-hitting catcher who went on to play several seasons with the Mariners, but his offensive production tended to be marginal, as he never hit more than five home runs in season or batted higher than

.278. The player to be named later was Ivan Calderon. Calderon was an outfielder and had batted .286 for Seattle in 1985, making minor contributions. After moving to Chicago, he burst out with twenty-seven home runs in 1987 and made the All-Star team in 1991, just a year before Bradley retired.

Following the trade of Calderon, the Mariners pulled off one of the most disappointing moves in team history when they sent outfielder Dave Henderson and shortstop Spike Owen to the Red Sox for cash, infielder Rey Quinones, and three players to be named later. The trade, done to dump high-profile players to a team that was contending, proved to be a disaster. Henderson, the Mariners first-ever draft pick, had been one of the few legitimate stars in Seattle during the early eighties, and he was shocked by the move. "When you get traded from the organization that drafted you No. 1 and was going to build around you, it hits you right in the stomach," he remarked about the trade.[70] Henderson went on to hit one of the biggest home runs in postseason history that year for the Red Sox, propelling them into the World Series. He also won a championship with Oakland in 1989.

Spike Owen, though not one of the game's elite shortstops, was a steady force defensively and had a respectable career with several teams before retiring after the 1995 season. The players the Mariners received in return made no significant contributions to the team. Quinones, though an offensive upgrade over Owen at shortstop, played only two seasons with Seattle before being traded to Pittsburgh. He was out of baseball by 1989. The three players Seattle received later were all playing for different teams by 1988.

The final disaster of 1986 came in December, when the team sent Danny Tartabull and a minor leaguer to the Kansas City Royals for pitchers Scott Bankhead and Steve Shields and outfielder Mike Kingery. Tartabull had risen through the Mariner system as an infielder, though he eventually moved to the outfield. In 1986, he hit twenty-five home runs and drove in ninety-five runs. Instead of embracing this newly found offense, the Mariners traded him. The next year in Kansas City, Tartabull hit thirty-four home runs. He would have five 100-RBI seasons in his post-Seattle career. Bankhead had enjoyed moderate success in Seattle, including a career year in 1989, but injuries and pitching in a hitter's park took their toll on his statistics. Shields pitched twenty games for the Mariners in 1987 and posted an ERA of

6.60. He left via free agency after the season was over. Kingery had a respectable 1987 season but was regulated to mostly part-time or pinch-hitting duties in 1988 and 1989 before leaving the team. The Mariners had traded away hundreds of RBIs and received little in return.

Phil Bradley was an exceptional athlete who showed flashes of power and speed. He hit over .300 for Seattle in 1984, 1985, and 1986. In 1987, he stole over forty bases and scored 101 runs. Those attributes made him increasingly more expensive as the years went by. Bradley had beaten the Mariners twice in arbitration, which he believed irritated the team's owners. Rather than resort to arbitration a third time, they traded him to the Phillies on December 9, 1987. In return the Mariners received outfielder Glen Wilson, pitcher Mike Jackson, and a minor leaguer. Wilson flopped in Seattle and was traded during the 1988 season. Jackson turned out to be a key acquisition for the Mariners, but he too would eventually be shipped to another team in possibly the worst trade in franchise history.

After the 1988 season, Mike Moore, considered one of the team's best right-handed starters, left via free agency and joined the Oakland A's. Moore won nineteen games for the A's in 1989 as they went on to a world championship. Black, Coles, Calderon, Henderson, Owen, Tartabull, Bradley, and Moore. Though not a list of Hall of Famers, they were all good players who went on to make major contributions after leaving the Mariners. The continuing parade of managers and loss of talented players fueled Mariners fans' animosity toward Argyros. Perhaps no move, however, infuriated fans more than Argyros's attempt to buy the San Diego Padres in 1987.

· · · · · · · · ·

In March 1987, Argyros was fighting with the city over a new lease for the Kingdome. He had just announced that the Mariners were close to signing free agent Tim Raines, the National League batting champion (though Raines's agent announced that Argyros knew Raines had ruled out going to Seattle months ago).[71] Suddenly on March 26, Argyros announced that he was putting the Mariners up for sale and purchasing the San Diego Padres. He said that personal issues required him to spend "an ever-increasing amount of time in Southern California."[72] Although he pledged to sell the team to a local owner, thus preventing the Mariners from moving out of Seattle, Argyros's announcement made him Public Enemy Number One in the Pacific Northwest. He was booed heavily on opening night at the Kingdome, and a police escort led him from the stadium.[73] Fans in the Kingdome began to cheer any time it was posted that the Padres were losing and referred to San Diego as "George's Other Team."[74] Things got worse for Argyros when, on April 16, he called Padres manager Larry Bowa to congratulate him on San Diego's victory over the Dodgers that night. Argyros was still the owner of the Mariners, and he had been warned not to contact any player, coach, or the manager of San Diego. Argyros's call might have gone unnoticed had National League president Bart Giamatti not been sitting in Bowa's office at the time of the call. Giamatti reported the incident to Commissioner Peter Ueberroth, who in turn slapped Argyros with a $10,000 fine.[75] Within weeks, the deal to buy the Padres fell apart. Argyros was no closer to home, stuck with a team he apparently didn't want, and surrounded by fans who apparently didn't want him.

By the winter of 1989, Argyros had had enough of Seattle baseball. The team had not improved since he had taken over, and the fans were not coming to the ballpark. The Mariners had finished last in attendance in 1988, further fueling the idea that baseball could not exist in Seattle. To some, the region would never support a team, even a successful one, because Seattle people simply weren't interested in the sport. This theory was supported by the absence of any local interest in purchasing the club when Argyros put it up for sale that winter. The threat of the team leaving, just as the Pilots had, hung in the air. Then came Jeff Smulyan, another wealthy businessman who appeared to be the savior of the Mariners. Like Argyros, Smulyan was an out-of-towner, coming from Indianapolis where he had made his money as a radio mogul. He purchased the team for $76 million.[76] Despite the lack of success that occurred on his watch, Argyros sold the team for $76 million, earning himself a $63 million profit. In retrospect, some of the harshest criticisms of Argyros may not be deserved. "He was portrayed as trying to extort the community, but that wasn't true. The columnists were always pointing out that he lived out of town. You couldn't blame George for all the difficulties, but after '87, the community couldn't think well of him," said George Armstrong, who served as the Mariners' team president under Argyros.[77] While Argyros certainly pinched pennies wherever he could, the fiscal condition of the team left him little choice in terms of keeping or signing high-quality players. Of course, the large profit he pocketed despite the team's financial straits and lagging attendance can also cause one to ask why more money was not available to improve the team.

· · · · · · · · ·

"There will be more promotions, more fun, and a better team," said Jeff Smulyan shortly after buying the team.[78] Like Argyros, Smulyan was greeted as a hero in Seattle. He announced his intention to go after marquee players and even to move the fences at the Kingdome back to make the field more pitcher friendly.[79] But as it was with Argyros, the honeymoon was short lived. Smulyan proved no different in terms of acquisitions. Under his ownership, Seattle made the worst trade in franchise history when the Mariners dealt pitchers Bill Swift, Dave Burba, and Michael Jackson to the San Francisco Giants for outfielder Kevin Mitchell. Mitchell would play one season in Seattle, during which he hit only nine home runs and became a clubhouse problem.[80] Eventually, rumors swirled that Smulyan was simply biding his time in Seattle before he could move the team to another city. By the winter of 1992, the Mariners remained unprofitable. Smulyan, who reportedly still owed creditors $39.5 million for the purchase of the Mariners, was forced to put the team up for sale. Luckily for Seattle, the team's lease with the city had a provision that said if the team was put up for sale, a 120-day window had to be left open for a local buyer to be found.[81] That clause probably saved Seattle baseball.

In 1991, the Mariners finally finished over .500. It was a joyous moment for a team that had known nothing but losing. Still, it was an example of how badly things had gone that the team was actually celebrating a .500 record as if they had made the playoffs. Shortly after the season ended, manager Jim Lefebvre was fired and Smulyan put the team up for sale. The joy of finally producing a winning season was washed away by the turmoil of off-season events. But the sale of the team, which some thought would spell the imminent demise of the Mariners, proved to be a blessing in disguise. The sale, along with other behind-the-scenes factors, would turn the Mariners from a laughingstock into the 1995 American League West champions.

· · · · · · · · · ·

During the winter of 1992, the prevailing belief was that the Seattle Mariners were headed out of town. Jeff Smulyan was informing other Major League owners of his plans to locate the team elsewhere—possibly Tampa, Florida—believing that no local buyer would risk the asking price for the team: $100 million.[82] In Seattle, a small group of people was banding together to try and save the club and wasn't having much luck. A group of local business owners appointed Herman Sarkowsky, the former part-owner of the Seattle Seahawks, to head up a committee to find a local buyer for the Mariners as well as to drum up local business support to increase revenue. "It was difficult," recalled Sarkowsky. "We formed a committee and contacted business people and some promises were made that they would buy commercials." But the deals fell apart in the end.[83] Trying to find a local buyer was even worse. Microsoft and Boeing were in the Mariners' backyard, but neither corporation showed any interest in purchasing the team. Finally, Slade Gorton, now a U.S. senator, thought outside the box. He went searching for an investor and found someone who had never seen a Mariners game in his life yet was willing to buy the team.

"When it became obvious that Smulyan was selling the team to Tampa, I thought of reaching out to Japanese investors," said Gorton, looking back at one of the most critical moments in Mariner history. "I'd thought of them before when Argyros was going to sell the team after he'd bought the Padres. I thought of Nintendo and had my secretary set up the meeting."[84] By 1991, Nintendo was a hugely successful Japanese video-game company that had an office located in Redmond, just outside of Seattle. The president of the American branch company was Minoru Arakawa, who just happened to be the son-in-law of Hiroshi Yamauchi, head of Nintendo Company Ltd. Arakawa, along with his senior vice president, Howard Lincoln, agreed to meet with the senator, though Arakawa was not particularly interested in baseball.[85] Gorton explained to them that the community had exhausted all possibilities and that while some local parties were interested, none of them could do it by themselves.

Gorton was looking for potential Japanese investors to buy the Mariners and hoped they could inform him of anyone they knew who might be interested.[86] When Arakawa relayed this message to Yamauchi, his father-in-law advised him to look no further, telling him, "I will do it."[87] Arakawa relayed the message to Lincoln, who had been a Mariners fan for years. Lincoln was flabbergasted. "You've gotta be out of your fucking mind," Lincoln replied. "Do you know what it's like to own the Mariners? He'll [Yamauchi] be greeted as a hero at first, but once the team goes downhill, he will be vilified."[88] Yamauchi didn't care. To him, it was a public relations gesture. The region had been very good to Yamauchi and his business, so he decided to give them something in return by keeping the Mariners in Seattle. On December 23, 1991, a very sick Slade Gorton got a phone call from Arakawa informing him that his father-in-law would purchase the team, and not just part of it, but would put up the entire $100 million asking price. "It was the greatest Christmas present I got in my life," said Gorton, who even sixteen years later still grinned from ear to ear just thinking about that moment.[89]

Gorton knew, though, that once the other baseball owners got a whiff of Yamauchi's proposition, they would try to stop it. Allowing a Japanese businessman to purchase a Major League team would be allowing someone into an extremely exclusive club that didn't particularly want him. There was a large concern, particularly at that time in the United States, that Japan was conquering certain aspects of the business world and threatening American supremacy in various areas. If one Japanese owner was allowed in, how soon would it be before others followed suit? How long would it be before all American teams were Japanese owned? Another concern was Yamauchi's vast wealth, estimated at over a $1 billion, and whether he would use this personal fortune to begin purchasing the game's best players.[90] Hoping to quell these concerns, Gorton met with Arakawa and Lincoln and informed them that they had to find local buyers to join Yamauchi, or it wouldn't work.[91] They all agreed, and so John Ellis, CEO of Puget Power & Light Company and a friend of Gorton's, was asked to become a part-owner. "I told them I wasn't a baseball guy and I didn't have that kind of money," said Ellis. They moved on, but shortly thereafter, they approached Ellis again, this time asking that he represent the group that intended to purchase the team. By now, the group included Yamauchi as majority owner, along with several other people as minority owners. Ellis agreed, mostly out of civic duty and because he didn't think it would be a long commitment. "But weeks turned into months," said Ellis.[92]

After a meeting with Commissioner Fay Vincent was canceled, the group of would-be owners decided it needed to get the public on its side and put pressure on the rest of the Major League Baseball owners. The group scheduled a press conference on January 23, 1992, in the ballroom of the Madison Hotel in downtown Seattle. There, John Ellis announced to the world "his" group's intention to purchase the Mariners. "I had never been in a meeting with so much press before," recalled then–Seattle mayor Norm Rice, who had also been involved in the search to find a local buyer. "They hung on our every word. That news conference really did bring on so much attention to the issue."[93] It especially caught the attention of the other Major League owners and Commissioner Vincent, who issued a statement that same day declaring that baseball "has a strong policy against approving investors from outside the U.S. and Canada" and that the chance of the deal going through was unlikely.[94] Public backlash against the MLB owners and Vincent was harsh as they faced charges of bigotry and racism. They eventually eased their position and made clear that they wouldn't oppose involvement of a foreign investor. The only question was how much involvement they would tolerate. Several of the would-be owners met with the MLB ownership committee in April and the committee made it clear that no one with even a connection to Yamauchi would be allowed to have control of the team. That included Arakawa and Lincoln. "It was made clear to us that they would only accept limited Japanese ownership," said Lincoln. "On the flight back from the meeting I thought of using John [Ellis] because they trusted him. That broke the dam and was considered acceptable."[95] Ellis would become the team's general managing partner, although MLB required that Ellis invest $250,000 in the purchase of the team. He accepted. Ellis, who had merely agreed to be the titular head of this group because he felt it was a civic duty that would not take up too much of his time, was now going to be in charge of the Mariners.

In the end, various aspects of the original deal were changed. Yamauchi reduced his ownership share to 49 percent and shifted part of his investment into a $25 million fund for the new owners to use for capital improvements. Lincoln, Arakawa, Ellis, Chris Larson, John

McCaw, Craig Watjen, and Frank Schrontz would form a seven-member board of directors, and ownership was divided up in such a way that prevented Yamauchi from having a majority control of operations.[96] Chuck Armstrong, who had been president of the Mariners from 1983 to 1989, returned to that position. By July 1992, the sale was official. "Yamauchi accepted all these restrictions with an 'OK' attitude," said Lincoln.[97] Yamauchi's attitude was remarkable, considering the xenophobia he faced for making what he considered a gesture of goodwill toward Seattle. Regardless, after fifteen long years, the Mariners now had a solid, locally based ownership that was going to change the way things happened in the Kingdome.

· · · · · · · · ·

"We concluded that all of the owners had to be treated as equal partners," said Howard Lincoln. "We held monthly ownership meetings where everyone would be heard from and free to express their views. We had new-owner syndrome where we all thought 'We can turn this team into a winner.'"[98] One of the first ways they decided to start becoming a winner was by getting a new manager.

Despite finishing .500 in 1991, the Mariners endured a horrific 1992 season that saw them lose ninety-eight games and attendance drop by half a million. Manager Bill Plummer was let go after just one season and the new ownership began a search for its first manager. John Ellis approached Chuck Armstrong and general manager Woody Woodward with a proposition. "I asked them to give me a list of their top ten choices for manager," said Ellis. The two were not to discuss or compare their lists to one another's before submitting it. Armstrong and Woodward complied, each listing ten choices. Only one name was on both their lists and coincidentally, they both had it listed as their number-one choice: Lou Piniella.[99] Not only was Piniella a proven manager who had taken bad teams and turned them into winners, but he was someone with credibility. Hiring him would show Mariner fans that these new owners were serious when they said they wanted to create a winner. Piniella wouldn't just make the team better, he'd get people in the seats, too.

Like so many others, Piniella did not distinguish himself as a player in his short time with Seattle, although he had a very successful career after leaving the city. He had been on the 1969 Seattle Pilots club but didn't make it out of spring training before being traded to the Kansas City Royals. There, he won the 1969 Rookie of the Year award, and he eventually made his way to the New York Yankees and became a key component of the "Bronx Zoo era" teams. Piniella played hard and was fiercely dedicated to winning. He had a penchant for clutch hits, including a ninth-inning game-winning single during the third game of the 1978 World Series. His playing career ended with the Yankees in 1984, and he became their manager two years later. Piniella's first go-around as a manager was not easy, as he became one of a string managers that had to contend with the intricacies of Yankees owner George Steinbrenner. Piniella made it through two complete seasons— no small task at the time—before being replaced by Billy Martin for the start of the 1988 season. Martin was fired halfway through the year, and Piniella returned to the dugout to finish out the season. He did not return in 1989, instead taking another position within the Yankee organization. In 1990, Piniella accepted a managerial position with the Cincinnati Reds. It was in Cincinnati that he cemented his reputation as a successful manager, leading the Reds to victory against the heavily favored A's in the 1990 World Series. He also cemented other aspects of his managerial style. Piniella engaged in a clubhouse fight with Reds relief pitcher Rob Dibble, and the entire incident was caught on camera. He was legendary for his outbursts at umpires, but his fight with Dibble displayed to the public what those who had played for him already knew: Piniella didn't take shit from anyone, not umpires, not coaches, and certainly not his own players. He could be especially hard on catchers. His dislike for pitchers, particularly those who couldn't find the plate, was also well known.

Though they slipped in 1991, the Reds rebounded to win ninety-two games in 1992 but fell short of making the playoffs. Piniella, in the final year of his contract, was hugely popular in Cincinnati and easily could have returned.[100] The Reds offered him an extension, but his mind was focused elsewhere. Unfortunately for Piniella, a series of business interests had soured during the course of the early nineties, and many of his partners went bankrupt. He felt he had to leave baseball for a while and return to his home in New Jersey to get his finances in order.[101] Little did he know that on the other side of the country, a few men were plotting to thwart his plans. After receiving both Woodward and Armstrong's managerial choice list, Ellis and others began making their play for Piniella. Woody Woodward knew Piniella from his days as a Yankee executive and asked him to come to Seattle to meet the new owners. "I'll come out," Piniella told Woodward, "but I have no interest in the job." Piniella told his wife, Anita, the same thing. He was only going out there as a courtesy.[102] Piniella met with Ellis, Woodward, Armstrong, and part-owners Chris Larson, Jeff Raikes, and Craig Watjen at Salish Lodge, a restaurant approximately thirty miles outside Seattle. "Some of the guys really grilled him," said a somewhat embarrassed Ellis, "but Lou handled it all well."[103] After dinner, Ellis told Piniella they really wanted him to be their manager. Piniella wasn't convinced yet. He liked Ellis, but he had committed himself to taking care of his financial obligations and knew his wife would not approve.[104] The next day, after Piniella had flown back home, Ellis called to tell him, "We would really like to see you as manager, but I'm not convinced this would be anything but a short-term job." By implying he didn't think Piniella could turn around the Mariners, Ellis was indirectly challenging his ability as a manager. The tactic worked. Piniella took the bait and, much to the disapproval of Anita, accepted the job. "I made him so mad that he would show me that he was up to it," said Ellis.[105]

"When Lou came in, you noticed the change immediately," said Jay Buhner,[106] who had been with the Mariners since 1988. Buhner had come from the Yankees, where winning was expected day in and day out. His experiences once he arrived in Seattle had shocked him. Not just the losing, but the attitude around the team and city that losing was okay. That changed when Lou Piniella arrived in the spring of 1993.

"Lou was very instrumental in [my] signing with the team," said Chris Bosio, a starting pitcher who had signed with the Mariners before the 1993 season. "I felt the team could win quickly [with Lou there]."[107]

Piniella swept into training camp like a hurricane, immediately making clear that the misgivings and sins of Mariners teams of the past would not be tolerated. After an early spring training loss, he ordered the food room in the Mariners clubhouse to be locked up. When players began griping about it, Piniella exploded. "I'm tired of this," he yelled in one of many memorable clubhouse tirades. "This isn't a fucking country club. We got the motherfucking sandwiches and the motherfucking pizza. We got the fucking mini-bars. I'm sick and tired of this shit."[108]

The tirades continued. The Mariners had to play all of spring training on the road in 1993 because their complex in Peoria wouldn't be complete until the next year. Constantly being on the road didn't ease the pressure. Neither did an early-spring-training losing streak that culminated when the Mariners lost a game in the ninth inning. On the bus afterward, Piniella sat up and, to no one in particular, began muttering out loud, "I can't believe this. There is no way these guys are this fucking bad. No way." As he kept muttering, Piniella spotted some kids playing baseball in a sand lot. "Stop the mother-fucking bus!" he shouted. "You see those guys, those guys can play the game. Maybe we could beat these motherfuckers!"[109] The tirades continued into the regular season. Some bordered on the comical, such as the time Piniella pushed over a postgame spread and the clubhouse carpet caught fire. Piniella kept yelling and didn't notice the flames before players doused them with milk.

But even the comical moments got their point across. Piniella was obsessed with winning, and he instilled that type of attitude into his players. "Lou came in [during] spring training and said, 'Within three years, we will be in the playoffs,'" said Mariners trainer Rick Griffin. "That started people thinking not about .500, but about the playoffs."[110] It was an attitude that had been lacking in the Mariners' clubhouse for fifteen years. "We're not going through the motions," Lou told his players. "I'm going to weed out everyone who does, and I promise you your ass won't be here."[111]

The attitude paid off, as the Mariners finished 82–80, an impressive eighteen games better than 1992. They lost the division to the Chicago White Sox, who clinched the title at home during the end of the season. That night, as the White Sox celebrated, Piniella gathered his players in the clubhouse. "What you are seeing and what you hear, that's why you play. That's never gonna happen again while I'm here," he told them.[112]

Almost as important, over two million fans came to the Kingdome that year. The new ownership and the new manager had created a buzz around Seattle. But there was another element that contributed to the new Mariners.

• • • • • • • •

The foundation for the Mariners' success was laid many years before 1993. Seattle's new owners and manager were able to cultivate the seeds that had been planted in the ground, oddly enough, by the previous owners and personnel of the team, who almost caused its ruin. The biggest seed was Ken Griffey Jr. "Junior" was the seventeen-year-old son of Major League outfielder Ken Griffey Sr., and in 1987 he was crushing the competition as a player at Moeller High School in suburban Cincinnati. That year, he hit .478 with seven home runs and twenty-six RBIs in just twenty-four games.[113] "He was the best player I ever had in forty years of coaching. Junior would make a play, and [opposing] players collectively would go, 'Oh my God.' You never heard that about other players," said Mike Cameron, Griffey's high school baseball coach.[114] Scouts were all over him and for good reason. "The major league scouting reports all said the same thing about this kid—tremendous tools, a man in a kid's body, the sky is the limit," said Mariners scout Tom Mooney.[115] The upside of all the Mariners' abhorrent finishes was continuously having the top-five pick in the amateur draft, and in 1987, they had the first pick. The Mariners hadn't squandered their first picks in previous years, but those players became too good for Seattle and would be traded or allowed to leave. The Mariners knew what they were doing in terms of scouting, and yet, because of the complicated state of the team, they almost passed on Junior. George Argyros was in the middle of trying to sell the Mariners and buy the Padres. To avoid possible conflicts of interest, Commissioner Ueberroth had stopped Argyros from managing the day-to-day operations of the team and allowed him only one phone call a day to club president Chuck Armstrong, but only if there was a witness in the room.[116] Argyros had hinted that he didn't want the talented young outfielder. Griffey hadn't done particularly well in school, and there were questions as to whether he had the psychological makeup to be a big leaguer. Instead, Argyros wanted to pick Mike Harkey, a pitcher from Fullerton State. Shortly before the day of the draft, Armstrong and Argyros had their daily call, this time with Commissioner Ueberroth listening in. Armstrong pleaded his case and Argyros relented, as long as Griffey wouldn't cost them too much money.[117] As fate would have it, Junior was more interested in being the first pick than in having a cushy contract. The Mariners and Griffey came to an agreement, and he was selected first overall.[118] Mike Harkey was selected fourth by the Cubs.

Griffey's selection altered the course of Mariners history. After just a year and half in the minors, he joined the big-league club and began dazzling fans with his abilities. The scouting reports turned out to be accurate, as Junior developed into the best all-around player in baseball. In the outfield, the grace and the sheer easiness with which he tracked down fly balls amazed fans across the country. At the plate, he had the smoothest left-handed stroke that many people would ever see. He swung with no extraneous motion, using no leg kick and little movement of his hands or arms. As the pitch came, he smoothly brought the bat through the strike zone before it quickly exploded, sending balls high and deep into the Kingdome's third deck. By 1990, just his second year in the league, he was a bona fide star. That season he took part in one of the more poignant moments in baseball history when he played alongside his father in the Mariners outfield, the first time a father and son had ever played on the same team. In a magical moment at the "Big A" in Anaheim, the two hit back-to-back home runs.[119] He was named to his first All-Star team in 1990 and would be selected every year for the rest of his Mariners career. He broke out in 1993, hitting what was then a club record forty-five homers. During the season he tied a Major League record by homering in eight consecutive games. Junior wasn't just the game's greatest player; he was the face of baseball in Seattle. With Griffey, the Mariners finally had someone that the team could build the franchise around. This wasn't just because of his playing ability. He also had an infectious smile that became just as much a part of his legacy as his statistics. Still young, he was, by many accounts, a big kid at heart. "He played [video] games in the hotel room. He ate jawbreakers, licorice. There wasn't a mean bone in his body," said teammate Chris Bosio.[120] His attitude, which could give off an aura of entitlement, sometimes drove a wedge between him and his teammates, but there was no doubting his ability and dedication to the game. "There was always something he did a couple times a game where you went 'Wow,'" said former teammate Darren Bragg.[121]

In addition to Griffey, the Mariners made other well-timed draft picks, including Edgar Martinez in 1982 and Tino Martinez in 1988.

Not every trade made was a disaster, either. In 1989, they had shipped away their best pitcher Mark Langston to the Montreal Expos, a move decried in Seattle as just another money-saving trade that would not benefit Mariner baseball in any way. As part of the deal, the Expos threw in a tall starter with horrible control problems, but by 1993 Randy Johnson had worked out his issues and become the game's most dominating left-handed pitcher. With Junior, Edgar, Tino, Johnson, and such others as Buhner, Bosio, and Mike Blowers, the 1994 Mariners were poised to capture the AL West division title. The season got off to a disastrous start, however, and after several tiles fell from the Kingdome ceiling, the team was forced to go on an extended road trip that lasted weeks. But the road trip invigorated the Mariners, who had the benefit of playing in baseball's worst division. On August 11, they had a 49–63 record but were miraculously only two games behind the division-leading Rangers. The possibility of playoff baseball in Seattle was real for the first time. Then, the strike came.

3

Bronx Bummers

"How would you like it if every time something went wrong, I just blamed you, the supervisor, huh? Let's just fire the supervisor! Then I'll hire some other guy, and something would go wrong and I'd fire him, and I'd probably rehire you! Then fire you again, bring in someone else, then fire him and rehire you again! Then fire and hire, back and forth until the whole thing's just a big joke! Is *that* the kind of owner you want? Some yammering nincompoop in a fancy suit? No way you take that road, 'cause before you know it, you'll probably be banned from running the entire company."

—*Saturday Night Live* skit, October 1990, featuring convenience
store manager Carl, played by George Steinbrenner,
reacting to his head supervisor Pete's comment that
when owners are unsatisfied, they fire people

For the New York Yankees, fate had chosen a far different course than that of the Seattle Mariners. The Yankees had already won a record twenty world championships before Marty Pattin threw the first pitch for the Pilots in 1969.[1] The 1977 Mariners sported such forgetful names as Kevin Pasley, Bill Laxton, Joe Lis, and Tommy Smith. The Yankees' roster throughout the years had included baseball legends like Babe Ruth, Lou Gehrig, Joe DiMaggio, and Mickey Mantle. While just reaching .500 was considered a laudable goal in the early days of Seattle baseball, anything less than a championship was deemed a failure for the Yankees. After more than a decade without a playoff appearance, New York made the World Series in 1976, although they were swept the Cincinnati's "Big Red Machine." The following year, despite constant clashes between outfielder Reggie Jackson and manager Billy Martin, among others, the Yankees won their twenty-first world championship. The coexistence and odd relationship of Jackson and Martin came to define what would be famously labeled as the Bronx Zoo era. It was a time in the team's history when players fought themselves as well as the manager, took shots at each other in the press, and gave the general impression that they did not like each other, and yet somehow, they still found a way to win. It was an element that separated the Bronx Zoo Yankees from other teams. Hatred equaled winning.

In 1978, the Yankees overcame a two-games-to-none deficit against the Dodgers to win their twenty-second world championship. Little did anyone know that as Thurman Munson squeezed the last out of the series in his glove at Dodger Stadium, it would begin a championship drought the likes of which no Yankees player, coach, or fan had ever seen.

· · · · · · · · ·

Stunned by the death of Munson, killed in a plane crash at age thirty-two, the Yankees failed to make the playoffs in 1979. They returned to the postseason in 1980 after winning the American League East, but were swept in the American League Championship Series by the Royals. They again made the playoffs during the strike-interrupted 1981 season. Because the strike had occurred in midseason and resulted in the loss of approximately one third of all games for each team, a playoff format was devised whereby the teams in first place before and after the strike would make the playoffs (or a wild-card team if the same team was in first place for the first and second half) and a third round would be added to the postseason. It was a novel concept at the time, deemed necessary because of the work stoppage. A similarly formatted playoff would have to wait fourteen years before becoming a permanent fixture in the game.

The Yankees eliminated the Milwaukee Brewers in the best-of-five divisional series. They then swept the Oakland Athletics, led by manager Billy Martin, in the American League Championship Series and climbed out to a two-games-to-none lead against the Dodgers in the World Series. It looked like they were well on their way to a twenty-third championship, but it was not to be. After Game 2, the Yankees headed to Los Angeles where they blew leads in Games 3 and 4 and lost the next two games, as well. Unbeknownst to anyone in the crowd of 56,513 at Yankee Stadium during Game 6 against the Dodgers, fans were witnessing the last postseason game played in the Bronx for a long, long time.

• • • • • • • • •

Unlike the Mariner teams of the same era, the Yankees teams of the 1980s were not necessarily bad ball clubs. In fact, the Yankees won more games during the eighties than any other team. The problem, however, was that during the 1980s, the Yankees' good teams were not good enough to win the division. After a sluggish 1982 season, they won eighty-eight games in 1983 and followed that with eighty-nine wins the next year. While the win totals were certainly nothing to be ashamed of, they were not good enough in the highly competitive American League East to earn first place.

Building on their respectable win totals of 1983 and 1984, in 1985 the Yankees constructed what on paper appeared to be their best all-around team since the late seventies, and they made a run for the division title that lasted until the end of the year. Trailing the division-leading Blue Jays by three games, the Yankees went to Toronto on the season's final weekend. A Yankees sweep would force both teams to play a single remaining makeup game against another team and extend the Yankees' season. A dramatic, two-out ninth-inning comeback during the first game of the series kept New York alive, but the following night, they fell 5–1 and watched as the Blue Jays celebrated their first-ever division title.[2] The following day, Phil Niekro won his 300th game and the Yankees finished the year with ninety-seven wins. It was six more wins than the eventual world champion Kansas City Royals had during the regular season.

While it was a disappointing result, the ninety-seven wins indicated that the Yankees were not far from a division title and left open the possibility that the team could attain first place in 1986. But for a variety of reasons, the subsequent Yankees teams of the eighties would never be as good as the 1985 team and would never reach first place. From 1986 to 1988, the Yankees averaged eighty-eight wins a season but were only able to manage second-, fourth-, and fifth-place finishes, respectively. By 1989, the team was in a complete downward spiral. It would finish below .500 that year and every following year until 1993. A once intensely proud franchise was reduced to a laughingstock of baseball. The mismanagement and mistakes of the past had finally caught up with the Yankees.

• • • • • • • • •

During his tenure as owner of the Yankees, George Steinbrenner was a sportswriter's dream, a manager's nightmare, and a player's sugar daddy. In the years during and following the Yankees dynasty of the late 1990s, Steinbrenner's persona and image would be that of an owner who would do anything for a winning club. Managers, players, and fans would praise him for this. But before this "era of good feelings," there was a much darker period in which Steinbrenner was viewed in a far different light.

Born on July 4, 1930, in a suburb of Cleveland, George Steinbrenner was raised under the domineering presence of his father, Henry, who demanded nothing but the best from his only son. Failing to finish first brought questions as to why George had come up short. George was required to answer his father properly: Yes, sir; no, sir.[3] When George ended up buying the Yankees, his father remarked that it "was the first smart thing he's ever done."[4] George was forty-two at the time. That type of presence would influence how George ruled the Yankees empire for years. "I was brought up by a very tough task master father," Steinbrenner once admitted, "[but] the things he taught me put me in a pretty good stead throughout my life."[5]

Steinbrenner attended Culver Academy in Indiana and graduated from Williams College in 1952. He spent two years in the air force, before being named assistant football coach at Northwestern University. He was fired shortly thereafter and eventually took a job with this father's company, the American Ship Building Company.[6] Steinbrenner would dabble in sports throughout the following years, buying the Cleveland Pipers of the National Industrial Basketball

League. Eventually, the team went bankrupt. He attempted to buy the Cleveland Indians in 1971 for $9 million, but in a moment that changed the course of baseball history, the deal fell apart and he was outbid for the team by Nick Mileti.[7]

As Steinbrenner was trying his hand at various sports ownerships, the New York Yankees were falling apart. The team was finishing toward or at the bottom of the AL East standings nearly every year during the late 1960s. Attendance was barely exceeding one million fans.[8] CBS, which had owned the Yankees since 1965, was receiving much of the blame for the Yankees' drop-off. By 1972, the corporation decided to put the team up for sale. On January 3, 1973, twelve investors led by Steinbrenner and minority partner Michael Burke bought the Yankees from CBS for $8.7 million.[9] By 2001, the Yankees were worth an estimated $730 million,[10] making Steinbrenner's purchase of the Yankees perhaps the greatest investment in history.

"We plan absentee ownership as far as running the Yankees is concerned. We're not going to pretend we're something we aren't. I'll stick to building ships," said Steinbrenner after the sale was announced.[11] His definition of absentee ownership proved slightly different from that of everyone else's. "I guess I overstated a little," Steinbrenner admitted years later, referring to his infamous decree.[12] Four months after purchasing the team, he forced Michael Burke out as general partner. Steinbrenner, nicknamed "The Boss," made Burke a consultant but apparently never consulted him.[13] As John McCullen, another former minority owner of the Yankees, once put it: "There is nothing so limited as being a limited partner of George's."[14]

Steinbrenner immediately became involved in all functions of the team, including trades and managerial changes. Once free agency entered baseball in the midseventies, Steinbrenner obsessed over signing the biggest names available. First,it was Catfish Hunter, then Don Gullet, then Reggie Jackson. Then in an especially peculiar move, just weeks after closer Sparky Lyle won the 1977 American League Cy Young Award, Steinbrenner signed Rich "Goose" Gossage to be the team's closer for 1978. While the acquisition improved the club, it was odd that a team would replace their existing Cy Young Award–winning closer with another closer, no matter how good that replacement was.

Free-agent signings were coupled with ongoing public feuding between Steinbrenner and manager Billy Martin, plus the occasional Steinbrenner quote in the paper criticizing a player for poor performance. There was even a nine-month suspension given to him for the 1975 season after he pled guilty to making illegal campaign contributions to Richard Nixon's 1972 reelection campaign.[15]

Steinbrenner's fingerprints were seen on every move the Yankees made. His bizarre and overbearing behavior made headlines on a near-daily basis. But because he delivered three pennants and two world championships within the first six seasons of his ownership, the fans were willing to give a pass to any erratic actions he took. During the eighties, however, his act wore thin, as his decisions began impacting the team negatively on nearly all levels. It began with his destructive relationships with his managers.

• • • • • • • • •

The number of managerial changes that occurred on the New York Yankees after 1977 is stunning if not laughable. Steinbrenner changed managers a remarkable seventeen times between the summer of 1978 and the summer of 1990. By comparison, the Mariners, who certainly had their share of managerial issues, changed managers only nine times in the same period. Yankees managers were hired, fired, rehired, and refired. They were promised they would manage for the entire season and fired without lasting a month. They included former big-name Yankees players, managers who had had success with other teams, and sometimes no-name, organizational men who thought they had caught a break getting to manage the sport's most successful franchise. No matter what their motives for taking the job, the result was always the same.

Billy Martin managed the team five times under The Boss's reign and was rumored to be inquiring about managing the team again at the time of his death on Christmas Day, 1989.[16] Martin, though no angel himself, was tormented by Steinbrenner. Steinbrenner made calls to the dugout during games questioning Martin's decisions, and he constantly questioned Martin's health while dropping not-so-subtle hints to reporters about it. When Martin felt Steinbrenner was siding with Reggie Jackson, who was also driving Martin crazy, he famously remarked, "They deserve each other. One's a born liar and the other's convicted."[17] The constant hirings and firings eventually became a joke and whenever Martin managed the team, there was always the specter of The Boss standing over him, waiting to fire him at any moment.

Bob Lemon held the position of Yankees manager twice. After winning a championship in his first stint with the club in 1978, Lemon stepped down during the 1979 season and was replaced by Martin. Lemon returned in 1981 to replace Gene Michael as manager, only to be replaced by Michael during the 1982 season. In between Lemon, Martin, and Michael was Dick Howser, who managed the Yankees to 103 victories during the 1980 season. But after the Yankees were swept by the Royals in the ALCS, Howser was let go.[18]

Michael, who had been asked to join the Yankees organization by Steinbrenner after retiring as a player, had a particularly rough time as manager. Because of the strike and the reformatted playoff structure, the Yankees had already clinched a postseason berth once the work stoppage concluded in 1981. But the team struggled after returning from the strike, and Steinbrenner was constantly phoning and second-guessing Michael. After a game in late August in Chicago, Michael finally had enough. "I'm tired of getting phone calls after games and being told it's my fault we lost," he explained to reporters. "I thought I knew what I was getting into when I accepted this job, but I didn't expect it to be this direct and this constant."[19] Michael was fully aware that his comments could get him fired and said he did not care. Steinbrenner, instead of immediately firing Michael, deployed one of his favorite torture techniques by having the front-office staff shut off all communications with the Yankees' manager.[20] Finally, a week later, Michael was let go.

Yogi Berra managed the team to eighty-seven wins in 1984. On February 20, 1985, Steinbrenner declared that "Yogi will be the manager the entire [1985] season, win or lose . . . a bad start will not affect Yogi's status."[21] That promised lasted sixteen games. The Yankees did get off to a slow start, and The Boss fired Berra after a particularly bad team performance in Chicago.[22] In response to his firing, Berra vowed never to return to Yankee Stadium again (a promised he kept until the two made peace in 1999). Berra was replaced by the man he had replaced as manager: Billy Martin. Upon rehiring Martin, Steinbrenner boasted, "he is one of the few managerial geniuses in the game."[23] Despite this glowing praise, Martin was fired after the 1985 season and replaced by Lou Piniella, who was replaced by Martin for the start of the 1988 season. In June of that year, Martin was fired for a fifth and final time and replaced, for a second time, by Piniella.

Piniella's turn as manager was every bit as tumultuous as the others'. Piniella had a cordial relationship with Steinbrenner and was regarded as one of the few people who could joke about the owner to his face. "I have a special relationship with George," recalled Piniella. "We've had a love-hate relationship at times, from both sides."[24] But, as happened with the others before him, Piniella's relationship changed once he became manager. There were the incessant phone calls from Steinbrenner before, during, and after games. The owner continued second-guessing managerial decisions in the papers. Things nearly came to a head when, after a loss in the 1987 season, Steinbrenner demanded that Piniella meet with him the following afternoon, which was ignored. The result was an infuriated Steinbrenner who employed the same tactic he had used against Gene Michael: ordering the front-office staff not to communicate in any way with the Yankees manager.[25] As the season progressed, Steinbrenner issued a series of press releases that made not-so-subtle jabs at Piniella. Once the season was over, Piniella agreed to become the Yankees' general manager for 1988. When Billy Martin was fired for the fifth and final time that year, Piniella went back to managing the team but left after the season was over.

Dallas Green replaced Piniella after the 1988 season. Steinbrenner expressed the hope that bringing in someone from outside the organization, especially one with Green's reputation for discipline, would bring order to the team. But things went sour from the start. Steinbrenner, who had promised to leave control of the team to Green and his staff, began making personnel decisions that irked the new manager. Steinbrenner brought back aging pitchers Ron Guidry and Tommy John, much to the chagrin of Green, who had not wanted them on the roster. He traded away pitcher Rick Rhoden, despite the Yankees' need for pitching, and failed to re-sign Claudel Washington, leaving the team with a hole in the outfield.[26] Eventually, Green began feeling the same hassles and pressures as his predecessors. He lasted only 121 games into the 1989 season before being fired. In a memorable tirade after being let go, Green blasted his former employer. "George doesn't know a fucking thing about the game of baseball," Green told reporters. "That's the bottom line."[27]

Green was replaced by Bucky Dent, the former Yankees shortstop and hero of the team's one-game playoff against Boston in 1978. Dent lasted forty-nine games into the 1990 season and was fired after the team posted an abysmal 18–31 record. He was replaced by Carl "Stump" Merrill, a coach within the organization. Under Merrill, who had little to work with, the team finished last in 1990 and then won only seventy-one games in 1991.

In addition to the constant firings, Steinbrenner's Jekyll-and-Hyde attitude toward his managers was also rather odd. After firing a manager, he would exhibit signs of guilt or remorse for his action and then offer to keep the recently departed within the organization. Some became general manager, some scouts, and some were named to a new, vague position. "I don't know why he does it that way," said one Yankees executive. "Whether it's [from] guilt or charity."[28]

Steinbrenner's constant managerial changes were mystifying. Even worse was the impact they had on the atmosphere of the team. New managers meant new perspectives and new attitudes on playing the game. Such changes occurring every few months can be a huge distraction for any team. In 1998, Don Mattingly was asked who had managed the team at the beginning of the 1988 season. He could not remember and added that "when you change that much, it's hard to build, to get continuity and get a flow working."[29]

The constant changes made people weary of coming to play or manage for the Yankees. Who knew what might happen to them under The Boss's watch? If a manager who won ninety-seven games during a season was deemed a failure, who would possibly wish to fill those shoes? Who would want to handle such elevated expectations? Even if a championship could be attained, was it worth the stress, knowing that that was the only acceptable outcome? It was a frustrating situation for personnel, players, and fans as the revolving door of managers shuffled in and out of the Bronx.

• • • • • • • • •

As harmful as the managerial moves may have been, the decisions made by The Boss regarding his players during the eighties were more impulsive and far more destructive to the team. Steinbrenner reacted to his players the way a fan might yell at them from the Yankee Stadium bleachers. But unlike a fan, Steinbrenner actually had the ability to act on his feelings. And act he did, many times strictly on impulse. Players who could not provide Steinbrenner instant gratification faced harsh scrutiny in both public and private.

Sometimes, the entire team fell victim. Following the Yankees' loss to the Dodgers in the 1981 World Series, Steinbrenner issued a public apology: "I want to sincerely apologize to the people of New York and to the fans of the New York Yankees everywhere for the performance of the Yankees team in the World Series. I also want to assure you that we will be at work immediately to prepare for 1982."[30]

No player was immune from a negative press statement. Reggie Jackson, Goose Gossage, Graig Nettles, and Dave Winfield all had shots taken at them. Pitcher Doyle Alexander was performing so poorly during the 1982 season that after a particularly bad start, Steinbrenner informed the media that "I am having Doyle Alexander flown back to New York to undergo a physical. I'm afraid some of our players might get hurt playing behind him."[31] The shots became so bad during the 1982 season that the players requested a meeting with Steinbrenner, asking him to tone down his comments to reporters.[32] Two years later, Steinbrenner sent twenty-three-year-old shortstop Bobby Meacham down to Double A after he made an eighth-inning error with two outs that cost the Yankees a victory against the Texas Rangers. It was only the fourth game of the 1984 season.[33]

Rash actions such as these were more evident in transaction after transaction. With few exceptions, the majority of free-agent signings by the Yankees during the eighties and early nineties were busts or borderline disasters. Steinbrenner made decisions based simply on a gut feeling and was the driving force behind adverse free-agent signings and trades, acquiring players who were at best above average and at worst, not prepared for the New York spotlight.

Steve Kemp drove in 100 RBIs twice in his first six seasons in the Major Leagues and made the 1979 All-Star team. Believing that Kemp's left-handed swing would be perfect for the short right-field porch at Yankee Stadium, the Yankees signed him to a five-year deal before the 1983 season. But Kemp was plagued by injuries, missing 121 games over the course of his two years with the club and hitting only nineteen home runs. He was traded to Pittsburgh following the 1984 season.

Ed Whitson was a starting pitcher who in 1984 led the San Diego Padres to their first-ever World Series appearance. The Yankees signed him in December 1984 to a five-year, $4.4 million contract.[34] It was a staggering amount, considering Whitson had won more than ten games in a season only twice in an eight-year career. Whitson's time in New York became the stuff of bad legends. Although he compiled a 17–10 record in a season and a half with the team, his 5.38 ERA was a more accurate reflection of his performance. On September 22, 1985, he got into a brawl with manager Billy Martin in a Baltimore hotel, breaking Martin's arm.[35] The following year, things were so bad that Whitson would only make starts on the road due to the incessant booing he received from the home crowd at Yankee Stadium. Whitson told reporters that he had a shoebox full of hate mail and that he feared for his family's safety at their home in New Jersey.[36] He was eventually moved to the bullpen before being traded back to the Padres in July 1986. Whitson retired in 1991, having rebounded to win a respectable fifty-eight games in his last five seasons, but his career would be forever scarred by his time with the Yankees.

Whitson was joined in Yankees obscurity by his former Padre teammate Andy Hawkins. Hawkins enjoyed a few relatively successful seasons as a pitcher in San Diego, including 1988, when he posted fourteen wins and a 3.35 ERA. Though not the numbers of a perennial starter, Steinbrenner and the Yankees offered him a multimillion-dollar contract and an opportunity to be the staff ace. Hawkins led the club with fifteen wins in 1989, but he also led them with fifteen loses. The Yankees planned on releasing him in early 1990, but an injury to pitcher Mike Witt forced them to keep him on staff.[37] All told, Hawkins posted a 20–29 record in sixty-six appearances with the Yankees. He also had the unfortunate distinction of throwing a no-hitter against the White Sox on July 1, 1990, and thanks to three errors, losing the game, 4–0. Hawkins was released a month into the 1991 season and won only four more games in his career.

Joining Hawkins on those 1989 and 1990 Yankees teams was Dave LaPoint. Like Hawkins, LaPoint enjoyed moderate success throughout the 1980s. He had been traded late in the 1988 season to the Pittsburgh Pirates and had pitched extremely well for them in the team's attempt to catch the division-leading New York Mets. Based on his success in 1988, the Yankees signed LaPoint to a three-year, $2.5 million deal.[38] He lasted two seasons in pinstripes, winning only six games in 1989 and seven in 1990. LaPoint was released in February 1991 and pitched only two more games in his career.

Pascual Perez was a flamboyant pitcher who was known for sprinting from the dugout to the mound, his gold chains and Jheri curls shaking in all directions. Hard up for pitching after injuries decimated the staff in 1989, the Yankees signed Perez to a three-year,

$5.7 million contract to join the team for 1990.[39] Perez lasted just three starts into the 1990 season, before a right-shoulder injury sidelined him for the year. Amazingly enough, in a testament to how flaccid the 1990 Yankees offense was, Perez still lost two of his three starts that year, despite giving up only three runs combined in the two loses. He returned in 1991, bringing excitement and entertainment to the mound, but injuries again got the better of him and he made only fourteen starts. Before the 1992 season, he was suspended a year for violating Major League Baseball's drug policy. He never pitched in the majors again.

· · · · · · · · ·

Steinbrenner's numerous managerial comings and goings and the failed free-agent signings were both culprits in the Yankees' decline toward the end of the 1980s. But there was no bigger culprit than the numerous trading away of prospects. The list of young, talented players the Yankees dealt away after their playoff appearance in 1981 reads like an All-Star ballot. It included a Cy Young Award winner, a National League MVP, a World Series MVP, a two-time batting champion, and borderline Hall of Famers.

The exodus of talent began coincidentally as the Yankees were winning their last playoff game of the 1980s. The day of Game 2 of the 1981 World Series, they traded Willie McGee to the St. Louis Cardinals.[40] The Yankees had selected McGee in the first round of the 1977 amateur draft. He had a wiry frame but possessed great speed and a respectable glove. Never making it to the Bronx, he was traded away to the Cardinals and made an immediate impact, finishing third in the Rookie of the Year voting in 1982 and helping the team to a World Series championship. McGee became a four-time All-Star, a three-time Gold Glove winner, a two-time batting champion, and the 1985 National League MVP. He played in the postseason six times. In return for McGee, the Yankees acquired pitcher Bob Sykes, who at the time had a 23–26 career record. After the trade, Sykes never threw another pitch in the Major League.

Fred McGriff was drafted by the Yankees in 1981. Due to an abundance of first basemen in the Bronx at the time, his chances of making the club were slim; therefore, he was traded in December 1982, along with Mike Morgan and Dave Collins, to the Toronto Blue Jays for

Dale Murray and Tom Dodd.[41] McGriff hit 493 home runs and played in the postseason five times. Dale Murray won only three games for the Yankees and retired before McGriff made his Major League debut. Tom Dodd was released by the Yankees without ever playing a game for them.

Otis Nixon was signed by the Yankees after being selected in the first round of the second phase of the 1979 amateur draft. He made his Major League debut with the team in September 1983 but played only thirteen games for New York. Nixon was traded along with George Frazier to the Cleveland Indians in February 1984 for Toby Harrah and Rick Browne.[42] Nixon stole 620 bases in his career, while Harrah hit just .217 in his only season in pinstripes. Rick Browne never made it to the Major League.

Jose Rijo made his first Major League appearance on April 5, 1984. Although the Yankees were crushed by the Royals that day, Rijo pitched an effective $5\frac{1}{3}$ innings of four-hit, one-run relief. There was hope that he could turn into a solid starter for the team, but it never worked out and he was traded, along with several other players, to the Oakland A's in a blockbuster deal that brought Rickey Henderson and Bert Bradley to the Yankees. Henderson was an All-Star in each of the five seasons he played for the Yankees. He was, however, already back with the A's by the time Rijo was named World Series MVP with the 1990 champion Reds. Bradley never pitched a game for the Yankees.

Doug Drabek made his Major League debut with the Yankees in 1986, pitching well and winning a respectable seven games. But with only one pitcher posting more than ten victories for the team that year, the Yankees were desperate for an established starter for 1987. That off-season they traded Drabek, Logan Easley, and Brian Fisher to the Pittsburgh Pirates for Rick Rhoden, Cecilio Guante, and Pat Clements.[43] Rhoden led the Yankees in victories in 1987, but he had already retired from baseball when Drabek won the 1990 National League Cy Young Award for the East Division champion Pirates. It was the first of three consecutive division titles Drabek led Pittsburgh to. The Yankees shipped Guante to the Texas Rangers in August 1988 and Clements to the Padres in 1989. Combined, Rhoden, Clements, and Guante won only thirty-nine games for the Yankees.

Bob Tewksbury was also a rookie in the Yankees' 1986 starting rotation. His nine wins that year tied him for second on the club. Like Drabek, there were high hopes for him going into 1987. Those hopes were quickly dashed when Tewksbury lost four of the first eight games he pitched. In July, he was traded to the Cubs along with two other players for pitcher Steve Trout. After completing the trade, George Steinbrenner told then manager Lou Piniella, "I just won you the pennant [by getting Trout]."[44] It was a gross miscalculation by Steinbrenner, as Trout fell apart in New York, going 0–4 and walking thirty-seven hitters in just over forty-six innings pitched. In one particularly memorable outing, he issued five walks and three wild pitches in less than four innings against the Indians.[45] As Trout was retiring from baseball in 1990, Tewksbury was establishing himself as a solid starting pitcher for the Cardinals. He averaged thirteen wins a year from 1990 to 1994 and made the 1992 National League All-Star team.

Dan Pasqua had a left-handed swing that seemed tailor-made for Yankee Stadium's short right-field porch. Six feet tall and 200 pounds, Pasqua made his way through the Yankees system and debuted in 1985. From 1985 to 1987, he hit forty-one home runs in 646 at-bats, showing the potential to put up dangerous power numbers. But the Yankees, again needing pitching, traded Pasqua and two others to the Chicago White Sox in November 1987 for pitchers Richard Dotson and Scott Nielson.[46] Dotson had enjoyed moderate success in Chicago, including the 1983 season when he won twenty-two games and finished fourth in the Cy Young Award voting.[47] At the time of trade, however, he hadn't had an ERA below 4.00 in three seasons. That trend continued in the Bronx, as he posted an ERA of exactly 5.00 in 1988. He pitched even worse in 1989, walking more hitters then he struck out and winning only two games. The Yankees released him in July of that year. Dotson won only three more games in his career.

Shortly after releasing Dotson, the Yankees traded Nielson to the Mets. Nielson had serious control issues and actually performed worse for the Yankees than Dotson. He walked fourteen hitters in just $20\frac{1}{3}$ innings with the team. While Pasqua never realized his full potential, he did provide the White Sox with respectable power numbers and run production in limited playing time. Simply stated, the White Sox got far more out of Pasqua than the Yankees did out of Dotson and Nielson.

Hal Morris was another sweet-swinging lefty brought up through the Yankees organization. A first baseman with a better-than-average glove, Morris made a handful of appearances for the club in 1988 and 1989. With Don Mattingly at first base and power-hitting lefty first baseman Kevin Maas waiting in the minors, Morris's future with the team appeared to be going nowhere. In December 1989, he was traded along with minor leaguer Rodney Imes to the Reds in exchange for Tim Leary and Van Snider.[48]

Outside of a seventeen-win season for the Dodgers in 1988, Leary had not made much of a mark in the Major League. He had been a highly touted Mets prospect who injured himself during his Major League debut in 1981 and missed the rest of the season.[49] But the Yankees were desperate for pitching and took a gamble. They lost, and so did Leary—in droves. Leary lost nineteen games in 1990, tying for the most losses by any pitcher in a single season in that decade. He struggled again in 1991, causing the team to move him to the bullpen. During a nationally televised game in Baltimore in 1992, Leary was caught on camera apparently chewing on a foreign substance in his glove. Although exactly what he was doing was never determined, it appeared he was chewing on a piece of sandpaper. Shortly thereafter, Leary was traded to the Mariners. In two and half years as a Yankee, he went 18–35. Snider never played a game for the Yankees. As Leary and Snider floundered in 1990, Morris batted .340 for the eventual world champion Reds. He hit .300 or better six times in his career.

While these moves were all costly, no trade better exemplified the Steinbrenner rule of the eighties than a deal made in 1988 with the Seattle Mariners: Ken Phelps for Jay Buhner.

• • • • • • • • •

Ken Phelps was typecast for the role of designated hitter. He was adequate defensively but had no speed, did not hit for average, and struck out frequently. His upside was a powerful bat, especially against right-handed pitchers, that produced impressive home-run–to–at-bat ratios. The Yankees were making a stretch run for first place in 1988, and sought to add a left-handed power hitter to the lineup. On July 21, they traded outfielder Jay Buhner to the Mariners for Phelps.[50] Buhner had appeared in thirty-two games with the Yankees and struck out in a third of his at-bats. He had potential to be a major power hitter, and he possessed a strong throwing arm. But in the win-now, win-at-all costs atmosphere of Steinbrenner, there was no time for that potential to materialize.

After the trade, Phelps hit ten home runs and drove in twenty-two runs for the Yankees as they finished the year three and a half games behind the first-place Red Sox. Phelps played for the Yankees in 1989 but did not remain with the team past the trading deadline in August. He was acquired by the A's, who were looking for a power hitter off the bench as they prepared for the playoffs. Phelps would get the championship ring he coveted that year but would play only one more season in the majors.

Buhner hit ten home runs and drive in twenty-five runs for the Mariners in 1988, amazing the home crowds with his cannon arm in right field and winning the respect of his new teammates with his style of play. "The attitude he brought here was great," said Scott Bradley, the Mariners' catcher that year. "[He] just lifted this whole team. He's a throwback to the old days."[51] In his first performance against the Yankees on August 19, 1988, Buhner crushed a three-run home run off John Candelaria that landed in the unused center-field bleacher seats at Yankee Stadium known as "the Black." At the time, he was only the fourth player to have hit a ball there since the stadium's renovation in the early seventies.[52] In a 1991 game against the Yankees at Yankee Stadium, Buhner hit a 479-foot home run to left field, one of the longest in the ballpark's history. Buhner exploded that year, hitting twenty-seven home runs and driving in seventy-seven runs. From that season on, he was regarded as one of the games' premiere power threats.

At the time it occurred, the Buhner-for-Phelps trade was not considered as lopsided as it would be in later years. "I was a better player than Jay at the time," Phelps proudly pointed out years later,[53] and he is correct. Phelps's impact on the 1988 Yankees was far greater than anything Buhner could have or would have contributed. But this was only short-term thinking. It was exemplary of the type of knee-jerk, poorly thought-out decisions that emanated from the Yankees front office, and more accurately, George Steinbrenner's mind, during the 1980s.

Lou Piniella, then the manager, was aware of the negative repercussions the trade would have. "George, we don't need Phelps," he explained to Steinbrenner before the trade. "You're going to cause me problems here."[54] Privately, Piniella had told Steinbrenner, "We need one [a left-handed hitter] who pulls the ball, not one who hits straightaway or to left like Phelps."[55] Publicly, however, Piniella tried to put on his best face, explaining about Phelps, "you look at the great Yankee teams; they've won championships with left-handed hitters taking aim at the short porch."[56]

In terms of immediate impact, the Yankees had little room for Phelps. Jack Clark was serving as the designated hitter, and Don Mattingly was the team's first baseman. "I remember walking into the clubhouse and wondering 'What do they need me for?' They had several guys embedded at first base," recalled Phelps.[57] His addition meant that if all three were going to play, someone was going to have to move to the outfield. Piniella even went so far as to tell Clark and Mattingly to be available to play the outfield if called upon.[58] "[Jack] Clark was upset," said Phelps.[59] Forced by the actions of Steinbrenner, the Yankees were actually telling baseball's best-fielding first baseman and their full-time designated hitter that they might have to play in the outfield. It was a ludicrous situation.

More baffling was that at the time, the Yankees' most pressing need was for a pitcher—a fact Phelps himself even admits. "They needed pitching, not a first baseman," recalled Phelps. "If we [the Yankees] had pitching, we could have won the division."[60] Despite this need, the Yankees showed no interest in acquiring right-hander Mike Boddicker from the Orioles. Baltimore sent Boddicker to the Red Sox for Brady Anderson, who by most accounts was a less-coveted prospect than Buhner. Boddicker went 7–3 in Boston and helped the Red Sox win the division.

In the long term, the Buhner-Phelps trade was questionable because Buhner might have had a spot with the team after another season or two. It could be understood why a player like Fred McGriff or Hal Morris were traded, as there were many roadblocks in their paths to joining the team. But at the time of the trade, the Yankees could have made a spot available for Buhner in the near future had they been patient enough. Although they would not know it when the trade occurred, Dave Winfield would miss the entire 1989 season due to a back injury, and Rickey Henderson would be traded. Buhner could have stepped into their spots if they—or, more accurately, Steinbrenner—had exhibited patience.

Despite having no position for Phelps to play, despite being in desperate need of a starting pitcher, and despite the potential that Buhner showed, the trade was still made. Though perhaps not the worst deal of the 1980s, it was the clearest example of why it was nearly impossible for the Yankees to have been in contention by 1989. Steinbrenner's deals depleted their farm system, and they had acquired little of value in return. The owner habitually signed numerous overpaid and underachieving free agents, constantly belittled his players in the media, and changed managers on an almost yearly basis. It got to the point where players simply had no desire to sign with the Yankees, and those who were already playing for the team were miserable. "You come here," said Mattingly during a rare outburst in the course of the 1988 season, "and you play and you get no respect. They treat you like shit."[61] Another player once stated that he was glad about Steinbrenner's increased business-flight schedule, because it meant there was a better chance he would perish in a plane crash.[62]

By 1990, the Yankees finished in last place for the first time in thirty-four years. Mattingly, their only legitimate star, was playing through a crippling back injury that caused him to post the worst numbers of his career. Their starting lineup included such forgettable names as Oscar Azocar and Hensley Meulens. Their pitching staff was in such shambles that no starting pitcher won more than nine games. The attendance dropped sharply, going from over 2.6 million in 1988 to slightly over 2 million in 1990 and down to just 1.74 million in 1992. Team moral sunk, and play on the field was awful. The Yankees went from being the greatest, proudest team to a laughingstock of baseball. Yet as the team sank deeper and deeper into mediocrity in the early nineties, three things occurred off the field that, unbeknownst at the time, would lead the Yankees back into contention in the American League and directly into their first-round divisional series matchup with the Mariners in 1995.

· · · · · · · ·

Dave Winfield was a remarkable athlete. He was drafted by four teams in three major sports: the San Diego Padres in baseball, the Minnesota Vikings in football, and the Atlanta Hawks of the NBA and the Utah Stars of the ABA in basketball. He chose the Padres, going straight to the big leagues without spending a day in the minors. Winfield hit for average as well as for power, and he had speed, a great glove, and a strong throwing arm. He posted All-Star–caliber numbers year after year in San Diego, but the Padres were going nowhere. A free agent after the 1980 season, Winfield was courted by several teams, but it was George Steinbrenner and the Yankees who won the battle. Steinbrenner, again fascinated with landing the biggest free agent available, signed Winfield to a then-record contract: $23 million over ten years.[63]

Landing yet another big-name free agent should have been a source of happiness for Steinbrenner, but things were shaky from the beginning. The Boss seemed to harbor resentment against Winfield, feeling the outfielder had outmaneuvered him in contract negotiations.[64] Making the situation worse was Winfield's 1–22 performance in the 1981 World Series. While he would rebound by averaging over 100 RBIs a season from 1982 to 1988, it still wasn't good enough for The Boss. During the stretch run in 1985, Steinbrenner entered the press box at Yankee Stadium to inform the writers that he had gotten rid of Reggie Jackson, known as "Mr. October," and brought in Winfield, who was "Mr. May."[65] The Mr. May title would never leave Winfield, causing even him joke about it, saying once after a particularly good April, "we go on to May and you know about me and May."[66]

The relationship between the two deteriorated to the point where in January 1989, Winfield sued Steinbrenner for failing to make an annual $450,000 contribution to Winfield's foundation, which helped underprivileged children. Steinbrenner countersued, saying that Winfield's foundation was guilty of fraud, wrongdoing, and misappropriations. The two sides eventually came to a settlement, but unfortunately for Steinbrenner, the story did not end there. The question of how he had obtained information about Winfield's foundation led directly to Howard Spira, a known gambler who was alleged to have ties to the mafia.[67]

Spira had done some public relations work for Winfield's foundation, but when Winfield spurned him, Spira reached out to several people with allegedly harmful news about the Yankees outfielder. One of those people was George Steinbrenner. The Boss allegedly paid Spira $40,000 to provide him with the negative information about Winfield.[68] Steinbrenner would later say the money was to protect Yankees personnel.[69]

By the summer of 1990, Winfield had already been traded to the California Angels, and his long and rocky history with the Yankees seemed over. But Commissioner Fay Vincent had been investigating the Steinbrenner-Winfield-Spira affair, and on July 30, 1990, he issued

his ruling: For being associated with and paying Spira $40,000, Stein-
brenner would be banned for life from the day-to-day operations of
the Yankees and he was to resign as the Yankees' general partner by
August 20, 1990. "He can no longer be involved in the management of
the team. Ever," announced Vincent.[70] Adding insult to injury, Vincent
noted in his report that after having listened to Steinbrenner testify
before him, he was "able to evaluate a pattern of behavior that borders
on the bizarre."[71]

Vincent's ruling sent shockwaves throughout baseball, as the idea
of the Yankees without George Steinbrenner seemed incomprehen-
sible. Many players thought the punishment was too much. "We were
prepared for a suspension," said Yankees pitcher Andy Hawkins, "but
this is beyond what we were expecting."[72]

"I think it's pretty harsh," commented Hawkins's teammate Dave
LaPoint. "I think it's pretty severe."[73]

One group that did not share that sentiment was the fans. The
Yankees were on their way to a rare victory against the Tigers the
night of July 30, and as news of Vincent's decision spread throughout
the stadium, fans began cheering and chanting "It's over! It's over!"[74]

"As the news flashed across the Yankee Stadium scoreboard
announcing that boss George Steinbrenner had been given the heave-
ho, fans spontaneously leaped to their feet and applauded and cheered
for a minute and a half," according to New York Newsday.[75]

"I can't believe it," declared Richie Zeisler, a happy Yankees fan then
residing in Virginia. "I've been waiting for this a long, long time." Zeisler
then celebrated by buying a round of beers for his friends.[76]

"I speak for all true Yankee fans when I say that getting rid of
Steinbrenner is the best thing that could happen to the Yankees,"
declared Bobby Ricci, a native of the Bronx.[77]

The fan reaction may have seemed harsh, but Steinbrenner's banish-
ment from the team's operations truly was a blessing for the Yankees.
Although Vincent later reduced the lifetime ban to a thirty-month
suspension, allowing Steinbrenner to return to the Yankees on March
1, 1993, it would turn out to be just enough time to allow the team
to correct itself. With The Boss gone, the Yankees were free to do
things that other successful teams had done. They could rebuild the
farm system, prevent young rising stars from being traded for aging
has-beens, sign modest contracts with stars who could handle the

spotlight, and avoid the overhyped overpriced signings of the past. To do this, the Yankees called on Gene Michael. Michael had been fired twice by Steinbrenner as manager and had been undistinguished as a Major League player. But his scouting ability and player-evaluation instincts were exceptional. On August 20, 1990, as Steinbrenner was parting ways with the team, Michael stepped in as general manager, ready to rebuild the ship that, ironically, the Cleveland shipbuilder had destroyed.

• • • • • • • • •

Gene Michael may have been better off playing basketball, his true love. His tall, skinny frame, which led people to call him "Stick," seemed better suited for the NBA, he was even offered a spot with the Detroit Pistons in 1962. But at the time, he was in the Pittsburgh Pirates minor-league system, having signed with the team in 1959. Afraid to break his contract with the Pirates, Michael turned down the offer.[78] He enjoyed some success at the minor-league level but languished there for years before finally making the big-league team in 1966. Michael turned out to be no match for big-league pitching, however, usually struggling to keep his batting average above the Mendoza Line (.200). He spent time with the Pirates, Dodgers, Yankees, and Tigers, but after eleven seasons in which he hit only .229 with fifteen home runs, Stick was done as a player.

Although his playing career was relatively unsuccessful, Michael gained a reputation as being unusually intelligent and perceptive about baseball. He had a sixth sense when it came to the game, picked up on things others missed, and was an amazing evaluator of talent. Shortly after retiring as a player, he met with Steinbrenner, who told him he needed to remain in baseball. The Boss hired him as a coach in 1978, moved him to manager of the team's AAA affiliate in 1979 and used him as general manager briefly in 1980. He then installed Michael as manager in 1981, fired him, rehired him in 1982, only to fire him shortly thereafter.[79]

Despite the firings and the constant changes of position, Michael maintained a close relationship with The Boss. After he resigned as manager of the Chicago Cubs in 1987, Steinbrenner brought him back to the Yankees as a scout. It was what Michael truly loved to do anyway. It was not in him to sit behind a desk filling out paperwork all day. He wanted to be out watching games, evaluating talent.[80]

In August 1990, as he was preparing to step down from the team, Steinbrenner began searching for a replacement for his general manager, Harding Peterson. Several suggestions were being thrown around, including Don Sutton, Whitey Herzog, and Tom Seaver.[81] These were all well-known, established names. Herzog had been a successful manager with the St. Louis Cardinals; Sutton and Seaver were both future Hall of Fame pitchers with over 300 career victories apiece. But for perhaps the first time, Steinbrenner decided against a marquee name that would have drawn big headlines. He stayed in house, naming Michael as the general manager.[82] "I have great confidence in him," said Steinbrenner as he introduced Michael at the press conference. "No one is more knowledgable in the organization."[83] What many people took that to mean was that Steinbrenner had put in place someone he could control while displaced from the team. In some circles, Michael was regarded strictly as a Steinbrenner "yes" man. Michael himself took exception to that idea and claimed that Steinbrenner never had any say or influence with him or the organization after leaving on August 20, until his return in 1993. "He never slipped me a note, never told me what to do, not once," asserted Michael, years afterward.[84]

Regardless of the motivations behind the move, Michael's hiring was a parting gift by Steinbrenner to the Yankees. Michael immediately set about cleansing the team of several elements. The first was an abundance of right-handed hitters.[85] In 1990, only two regulars in the Yankees lineup batted from the left side. It was an extremely low number for a team that played eighty-one games a year with one of the shortest right-field fences in baseball. Additionally, Michael sought out players who excelled in his favorite statistical category, on-base percentage.[86] He looked for players with high numbers of extra-base hits, not just those who hit home runs. Right field may have been short at Yankee Stadium, but left-center field, known as Death Valley, was almost 400 feet from home plate. It was a hot spot for doubles, even triples, especially for left-handed hitters who could take the ball to the opposite field. By 1993, Michael had acquired two such hitters in third baseman Wade Boggs and right fielder Paul O'Neill. He had also picked up the little-used catcher Mike Stanley in 1992. Stanley became a fan favorite, as he sprayed the ball to all fields for average and for power.

Michael also sought to rid the team of negative-impact players. He focused on those who were in it more for themselves than for the team, and on players who were so used to losing in New York they had no ambition to create a winning atmosphere. Those who had made substantial contributions in 1990, 1991, or 1992, but whose attitude negatively impacted the team, were traded or not re-signed. Pitchers were dropped at such a rapid rate that not a single pitcher from the 1990 staff appeared on the Yankees' 1993 opening-day roster. Instead of seeking the biggest names on the market, Michael went after pitchers who ate up innings and won games at a respectable, steady pace. Jimmy Key was not regarded as one of baseball's premier pitchers, but he had won at least twelve games a season every year from 1985 to 1992. Key had also proved he could pitch in big situations, helping the Blue Jays to a World Series championship in 1992. Michael signed him to be the Yankees' number-one starter for 1993 and Key responded by winning eighteen games and finishing fourth in the American League Cy Young Award voting.

Most important, Michael allowed prospects to develop in the minor leagues. Players such as Bernie Williams, Scott Kamieniecki, Mariano Rivera, and Andy Pettitte were able to move through the minor-league system at a pace that would prepare them for the Major League. There was temptation to trade them. Teams had inquired about the Yankees' prospect Bernie Williams, but Michael would not budge, refusing to relinquish the young outfielder.[87] Instead, he called Williams up to the big leagues for a period during the 1991 season and called him up for good in midseason in 1992. Michael was confident enough in Williams's ability that he actually had Roberto Kelly, the team's only representative at the All-Star Game that year, moved over to left field so that Williams could play center. By 1993, Kelly was gone and Williams would be the Yankees' everyday center fielder for another decade.

Michael's ability to evaluate talent never seemed to fail. Even signings that did not work out as planned, such as Danny Tartabull, were not the complete failures that had been seen in the 1980s. And luckily for Michael, George Steinbrenner was not there to second-guess every move or to put pressure on Michael to make big deals or sign ridiculous contracts. Michael had taken the Yankees from being the American League's worst team in 1990 to being in contention with the Blue Jays for the 1993 AL East Division title. The offense in 1990 had driven in a stunningly low 561 runs over the entire season. In fact, the 1990 Yankees finished last in the American League in runs scored, base hits, doubles, walks, batting average, on-base percentage, and slugging percentage. By 1993, they had reversed course in all categories, finishing first in base hits and batting average and finishing fourth or higher in runs scored, doubles, walks, on-base percentage, and slugging percentage. They went from sixty-seven wins in 1990 to seventy-one in 1991 to seventy-six in 1992 and eighty-eight in 1993. It was an impressive turnaround in just three years' time.

The suspension of Steinbrenner and the hiring of Michael as general manager had taken the Yankees far, but one more element was needed to get them back to the postseason. The team needed a manager who could provide long-term stability and reinstall a winning attitude in the clubhouse. Michael, as Steinbrenner had once done with him, looked in-house for the answer.

• • • • • • • • •

The Yankees had slogged through a thoroughly unimpressive 1991 season with Stump Merrill as manager. Merrill, a member of the organization for years, was given the managerial position in 1990 after the firing of Bucky Dent and had watched the team finish in last. Under Merrill, the Yankees faired little better in 1991, winning only seventy-one games and enduring a season that saw constant bickering and complaining from the clubhouse. The clubhouse emitted an aura of unpleasantness as veterans complained to reporters about their playing time or the Yankees' constant lack of winning. Merrill, the stereotypical picture of a big-league coach or manager, with his large beer gut and lip full of tobacco, made matters worse when he benched captain Don Mattingly in mid-August for failing to adhere to a team policy regarding players' hair length. Eventually, the "players formed an anonymous mutiny against Merrill, even imploring reporters it was 'your job' to get him fired."[88] By season's end, it was apparent to all that Stump's days were numbered. Barely a week after the Yankees finished the year with a paltry .438 winning percentage,

Merrill was fired, along with his entire coaching staff. Included in the purge was third-base coach Buck Showalter.

"Gene called me and said I would not be the manager and that I was free to explore work elsewhere," said Showalter. Though Showalter had received glowing reviews from players, Gene Michael did not originally consider him to manage the team.[89] Michael wanted to look outside the organization, as each of the Yankees' previous three managers had either been coaches or executives with the team at the time of their hiring. Additionally, as he informed the media after the firings, "we want somebody who's been a major league manager."[90] Weeks after firing Merrill, however, Michael sat in a meeting with Yankees general partner Robert Nederlander and chief operating officer Leonard Kleinman. The team had yet to find a manager, and Michael's suggestions of former managers Doug Rader and Hal Linier did not appeal to the Yankees brass.[91] Kleinman and Nederlander wanted Michael to reconsider Showalter, as no one else seemed to fit the bill. Michael consented and reached out to the recently fired third-base coach. Showalter, not knowing about the change of heart that had occurred, was "so flabbergasted by the turn of events [when Michael called to offer the managerial position] that there was a long silence from his end of the phone. Michael, realizing Showalter's surprise, said, 'I'll tell you what. I'll call you back in 10 minutes.'"[92]

For Showalter, it was hardly a difficult decision. He had been a Yankee every moment of his professional baseball career. He was an outfielder in the team's minor-league system for years but failed to make it to the big leagues. He retired in 1983 and became a coach for the Yankees' Class A team in Fort Lauderdale and, in 1985, became manager of the team's Class A club in Oneonta. Showalter managed five years in the minors, compiling an impressive 360–207 record, as his teams finished in first place four out of those five years. He became a coach for the big-league club in 1990 and was Merrill's third-base coach throughout the 1991 season.[93] He had lived and breathed the Yankees his entire career and, having been a minor-league manager in the system for years, was well acquainted with the numerous up-and-coming younger players. On October 20, 1991, the Yankees made it official, announcing Showalter as the team's new manager. At thirty-five, he was the youngest manager in the game and the youngest manager of the Yankees in seventy-seven years.[94] The change of heart by Gene Michael, thanks to some prodding, was a critical juncture for the team, as Showalter would drastically change the appearance, the structure, and the dignity of the Yankees.

· · · · · · · · ·

"Gene and I knew there had to be a culture change," said Showalter, referring to the atmosphere in the clubhouse.[95] In 1991, the team had been full of players who made excuses, whose presence alone negatively impacted those around them. "Guys used to be in the clubhouse watching TV during the game. That didn't happen when Buck came in," said Jesse Barfield.[96] Working together gradually over the course of the 1992 season and into 1993, Showalter and Michael rid the team of this group of individuals. In their place came players such as Mike Stanley, Spike Owen, Mike Gallego, and Steve Farr, none of whom were the greatest at their positions but all of whom were dedicated to the team concept.[97] Showalter didn't just eliminate the negative element, but he did his best to implant the team concept in the minds of his players. "Buck would constantly be saying it's about us [the team], not me [the individual]," said former Yankees coach Brian Butterfield.[98] Additionally, the Yankees not only needed to play great on the field, but Showalter felt they also needed to emit an aura of greatness and respectability in appearance off the field. Showalter made improvements to the clubhouse to enhance its overall appearance, and he was personally a meticulous dresser, always attempting to present himself in a dignified manner becoming of a New York Yankee—in sharp contrast to his predecessor, Stump Merrill.[99] To Showalter, being a Yankee was an honor, a special gift bestowed on a chosen few, and those who were chosen needed to act the part. Buck also had an intensity about him that projected an image of success not seen in Yankees managers for some time. Though not on a level with Billy Martin or Lou Piniella in terms of blowing up at umpires, players, or even George Steinbrenner, Showalter was not afraid to pick a fight when needed. During a 1992 game against the A's at Yankee Stadium, he charged from the dugout to directly confront A's manager Tony LaRussa behind home plate, precipitating a bench-clearing brawl.[100]

In addition to his concerns about atmosphere and attitude, Showalter was a micromanager who paid attention to the most minute of details. "Buck was thoroughly prepared . . . [and] amazingly detail oriented," recalled pitcher Jim Abbott, who played for Showalter in 1993 and 1994. "He had a terrific sense for putting people into situations where they could succeed, especially on the offensive side of things."[101] Showalter's office was full of charts, stats, facts, and figures about other teams, and he was constantly thinking of ways to outsmart his opponent, even through unconventional measures.[102] Showalter pushed any button, attempted any maneuver, to give his team even the slightest of edges. "Buck did a lot to give catchers the best opportunity [to throw out a runner]," said Mike Stanley, referring to Showalter's constantly calling for throws to first base in order to keep base runners close to the bag.[103] The throws drove fans crazy due to the delays they caused in the action, but to Showalter, it was a necessary part of the game, done to keep the other team from gaining any advantage. He even once drew the ire of Tigers manager Sparky Anderson when, in a May 1993 game in Detroit, Showalter had Pat Kelly steal second base with the Yankees leading 6–0. Showalter assumed no lead was safe, and he played to win (he was right about the lead, as the Yankees lost that game 7–6).[104]

Under Buck Showalter, the overall improvement in the players' morale, their appearance, and the manner in which they carried themselves on a day-to-day basis immediately became noticeable as the Yankees began winning again in 1993. By then, the team that Gene Michael put together and Showalter skippered made a run at the division title, falling just short. Even the reemergence of George Steinbrenner, whose lifetime ban had been lifted in March 1993, did not set the team adrift, as The Boss returned somewhat milder in attitude, at least in public. By 1994, the Yankees had all the pieces they needed. Showalter became a fan favorite, adored for his managerial style and the respectability he brought back to the franchise. He won the American League Manager of the Year award that year, Paul O'Neill led the league in batting average, Don Mattingly hit .300 for the first time in five years, and Jimmy Key was barely edged out by David Cone for the Cy Young Award. The Yankees posted the best record in the American League and were 6½ games ahead of second-place Baltimore on August 11. Fans were finally returning to Yankee Stadium, and the team was well on its way to the playoffs for the first time in over a decade. Then, the strike happened.

4

Strike

"Baseball games are won and lost because of errors. This will go down as the biggest 'E' of all. The losers are the fans, and there is no winner."
—Former baseball commissioner Peter Ueberroth on the cancellation of the 1994 World Series due to the players' strike

On August 12, 1994, the Major League Baseball players went on strike. It was the eighth time in twenty-three seasons that a work stoppage occurred, so the strike itself was not a rare occurrence.[1] Still, this one seemed more serious than the others. Years of pent-up frustration, resentment, and deep mistrust had built up between the owners and the Major League Baseball Players Association. Much of it stemmed from the period of 1985–1987, when owners colluded with each other not to sign free-agent players in an attempt to keep salaries down.[2] The owners were eventually caught and forced to pay the players $280 million in damages.[3] Both sides never truly trusted each other from then on. When the owners essentially forced Commissioner Fay Vincent to resign in 1992, only to replace him with an owner (Bud Selig, of the Brewers), the tension grew worse.[4]

When the collective bargaining agreement between the owners and players expired in 1994, the tension came to a head. The average salary for a ballplayer stood at $1.2 million, nearly twenty times what it had been in 1976.[5] Claiming fears that escalating salaries would eliminate competitive play and crush small-market teams, the owners wanted to institute the sport's first-ever salary cap.[6] The Players Association, which had gradually gained strength since the inception of free agency in the 1970s, refused to agree to one. Its stand was not just one of principle. It simply didn't believe the owners' claims that baseball was in financial difficulty, considering that revenues from the game had gone from $625 million in 1985 to $1.8 billion in 1994.[7] The two sides discussed a new agreement throughout the 1994 season, but by July 28, they were far apart on negotiations. It appeared the owners might simply impose a salary cap upon players, which they could do if the season ended without a new agreement. To gain leverage in that contingency, the players set a strike date of August 12.[8] The deadline came and went without a deal. In fact, on August 11, negotiators on both sides never even met.[9] On August 12, the season was halted. "There is no doubt in my mind the players are united, as always, and the owners are united this time for a significant series of reasons," said Acting Commissioner Bud Selig. "But having said that, now we have to figure out a way to solve this thing."[10] The potential fallout from the strike was so alarming that even President Bill Clinton weighed in, saying, "There are a lot of little kids out there who want to see this season come to a close and there are a lot of not-so-little kids out there who know this is the most exciting baseball season in forty years."[11]

But the stoppage continued for days, then weeks. Finally, on September 14, Selig announced the cancellation of the World Series and, thus, the official end of the 1994 season. Fifty-two days and 669 games were lost.[12] For the first time since 1904, there was no postseason. The contentiousness on both sides was clear, as player representative Donald Fehr noted, "I have every reason to believe, given the calmness with which [Selig's] announcement was preceded, it was something the owners had long since come to accept as necessary."[13] Though fans were angry over the strike in general, the cancellation of the season was unfathomable and the backlash severe. Players were seen as greedy and vilified across the country. Many fans did not know or care to know the intricacies of the strike or the Players Association's position. "There came a time when you just threw up your hands trying to explain your position. I remember the fans I spoke to didn't want to hear any of it. They just looked at us and the owners as millionaires fighting with billionaires," said Tony Gwynn.[14]

Fans were also repulsed at the cancellation of what was becoming one of the greatest seasons in recent memory. Ken Griffey Jr. and San Francisco Giants third baseman Matt Williams were both challenging Roger Maris's single-season record of sixty-one home runs. Tony Gwynn, hitting .394, was attempting to become the first player since 1941 to bat over .400 in a season. Albert Belle of the Indians and Frank Thomas of the White Sox each had legitimate shots at becoming the first Triple Crown winner in twenty-seven years.[15] The Montreal Expos, who had struggled with subpar attendance and only made the postseason once in their existence, had baseball's best record. The Yankees, who hadn't made the postseason since 1981, stood atop the AL East. The Cleveland Indians, perennial losers of the American League, were in second place, challenging for the wild card and selling out every home game at their brand-new facility, Jacobs Field. The Texas Rangers were on the verge of their first postseason appearance. The wild card, the brainchild of Bud Selig whereby the teams in the American and National League with the best record not to finish in first place in their division made the playoffs, had allowed many teams to remain in the postseason hunt. It was all washed away. Once the World Series was canceled, many fans vowed never to return after—or even if—the strike was resolved. Assuming it ever ended, Major League Baseball would be facing its biggest crisis since the "Black Sox" scandal of 1919. As the months dragged on and the strike continued into the winter months of 1995, people began wondering if baseball or the fans would ever return.

· · · · · · · · ·

By February 1995, no resolution to the strike had been reached. With the season fast approaching, the owners resorted to a drastic measure that had long been discussed but few thought would actually be implemented: replacement players. The idea had been broached as early as the summer of 1994 as a way to keep that season going should the strike happen. But owners found the cost of using replacement players to continue the season prohibitive.[16] Even to disappointed fans, the thought of replacement players was abhorrent. Striking ballplayers were quick to discourage anyone that would dare cross picket lines. The Mets' Bobby Bonilla said that replacements "could end up in the East River."[17]

But without their professional players and somehow believing the idea would draw in revenue, the owners began recruiting to spring camp anyone they thought could play. The result was a mixture of semipro ballplayers, average joes, and far-below-average joes showing up at training facilities throughout Florida and Arizona. There was 270-pound Matt Stark, who would be replacing Don Mattingly as first baseman of the Yankees. Stark was so big, he accidentally crushed a metal folding chair by sitting on it.[18] There was Bubba Wagnon, who enjoyed time at second base for the Mets. Bubba had worked at B & B Landscaping in Alabama before making the "big leagues."[19] Some teams reached out to retired major leaguers. A Phillies employee called former pitcher Andy McGaffigan asking him to play in a golf tournament but instead made a different offer. "Can you throw?" asked the employee. "We are looking for guys, guys who have had time in the big leagues, guys on the bubble the last few years. We're looking to fill rosters."[20] McGaffigan turned him down. Other former players, such as Von Hayes and Dan Gladden, also rejected offers. Pitcher Lee Guetterman was asked by the Mariners to cross the picket line. He refused.[21] Some, including Doug Sisk and Dennis "Oil Can" Boyd, took the offers.[22] Eventually, rosters were weeded down and spring training games began.

The experiment was a disaster, as the majority of replacement players were simply not of Major League caliber. "Nobody could hit the ball out of the ballpark. They had warning-track power at best. Game after game, and balls would just die. There was just no power on display," said David Cohen, the Yankees' play-by-play announcer in 1995.[23] Some were great and would even make it to the big leagues one day. Most, however, would not. The majority of fans were not buying it either. "I will not pay to see the replacement Braves play," wrote one Atlanta fan. "I'm through with spending money on baseball."[24]

"It sickens me to think that the 1995 baseball season might start with replacement players," said another Braves fan. "In fact, if the regular players are not playing by opening day, I will penalize major league baseball and the Atlanta Braves by not attending any games during the 1995 season."[25]

Sparse crowds, some no bigger than a few hundred people, showed up for the games. The Dodgers' spring opener drew 700 fans. They had drawn over 6,600 to their spring opener the year before.[26]

A Mets-Yankees game drew 2,323 people, approximately 3,000 fewer than the game normally would have drawn with regular players.[27] Baltimore Orioles owner Peter Angelos maintained that he would not start the season with replacements, because they were an inferior product.[28] Due to Ontario labor laws, the Toronto Blue Jays were prohibited from using replacement players and would have to play their regular-season home games at their spring training facility in Dunedin, Florida.[29] *Sports Illustrated*'s Tim Kurkjian and Tom Verducci summed up that spring as the "freak show known as replacement players, where the crowds are small and lifeless, and the play is unremarkable, except for the lack of speed, power and quality of pitching."[30]

For managers and coaches, caught between the owners who wrote their checks and the players they were loyal to, it was especially awkward. "It was a part of your career that you try to forget," said Yankees first-base coach Brian Butterfield.[31] "It was the worst part of my baseball career," said Yankees hitting coach Rick Down.[32] Most managers and coaches begrudgingly reported to camp. Braves manager Bobby Cox lamented, "when you work for a person, you have to work, there is no choice."[33] When the Reds signed forty-eight-year-old former Major League pitcher Pedro Borbon, Pirates manager Jim Leyland ripped into them and the entire situation. "I don't care what the reason is [for signing him], to me, you're insulting the game," said Leyland.[34] Tigers skipper Sparky Anderson didn't show up to spring training, refusing to manage replacements.[35] Most managers knew that many of these substitutes were just trying to live out a dream, and they appreciated that. "It was tough 'cause it was the dream for a lot of these guys, and you didn't want to crush their dream," said Buck Showalter. Still, Showalter and the other managers missed their pros. "The team wasn't good. It was a fake spring training. Everyone was down but these guys [the replacement players]."[36]

As March went on and the "games" continued, the players and owners were no closer to an agreement. The hours until opening day ticked away. On Friday, March 31, the Yankees helped open the Colorado Rockies' new home, Coors Field. The Mariners were playing an exhibition game against the Blue Jays in Dunedin. Back in New York, the National Labor Relations Board had filed suit against the owners for committing unfair practices.[37] It was perhaps the last hope to end the strike before the start of the season. People across the country awaited a decision on the suit from Judge Sonia Sotomayor of the United States District Court in Manhattan. "Lou [Piniella] told me that if you see me walking down the right-field line [during the game], the strike is over," said Mariners radio announcer Dave Niehaus. "During the seventh inning, I see Lou walking down the right-field line."[38] Buck Showalter walked into the clubhouse at Coors Field and also received the news. Judge Sotomayor had issued an injunction against the owners, which prevented them from establishing new work rules in the absence of a new collective bargaining agreement.[39] With the owners now stripped of their ability to impose a salary cap, the players ended their strike.

The replacement players packed their bags and left, most never to be heard from again. Had they made the opening-day roster, each player would have been entitled to $5,000 and a league-minimum salary of $109,000 a year. Many returned home without these bonuses, though some teams decided to give them the $5,000 anyway.[40]

Baseball—real baseball—was back. And no one was more relieved than the players. Wade Boggs was in the middle of fishing tournament when he found out. Paul O'Neill was already in Florida and rushed to camp, one of the first players to arrive. Jim Leyritz had just bought a new home and was in the process of ripping up and replacing the floors. Edgar Martinez came in from Puerto Rico. Randy Velarde and his wife packed their belongings and drove straight from Texas to Fort Lauderdale, a nearly twenty-four-hour drive. An abbreviated spring of three weeks would take place, followed by a truncated 144-game regular season. To make up for the short spring, teams would be allowed to carry twenty-eight players, as opposed to twenty-five, once the season began.[41] The union set up a camp for players who remained unsigned or were, because of the strike, uncertain as to what their contract status was. The Homestead Camp, named for the Florida town in which it was located, included Vince Coleman, Dave Stewart, Tim Belcher, and Mickey Tettleton.

The Yankees looked forward to 1995 as much as any team. They had been in first place when the strike began, and many of the players from that squad felt that the 1994 team was the best they had ever played on. And the Yankees had only improved since then. During the off-season, they added an ace starting pitcher in Jack McDowell, a closer in John Wetteland, and a shortstop in Tony Fernandez. "Last year we had a great team, and we've just gotten better. You don't shake the tree and have a Jack McDowell fall off the branch every day," said Wade Boggs during the spring.[42]

Many predicted the Yankees would run away with the American League East. The *Baltimore Sun* stated they would be going "to the playoffs for the first time since 1B Don Mattingly joined the team in 1982."[43] "Make plans for October if . . . everybody on the Yankees does his job," stated the *Rocky Mountain News*.[44] The *Boston Globe*'s Peter Gammons ranked the Yankees the best team in all of baseball.[45]

The Mariners wanted to build off the momentum of their one-month team-bonding road trip that ended the strike-shortened season. The main ingredients—Randy Johnson, Ken Griffey Jr., Edgar Martinez, and Jay Buhner—all returned. Though the Mariners, unlike the Yankees, had not made any blockbuster off-season deals, they were confident that their team was good enough to compete for and even win the American League West.

While the players reported and the real spring-training games got under way, one question remained: would the fans come back? Initial indications were no, they wouldn't. Though many teams sold out opening day rather quickly, various media outlets reported a harsh backlash from the fans. One Phillies fan went to the team's ticket office so that he could personally deliver his season-ticket cancellation.[46] *New York Newsday*'s Lawrence Levy called for a National Fan Strike Day. "National Fan Strike Day must happen because the baseball strike didn't have to. . . . National Fan Strike Day must happen because the baseball walkout wasn't the first time the owners and players showed how little they care," wrote Levy.[47] Fan groups such as Foul Tip and Fan Out advocated for boycotting games.[48] A preseason game between the Angels and Padres at Anaheim Stadium drew only 2,000 people.[49] A *USA Today* poll conducted just after the strike ended found that 69 percent of fans were now less interested in the game than they were the year before, and only 40 percent identified themselves as fans as compared with the 55 percent who had identified themselves as fans the year before.[50]

Many teams tried to combat these problems through promotions and giveaways. The Mets announced that team yearbooks would be given out for free at their home opener.[51] Six teams lowered their ticket prices.[52] The Dodgers lowered their prices to 1958 levels, the year in which they moved from Brooklyn to Los Angeles.[53] The Angels sold all opening-day seats for a dollar.[54] Major League Baseball began a multimillion-dollar national campaign to enhance the game's image.[55] "The fans need to know this season won't be interrupted [by another player's strike] if they want to come back and take the game seriously," said Don Mattingly. "We need to mend fences with fans. We have to respect them. . . . More and more we're going to have to reach out to the fans."[56]

Still, there was no doubting the deep wound the strike had left with the fans. Promotions and free souvenirs might help, but it was going to take a lot more than that to draw people back. Fans were going to need a reminder of why baseball was such a great game. Pretty soon, they would get it.

5

Baseball Returns

"Baseball is fun, and what's happened is that it stopped being fun. We're reminding people how much fun it is."

—MLB spokesman Jim Small during the
first week of the 1995 regular season

For one beautiful April day in the Bronx, the hurt feelings and fallout from the strike all but disappeared. Coaches, managers, and players suited up and played ball. A crowd of 50,245 showed up for opening day between the Yankees and the Texas Rangers. Danny Tartabull and Bernie Williams homered, Jimmy Key pitched well, and John Wetteland got a save in his Yankee debut. In the stands, a fan held up a sign that read, "What Strike? Go Yanks!" The next day, 3,000 miles away, the Mariners returned to the Kingdome and shut out the Tigers 3–0. Judging from their opening-day results, it was totally conceivable that these two teams would meet up in the postseason. But within weeks, things began to go downhill for both teams, and the possibility that either team would make the playoffs greatly diminished. Moreover, the fans who returned in droves for opening day disappeared just as quickly in protest.

• • • • • • • • • •

Despite the serenity in the Bronx and Seattle on opening day, things did not go so well in other parts of the country. In Queens, three fans wearing shirts with the word "Greed" on them ran onto the field at Shea Stadium during the Mets' opener against the Cardinals. The trio threw nearly $150 in singles at players on the field, drawing an ovation from the crowd. During the second inning of the Reds' opener in Cincinnati, a plane flew over the stadium with a banner reading "Owners + players—To hell with all of you!" In Pittsburgh, fans threw sticks bearing Pirates pennants onto the field after the home team committed several errors. At Wrigley Field, Cubs fans threw magnetic schedules onto the field.[1] After drawing 42,125 fans to opening day, the Marlins saw just 18,857 attend the second game of the season. It was an indication of fan backlash that would continue through the season.

· · · · · · · · ·

After their opening-day victory, the Yankees aggressively surged ahead, winning ten of their first fifteen games. There was some visible shakiness caused by the abbreviated spring training, but nothing that drew immediate concern as the Yankees appeared to be on their way toward the division title. But within weeks, injuries sidelined pitchers Jimmy Key, Scott Kamieniecki, and Melido Perez. By the end of June, the Yankees were without three-fifths of their original starting rotation. Key was finished for the season, and Perez pitched only one more inning the rest of the year. Don Mattingly was afflicted by an eye infection that weakened his ability to distinguish between pitches. The Captain hit a big home run against the Red Sox on May 4 but then went nearly two months without hitting another. Tony Fernandez, a key off-season acquisition to fill a hole at shortstop, went down to injury. So did second baseman Pat Kelly and outfielders Danny Tartabull and Paul O'Neill.[2] "The injuries really hurt us," recalled manager Buck Showalter. "We didn't really have our true team together until July."[3] Those who were healthy played far below expectations. Bernie Williams batted just .194 in May. Wade Boggs batted just .259 that same month. Jack McDowell, considered the team's number-one starter, went winless in May and posted a 5.75 ERA in June.[4] On June 10, the Yankees stood ten and a half games out of first and were in last place in the American League East. The drop in the standings was largely the result of a disastrous series of road and home games against the West Coast teams in which the Yankees went just 4–15. Particularly devastating was a loss in Seattle where Rich Amaral hit the first of his only two home runs of the season in extra innings to end the game.[5] Another heartbreaking loss occurred when Luis Polonia was thrown out trying to steal second to end a game against the Angels at Yankee Stadium.[6] Off-the-field distractions, such as a ban on goatees by George Steinbrenner, did not help, either.[7] Moreover, the Yankees were playing their home games in front of increasingly sparse crowds. It was a clear sign that even in baseball's biggest market, many fans were making good on their promise not to come back to the game. After 50,245 spectators attended opening day, only 17,412 showed up for the second home game of the year. The dismal number was made worse by the fact that the game was against the Red Sox, the Yankees' archrivals. As the weeks went along, the attendance figures failed to climb. For the month of May, the Yankees failed to draw more than 26,000. In June, no crowd topped 29,000. Those that did attend were treated to mediocre play. A June 20 loss to the Orioles kept the Yankees in last place. The team that nearly everyone predicted to cruise through the regular season was struggling just to make it out of the AL East basement.

• • • • • • • • •

The Mariners' 3–0 victory on opening day, their first-ever opening-day shutout, gave every indication that good things were happening. They proceeded to win six of their next nine games and had some people believing that just maybe the Mariners would be the team to beat in the AL West. That hope tapered off, though, as Seattle fell to third place by May 25, and three and a half games out of first. The next night, hope for the 1995 season was nearly lost for good. In the seventh inning of the series opener against the Orioles, Baltimore's Kevin Bass drilled a Randy Johnson fastball to deep right-center field. Ken Griffey Jr. sprinted to his left, lunged, and snagged the ball just before crashing into the solid concrete wall. He bounded back, but it was clear that something was wrong. He started walking toward the infield, grabbing his left wrist, while fellow outfielder Alex Diaz frantically called for help from the Mariner bench. Trainer Rick Griffin immediately headed out to center field. "I think I broke my wrist," Junior told him. "How can you tell?" asked Griffin. "I felt it snap," said Junior.[8]

Griffey was right. He had a spiral fracture of bones in his left forearm and would miss the next two months of the season. It was a devastating loss for Seattle. "Lou [Piniella] told me in the clubhouse that Junior broke his wrist and I thought, 'It's just May [and] we lost Junior,'" said Mariners third-base coach Sam Perlozzo. "It turned out to be a good thing, though, because each guy had to contribute and it brought the club together."[9] Instead of engaging in self-pity, several role players, such as Rich Amaral, Alex Diaz, and Doug Strange, filled the gap left by Griffey's absence. "There was an overwhelming feeling that things wouldn't be easy, but Lou didn't make a big deal of it. We just moved on as a team," said Tim Belcher, who had just joined the Mariners at the time of Griffey's injury.[10]

The Mariners hovered around .500 for the next month and a half of the season, no small accomplishment considering the loss of baseball's best player. Though their .500 play kept them from falling completely out of the race, they failed to accumulate any prolonged winning streaks or gain any momentum. At the All-Star break, they were one game under .500. Fortunately for the Mariners, even with a losing record they were still just five games out of first place, allowing hope to linger that they could make a playoff run. The hope of success on the field took a whole new twist, however, when the fate of the team off the field was revealed to be in serious jeopardy.

• • • • • • • • •

The Kingdome was considered a marvel of modern engineering when it opened in 1977. It was a multipurpose stadium capable of hosting NCAA basketball games and rock concerts. As the years went by, however, the structure aged rapidly and became an albatross. In an era when new ballparks like Camden Yards and Jacobs Field were attracting millions of patrons with their retro style, the Kingdome was old, antiquated, and gloomy. "It was like playing in your basement," said Darren Bragg.[11] Artificial turf was fast becoming a thing of the past in baseball. It was symbolic of the unattractive cookie-cutter stadiums of the 1960s and 1970s. The Kingdome's turf was known for being in poor condition, as it was thin with cuts and divots. Despite adjustments over the years to the fences, the playing field remained rather drab and the dimensions plain. "The Kingdome was a very sterile place to play. Not much character or personality. Lots of gray concrete," recalled umpire Jim Evans.[12] "A giant mausoleum," said pitcher Lee Guetterman, who played for Seattle in 1984–1987 and 1995–1996.[13] One of the few aspects of the Kingdome that most players liked was that the weather never changed inside the dome. There was no wind, the lighting was always the same, and it was temperature controlled. This attribute, while great for the players, was one of the main reasons fans stayed away. Despite the stereotype of being a rainy, dreary city, Seattle in fact has some of the most mild, beautiful summers in the country. Few people wanted to waste a warm, sunny summer day stuck inside a dark dome watching a subpar baseball team.

The lagging attendance had created financial issues for the Mariners' original owners, then for George Argyros, then for Jeff Smulyan. It was now creating problems for the newest ownership. In 1993, the Mariners finished ninth in the American League in attendance. In 1994, they finished eighth. The strike only made matters worse in 1995. A nine-game home stand in late May saw the Mariners average just 13,000 per game. A June 27 home game against the A's brought only 9,767 to the Kingdome, and a weekend series against the Rangers in early July averaged just over 15,000 fans. By the end of the 1995 season, the team was projected to lose more than $67 million over a four-year period.[14] The strike and the Mariners' lackluster play did not help attendance figures, only adding to the existing burden of playing in an outdated, desolate stadium. The Mariners owners knew that for baseball to survive in Seattle, their team was going to need a new home.

No incident made further apparent the need for a new Mariners' home than one that occurred on July 19, 1994. Shortly before a home game against the Orioles, four insulating ceiling tiles fell from the Kingdome roof and smashed into what were, fortunately, empty seats.[15] The incident drew new awareness to the Kingdome's problems, as Seattle was forced to play the rest of the strike-shortened season on the road. In the meantime, King County executive and future Washington governor Gary Locke formed a committee to determine if it was more feasible to build the Mariners a new home or to make improvements to the Kingdome. The committee concluded that a new stadium was the best option.[16] But how to pay for such a stadium became a matter of intense debate. By the summer of 1995, the state legislature devised a proposal, approved by the King County Council, which called for a referendum to be placed on the ballot to raise the sales tax from 8.2 percent to 8.3 percent for a period of twenty years solely in King County (the location of Seattle). The sales tax increase would generate $240 million for a retractable-roof stadium as well as $160 million for improvements to the Kingdome.[17] The vote was scheduled to take place on September 1 and be held solely in King County.

• • • • • • • • •

With their season spiraling out of control, the Yankees turned a corner at the end of June. They won nine of twelve games, jumped to third place, and gained momentum just before the All-Star break. Led offensively by Paul O'Neill and Mike Stanley, the Yankees steadily improved their record and made up ground on the division-leading Red Sox. They caused a minor stir by signing former Mets All-Star Darryl Strawberry, who had issues with drugs and alcohol and hadn't played a full season in four years. By July 27, they were four and a half games out of first. Then the Yankees made two blockbuster trades that changed their season. The first was acquiring reigning Cy Young Award winner David Cone from the Blue Jays. The second was trading Danny Tartabull for power-hitting outfielder Ruben Sierra. Scott Kamieniecki returned from the disabled list, and pitcher Andy Pettitte emerged as a potential Rookie of the Year candidate. Their midsummer surge had the Yankees back in the hunt for the AL East and right in the thick of the wild-card race. Then came a road trip in mid-August to the West Coast, a place that had never been kind to the Yankees. Their disastrous trip in May had proven as much. When they headed west for the second time, it nearly resulted in the complete destruction of their season. Though they won the first game of the trip in Anaheim, the Yankees lost the next two games to the Angels, including a heartbreaker where a potential ninth-inning game-tying home run off the bat of Darryl Strawberry was taken away by a leaping grab from Angels left fielder Garrett Anderson.[18] The Yankees moved on to Oakland and proceeded to lose all three games to the A's. They were now down by fourteen and a half games in the American League East and by four and a half in the wild card as they headed to the Kingdome for a four-game series with Seattle.

• • • • • • • • •

On July 19, the Mariners were two games under .500, eight games out of first, and five games behind in the wild card. They had two months to turn around public opinion on the new stadium, which in July was tepid at best. Few taxpayers wanted to see an increase in taxes for any reason, much less to support a team that had brought them little to no success. If the Mariners couldn't turn this opposition around, John Ellis had made it clear that they would most likely have to leave the Pacific Northwest. For many, the obvious relocation choice appeared to be Tampa, where an empty stadium stood waiting to be used. The threat that the Mariners would be heading there was so serious that players began getting pamphlets from the Tampa Chamber of Commerce and looking at schools and homes in the area.[19] Not only were the Mariners going to have to fight to save their season, they were going to have to fight to save baseball in Seattle.

The team's management was keenly aware of what was at stake. So when general manager Woody Woodward approached Ellis at the trade deadline and sought permission to acquire key players instead of trading them away, Ellis acquiesced. Finally, the Mariners were going to be buyers and not sellers. Woodward followed through on July 31 by acquiring pitcher Andy Benes from the Padres. Two weeks later, Woodward traded for Vince Coleman, filling a crucial gap that existed in the Mariners' leadoff spot. News of the recent acquisitions brought a joyous response throughout the Mariners clubhouse. "We went out and got veteran guys that knew how to win and were no nonsense," said Jay Buhner, who had seen his share of good players traded away from Seattle since 1988.[20]

The moves by Woodward had little immediate impact, though. The Mariners did reel off six straight wins in early August, but they were not gaining any traction in the AL West race. They were also barely managing to stay in competition for the wild card. Seattle stood at 54–55 on August 24 as the Yankees came to town.

• • • • • • • • •

The Yankees' season was on life support as the team began the first game of a four-game series with the Mariners in Seattle. In just one hellish week on the West Coast, New York dropped five games in the AL East standings and now desperately needed a lift from starting pitcher David Cone. The Mariners, meanwhile, were still in the wild-card hunt but were one losing streak away from playing out the stretch for yet another season. Despite their recent additions, they had only been able to hover around .500 for weeks and were eleven and a half games behind the first-place Angels. Though there was still hope for the wild card, time was running out for someone on the Mariners to ignite the spark that would send them to the postseason.

Just 17,592 spectators showed up that Thursday to witness what would be one of the most important games in Mariner history. Things could not have started out worse for the Yankees, as Jay Buhner hit a two-out first-inning grand slam off Cone. It was an all-too-familiar sight for the Yankees, as they appeared destined to lose their sixth consecutive game of the trip. Momentum swung their way in the fourth inning, though, when they exploded for seven runs off Andy Benes. Cone recovered from his first-inning difficulties and pitched eight innings, giving up two additional runs. That brought the game to the bottom of the ninth with the Yankees clinging to a 7–6 lead. John Wetteland entered to finish what would be a crucial victory for the Yankees. For Seattle, a loss would drop them further behind in the wild card and a seemingly insurmountable twelve and a half games behind the Angels in the AL West. Wetteland quickly got two outs, then walked Vince Coleman. Coleman promptly stole second and third base, putting himself ninety feet away from tying the game.[21] Joey Cora then hit a soft line drive toward short for what looked like the game's final out. Tony Fernandez, however, misjudged the speed of the ball and it deflected off his glove and into left field. Coleman scored easily, eliminating the Yankees' lead. Though it was ruled a single, even Fernandez admitted that his "son could've made that catch."[22] The shock of Cora's two-out single had barely lifted when on the very next pitch, Ken Griffey Jr. launched a fastball into the stands in right field, giving Seattle a 9–7 victory. The Mariners exploded out of the dugout, euphorically jumping around like Little Leaguers. The

Yankees, meanwhile, walked sullenly off the field. They had been just one out away from a win, but their lead and a possibly momentum-gaining victory had disappeared in mere moments. Afterward, a funereal quietness hung over the visitors' clubhouse. "A backbreaker," said David Cone of the game.[23]

· · · · · · · · ·

For the Mariners, the victory propelled them toward a historic run. They won two of the next three games against New York and headed to Boston, having picked up two games on the Angels. Though the fans didn't immediately get caught up in the aftermath of the Mariners' thrilling come-from-behind victory, the team went on a tear. It won two of the next three from the Yankees in New York, then two of three from both the Red Sox and the Orioles. Remarkably, while the Mariners kept winning, the Angels kept losing. After sweeping the Royals and taking two of three from the Twins and the White Sox, the Mariners stood just three games out of first place, thanks to a four-game losing skid by California. Suddenly, it was not the wild card but rather the AL West championship that the Mariners were shooting for. "They posted the wild-card race standings up in right field, and Jay Buhner complained about it," said Mariners communications director Randy Adamack. " 'We aren't playing for the wild card,' he said, 'We are playing for first place.'"[24] While the Mariners kept winning, the Angels just kept losing. "We'd laugh about it. We'd look at the scoreboard and say, 'Jesus Christ, how did they [the Angels] lose this time?'" said Buhner.[25]

The race was becoming ever so much closer, and people in Seattle finally began to take notice. "We were getting ready to take batting practice late in the year, and I looked out in center field and noticed a guy with a little sign," said Mariners hitting coach Lee Elia. "The sign said 'Refuse to Lose.'"[26] It was not a new slogan, but at some point in September 1995, "Refuse to Lose" became the mantra of the Pacific Northwest and spread like wildfire. Mark Schuppisser, who ran an athletic apparel store out of Redmond, Washington, began mass-producing the slogan. At one point in mid-September, his company shipped approximately 10,000 "Refuse to Lose" T-shirts to outlets across the Northwest in just over a week.[27] The T-shirts were joined by hats and cardboard signs that were plastered all around Seattle. Players who had gotten used to the lack of baseball enthusiasm suddenly saw "Refuse to Lose" signs everywhere they went in the city. "I first got called up in June, and we were playing in front of 12,000, maybe 18,000 people. Earlier in the year, I had hit my first career home run into an empty seat in left field. Then suddenly it was 40 or 50,000 people in the seats and 'Refuse to Lose' was everywhere. It was a complete 180 from the time I was called up until September," said catcher Chris Widger.[28]

"The atmosphere [around Seattle] totally changed," said Mariners broadcaster Rick Rizzs. "I remember watching the news and they asked a random person on the street when they became a Mariners fan and the guy said 'last Thursday.'"[29] It was truly amazing. After eighteen years of lackluster support, baseball fans were suddenly popping up everywhere and every day in Seattle. It had never happened before in the Pacific Northwest.

The outpouring of support for the Mariners had an effect on public opinion too. As late as September 1, polls showed that only 33 percent of voters in King County planned to vote in favor of the new stadium referendum.[30] Now suddenly, public opinion shifted and it seemed possible that the vote would pass. "It is the most incredible thing I think I've ever seen," said Doug Strange. "Seattle became a baseball town."[31] With just days to go before the vote on the stadium, the Mariners became unstoppable. They won on Monday, September 18, and on September 19, they brought an unparalleled moment of drama to their game. As referendum votes were being tallied, the Texas Rangers, who were also in contention for the wild card, held a 3–1 lead over Seattle heading into the bottom of the ninth. With one eye on the incoming election returns and another on the game, Seattle politicians, Mariners ownership, and team fans watched as Lou Piniella sent Strange to pinch-hit as the potential tying run. In a string of improbable moments, Strange drilled a Jeff Russell pitch into the right-field stands, tying the game. Two innings later, Griffey lined an opposite-field single to score Strange and give the Mariners the victory. Almost as improbable as Strange's home run, after the game, the Mariners watched as the returns showed that the new stadium measure was actually passing.[32] It appeared that the Mariners had saved themselves. The jovialness of that night, however, would be derailed by an unfortunate fact.

· · · · · · · · ·

The West Coast trip nearly signaled the death knell of the Yankees' 1995 season. They had left for Anaheim nine and a half games out of first place and returned to New York fifteen and a half games out. They had also dropped by three and a half games in the wild-card standings and were trailing four teams for the last playoff spot. "We got the first victory in Anaheim and we all felt it would be different out here this time," said Mike Stanley, referring the Yankees' first disastrous trip to the West Coast in May. "Guess we were wrong."[33] Though no one would admit it publicly, there was a feeling that the season died out west. The team mercifully returned to the Bronx on August 28, only to suffer another heartbreaking loss, this time to the Royals, 4–3. After that loss, however, the Yankees turned a page and went on a remarkable run that saw them lose only six more games the rest of the season. The cascade of victories began with a three-game sweep over the Angels, highlighted by Paul O'Neill's first three-home-run game of his career. The Yankees then took two of three from both the A's and the Mariners. Led by their rotation of Cone, McDowell, Pettitte, Kamieniecki, and Hitchcock, the Yankees got into the thick of the wild-card race and gradually leapfrogged over the other teams in contention. They won four of seven on a road trip to Cleveland and Baltimore and then, thanks to a huge eighth-inning home run by Ruben Sierra, completed a four-game sweep at home against the Blue Jays on September 21. The victory put the Yankees a half-game out of the wild-card lead with eight games to play. They followed the sweep of Toronto by winning two out of three from the Tigers, moving them a half-game ahead of the Angels for the wild card. The Yankees then embarked on a year-ending five-game road trip, where they began by winning both games of a two-game series against the Brewers in Milwaukee. They now stood one and a half games ahead in the wild-card race and were on their way to Toronto for the final three games of the year. A decade earlier, Don Mattingly and his teammates had been in the same position: a critical year-ending three-game series in Toronto where each game was a must-win. Unlike the outcome in 1985, though, this time the Yankees wouldn't lose.

• • • • • • • • •

The King County referendum for a new stadium failed by less than 1 percent. Absentee ballots that were cast before the Mariners started their winning ways had been overwhelmingly against the measure, erasing the Election Day lead. In the end, the final vote was 246,500 against and 245,418 in favor.[34] Had the team started to catch fire weeks or perhaps even days earlier, the measure might have passed. It hadn't, and now it would take an act of the state legislature to pry loose the last nail from the Mariner's coffin, because John Ellis had issued his ultimatum. In a letter to King County executive Gary Locke shortly after the results were final, Ellis stressed that the current ownership had bought the team to keep the Mariners in Seattle "and we have committed our time, dollars, and our hearts to make that happen." Various elements, however, had made it so that the current owners "simply cannot continue as owners under the current circumstances." This comment was in no doubt referring to a substantial loss in revenue the owners had faced. Ellis gave local officials until October 30 to devise a way to provide for a new stadium or the team would be up for sale.[35] Everyone knew that new ownership most likely meant the Mariners would be leaving Seattle. "We weren't playing a game. It was not a threat," said Ellis, looking back years later on his ultimatum. "It was a fact."[36] But convincing the legislature to find funding would not be easy. To do that, the Mariners were going to need more than just late-inning victories. There were going to have to make the playoffs.

Mariners players tried to ignore the off-the-field distractions and simply kept winning. "People just stepped up. Every night it was someone new on the roster coming through," said Jay Buhner.[37] Just as important, the Angels kept on losing. Seattle's September 19 victory over Texas, coupled with the Angels' loss that night to the A's, reduced the Angels' lead to just one game. The next night, the Mariners won again and the Angels lost again. There was now a tie atop the division with just nine games left in the season. In exactly one month, the Mariners had gone 19–11 and erased the Angels' twelve-and-a-half-game lead. The weekday series against the Rangers had drawn a total of 75,000 fans, the largest total during the year at the Kingdome to that point. That paled in comparison to what happened starting Friday night, September 22. The largest crowd at the Kingdome since Seattle's 1994 home opener, 51,500 fans, witnessed the first game of a three-game series against the A's. They got their money's worth. After falling behind by the third inning, 6–0, the Mariners rallied for two runs in the bottom of the fourth. Then Vince Coleman came to bat with the bases loaded, representing the tying run. Coleman had never hit a grand slam in his career, but he drilled a Todd Van Poppel pitch into the right-field stands, tying the game.[38] In the bottom of the eighth, down by one run, the Mariners rallied again. Edgar Martinez led off with a game-tying home run. Then, with one out and two runners on, Alex Diaz pinch-hit for Luis Sojo and crushed a go-ahead three-run home run, and the Mariners went on to win. Down in Arlington, the Angels lost 8–3, pushing the Mariners into sole possession of first place. It was, by far, the latest in any season the Mariners had ever been in possession of first place.

The drama of Diaz's home run was eclipsed two days later. After a 7–0 shutout victory the day before, which had increased their lead to two games, Seattle held a 7–6 lead going into the ninth inning against Oakland. But Norm Charlton surrendered a two-run home run to Danny Tartabull, giving the A's the lead. At this point, even some members of the Mariners had to concede that they simply couldn't come back every time they were losing. They were wrong. With one out in the bottom of ninth, Tino Martinez hit a two-run home run into the right-field stands, capping yet another dramatic come-from-behind win for Seattle. It was the sixth time in their last thirteen games that the Mariners had won in their final at-bat. Tino's home run was crucial, because the Angels won their ballgame that night. California then came to Seattle for a two-game miniseries, trailing the Mariners by two games. But the series against California proved anticlimactic. The Mariners clobbered the Angels in the first game, giving the home team a chance to clinch at least a tie for the division title the next night. But in game two, the Angels scored two first-inning runs, which proved to be all they needed in a 2–0 victory. A split of the series left the Mariners two games in front of the Angels with just four games left in the season. The Angels returned to Anaheim for a four-game series against the A's and the Mariners flew out to Arlington to face the Rangers.

• • • • • • • • •

On Friday night, September 29, the Yankees found themselves down, 3–0, to the Toronto Blue Jays in the top of ninth inning. A loss would mean a tie for the wild card with the Angels, making the next two games even more critical. The Yankees hadn't rallied to win a game in the ninth inning once all season, and this night seemed no different.[39] Don Mattingly led off with a single and Jim Leyritz walked, but Randy Velarde hit a ground ball to short that should have killed the Yankees' momentum. Instead, Blue Jays shortstop Alex Gonzalez booted the ball, allowing Mattingly to score, Leyritz to go to third, and Velarde to reach base. Gonzalez's error was the twist of fate that had eluded the Yankees all year until now, and they took full advantage. A Mike Stanley sacrifice fly made it a 3–2 game and brought Pat Kelly to the plate as the potential go-ahead run. Kelly, fourth on the team in seniority, was a hard-nosed second baseman with an outstanding glove. Injuries had constantly befallen him, though, and reduced his playing time. After showing signs of improvement offensively in the 1993 and 1994 seasons, he regressed in 1995, slumping badly most of the year. As Velarde, Strawberry, Sierra, Dion James, and Williams all jockeyed for playing time, Kelly watched many games from the bench. Now, here he was in the biggest at-bat of the season, battling Blue Jays reliever Tony Castillo for six pitches. Finally, on the seventh pitch, Kelly drove a breaking ball high and deep to left field.[40] Thinking he'd merely popped out, Kelly threw his bat away in disgust and began slowly trotting toward first base. Out in left field, however, Joe Carter couldn't track down the ball and watched as it landed behind the left-field fence, giving the Yankees a 4–3 lead. Kelly rounded first base and raised both arms in triumph. It was only his fourth home run of the year and his first since May, but it was the biggest home run any Yankee had hit since Bucky Dent's famous shot at Fenway Park.[41] John Wetteland entered in the ninth inning and retired the side in order. It was a game they desperately needed, and the Yankees had come through with big pitching, clutch hitting, and a little luck.

The next day, Scott Kamieniecki turned in his best performance of the season, going all nine innings as New York won, 6–1. The Angels won that day as well, but the Mariners lost. That meant that the Yankees, with the same record as Seattle and one more win than California, had ensured themselves at least a tie for the wild card and a one-game playoff. The one-game playoff, however, was contingent upon their losing the last game of the year and upon both the Mariners and the Angels winning their games. Regardless, the Yankees controlled their own destiny. A win on Sunday would ensure them the wild card, no matter what the Mariners or Angels did.

In the biggest regular-season game of his managerial career, Buck Showalter went against the odds. He had ace pitcher David Cone available but, instead, opted to go with Sterling Hitchcock. The decision irked George Steinbrenner to no end. The Boss had been calling Showalter all weekend, pleading with him to start Cone. Showalter wouldn't relent, knowing that even if the Yankees lost, they would still have Cone to pitch in a one-game playoff if needed. His gamble worked. By the second inning, the Yankees had a 4–0 lead and Hitchcock was pitching great. Fittingly, the two men who had been with the team the longest both hit home runs. In the fifth inning, Don Mattingly lined a ball off the foul pole in right field for the last of his 222 career regular-season home runs. In the eighth inning, Randy Velarde lined a home run to left field which, unbeknownst to him, would be his last as a Yankee.

With a 6–1 lead in the ninth inning, Showalter called on Steve Howe to officially put the Yankees into the postseason. Howe was the senior member of the Yankees' pitching staff, having signed with the team in 1991. It had been a risky move, as Howe had served several suspensions for violating Major League Baseball's drug policy. In fact, he had to serve another suspension in 1992, but he returned to the team and became the closer late in the 1994 season, pitching extremely well in that position. In 1995, though, Howe had been hit hard all year, and even a five-run lead seemed unsafe in his hands. But the pitcher, who was known for talking his teammates' ears off, came out to silence the Blue Jays. Howe walked a batter, but with two outs, got Randy Knorr to hit a ground ball to Tony Fernandez, who easily gloved it and tossed to Pat Kelly at second base for the final out. The Yankees, who had been in last place in June, had made the playoffs for the first time in fourteen years. Almost as important to some, Don Mattingly finally made it to the postseason. Once the final out was recorded, Mattingly began trotting toward the pitcher's mound, then stopped, dropped to one knee, and pounded the artificially turf with his left hand. It was a telling moment from a player who rarely wore his emotions on his sleeve. It yelled out what Mattingly, his teammates, George Steinbrenner, and millions of Yankees fans were saying at that moment: finally!

On the mound, a subdued celebration ensued. The wild card was brand new, so no one was certain how boisterous the celebration should be. Most players hugged each other, acknowledged the many Yankee fans who had made their way north of the border to Toronto, then headed into the clubhouse. There, alcohol was modestly sprayed around while the music of Boston played in the background.[42] Players sipped beer as they donned wild-card hats and T-shirts. Meanwhile, George Steinbrenner entered the coaches' room. Instead of offering congratulations, he told those assembled, "If you fuckers don't get to the World Series, you're all out of here."

Though offering nothing but praise publicly about his manager, in private, Steinbrenner never thanked or praised Showalter for his decision to hold off on starting Cone. Meanwhile, much of the postgame attention shifted to the Yankee captain. "I had kept hearing about all the games [we] played without making the playoffs, so it was nice to know we were finally going to make it. During that month, we felt we had to win every game, like it was the NCAA tournament. It was a great feeling to know what we'd accomplished," said Mattingly.[43] The celebration continued until the Yankees finally boarded the flight home to New York. What should have been an exciting celebratory flight home turned into a nightmare for Buck Showalter. "My people all have their regular seats [on the plane]," the manager told reporters shortly after the flight was over. "He moved everybody around. Sat right next to me. Worst flight I ever took."[44] The "he" Showalter was referring to was George Steinbrenner.

• • • • • • • • •

The Mariners, who had swept the Rangers just eight days earlier, could clinch the division title by winning three of their final four games. After winning the first two games, they appeared well on their way. But the Angels won their first two games against the A's, and the Mariners' lead remained at two. On Saturday, September 30, the Angels won their fourth game in a row, and the Mariners lost. The Mariners were now just one game up with only one game left in the season. They just needed to win on Sunday or for the Angels to lose, and the division was theirs. But in Arlington, the Mariners found themselves down 3–0 after the first inning, then 7–1 after five. Mike Blowers homered in the sixth, but Texas answered right back with another two runs in the bottom half of the inning. Seattle succumbed to a 9–3 defeat. Their fate undetermined, the Mariners returned to the visitor's clubhouse to watch the Angels–A's game. The news was bad there too. The Angels were pounding A's pitcher Todd Stottlemyre for six runs. "The A's looked like they were just playing out the string," said one Mariners official, who was watching the game in a bar at the Ballpark in Arlington. "The A's just played their scrubs," said another. The Angels won, remarkably saving their season for another day. After dramatically coming back from a twelve-game deficit, the Mariners had actually blown a three-game lead and now had to pull out one more victory. Fortunately for them, they would attempt to do it with the game's best pitcher on the mound and the rowdiest crowd Seattle sports had ever seen.

· · · · · · · · · ·

Two weeks before the end of the regular season, Major League Baseball held a series of coin tosses to determine home-field advantage for all one-game playoff scenarios among the teams still in playoff contention. The Mariners won the toss against the Angels; therefore, the biggest game in team history would be played in front of the hometown faithful at the Kingdome.[45] Not having known if the game would be needed, the Mariners did not begin selling tickets for the playoff game until after the Angels defeated the Rangers that final Sunday. "The game was at 1:30 P.M. on Monday and no tickets were sold. There was a football game [in the Kingdome] that Sunday too, so everything had to be converted [overnight]," said Randy Adamack.[46] Remarkably, 52,000 tickets were purchased in a matter of hours, making the game a sellout.

The Mariners had the home-field advantage and a stadium full of screaming fans, but their biggest asset would be standing on the mound. Six-foot, ten-inch Randy Johnson got the start in Seattle's biggest game. Johnson had come to the Mariners via the biggest trade in team history, but originally, it wasn't because the deal involved Johnson. Johnson, along with Gene Harris and Brian Holman, came to Seattle from the Montreal Expos in exchange for Mark Langston in May 1989. "Originally, I wanted John Dobson [a prospect in the

Expos' system], not Johnson," conceded Chuck Armstrong of the deal that brought him the tall lefty.[47] The trade was decried across the Pacific Northwest. Langston had been the best pitcher in the Mariners' history, finishing second in the Rookie of the Year voting in 1984 and leading the American League in strikeouts three times. Though he had openly feuded with managers and team management, Langston was a fan favorite and had enjoyed his time in Seattle. Upon hearing of his trade to Montreal, Langston cried. He wasn't the only one. Team president Chuck Armstrong, perhaps growing weary of constantly having to trade away top talent, was equally upset.[48]

Johnson was not deemed a key acquisition. He possessed a blazing fastball and a sharp slider but lacked any semblance of control over either. In 1989, he walked ninety-six batters in just 160 innings. In 1990, despite throwing the first no-hitter in Mariners history, he walked 120. In 1991, he walked 152. Gradually, Johnson learned to control his pitches, which in turn made him the most dangerous pitcher in the game. His fastball constantly approached 100 miles per hour, and his slider was so devastating that few managers would play even their best left-handed hitters against him. During the 1993 All-Star Game, Johnson unleashed a fastball that sailed several feet behind the head of left-handed hitter John Kruk. Kruk, visibly shaken, began playfully patting his chest and breathed a visible sigh of relief before striking out. Johnson's repertoire of pitches was only one aspect of his game. He was among the tallest pitchers in history. It was an edge that allowed Johnson to appear to hitters as if he was delivering the ball right on top of them. In addition to the speed and the height, he had an intimidation factor unmatched by any other player. Johnson would place his glove in front of his face before delivering each pitch, his eyes staring daggers at the hitter from above the mitt. Behind him, a long shock of blond hair protruding from the back of his cap would fly wildly with every pitch he delivered. Taken together, all Johnson's attributes scared the hell out of most hitters. "Randy was the most intimidating pitcher I have ever seen," said teammate Rich Amaral. "He wanted to win. He doesn't even like to lose off the field, even playing cards."[49]

Johnson's intimidation factor was not simply an act put on to trick hitters. In the clubhouse, he could be ornery and aloof to his teammates. "You didn't talk to Randy on game day," recalled a former teammate. "He'd get in his zone and just focus. He might be friendly afterward, but not on game day." Still, Johnson's teammates had total respect for his ability and determination. "You may not like Randy, but every fifth day you were gonna love him. He's the best pitcher I have ever seen," said Norm Charlton. On the mound, Johnson wore his emotions on his sleeve, pounding his chest or shouting after a big strikeout. The sliders, the staring, the shouting, just the pure sight of him, all contributed to make Johnson, referred to as the "Big Unit," the most dominating pitcher in baseball. "It's the most fitting nickname ever. He was scary dominant," said Tim Belcher.[50]

In 1995, Johnson ascended to another level in terms of pitching. He lost only two games all season, and Seattle won every start he made after August 11. Johnson's being in line to start the one-game playoff was no coincidence. During the stretch run, Lou Piniella deliberately adjusted his rotation so that Johnson would be the starter for either Game 1 of the postseason or a one-game playoff.[51] That move now seemed prophetic. Johnson was to get the ball for the 1:35 P.M. (PST) nationally televised start. In the coincidence of coincidences, the man he opposed on the mound was the very man he'd been traded for six years earlier: Mark Langston.

• • • • • • • • •

The Kingdome was packed and loud—so loud, in fact, that players could barely hear one another on the field or even in the dugout. "It was the loudest game I have ever heard. Nothing comes close," said Angels pitcher Scott Sanderson.[52] It hardly seemed like the same stadium where, for years, crowds were so scarce that players could hear the individual taunts of fans from every section of the Kingdome. From the first pitch, it was clear that Randy Johnson was on his game. He retired the first six Angels in order. Then in the third inning, he struck out Garrett Anderson, Andy Allanson, and Rex Hudler—all swinging. In the fifth inning, he struck out the side again. Johnson did not allow an Angel to reach base through the first five innings. Langston wasn't performing badly, either. He'd allowed a few Mariners to reach base but prevented Seattle from scoring through four innings. Finally, in the bottom of the fifth, the Mariners broke through. Vince Coleman, who earlier had been caught stealing at a key moment, singled in Dan Wilson to give Seattle a 1–0 lead. Langston escaped further damage, but with the way Johnson was pitching, that one run just might prove to be enough to give Seattle the victory.

Johnson lost his perfect game in the sixth inning when Hudler singled, but the Mariners still led, 1–0, in the bottom of the seventh inning. With two outs, Seattle loaded the bases for shortstop Luis Sojo. Though there were better hitters in the lineup, there were few hitters that anyone wanted up in this situation other than Sojo.

· · · · · · · · ·

If you met Luis Sojo on the street, you'd never have guessed he was an athlete. His doughy physique didn't fit that of a major leaguer and though only thirty years old, Sojo took constant ribbing from his teammates for his seemingly aged appearance. "Rumor had it that Luis was collecting a pension his rookie year," joked teammate Chris Bosio.[53] Sojo took this kind of ribbing all in stride, and he had an ever-present smile on his face. Despite the cracks about age and appearance, Sojo was an exceptional athlete with a knack for coming through in big situations. Now, he was in the biggest situation of his career: bases loaded, two outs in the seventh inning of a one-game playoff. Even with the way Johnson was pitching, the Mariners would feel more secure if Sojo could add to their 1–0 lead. In Sojo's first two at-bats, Langston had thrown him mostly fastballs. "I thought, 'If he does it again, I'm gonna swing.' On the first pitch, he threw me a two-seamer in and I swung," said Sojo.[54] Sojo slapped the outside fastball down the first-base line. The cue-shot ground ball cut away from one of the game's best-fielding first basemen, J. T. Snow, narrowly eluding his glove and squirting down the right-field line, where it settled underneath the bench in the Angels' bullpen. Two runs scored easily and a third was fast approaching. The ball came in from right field and was cut off by Langston, who spun and fired toward home plate, but the throw eluded catcher Allanson and went to the backstop. A third run scored easily. In the dugout, several Mariners began frantically waving their arms, telling Sojo to go home. Allanson recovered the ball and flung it to Langston, who was covering home plate. Sojo slid in safely as the ball arrived too late. "*Everybody scores!* And the Mariners take the lead, 5–0. This place is going wild!" screamed announcer Rick Rizzs. Sojo bounded up from home plate and pumped his fists through the air in a move that became known throughout Seattle as "the Sojo." As Sojo danced, Langston lay on his back sprawled across home plate, staring in disbelief at the Kingdome roof. The Angels season had just collapsed on one play. Langston knew, as did everyone watching, that a five-run Mariners lead would be insurmountable.

The Mariners scored four more runs in the eighth inning to take a 9–0 lead. Johnson gave up an inconsequential home run in the ninth inning, and with two outs, the Big Unit stared down the Angels' Tim Salmon. Johnson got two strikes on Salmon, and with the Mariners teetering on the brink, the noise inside the Kingdome became deafening. It got so loud that people in the stands couldn't hear those seated right next to them. With the fans on their feet, Johnson reared back and fired his 125th pitch of the day. It was a fastball that home-plate umpire John Shulock called for strike three. Catcher Dan Wilson couldn't hear Shulock's call. He had to momentarily peek back just to make certain it was strike three.[55] Wilson leapt in celebration and sprinted toward the mound. Johnson smacked his chest with his glove then pointed toward the sky before Wilson and the rest of his teammates engulfed him in celebration. The remarkable comeback that began six weeks earlier was complete.

But would it be enough to keep the Mariners in Seattle? Hours before the one-game playoff started, John Ellis had met with Washington governor Mike Lowry and members of the legislature to reiterate the Mariners' stance. If there was no plan in place for a new, retractable-roof stadium by October 30, the team would have to leave Seattle. "The question is, does the community, does the state, want to maintain competitive major-league baseball here for my lifetime and your lifetime?" said Ellis after the meeting.[56] Governor Lowry and the legislature had to work under a pressing deadline, and even though the Mariners had just won the biggest game in their history, the legislature was still split on the issue. Seattle was going to need even more excitement than it had already produced to bring enough of the state's lawmakers on board.

• • • • • • • • •

As the legislators worked on a way to finance a new stadium, the Yankees and Mariners prepared to face one another in the first round. At that time, the playoff matchups were predetermined every season. In 1995, the American League West champion automatically played the wild-card winner. That meant that even though they had the best record in the league, the Cleveland Indians would be playing the AL East champion Red Sox and not the wild-card Yankees. The Mariners would play the Yankees. The teams were more than familiar with each other. They had played thirteen games against each other during the regular season, with the Mariners winning nine times. Seattle took six of the seven games played at the Kingdome, including the critical August 24 game that changed the season for both teams. There was also tension between these two clubs, thanks to an incident that occurred in Seattle on May 30. Trailing by two runs in the sixth inning, Randy Johnson had hit Jim Leyritz on a 3–0 pitch. The ball nailed Leyritz in the wrist before striking his left cheekbone. It was believed to be in retaliation for Steve Howe's having hit Felix Fermin the previous night. Regardless of the motive, Leyritz was mad and so were his teammates. Both benches emptied. "I'll see you afterward," Leyritz told Johnson as he made his way to first base.[57] Both Buck Showalter and Jack McDowell shouted at Johnson, but no fighting occurred. Order was restored, but the hurt feeling did not subside. Leyritz waited for Johnson outside the Yankees' clubhouse after the game, but Johnson never showed, and Kingdome staff eventually had to tell Leyritz to leave.[58] That animosity would carry over into the Division Series.

Despite the Mariners' 9–4 record against the Yankees during the season, the Division Series promised to be evenly matched. The Mariners had an explosive offensive, while the Yankees had better starting pitching. The Yankees were able to align their starters just as they wished, while the Mariners would have to hold off on using Randy Johnson until Game 3. The bullpens for both teams featured dominant closers, but the remaining relievers were all questionable. Predictions from papers across the country favored New York. The *St. Petersburg Times*, Portland *Oregonian*, *Chicago Sun-Times*, *Chattanooga Free Press*, *Buffalo News*, and *Austin American-Statesman* all picked the Yankees in five games.[59] Few were giving the Mariners a chance. And those were just the kind of odds Seattle wanted.

But more was at stake for both teams than just this playoff series. For the Yankees, numerous player contracts were up after the season was over. Who would and would not be returning might very well be determined by these games. And for the Mariners, nothing less than the future of the entire ball club rested on what they did in this divisional playoff.

6

Game 1: The Bronx, Baseball, and Beer Bottles

"All season long we heard how baseball was dead. A dinosaur, a relic. Hogwash. Baseball is alive and well. Thank you. Yankee fans proved that. There have to be many sore throats and tired legs this morning. So many people were roaring and standing . . . there was electricity. There was excitement with every pitch. What wasn't there last night was resentment. There was no anger. Just baseball. Just cheers. Just boos. Just baseball."

—*Newsday*'s Rob Parker in a column
published the day after Game 1

The evening of October 2, 1995, was cool, comfortable, and pleasant in the South Bronx. It betrayed the electric buzz swirling around New York City that day. For the first time in fourteen years, the Yankees were playing in the postseason. The excitement had ripped through the tristate area like a tornado. As with most ballparks in the country, New Yorkers had not come back to Yankee Stadium once the strike ended. Even down the stretch, as the Yankees fought tooth and nail for the wild-card spot, games were played in front of a nearly empty stadium. The final home game of the regular season, which might have been Don Mattingly's last at Yankee Stadium, saw only 34,848 in attendance. Years earlier it would have been implausible to think that what was possibly Mattingly's last day at Yankee Stadium would not be a sell-out, but nearly 23,000 empty blue seats stuck out that day as a stinging reminder of the damage the strike had done. It was bad for the Yankees and even worse for Major League Baseball. If the league's biggest market could not lure fans back to the ballparks, what chance did other, small-market teams have to regain their fan base? The poor attendance in such traditional baseball havens as New York, Chicago, and St. Louis had cast the future of the game in serious doubt throughout the abbreviated 1995 regular season.

The playoffs changed all of that. In clinching the wild card, the Yankees created a baseball reawakening in New York. Bud Selig, harshly criticized by many throughout his tenure as commissioner, truly deserved credit for coming up with the wild-card slot. Originally derided by baseball purists, his brainchild was now resurrecting the game in the Big Apple. The wild card was causing 57,178 people—a record crowd for the newly remodeled Yankee Stadium—to cram into the ballpark in the Bronx on a beautiful fall evening.[1] It was a far cry from the minuscule crowds of fewer than 20,000 people the team had drawn during the summer. As the fans filed in and found their seats, there was an aura of good feeling around the stadium. In 1995, there were twenty-eight teams in baseball, and excluding the expansion Rockies and Marlins, only three teams (Indians, Mariners, and Rangers) had gone longer without making it to the playoffs than the Yankees. For millions of Yankees fans, Game 1 was a mass cathartic event. Older fans saw it as a return of what they had come to expect nearly every year decades earlier. Younger fans saw it as their first encounter with postseason baseball. Joe Pascucci of Bridgeport, Connecticut, and several of his friends had jumped into a car in the early morning hours the day before and headed to the stadium looking for tickets. "We didn't want to be the ones who missed the playoffs. . . . It's awesome," he said.[2] Katie Brinn and her friend Elaine Chamber drove down from Boston to see Game 1. Paul Amoroso, a history teacher at Pompton Lakes High School in New Jersey, nearly came to tears explaining to his classes what it meant to him that he had tickets for Game 1. Ken Jones came all the way up from Atlanta to cheer on the Yankees. When he couldn't get tickets for Game 1, he watched the telecast at a bar across the street from the stadium. "This is just electric . . . there is nothing like being in New York when the Yankees are winning," said Jones.[3]

Whether young or old, they had all endured the endless Steinbrenner rants, the trades, the free-agent flops, the lost no-hitters, the managerial musical chairs, and years of the Mets being New York's premier team. This night, that was all going to be washed away. It was time to shed the memories of Kemp, Meacham, Hawkins, and Merrill, and focus on getting back to the World Series.

• • • • • • • • • •

Though seventy-two years old, Yankee Stadium showed no ill effects of age. One of baseball's cathedrals, the stadium was known for its inverted horseshoe shape, steep upper deck, and outfield facade. Located behind the left-center-field wall was Monument Park, where plaques and monuments honoring legendary Yankees were placed, along with retired uniform numbers. It was a site that emanated history and could be imposing to players. In preparation for the playoffs, red, white, and blue bunting adorned the facades of the upper deck and the mezzanine, and the divisional series logo was painted on the grass behind home plate. The advertising box behind home plate, an unseemly bright-colored blotch in a sea of blue walls, was covered with a blue tarp. In right and left field, the "Bleacher Creatures" began assembling. These fans were known throughout the league as among the roughest for an opposing player to deal with. The bleachers at Yankee Stadium consisted of some of the cheapest seats in the house and were generally filled with loud, sometimes obnoxious fans, who yelled at players and even attacked one another. The "creatures" moniker aptly fit. At a time when alcohol was still permitted in these sections, the Bleacher Creatures were going to be the source of amusement, shame, and borderline criminal behavior for the next two nights.

Just above the second level of the stadium and to the left of home plate, George Steinbrenner sat in the owner's box. This moment was just as big for him as anyone else. He had been exiled from the game only five years earlier. Now, The Boss basked in the glow of his team having made the postseason. "It feels tremendous to be back," he informed the media. "We forgot all about how to do this. We had to get some new bunting. The old bunting had moths."⁴ It was true that he didn't care much for a wild-card berth. After all, it was a championship that Steinbrenner longed for. Still, this was an important first step, and he certainly was pleased, after years of failure, to finally have a playoff team again.

· · · · · · · · ·

John Ellis, Chuck Armstrong, and Woody Woodward traveled to the ballpark together. For Ellis, it was his first visit to Yankee Stadium. Upon his arrival, he was greeted by security personnel, who informed him that they would be with him at all times throughout the course of the next two games, even when he went to the bathroom. It was a shock to Ellis, but decked out as he was in full Mariners apparel, he was going to need that security.⁵

For the Seattle Mariners, Game 1 was the culmination of one of the most exciting stretch drives in baseball history. The last few days had been exhausting. Wednesday, they had played at home against the Angels. Thursday, they had moved to Arlington, Texas, for their four-game series with the Rangers. Sunday night, they had flown back to Seattle for the one-game playoff. Monday night, after celebrating their victory against the Angels for hours in the clubhouse, they hopped a plane to fly to New York, not arriving until early Tuesday morning. In the last five days, they had flown over 6,000 miles, crossed through seven time zones, and spent over twelve hours on planes. As daunting as all that had been, to the players, the end justified the means. Yes, they were tired as hell, but for a chance to play in the postseason, sleep didn't seem to matter. The adrenaline alone was enough to overcome any drowsiness. They arrived at their hotel in New York at four in the morning, still giddy over their thrilling win against the Angels.⁶ "It wasn't really that bad. I was in bed by 4 A.M. and got six hours sleep. That's better than a lot of trips," said Edgar Martinez.⁷ Most players tried to get some sort of rest and relaxation before the 8:00 P.M. start, but like millions of Americans, many of them instead sat in front of TVs early that afternoon to watch a jury declare O. J. Simpson not guilty of murder. Mariners fans in the Portland area would actually miss the first inning of Game 1 because the NBC affiliate there decided to air extended coverage of the verdict and then cut into the game already in progress. As a result, the station received hundreds of calls expressing disapproval at their decision.[8] After the announcement of the verdict, the players shuffled off to Yankee Stadium. In order to keep his team relaxed, Lou Piniella had pizzas delivered during batting practice.[9]

Few Mariners had postseason experience. Even those who did, such as Tim Belcher, Norm Charlton, and Vince Coleman, had never played at Yankee Stadium in the playoffs. They were all about to find out how intense it could get. Still, for many of them, being in the postseason was a dream come true. For Jay Buhner, this was where he had started his career. The Yankees were the team that had given up on him so quickly. What better way to exact revenge than eliminating them from the postseason? The same could be said for Ken Griffey Jr., whose experiences as a child at Yankee Stadium, when his father played for the team, were less than pleasant. "We [Yankees] had no father-son game, no playing pepper with Dad, no shagging during batting practice. I never even got into the dugout here. One time Dad brought us into the dugout, and they threw us out. I don't forget things like that," said Griffey.[10] Then there was Lou Piniella, who for years had been a favorite of Yankees fans, first as a player and then as a gruff no-nonsense manager. Now he stood in the opposing team's dugout, and despite a congratulatory phone call from George Steinbrenner before the game, he still sought to outwit and eliminate the team and owner who had put him through hell in the late 1980s.[11]

• • • • • • • •

For the Yankees, Game 1 represented relief. They were supposed to be in the postseason, or at least that's what most analysts had said in spring training. Their stretch run had been every bit as hectic and grueling as the Mariners' and had erased their horrific start to the season. But unlike the Mariners, the Yankees were well rested heading into Game 1. Having clinched the wild card on Sunday in Toronto, they were able to return home Monday and enjoy a day off while basking in the glow of being hometown heroes. Making the playoffs was enjoyable for everyone, but it had been especially satisfying for a few specific players on the team. Steve Howe could not have imagined that he would be back in this position. Howe was the only player on either team's postseason roster to have actually played a playoff game at Yankee Stadium. In fact, Howe was the last player to throw a pitch in Yankee Stadium during the playoffs, having been on the mound for the Dodgers when they clinched the 1981 World Series against New York. Since then, his life had been through chaotic ups and downs. He had been suspended several times for violating baseball's substance-abuse policies, and by 1991 most teams wouldn't touch him. The Yankees took a chance, though, and five years later, Howe was again going to be a part of postseason baseball in the Bronx, only this time wearing a Yankees uniform.

Other players, such as Scott Kamieniecki, Pat Kelly, Jim Leyritz, and Randy Velarde had toiled for years in the Yankees' minor-league system or as members of some of the worst Yankee teams in history. For them, Game 1 represented a magnificent payoff for years of struggling in pinstripes.

No player on either side, however, was more symbolic of what this day meant than Donald Arthur Mattingly. Shortly before game time, Mattingly emerged from the Yankees' dugout to perform his pregame stretching. As he bounded up the dugout steps and his number 23 became visible to all in the stadium, the crowd let loose with a cheer of appreciation that had not been heard in years. "It was an unbelievable feeling. They were jacked up before I came out. It felt like I was floating," recalled Mattingly.[12] Out in right field, the Bleacher Creatures unraveled a large banner that contained a drawing of Mattingly rounding the bases. His uniform had been replaced with the outfit of Batman, including the flowing cape. Next to the picture read the words, "Batman Forever," a reference to the hit movie released that summer. For the remainder of the time Mattingly was on the field, the cheering did not cease and the flashbulbs didn't abate.

• • • • • • • •

A beautiful October night set in as Bob Sheppard took his place behind the public address microphone. His voice was another staple of Yankee Stadium. Sheppard first became public address announcer at the stadium in 1951, and his style was known throughout the country.[13] Blessed with a deep, booming voice, Sheppard made his pronunciations in crisp, clear English, spacing out the words just right. Equally as famous was the reverberation of his voice as it echoed across Yankee Stadium. Reggie Jackson once remarked that Sheppard's was the voice of God.[14] "Good evening . . . ladies and gentlemen. Welcome to Yankee Stadium," announced Sheppard, in his familiar tone. It was an announcement he had made hundreds, perhaps thousands of times in his life. Yet this night, the words took on a new meaning to the home crowd. They signaled the official return of postseason baseball to the Bronx and, hopefully, the ability of everyone to put the mess of the strike behind them for good.

After his customary welcome, Sheppard moved on to pregame introductions, beginning first with the Seattle Mariners. Some players received mild acknowledgment, but most, especially Ken Griffey Jr., were booed lustily. Some fared even worse. While warming up in the visitor's bullpen in preparation for his start, Chris Bosio endured merciless taunting from fans sitting in the left-field bleachers. Eventually, someone poured a beer on him. "Fans were telling me 'we're gonna hunt you down' or 'we're gonna skin you alive.' I loved it. During warm-up I got hit with a battery, beer, soda, ice, whiskey, and money. I wish I could have gotten some of it—maybe I could have paid some of my bills with it. Buhner and Griffey collected $5 in quarters during batting practice. It was unreal," said Bosio.[15]

Obviously, the Yankees were received more warmly. Each player, even those who had their struggles during the season, was the recipient of enthusiastic applause. Two people, however, received noteworthy introductions. Having introduced the coaches and bench players, Bob Sheppard moved on to the Yankees' manager, whose appearance received thunderous applause throughout the stadium. Yankees fans had taken a strong liking to the man who had guided their team back to the playoffs, and he was now their hero. In return, Buck Showalter enthusiastically waved his cap over his head, further inciting the crowd, before reaching home plate and shaking hands with Lou Piniella. "There was passion and energy in the ballpark. I can't describe how loud it was," said Showalter.[16] It was great theater, and watching it all from above was George Steinbrenner. Showalter's contract expired after the season, and The Boss was going to have to make a decision on whether to bring back the longest-tenured Yankees manager under his watch (excluding Billy Martin, whose tenures were stretched out over the course of five managerial turns, not in consecutive seasons). With his own eyes, Steinbrenner witnessed just what Yankees fans wanted him to do come the off-season. Of course, the Yankees' owner had never let the wishes of others dictate his own decisions. It remained to be seen whether the punishment meted out to him earlier in the decade would constrain his decision making when it came to the Yankees going forward.

No matter how loud Showalter's reception was, it could not match what awaited Don Mattingly. "At first base, number twenty-three, Don Mattingly," announced Sheppard as Mattingly came bounding out of the dugout to a voluminous, boisterous wall of applause. As Mattingly greeted his teammates along the first-base line, even Lou Piniella, his former teammate, coach, and manager, could be seen applauding. "It was an unbelievable feeling. There was no soreness, just energy in my body," said Mattingly.[17]

With the introductions out of the way, Robert Merrill stepped behind a microphone set up at home plate. Much like Bob Sheppard, Merrill was a staple at Yankee Stadium over the years. The gray-haired opera singer with a deep, baritone voice was generally brought out to sing the national anthem for special occasions at Yankee Stadium, and what could be more special than this one? As was his custom, he asked fans to "Join me, please," and then delivered a loud, booming rendition of "The Star-Spangled Banner." After Merrill departed from behind home plate, another staple of Yankee Stadium, Joe DiMaggio, came onto the field to throw out the first pitch. With Sheppard, Merrill, and especially DiMaggio participating, no one could accuse the Yankees of not putting on a show even before the game started.

Theatrics aside, both teams got down to business. Piniella had assembled a strong Game 1 lineup, consisting of Vince Coleman, Joey Cora, Ken Griffey Jr., Edgar Martinez, Tino Martinez, Jay Buhner, Mike Blowers, Dan Wilson, and Luis Sojo. This lineup contained no surprises, and each of these hitters represented a potential offensive problem for an opposing team. Buck Showalter countered with a lineup featuring Wade Boggs, Bernie Williams, Paul O'Neill, Ruben Sierra, Don Mattingly, Dion James, Mike Stanley, Tony Fernandez, and Randy Velarde. There were no surprises in this lineup either, and while not nearly as powerful as the Mariners, each Yankees hitter represented a potential offensive problem for an opposing team. The starters, however, were a sharp contrast. Without Randy Johnson, Tim Belcher, or Andy Benes available, Piniella called on the veteran Chris Bosio to start the first postseason game in the Mariners' history.

• • • • • • • • •

Chris Bosio was "the strongest player I ever played with," said Chris Widger.[18] Though not overpowering like Randy Johnson, the six-foot-three, 225-pound Bosio was a bulldog on the mound. A big man who used his size to intimidate, Bosio threw a variety of off-speed pitches and a sinking fastball to get hitters out. He had a slow, smooth motion where he would slide his right leg along the rubber before delivering, and he relied on intensity to get him through games. He began his career with the Milwaukee Brewers in the mid-1980s, pitching successfully for several years and winning sixty-seven games over six seasons. A free agent after the 1992 season, Bosio saw that the Brewers were not going to bring back several key players, including Paul Molitor and Dan Plesac, which caused him to leave Milwaukee. He signed with the Mariners, attracted by the team's strong defense and their manager, Lou Piniella.[19] In just his fourth start with Seattle, Bosio threw the second no-hitter in the Mariners' history. But injuries took their toll on the big righty, and by 1995 he was pitching on two badly damaged knees. Still, he managed to win ten games for the American League West champions.

Many teammates, however, felt Bosio's most important attribute was not his pitching, but his presence in the clubhouse. Like his manager, Bosio detested losing or anyone who didn't give their heart and soul for the game. "He was hard as nails. Nobody was more competitive. You wanted him in your trench when you were going to war," said coach Lee Elia.[20] Because he had to endure the pain of two bad knees every time he pitched, Bosio couldn't stomach those who didn't go all out. "He was a mean SOB, but in a good way," recalled trainer Rick Griffin. But behind the rough exterior was a compassionate teammate and clubhouse leader, who took under his wing anyone who was willing to learn the game. "He was generous. He'd take pitchers out on off days and would organize get-togethers. He was a big ole grizzly bear with a big heart," said Griffin.[21] One of those that Bosio took a liking to was Andy

Benes, who had joined the team in midyear. "He was like my personal coach. He taught me what to expect, taught me the [American] League. He made my transition easier," said Benes, who became inseparable from Bosio during the year.[22] The tough, gritty Bosio was an appropriate Game 1 starter for the tough, gritty Mariners.

* * * * * * * * *

Born and raised just outside of Kansas City, the Yankees' Game 1 starter David Cone was drafted by his hometown team, the Royals, in the early 1980s. After pitching eleven games in relief for Kansas City in 1986, he was sent to the New York Mets along with another player in exchange for Ed Hearn, Rick Anderson, and Mauro Gozzo in one of the most lopsided trades in baseball history. Cone flourished in New York, winning twenty games in 1988 and leading the Mets to the division title. He became one of the game's dominant pitchers, fooling hitters with an array of fastballs, sliders, and splitters, which he threw from several different angles. Particularly harmful was his two-strike side-arm slider, known as "the Laredo," which dipped violently away from right-handed hitters. Throughout the late 1980s and early 1990s, Cone constantly finished among the league leaders in strikeouts and innings pitched. But with the innings pitched came hundreds upon hundreds of pitches thrown. During one stretch in 1992, Cone averaged 142 pitches per game over six starts, including one game in which he threw 166 pitches against the Giants.[23] These high pitch counts were due largely to Cone's mentality of never giving in. He constantly searched for the perfect pitch to get a hitter out, even if it meant throwing seven or eight pitches per batter to do it. He was, as Buck Showalter pointed out, perfect to a fault.[24] From a distance, this kind of pitching seemed reckless. Jack McDowell used to think Cone looked unprepared on the mound, at least from the opposing side. But when he and Cone became teammates, McDowell saw one of the most prepared and focused players in the game. He learned that Cone had high pitch counts because he knew so much about each hitter that he avoided their strengths at all costs.[25] The constant nibbling at corners was sometimes maddening to fans as the pitches mounted, but few could argue with the success Cone exhibited.

Cone was traded by the Mets to the Blue Jays during the stretch run in 1992, earning him a reputation as a hired gun. In Toronto, Cone led the Blue Jays to their first World Series appearance, and he was the starting pitcher in Toronto's series-clinching Game 6 victory. The following season, Cone headed back to Kansas City, where he won the 1994 American League Cy Young Award. But the season was marred by the strike, and as one of the most visible representatives of the player's union, Cone was vilified by fans. He left Kansas City that off-season to rejoin the Toronto Blue Jays, but before the trade deadline in 1995, he was traded to the Yankees. The move only further enhanced Cone's hired-gun reputation.

The trade rejuvenated the Yankees both on the field and in the clubhouse, as Cone immediately stepped in as a team leader. Even though he was brand new to the team, "he started running the pitcher's meetings," recalled McDowell.[26] Cone was media savvy and handled public relations better than just about any major leaguer, easing the pressure on players who did not wish to spend time with reporters. "He could talk to the CEO of a company, then go hang out in the bleachers," said Dion James of Cone's personal appeal.[27] On the mound, Cone went 9–2 in thirteen starts, becoming a vital part of the September run for the wild card. "Coney was huge. Every time he pitched it was unbelievable. You felt like you'd win every time. He was a stud, a bona fide number one," said Don Mattingly.[28] Fans embraced him and "Coneheads" started popping up across Yankee Stadium. During the final weekend in Toronto, Buck Showalter had resisted immense pressure from George Steinbrenner to start Cone. Because of that, the "hired gun" would throw the first postseason pitch at Yankee Stadium in fourteen years. Though Cone had a blister on his throwing hand, nothing was going to stop him from making this historic start.

• • • • • • • •

Game 1 was being broadcast on the Baseball Network. In fact, all the playoff games were being broadcast on the Baseball Network—at the same time. There were three other postseason series taking place: Red Sox–Indians, Braves–Rockies, and Reds–Dodgers. Oddly, Major League Baseball scheduled all of the games to take place at the same time. That meant a 5:00 P.M. start in Los Angeles, 6:00 P.M. in Denver, and 8:00 P.M. in Cleveland and New York. Since all the games were taking place at once—and the same network was covering all four of them—it also meant that the games would be regionalized, and fans would not be able to see every game. The network would interrupt whichever game fans were watching to provide updates of the other games. There would be times over the next few days when the Baseball Network would even use split screens or sometimes leave games all together to show coverage of another series. It was a horrific system that was corrected the following year, but in 1995, fans could only watch one division series game a day.

• • • • • • • • •

After a hectic, strike-shortened season in which attendance plummeted and loathing for players reached all-time highs, the postseason began in front of 57,178 spectators at Yankee Stadium. David Cone squared off against his former teammate Vince Coleman and quickly jumped ahead of him, one ball and two strikes. Cone's somewhat herky-jerky motion was firing fastballs to start off, and Coleman watched a called strike three whiz by him. An ecstatic crowd sarcastically cheered Coleman as he made his way back to the dugout. Cone quickly retired Joey Cora, bringing Ken Griffey Jr. to the plate. It was an exciting moment for the Mariners' center fielder. "Of all the places to play your first playoff game, this is probably the one place you'd want to start. I'm not in awe of this place, but it is very special," said Griffey.[29] Years of having to play in front of nearly half-empty stadiums and a lethargic fan base finally paid off for Junior. As he stepped in, Griffey received the Bronx cheer that he had grown accustomed to, because Yankees fans despised him. Some claimed to hate Griffey because he wore his baseball cap backward. Some claimed to hate him for his showiness, particularly his habit of standing at the plate and watching his home runs. Most, however, hated him simply because Griffey had beaten the hell out of the Yankees for the last six years. Many remembered the night in 1990 when he made a leaping one-handed grab over the center-field fence at Yankee Stadium to rob Jesse Barfield of a home run. The play became a staple of defensive highlight reels. More recently, fans could point to the August 24 game, where Griffey homered off John Wetteland in the ninth inning at Seattle. All told, Griffey entered the postseason with a career .315 average against the Yankees, hitting .362 with seven home runs at Yankee Stadium.[30] The backward cap and the swagger were just excuses. Yankees fans booed Griffey because he was so damn good. "They've been all over me since I was a rookie," said Griffey before Game 1. "I don't pay any attention. When they get to throwing things, I just scoot over to left-center where there are no seats behind me. It just means I have to run a little longer for some balls to right or center."[31]

The excitement of Griffey's first postseason at-bat was short lived. He popped out to first base, ending the inning and drawing an enthusiastic cheer from the home crowd. It was a far cry from Cone's first inning the last time he had faced Seattle. In that game, Cone gave up a grand slam to Jay Buhner. Now, in Game 1, Cone couldn't have performed stronger.

• • • • • • • • •

Chris Bosio headed out to the Yankee Stadium mound to begin the bottom half of the first inning with his uniform soaked in beer. If Cone was going to pitch all night like he had in the first inning, the big, burly righty needed to be at the top of his game. Bosio looked shaky, though, as leadoff hitter Wade Boggs flied out to deep center field and Bernie Williams hit a line shot that Vince Coleman snared in left field. Two batters, two hard shots, but luckily for Bosio there were two outs. To the plate stepped Paul O'Neill, whom Bosio considered the Yankees' toughest out.[32] With the count at 1–1, O'Neill lined a sinker to right field for a single. It looked liked Bosio wasn't fooling any of the Yankees hitters with his stuff. Yet he rebounded to strike out Ruben Sierra on three pitches. Despite the shakiness, Bosio managed to get through the first inning on just eleven pitches, matching Cone's total.

The ever-dangerous Edgar Martinez began the second inning for the Mariners. Like most of his teammates, Martinez was making his first appearance in the postseason. Despite being the game's best hitter at the time, he was relatively unknown outside of Seattle. A breakout performance in front of the nation's largest media market would go a long way toward getting him the recognition he deserved. The breakout, though, would not come in this at-bat, as Martinez lined out to left field. Tino Martinez then flied out to right field. That brought Jay Buhner to the plate with two outs.

For Buhner, the Game 1 experience was surreal. "The Bone" as teammates lovingly referred to him, had come up with the Yankees organization in the mid-1980s. While eating breakfast one morning with his AAA batting coach, he read in the paper that he had been traded to Seattle in the infamous Ken Phelps deal.[33] Though the move meant increased playing time, Buhner was shocked at the difference in clubhouses. New York featured a win-at-all-costs atmosphere, while Seattle barely scratched a competitive mentality. Still, the lack of success in Seattle shone attention on Buhner for his standout play, and he immediately became a fan favorite. With his goatee and shaved head, Jay looked more like a biker than like a baseball player. Seattle ate it up. The Mariners held promotional nights in which fans who shaved their heads, sometimes with Buhner himself doing the cutting, would get discounted or free tickets.

In the clubhouse, Buhner was a prankster who sometimes mimicked vomiting so he could induce one of his coaches into actually throwing up.[34] "Jay walks to the beat of a different drum," said one former teammate with a laugh. But for all the practical jokes, few players took the game more seriously than Buhner. He never hesitated to call out a teammate who he didn't feel was giving his all, and he had a deep affection for Lou Piniella. His style of play produced impressive offensive numbers, including his forty-home-run performance in 1995. Buhner also had one of the strongest outfield arms in the majors and was a daunting presence in right field.

While Buhner loved Seattle, he maintained an affinity for New York. Part of it was his sometimes-hilarious love-hate relationship with the fans, for few players took more abuse from the Bleacher Creatures than Buhner. "Me, Junior, and Edgar were hated. They would start chanting 'Buhner loves Edgar' or 'Buhner takes it up the ass, do-dah, do-dah' or 'Fuck you Jay. Fuck you baldy.' They are great though. As long as I wasn't getting hit with anything, it was fine," said Buhner.[35] Now he stood at home plate, a reminder to every Yankees fan, especially one sitting up in the owner's box, of what might have been. It would have been something out of a Hollywood movie had Buhner homered in this situation. But he was not fond of hitting against Cone, despite his grand slam off the righty in August. "I hated [Cone]. He had a nasty slider and knew how to pitch. He was filthy. With Cone, you just had to hope for a mistake over the plate," said Buhner.[36] Cone made no such mistake and induced Buhner to ground out to Wade Boggs. Cone, who normally extended innings as well as his pitch count by trying to outwit hitters, had thrown a conservative twenty-five pitches through the first two innings. More important, he had retired all six hitters he'd faced.

• • • • • • • • •

"Now batting for the Yankees, the first baseman, Don . . . Mattingly . . . number 23." Bob Sheppard's announcement echoed across Yankee Stadium and continued into the Bronx night. For some, it was the sweetest introduction they had ever heard. Don Mattingly had waited 1,785 regular-season games for this moment. While strikingly different from any situation he had ever been in, it was also in many ways just like any other time he had batted in his career. The goal was still the same: see the ball; hit the ball.

As with Buhner, it would have been a moment straight out of Hollywood if Mattingly could hit a home run in this, his first postseason at-bat. Even a bunt single would drive the fans crazy. Instead, Mattingly lifted a Bosio sinker to right field. The initial contact and sight of the ball headed toward right field got a momentary stir out of the fans, who thought for a second that the ball might be going out. But it was nothing more than an easy fly ball to Buhner. The moment having passed, Mattingly received a warm ovation as he returned to the dugout. Despite the uproar over Mattingly's first at-bat, Bosio remained focused on the hitters. He quickly retired Dion James and Mike Stanley, and the inning was over.

• • • • • • • • •

David Cone walked hitters. A lot of them. It was something he had done throughout his career. So when he walked Mike Blowers to lead off the top of the third inning, no one was surprised. Nor was anyone worried. In the short time Cone had been with the team, Yankees

fans realized that just because he was walking hitters didn't necessarily mean he was losing control. The odds were that he was being
stubborn, refusing to give in to a hitter no matter what. With Blowers
on first, Cone struck out Dan Wilson on a sharp slider, momentarily
halting the Mariners' momentum. But Luis Sojo, enjoying his day of
glory as Seattle's hero, followed the Wilson strikeout with a single
into right field. Suddenly, what had been a quiet game grew interesting as Cone faced his first crisis. Remaining calm, Cone easily
worked out of the jam by inducing both Coleman and Cora to fly out.
The Mariners missed their first opportunity to take the lead.

With one out in the bottom of the third inning Randy Velarde
made his way to the plate. Though it was not nearly as loud as
Mattingly's, he received a warm ovation. Second on the team in
seniority only to Mattingly, Velarde had also waited a long time for
this moment. Making the most of it, he ripped a Bosio fastball into
center field for a single. The lineup turned over, and Boggs batted for
the second time.

By 1995, Boggs had already established himself as a first-ballot Hall
of Famer. Earlier in the season, he had collected his 2,500th career base
hit in just his fourteenth year. He was a five-time batting champion
who once recorded seven consecutive 200-hit seasons. Coming into the
1995 postseason, he was a career .334 hitter, one of the highest batting
averages in baseball history.[37] Boggs's hitting style was admired across
the league, and his name always came up in discussions regarded
baseball's best pure hitters. He batted lefty, with the bat held straight
and nearly perpendicular from his body, and used a minuscule leg
kick. While capable of producing power numbers, he refused to do
so, believing it would mean a significant drop in his batting average.
Boggs had an astonishing ability to turn on inside pitches that would
jam most hitters, sending them into left field for a single or double,
a technique known as inside-outing the ball. He also became a more
dangerous hitter with a two-strike count, as he would foul off or take
close pitches until finally receiving a ball he could drive for a hit.

These talents served Boggs well as a member of the Boston Red Sox,
where he spent his first ten seasons. After hitting a career-worst .259 in
1992, the first time Boggs's average had ever fallen below .300, Boston
opted not to re-sign him. The Yankees, meanwhile, desperately needed
a third baseman after they lost Charlie Hayes to the Colorado Rockies

in the expansion draft. But there were serious concerns expressed by both Buck Showalter and Gene Michael regarding Boggs.[38] They had heard stories about his being a difficult teammate and that people in Boston were only too happy to see him leave. There were also concerns about the plummet in batting average. Still, the Yankees needed a third baseman and signed Boggs to a three-year deal. The signing caused immediate excitement in the Bronx, as Yankees fans quickly forgot their animosity toward Boggs from when he'd been a member of the hated Red Sox. During that time, he had dueled Don Mattingly for the American League batting title throughout the 1980s. Now they were playing the corner positions on the same team. Boggs regained the stroke that had been missing in 1992 and hit .302 in 1993. He followed that up by hitting .342 in 1994 and .324 in 1995. Boggs returned to form and squelched any doubts about his being able to hit in the cavernous Yankee Stadium. Additionally, Boggs brought with him a style and work ethic that served as a shining example to many of the Yankees' younger players. Boggs took the game of baseball very seriously and expected others to do the same. He worked hard at honing his hitting and defensive skills and exuded all-out hustle and dedication on the field. Some saw his attitude as selfish. Boggs made no secret that he wanted to play baseball until he got 3,000 hits, a goal that could have been interpreted as self-serving. But the truth was that in pursuit of that goal, he was going to do everything he could to ensure that his team would win, and he wasn't going to allow any personal goals to deflect from team goals. The criticism of Boggs as selfish and unpopular that had festered in Boston dissipated in New York.[39]

In addition to his hitting ability and work ethic, Boggs also drew attention to himself in another way. Few, if any, players in baseball were as superstitious as he was. Jokingly referred to as "Chicken Man" by his teammates, Boggs had a ritual of eating poultry before every game, and he also took exactly 150 ground balls during infield practice. He had an obsession with the number seven, because he dreamed of going seven for seven in a game, so for night games, he always began warming up at 7:17. Before each at-bat, he would draw the Hebrew sign for life in the dirt near home plate with his bat.[40]

Boggs's quirkiness had paid off as he stepped into the box against Bosio in the third inning. It was an at-bat many thought Boggs would not have. A week earlier in Milwaukee, he was running out a ground ball when he felt a pop in his left hamstring. It was severe enough that even with the wild card on the line, Boggs had to sit out the final series in Toronto. He even missed batting practice for the first time in his career as a Yankee.[41] But he received medication and treatment for the injury, and though he admitted to not being completely healthy, he felt well enough to play in Game 1. Despite hitting just under .200 for his career against Bosio,[42] Boggs had gotten a good swing off the Mariner pitcher in the first inning, nearly hitting a home run to center field. In this at-bat, Bosio's second pitch, a fastball, got too much of the plate, and Boggs lined the ball hard and deep to right-center field. Buhner chased it, but the ball cleared the fence just to the right of the 385-foot marker. Boggs watched the ball leave the park, then enthusiastically pumped his fist as he gingerly trotted around the bases. Bosio immediately called out catcher Dan Wilson to discuss the pitch, though Wilson could barely hear him. The crowd was enthralled. Afterward, Boggs was almost apologetic about his two-run shot. "A home run for me is a mistake," he explained. "If I'm out in front of a pitch far enough to hit it out, that usually means I was fooled or I didn't see the pitch or something like that."[43] Even if it was a "mistake," Boggs had given the Yankees a 2–0 lead. His home run was merely a prelude of the type of power that would be on display throughout the series.

Unperturbed, Bosio quickly retired Bernie Williams and Paul O'Neill to end the inning. The crowd had barely calmed down from the excitement of Boggs's home run when Griffey hit Cone's fifth pitch of the fourth inning high and deep to right field. Cone's forkball had failed to dip down, staying over the plate, and Griffey turned on it with his smooth, picturesque swing. The ball slammed against the Bud Light advertisement sign that adorned the facing of the upper deck, then plummeted back onto the playing field. Griffey's first postseason home run, a 401-foot shot, calmed down the rowdy crowd.[44] He quietly, slowly rounded the bases with a swagger all too familiar to those in the stands. With just a 2–1 Yankees lead, Edgar Martinez popped a broken-bat single into right field. Tino Martinez then walked. It looked like the Mariners' offensive juggernaut was about to rev into full gear. Batting next was Buhner, who had already roughed up Cone for a grand slam at the Kingdome in August. Buhner got hearts around the stadium racing when he sent a first-pitch breaking ball deep to right-center field. But Bernie Williams gracefully tracked the ball down just before the warning track and fired the ball back to the infield. With the Mariners still threatening, Cone struck out Mike Blowers, seemingly ending the potential crisis. But Dan Wilson drilled the first pitch he saw for what looked like a game-tying single into left field. Wade Boggs, still sporting the sore hamstring, lunged to his left, dove, and in a full-out extension, snared Wilson's line drive before crashing full body onto the infield dirt. Boggs got up, soft-tossed the ball to the mound, then headed to the dugout where he received congratulations from his teammates. His remarkable play saved the lead for New York.

• • • • • • • •

His teammates having cut the deficit in half, Chris Bosio wanted to keep the momentum on Seattle's side. Boggs's home run and the rowdy crowd could easily have disturbed another pitcher. But Bosio was unfazed. He cruised through an easy fourth inning, retiring the side in order and throwing only six pitches. David Cone bested him, needing only five pitches to get through the top of the fifth. Bosio worked through mild trouble in the bottom of fifth inning. With one out, Tony Fernandez battled Bosio for eight pitches before finally drawing a walk. Fernandez was left stranded when Velarde and Boggs both flied out. Moving along at a brisk pace, the game headed to the top of the sixth inning.

• • • • • • • •

David Cone was in trouble. He easily retired Griffey to start the top of the sixth inning, but then Edgar Martinez singled into left-center field. "I came up and in with a fastball and broke his bat [in the fourth inning] and he fought it off, got the bat out, and got it over the infield into right-center," said Cone. "I said 'OK, I went hard in, so let's go down and away with soft stuff.' I threw a good splitter [in the sixth inning] and [Martinez] went down, got the bat on it and lifted it into left-center. I'm thinking, 'OK, now what?'"[45] Edgar was perplexing Cone, and the pitcher may not have been able to shake that frustration, as he then walked Tino Martinez. Buhner next lined a single into left field, but he hit the ball so hard that Edgar Martinez had to remain at third base. The bases were loaded for Mike Blowers, as dangerous a hitter with three men on base as there was in 1995. In August, Blowers had gone on a tear, hitting three grand slams in a fifteen-day period. On the flip side, he could not touch David Cone. Including his first two at-bats of Game 1, he was a career 0–11 against the Yankees right-hander. With a tense stadium observing, Blowers fouled off several fastballs and pushed the count full. Refusing to give in, Cone opted to throw a slider instead of a fastball. The pitch darted down and away from Blowers, who swung over it for the second out. "I was expecting a fastball for a strike and I got a slider outside. He made a good pitch," said Blowers. Cone didn't think the pitch was so good. "I was lucky," he said of it.[46] With two outs, the crowd grew overbearingly loud. Extending the Mariners' rally fell into the hands of their number-eight hitter, catcher Dan Wilson.

• • • • • • • • •

When Wilson was traded from the Reds to the Mariners in November 1993, he looked at it as a great opportunity. "I had a chance to show Lou [Piniella] what kind of player I was [when they were both] with the Reds. The Mariners had a staff I knew and could trust, and I knew there would be an opening behind the plate for me," said Wilson.[47] The trade did pay off, as Wilson became the Mariners' full-time catcher and one of the best defenders in the league. He earned the accolades of his teammates, who named him the team's unsung hero in 1995, no small achievement considering the various key players on the team. "He was a smart receiver who understood the game," said Andy Benes. "People told me when I got traded [to Seattle] that I was gonna love throwing to him."[48] But Wilson's success came with a price, because no one was harder on catchers than Lou Piniella. Catchers were the "pincushion" of the team when Piniella was manager, recalled one former player. He would constantly question their game-calling and blame them for just about anything that went wrong. "Every catcher had to take Lou's shit. But Dan took it like a man," said Joey Cora.[49] Despite the intense pressure, Wilson handled it well and never took it personally. "[Piniella] was hardest on pitchers and catchers, but he does it because he wants them to improve. I'm grateful for the instruction and for Lou making me into [a] better player," said Wilson.[50]

Offensively, Wilson had improved greatly since first coming up the majors, thanks in part to his working with hitting coach Lee Elia. "Lee Elia has done a heckuva job with him," said Piniella before Game 1. "Danny has become a very tough out."[51] The Mariners now needed Wilson to become a tough out against David Cone. Wilson quickly fell behind the count with no balls and two strikes. The crowd eagerly awaited the strikeout they were certain was coming. In the park, 57,000 people stood on their feet, enthusiastically cheering for a third strike. "In the sixth inning when the crowd was screaming for David Cone to get that strikeout, I couldn't hear myself think," said Wade Boggs.[52] Cone, however, choose not finish Wilson off with fastballs and instead went exclusively to his slider. After a ball, Wilson fouled off a pitch before Cone again threw a slider. Wilson at first went after the pitch but then checked his swing. The crowd began screaming wildly, believing Wilson had swung for strike three. Both Cone and catcher Mike Stanley immediately pointed toward first base, asking home-plate umpire Mike Reilly to appeal to first-base umpire Dale Scott on whether Wilson had swung or not. "Did he swing?" Reilly asked Scott. Scott extended both arms out from his body, perpendicular to the ground. No swing. The call enraged the crowd, which immediately exhaled a loud groan of disapproval that reverberated across New York City. Next to the Yankees' dugout, New York mayor Rudy Giuliani's son Andrew stomped and gestured.[53] Cone turned his back to home plate and faced center field, disgusted with the call. In the owner's box, George Steinbrenner fumed in disbelief. When he saw the replay of Wilson's check swing on NBC, he became incensed. Leaving the owner's box, Steinbrenner headed toward the press box and launched into a severe tirade, even by Steinbrenner's standards. "They shouldn't put an umpire like Rich Garcia, the most experienced umpire out there, down the left-field line. On first, to make that call, there should be some kind of merit system. It's almost criminal."[54] The impromptu press conference continued, with Steinbrenner putting blame on American League President Gene Budig for the umpires that had been selected. "It stinks. [Scott] blew that call or we're out of the inning. It's awful to put a rookie in a playoff series. Budig should know better than that."[55] Someone in the press informed

The Boss that Dale Scott was not a rookie umpire but had in fact been calling games since 1986. "OK, so he's not a rookie," said Steinbrenner, "but he shouldn't be the first-base umpire when you've got a guy like Richie Garcia down the left-field line. We have enough problems with the game. We have to make sure we get the best umpires doing these games."[56] When Wilson walked to tie the game, the crowd's indignation showered down on Dale Scott. Cone, himself disappointed in the call, induced Luis Sojo to fly out to deep right field, ending the inning without further damage.

• • • • • • • • •

The Yankees didn't have time to dwell on possible missed calls. It was the sixth inning, the game was tied, and they needed to regain the lead. Bernie Williams started off by poking a "seeing-eye single" between third base and shortstop. Williams was a threat to steal, but Bosio paid him mild attention, choosing instead to focus on Paul O'Neill. He induced O'Neill to ground out to second, but Williams moved up on the play, putting himself in scoring position with just one out. But Ruben Sierra popped up to Dan Wilson for the second out. The Yankees now needed a two-out hit from Don Mattingly to take the lead. Mattingly had done well against Bosio throughout his career, batting .333 with a home run. "Donny was a tough out because he was flexible. He stayed inside the ball. I would change speed on him, and he would adjust and spoil my best pitches," said Bosio.[57] But in his previous two at-bats against Bosio, the Yankees captain had only mustered two weak fly balls to the outfield. Now he sought his first postseason hit and in a crucial situation. Bosio fell behind in the count, allowing Mattingly to sit on a fastball and lash it into right field for a single. Running on contact, Williams easily scored and the Yankees recaptured the lead. As Mattingly received congratulations from first-base coach Brian Butterfield, Yankee Stadium shook to its foundation. It was a big moment in the career of the Yankees captain, made even bigger because it gave the Yankees a 3–2 lead. Bosio tried to settle down but gave up a single to Dion James. It was his last batter of the night. Piniella emerged from the dugout and signaled for right-handed Jeff Nelson. Bosio's final pitching line would betray a tough, gritty performance in front of an especially hostile crowd. In a beer-soaked jersey, Bosio had kept the Mariners in the game all night.

Nelson entered Game 1 and was greeted by a Mike Stanley single into left-center field. Don Mattingly trotted in from third base and scored, giving the Yankees a 4–2 lead. The stadium continued to shake as fans refused to sit down. Even Tony Fernandez's inning-ending groundout could not dampen their spirits. A two-out rally led by their captain made them giddy over the prospect of the Yankees' first postseason win in over a decade.

• • • • • • • •

David Cone had his lead back and quickly retired Coleman to begin the seventh inning. He then walked Cora, putting himself in yet another precarious position as Griffey strode to the plate as the tying run. The fourth-inning home run that had bounced off the upper deck was still fresh in everyone's mind as Cone delivered a first-pitch fastball to Griffey. Like the forkball that didn't dip in the fourth inning, this pitch stayed out over the plate. Griffey extended his powerful arms and drilled the ball. The mere sound alone sent a hush through the crowd. Fans stood in shocked silence as Cone's misplaced fastball sailed deep into the lower level of the right-field stands. The game was tied at four. A fan behind the Mariners' dugout had been waving his wrist gingerly at Griffey every time he returned after making an out, trying to hint that Junior had yet to fully heal from his injury. When Griffey returned to the dugout this time, the same fan started bowing to him.[58] Before the game, Junior had been greeted in the clubhouse by Reggie Jackson, whom he openly referred to as "Mr. October." Someone in the clubhouse asked Griffey if he wanted to inherit the title. Junior told him, "I'm going to go rub my bat against him [Jackson] for good luck."[59] The pregame move paid off, as he was now responsible for three of the Mariners' four runs.

Knowing he had missed his spot, Cone stood on the mound shaking his head as Griffey again slowly trotted around the bases. After watching the ball land into the right-field seats, he bent down and grabbed a hand full of dirt, which he slammed back to the ground. "I'd like to blame them on the blister," Cone said after the game. "But that wasn't a factor. . . . He's just a great hitter."[60] Yankee Stadium, jovial only minutes earlier, was filled only with the cheers of Seattle players and owners. As quickly as they had regained the lead, the Yankees had given it up, and the game was tied yet again.

Edgar Martinez followed Griffey's home run with a walk, and those in the crowd began to stir, wondering if their hired gun was running out of steam. Cone answered by striking out both Tino Martinez and Buhner to end the inning. But again, the Mariners had clawed back to tie the game. The Yankees returned to their dugout looking to reclaim the lead. "We got a game again, so let's go," yelled Don Mattingly to his teammates.[61]

• • • • • • • •

On the third pitch of the bottom of the seventh inning, Jeff Nelson's fastball slammed into Randy Velarde's left arm. With the game tied, there was no way Nelson was intentionally trying to hit Velarde. He threw a slider that simply didn't break, and now the Yankees had their leadoff hitter on base. But having not forgotten the incident between Randy Johnson and Jim Leyritz in May, Yankees fans serenaded Nelson with a loud chorus of taunts and boos. Piniella decided Nelson had had enough and called on Bobby Ayala. In Seattle, millions of Mariners fans began to shudder. Ayala, who earlier in the year had been the team's closer, was in Mariners fans' doghouse for his mid- and late-season struggles. It began on July 4 when he blew a save in Detroit. From that point on, he allowed at least one run in eleven of fourteen appearances and saw his ERA balloon above 4.00.[62] Though Ayala was, by all accounts, one of the nicest people in the game, his performances became irksome and so unreliable that he lost the closer's position to Norm Charlton, and fans began booing him when he appeared out of the bullpen. Piniella choose Ayala in this situation because the pitcher's forkball and split-fingered fastball were extremely difficult on left-hand hitters like Boggs. But that was only when they were working. If Ayala threw those pitches too hard, they didn't break and hitters clobbered them. Piniella could not have been pleased when Boggs greeted Ayala by ripping a single into center field, sending Velarde to third base. The crowd got back on their feet as the Yankees set up to take the lead. Needing even just a weak ground ball to score the go-ahead run, Williams drove a ball deep into left-center field. The ever-reliable

Griffey initially misjudged how hard Williams had hit it, and before he could get a good break, the ball sailed over his head and went all the way to the wall. Ironically, before the game, Williams had told the media that "when Griffey plays center, you have to hit the ball out of the park to get it past him."[63] Bernie had proven himself wrong and cruised into second base with a double, Boggs went to third, and Velarde scored easily. The Yankees took their third different lead of the game. O'Neill then lined a hard shot to left field. Coleman charged, nearly overrunning the line drive, and caught the ball over his right shoulder while moving to his left. Boggs, even with the sore hamstring, scored easily, and the Yankees had their two-run lead back. Although Ayala was getting hit hard, Piniella opted to let him face designated hitter Ruben Sierra. The salsa music came blasting over the PA system as Sierra came to bat with one out and a runner on second. The Yankees wanted to put the game away, and these were the types of situation that Sierra lived for.

• • • • • • • •

Sierra was a rising star in baseball during the late 1980s. He was a five-tool player, capable of massive home runs. Patrolling the outfield for the Texas Rangers, Sierra was one of the game's premier players beginning in 1987, when he hit thirty home runs and drove in 109 runs in just his second season. Over the course of the next several years, he continued to post impressive numbers, leading the American League in RBIs in 1989 and making the All-Star team four times. In 1992, he was involved in one of the biggest trades of the decade when the Rangers sent him and pitchers Bobby Witt and Jeff Russell to the Oakland A's for outfielder Jose Canseco. In Oakland, Sierra made the postseason for the first time as the A's won the AL West, but they were then defeated by David Cone's Blue Jays in the American League Championship Series. Sierra enjoyed successful 1993 and 1994 seasons with the A's, but by 1995, things began to sour. Sierra's offensive numbers dropped, and he was no longer the threat he'd once been. Once a decent outfielder with a strong throwing arm, he instead became a defensive liability. He openly feuded with Oakland's top personnel, including manager Tony LaRussa. Sierra's personality, which was nothing if not interesting, made matters increasingly worse, as he made no secret of how miserable he was. By the summer of 1995, Sierra was a loud, distracting problem, and the A's sought desperately to dump him. On the same day the Yankees traded for David Cone, they traded disgruntled outfielder Danny Tartabull to the A's in exchange for Sierra. It was largely viewed as a trade of one team's headache for another's. Tartabull, signed to a large contract in 1992, had never lived up to his potential, at least not in the eyes of Yankees fans and team personnel. He was often injured (many times those injuries were questionable), and by 1995, his production had dissipated to a paltry six home runs in just over 200 at-bats. The Yankees and Tartabull gladly parted ways, as did Sierra and the A's.

Sierra's acquisition was at first viewed as an afterthought, as Cone was making all the headlines. In fact, Sierra's role with the team was not clearly defined. Darryl Strawberry was expected to be called up any day from the minor leagues, which would create a backlog of DHs and outfielders on the team. Showalter made room for Sierra, and away from the distractions of Oakland, he began producing like the all-star of old. Thrown into the lineup solely as the DH and hitting in the cleanup spot, Sierra responded by driving in forty-four runs in just fifty-six games. He also, despite fan sentiment to the contrary, produced continuously in clutch situations, including an eighth-inning home run against the Blue Jays on September 21 that sparked a crucial come-from-behind victory.[64] In addition to the offensive production, Sierra brought a swagger and self-assuredness to the Yankees not seen since the days of Reggie Jackson. Sierra's home-run trots bordered on the comical, if not insulting to some, as he would remain at home plate, gazing admiringly at the shot he had just hit. Once he finally decided to move, Sierra took a roundabout way of getting around the bases, sometimes taking a turn so wide at first base people joked that he could high-five all his teammates sitting in the dugout. While some felt this style did not exemplify that of the New York Yankees, many felt that Sierra didn't do it maliciously or with the intent of showing anyone up. Rather it was just one aspect of an overall colorful personality. "Ruben had shoes for every outfit," said Don Mattingly with a laugh, describing the somewhat eccentric behavior of his onetime teammate.[65] Despite throwing him batting practice nearly every day after Sierra joined the Yankees, Yankees bullpen catcher Glen Shurlock couldn't get him to remember his name. "He never knew it. He would just call me guy. 'Hey guy, throw the fastball,'" said Shurlock.[66]

So the man with the funky suits who didn't know Glen Shurlock's name strode to the plate in the seventh inning with one out and one runner on. Hitless so far in Game 1, Sierra jumped ahead in the count, with two balls and a strike. Ayala's next pitch badly missed its intended spot, and Sierra crushed it deep into the right-field stands. In typical fashion, Sierra dropped the bat and did his "two-step backward shimmy [which he finished] with a little pluck at his shirtfront . . . and only then the unsmiling, nothing-to-it, slow-and-then-slower tour of the bases."[67] Such a display might have normally triggered anger in Lou Piniella and the Seattle team, but now they had bigger concerns. The fans, who had mostly kept their intrusions to some beer throwing and taunting, littered the field with all sorts of debris in jubilant celebration. Some items were as harmless as a program, while others were more severe. "You name it, I had everything from quarters to batteries thrown at me," said Mike Blowers.[68]

Bob Sheppard came on the PA system and asked the fans to refrain from throwing anything else onto the field. "[Sheppard] tells them to act like the great fans they are and right after that a golf ball goes whizzing by Joey Cora's ear at second base," said Jay Buhner. "They threw everything. There was a tomato, spit cups, coke bottles . . . you could have opened a convenience store. Someone threw a Sony Walkman and the damn thing still worked."[69]

"I am standing near second and a golf ball lands right in front of me," recalled Joey Cora. "I picked it up and showed it to the umpire. He looked at me and said there was nothing he could do. Buhner came in from right field with a bottle of rum. I thought to myself, 'What the fuck are we getting into?'"[70]

Players, who always had to be on guard in the Bronx, now had legitimate safety concerns while standing out in the field. Shortly after order was restored, a fan ran onto the field and was tackled by an army of security guards.[71] It was a black eye for the Yankees and their fans but merely a hint of more shenanigans to come. Play resumed with the Mariners facing the reality that the game was slipping away from them. Ayala promptly surrendered an opposite-field double to Don Mattingly. That was enough for Piniella, who mercifully lifted Ayala and replaced him with Bill Risley. "He was finding some bats, wasn't he," said Piniella somewhat wryly of Ayala's performance. "That was his biggest problem."[72]

Risley was lucky to be pitching in Game 1. During batting practice before the game, he had been shagging fly balls in the outfield and was about to catch one when teammate Bob Wells cut in front of him also trying to make the play. The ball went off the end of Wells's glove and nailed Risley in the left ear.[73] He was momentarily shaken up and needed medical attention, but it turned out to be nothing more than a small cut and he begged Piniella to let him stay at the ballpark.[74] Showing no ill effects from the incident, Risley retired the only two hitters he faced to end the seventh inning, but the Yankees had broken the game open and, they hoped, had finally put it out of reach.

• • • • • • • • • •

Twice in Game 1, David Cone had given away the Yankees' lead. Now, staked to a four-run lead with just six outs to go, he had no intention of letting things slip away from him again. Cone easily retired Blowers, Wilson, and Sojo in the top of the eighth inning. The hired gun had been erratic throughout various parts of the night, but he'd pitched well enough to allow the Yankees to obtain the lead. Almost as important, he had pitched long enough to allow Buck Showalter not to have to dip into his questionable bullpen. The eighth inning was Cone's last in Game 1, and the Yankees provided even more breathing room for his replacement by adding a run in the bottom of the inning. Bob Wells, who had narrowly missed being hit in the head with a bottle of Jaegermeister while warming up in the bullpen (backup catcher Chris Widger was hit with a lighter), replaced Risley on the mound.[75] Wells quickly retired the first two hitters, but he eventually gave up an RBI single to Bernie Williams, giving the Yankees a seemingly insurmountable five-run lead. Wells escaped further damage

The combination of a 9–4 lead and the 134 pitches he'd thrown meant David Cone's night was over. Up by five runs, Showalter could have gone to one of his lesser-used or more-ineffective pitchers. Instead, Showalter called upon his closer, John Wetteland. Wetteland, who hadn't pitched in four days, immediately ran into problems with the Seattle lineup. Leading off the inning, Coleman fought Wetteland through a nine-pitch at-bat before walking. With a five-run lead, there was no immediate cause for concern, especially after Cora flied out. But Griffey followed with a single to right field, and Edgar Martinez dropped a broken-bat single into right field. Coleman scored easily, and suddenly, the tying run was in the on-deck circle. Yankees fans were not panicking yet, but Tino Martinez then singled into center field, driving in Griffey and making it just a three-run game. The crowd began to stir. Williams's eighth-inning single was supposed to have made this game a laugher. Now, with the tying run at the plate, that RBI represented a critical run. Fans had gotten used to Wetteland's nail-biting performances, but this was the playoffs and they wanted no part of this gut-wrenching tension. When Buhner popped up to third for the second out, the stadium breathed a collective but only temporary sigh of relief. The tension was still thick in the air as Blowers came to the plate. Despite his struggles against Cone, Blowers was more than capable of tying the game with one swing. With Game 1 now on the line, Blowers quickly fell behind, no balls and two strikes. Wetteland reared back and fired a blistering fastball. It flew past Blowers, who swung and missed. After three and a half suspenseful hours, Game 1 was officially in the books, and the Yankees held a 1–0 lead in the series.

· · · · · · · · ·

Afterward, the Yankee Stadium crowd was as much a topic of discussion as the home team's victory. "It was wild . . . I've never seen it quite like this," said Don Mattingly during the postgame interviews. "I can't imagine a better place in the world to be. It was a great feeling and it lived up to everything I expected. Actually, it was better than I imagined."[76]

"I can honestly say it was the most amazing crowd I've ever seen," David Cone told the media. "They were chanting with every pitch. It was very similar to my experience at Shea in 1988."[77]

"I told Buck Showalter it was the loudest I've seen it in a long, long time," said Lou Piniella. "They were up for this game. It's been awhile."[78]

At the end of the night, Ken Griffey Jr. put it all into perspective. "We lost and that's tough, but we've got tomorrow."[79] And what a day tomorrow would be.

7

Game 2: A Classic in the Bronx

"This one by Mattingly . . . ohhhh hang on to the roof!"

—NBC broadcaster Gary Thorne calling
Don Mattingly's Game 2 home run

Andy Pettitte was not nervous. He should have been, but he wasn't. The left-handed rookie pitcher had lost out on the number-five spot in the Yankees' rotation in spring training. Now he was the starting pitcher for New York in Game 2 of the Division Series. Buck Showalter was asking Pettitte to get the Yankees a two-games-to-none lead before heading across the continent to the ever-imposing Kingdome. No problem, Pettitte thought to himself.[1]

The Yankees drafted Pettitte out of Texas in 1990. While coming up through the system, Pettitte struggled with weight problems that some believed was a result of poor training on his part. Buck Showalter saw enormous potential in the young player and couldn't figure out why someone with such talent would seemingly let it go to waste. He took Pettitte aside one day. "Son, there are three ways you can get yourself out of this game," Showalter told him. "You can eat your way out, you can talk your way out, and you can fuck your way out." Looking sternly now at Pettitte, Showalter advised him, "don't eat your way out." Pettitte began taking better care of himself. He worked his way through the minors, performing exceptionally well at each level. By 1995, some in the organization felt he was ready for the big-league club. He made the team, but only as a reliever, having been beaten out of the fifth spot in the rotation by Sterling Hitchcock. On opening day at Yankee Stadium, Pettitte was introduced to only a smattering of applause from the hometown fans. Most were probably asking themselves, "Andy who?" Pitching his first few games out of the bullpen, Pettitte was moved into the starting rotation when injuries decimated the Yankees' starting rotation. Initially, he was hit hard, giving up fifteen runs in his first thirty-one innings and going 1–4. He began throwing a cut fastball in August, but in his rookie year he relied more on a fastball, curveball, and a changeup.[2] Early on, these pitches did not fool hitters, but late in the season when the Yankees needed it most, Pettitte caught fire. After a horrific start at the Kingdome during the Yankees' nightmarish August West Coast trip, he went 6–1 to finish the season. In September, Pettitte became the team's most reliable starter. He also unveiled a pickoff move that was second to none in baseball. It was difficult for even the best base runners to distinguish between Pettitte's move to home plate and his pickoff move to first. Many were so confused that they got picked off even when not attempting to steal. Don Mattingly recalled a base runner who asked him how Pettitte's pickoff move was. "It's alright," Mattingly told him. The runner was picked off on the next play.[3] As word of Pettitte's move began spreading around the league, leads against him became shorter and shorter. Still, by year's end, he managed to pick off twelve runners.

Despite his natural ability, no one was harder on himself than Pettitte. It was not rare to see the rookie pitcher chastise himself after making the wrong pitch or missing his spot. "Andy was a perfectionist. He never wanted to walk a guy or give up a hit," said Jim Leyritz, who became Pettitte's personal catcher during the 1995 season.[4] There was such intensity to Pettitte's self-deprivation that it sometimes drew the laughter of his own teammates. He was a pitcher's version of his intensity-driven teammate Paul O'Neill. For Game 2, though, that intensity would have to be controlled. Pettitte had never pitched before a crowd of this size, nor had he faced many offenses as potent as the Mariners'.

• • • • • • • • •

Unlike his opponent on the mound, Andy Benes was no rookie. In fact, he had been a solid starting pitcher for years. Still, like Pettitte, he was making his postseason debut. Benes grew up in Evansville, Indiana, six years younger than its most famous resident, Don Mattingly. He emerged with the Padres in 1989 and became an effective pitcher, winning between ten and fifteen games a year and posting respectable ERAs. But the Padres were not competitive, and Benes never came close to the playoffs. He was a free agent at the end of the 1995 season, and with the Padres again not in contention, Benes was aware that he was going to be traded at the July 31 deadline. On that day, he returned from dinner with his wife and children to find three messages on his answering machine from Padres general manager Randy Smith. All of them said Benes needed to call him immediately.[5] Smith informed him that he had been sent to Seattle. Benes recovered from the initial shock and welcomed the trade to a team that was still in contention. But he did not welcome the trade as much as members of the Mariners did, because it was the first time Seattle had made a deal to acquire a quality player at the deadline, as opposed to giving one away.

For the Mariners, the trade was just as important mentally as physically. "It sends a message to the players that ownership is doing what it can to give us a chance to get into the playoffs," said Chris Bosio upon hearing of the trade.[6] Benes initially had difficultly adjusting to the American League, and his ERA rose to nearly 6.00. But the Mariners always came through offensively, and Benes posted a 7–2 record. "He'd give up four runs, we'd score five. We knew we were gonna win with him on the mound. It was like he knew how many runs we would score," said Norm Charlton.[7]

For Game 2, Benes was pitching on three days' rest. But, he had only thrown thirty-five pitches in his previous outing against Texas in which he'd gotten hit hard. "It was like a throw day between starts more than a start itself," said Benes.[8] While warming up in the bullpen before Game 2, he had a beer dumped on him. He had to change shirts before heading out to the mound.[9]

• • • • • • • • •

Buck Showalter made one change to his Game 2 lineup: Jim Leyritz was catching instead of Mike Stanley. Lou Piniella made a few changes to his lineup, putting Luis Sojo in the number-two spot behind Vince Coleman. Joey Cora was pushed all the way down to the ninth spot. Tino Martinez, who normally batted fifth behind Edgar Martinez, was moved into the seventh spot, and both Jay Buhner and Mike Blowers moved up a spot.

It was a warm October night, with temperatures hovering around seventy degrees. The threat of rain hung over New York City all day and continued into the night, leaving some to question if Game 2 would even be played. The theatrics continued at Yankee Stadium as Phil Rizzuto, the Yankees' Hall-of-Fame shortstop, threw out the first pitch before yet another boisterous crowd. The Yankees had planned on holding pregame introductions for a second straight night, but Lou Piniella wanted nothing to do with it, refusing to have his players to get booed and then watch while the Yankees got cheered.[10] The introductions were canceled.

Coleman stepped in and took a first-pitch ball from Andy Pettitte. Three pitches later, he grounded out weakly to shortstop. The out drew a round of applause from the crowd, which was no less enthusiastic than the night before. Sojo, replacing Cora in the number-two spot, also grounded out. Ken Griffey Jr., the Mariners' Game 1 MVP, received his customary Bronx cheer as he approached the plate with two outs. The booing was made more intense by Griffey's Game 1 performance, which still irked Yankees fans even if their team had won. They were appeased when Griffey flied out to short center field. Pettitte worked quickly and economically, throwing only ten pitches and easily retiring the Mariners in order.

• • • • • • • •

Andy Benes knelt down behind the mound and said a prayer that he be able to do the best he could with the ability he was given.[11] Then he toed the rubber and delivered his first pitch of the night. Benes had only faced the Yankees once before, as the starting pitcher in the now-infamous August 24 game at the Kingdome. He had never pitched in Yankee Stadium. Outside of that one August start, few Yankees had any experience against the righty, except those who previously played in the National League. Wade Boggs was one of the inexperienced. The hero of Game 1 by going three for five, Boggs flied out to deep center field. Bernie Williams popped out to short, quickly giving Benes two outs. Paul O'Neill, having spent eight seasons in the National League, was one of the few Yankees who had faced Benes a multitude of times, and he had posted good numbers against the righty. O'Neill's familiarity was evident as he ground a first-pitch fastball into center field for a single. But Rubin Sierra flied out to end the inning. Benes had matched Pettitte, and the game moved scoreless into the second inning.

• • • • • • • • •

Besides the Yankees, there was a great deal going on in the New York area this Wednesday. The fallout from the O. J. Simpson trial was still a topic of discussion in nearly every bar, barbershop, and workplace. Mayor Rudy Giuliani was in a battle with the New York City Board of Education over who the next schools chancellor would be. In fact, just the day before, Giuliani had suggested abolishing both the Board of Education and the chancellor position altogether.[12] That morning, a task force appointed by New York governor George Pataki to recommend changes in the how the state's health care system was financed met for the first time.[13] The biggest news, however, was the first visit to New York City in sixteen years by Pope John Paul II.[14] The pope first landed in Newark, New Jersey, in the afternoon before eventually flying by helicopter to New York. He arrived at the Wall Street Heliport, where he was greeted by Mayor Giuliani, his wife, and his son. The mayor was New York's biggest and most visible Yankees fan. Even a visit from the Holy Father could not distract him from the pride he felt in his hometown team: his son presented the pontiff with a Yankees cap.[15] The New York Post drew a cartoon featuring Pope John Paul whispering to his aides, "If we make this snappy, we'll catch game 3 in Seattle."[16] Even the pope was not immune to the hysteria surrounding New York over the Yankees' postseason appearance.

• • • • • • • •

Jay Buhner was well aware of Pettitte's pickoff move. When the Mariners right fielder walked with one out in the second inning, he was careful not to venture too far off first base. Blowers, who had struck out three of the six times he faced Pettitte during the year, battled the lefty through a long at-bat, fouling off several pitches. After the eighth pitch, it appeared Pettitte was paying little, if any attention, to Jay Buhner at first base. Before delivering pitch number nine, however, Pettitte veered his right leg toward first base and fired over to Mattingly. Buhner wasn't going on the pitch. In fact, he barely had a lead off first base. Still, when Pettitte threw over, Buhner was frozen. "I didn't even know he had thrown over," said Buhner. "I was looking down and then bam, Mattingly had the ball. Andy watches you out of the corner of his eye. I was totally shocked."[17] Knowing he had been caught, Buhner inched toward second base, avoiding Mattingly's tag. After several throws back and forth between Yankees infielders, Buhner finally ran out of gas and was tagged out by Wade Boggs. Yankees fans delighted in Buhner's misfortune, which was made worse when Blowers finally walked and Tino Martinez then singled into right field. Instead of the bases loaded, or perhaps runners on first and second and a 1–0 Mariner lead, the Mariners now needed a two-out hit to score a run. But Pettitte squelched the rally by inducing Dan Wilson to ground out. The Yankees got through their first jam of the night without falling behind.

Leading off the bottom of the second inning, Don Mattingly was greeted with an ovation just as loud and emotional as any he had received the night before. The Captain had come through solidly in the first game, going two for four. Now facing a fellow native of Evansville, Indiana, Mattingly lined a first-pitch single into center field. Mattingly was three for three in his last few postseason at-bats, and every hit only further incited the crowd. The successive Yankees, however, could not build on that momentum. James, Leyritz, and Fernandez went down in order after Mattingly's single, leaving him stranded. After two innings, the game remained scoreless.

• • • • • • • • •

Pettitte had escaped trouble in the second inning, but he had needed twenty-six pitches to do so. Considering his bullpen's collective shakiness, Showalter wanted to get plenty of innings out of Pettitte, and the pitch count wasn't helping. Even when Cora grounded out to lead off the third inning, Pettitte needed six pitches to make it happen. He threw another five to Coleman, who worked the count full. On the sixth pitch of the at-bat, Coleman drilled a fastball deep toward right field. O'Neill, running and tracking the ball at the same time, glanced up and watched as the ball dropped behind the fence, bounding high off the concrete floor between the right-field seats and the right-field bleachers. A jubilant Mariner dugout shouted while thousands sat still in the stands, shaking their heads. Coleman, though well muscled and built like a running back, had hit only twenty-seven home runs in his entire career. He had never homered in any of his previous seventy-three postseason at-bats. His home run, a deep drive to the opposite field by a guy with only two home runs from the right side all year, was the first in a string of oddities that were going to spring up during the course of Game 2.

Now down 1–0, Pettitte retired the next hitter, but Griffey then singled up the middle and Edgar Martinez walked on four pitches. As in the second inning, Pettitte was painting himself into a dangerous corner. Buhner could easily make it a 4–0 lead for Seattle. But Pettitte jammed the Mariner right fielder on a first-pitch inside fastball, and Buhner popped up to shortstop to end the inning. The damage had been contained to just Coleman's home run.

• • • • • • • • •

Benes continued to fluster New York in the bottom of the third inning. Velarde led off with a four-pitch walk, but Boggs and Williams both popped up. O'Neill, the only Yankee to get a hit off Benes so far, struck out swinging on a curveball. Benes had now hurled three scoreless innings, and the Mariners maintained their 1–0 lead.

Pettitte, who had needed twenty-one pitches to get through the third inning, retired the Mariners in order in the top of the fourth inning. In the process, he threw another fifteen pitches. Pettitte's pitch count was steadily rising. He was not getting shelled by the Mariners' potent offense, but he was laboring through each inning and each at-bat.

Sierra led off the bottom of the fourth inning and struck out. Mattingly followed with a four-pitch walk. Dion James came to the plate hoping to get the Yankees back in the game. With a 2–2 count, Benes came up and in with a fastball. James backed off the plate, raising his arms simultaneously above his head to avoid being hit by the pitch. The ball landed in Wilson's glove a few inches beneath James's left armpit. Dale Scott raised his arms too, calling the pitch a third strike. Though normally mild-mannered, James erupted and rushed Scott, boisterously shouting nose to nose in his face. "It was a ball inside by about a foot. I almost had a stroke," said James, who recalled the incident with a laugh.[18] In the process, James also bumped Scott. Had this been a regular-season game, James would have been ejected within seconds. Scott, however, let James have his say. The left fielder got his money's worth, continuing to scream violently in Scott's face. Buck Showalter emerged from the dugout to save his player from ejection. Sticking himself between the two, Showalter pushed James back to the dugout. On his way, James threw his bat and helmet. Showalter then expressed his displeasure with Scott's call before heading back to the dugout himself. "Dale got shell-shocked during that series," said one member of the Yankees. "He wouldn't call things . . . he was scared to death." Benes retired Mike Stanley to end the inning, and the Mariners walked off the field still leading 1–0.

Two levels above the playing field, George Steinbrenner fumed, again wondering why Rich Garcia was manning one of the outfield foul lines instead of calling balls and strikes. "You know why?" the owner asked reporters before answering his own question. "Because that way he'll rotate behind the plate in case there's a fifth game in this series. Isn't that good reasoning? That's the kind of thing that gives baseball problems." Incredibly, Steinbrenner then went on to suggest that Scott was in fact biased toward the Mariners because of where he lived. "You know where that guy's from? Oregon. I seem to recall my geography class tells me that's close to Seattle."[19] It was a baseless charge that no one listening took seriously, but it showed the extent of the accusations Steinbrenner was willing to make when he felt his team was being treated unfairly.

• • • • • • • •

Joey Cora led off the fifth inning with a ground ball deep in the hole between third and short. Tony Fernandez lunged to his right, snared the ball, and in one motion whipped a strong sidearm throw to first. Mattingly stretched for the throw as Cora lunged for the bag. Everything converged at once. First-base umpire Jim McKeon signaled safe, and yet another lustrous groan from the crowd echoed across New York. Mattingly threw his arms up in disbelief and Fernandez shouted obscenities while turning his back to first base. Showalter shot out from the dugout, yet again, to confront McKeon, and a mild shouting match ensued. Meanwhile, those watching the replay on television, including Steinbrenner, saw that while the play was close, Cora had been out. Steinbrenner, Showalter, and just about everyone in the crowd were reaching a boiling point with the umpiring crew, as they had now seen three close calls go against their team in two days.

Overlooked in all the hysteria was the athleticism displayed by Tony Fernandez. His was the first of several outstanding defensive moments to come in Game 2, on both sides. It took no longer than the next hitter for the Gold Glove work to continue. With Cora on first, Coleman grounded a breaking ball for what looked like a seeing-eye single to left field. Boggs, however, lunged to his left and made a diving stab of the ball, quickly getting up and throwing out the speedy Cora at second base. Velarde spun and fired to first base, but Coleman beat the throw to avoid a double play. Pettitte kept a close eye on Coleman at first base and was able to retire Sojo and Griffey without further trouble. Pettitte threw another seventeen pitches in the fifth inning, adding to an already escalating total.

· · · · · · · · ·

Tony Fernandez led off the bottom of the fifth inning by lining a shot into the left-center field gap for a hit. He wanted to get himself into scoring position with no outs so that the Yankees might be able to tie the game without the benefit of getting another hit. As he rounded first and dug hard for second base, Griffey fielded the ball, spun, and fired a missile to second. The throw easily beat the hustling Fernandez, who was called out. Disgusted by yet another outstanding play by the Mariner's center fielder, the Bleacher Creatures began chanting "Fuck-You-Junior" repeatedly and loud enough for it to be easily picked up on NBC cameras and heard on television. Junior's defensive play became even larger when Boggs drew a two-out walk. The Yankees needed a big hit from Williams to tie the game. Williams delivered, lining a fastball deep to left-center field.

The ball dropped between Coleman and Griffey and headed toward the wall. Boggs scored easily, tying the game. Finally, the Yankees dented home plate. Benes escaped further harm.

· · · · · · · · ·

The game remained tied at one for all of four hitters. Edgar Martinez started off the sixth inning by drilling a Pettitte fastball down the left-field line just out of the reach of a diving James for a double. Buhner moved Martinez to third with a deep fly ball out to right field. The Mariners were set up to take the lead. Showalter had Boggs, Fernandez, Velarde, and Mattingly all come in a few feet. Edgar Martinez took notice and decided he would hold up at third base should the next hitter, Mike Blowers, hit a ground ball. On the first pitch to him, Blowers did just that, sending a ground ball up the middle for what appeared to be a tie-breaking single. Fernandez charged to his left, dove, and gloved the ball. He fell to the ground and, realizing he did not have enough time to stand and throw out Blowers, instead flipped the ball to Velarde. Velarde then turned and threw Blowers out at first for an atypical 6–4–3 groundout. Martinez, who held on contact, failed to score. He had remained at third, watching the play unfold and staring perplexed at how Blowers's ground ball had not snuck out of the infield. Several outstanding defensive plays had already occurred in Game 2, and there were more to come, but Fernandez's play was the best of them. "Nobody in the press box had ever seen it done before," wrote Roger Angell.[20]

The joy over Fernandez's play was short lived as Tino Martinez then singled into left field. Edgar Martinez scored easily, negating the outstanding work by Fernandez and quieting the crowd. The Mariners recaptured the lead, 2–1. Seattle's two-out momentum was tempered when Pettitte picked Martinez off first base before even throwing a pitch to the next hitter. Like Jay Buhner in the second inning, Tino was not even attempting to steal. He'd taken a marginal lead off first base and was simply deceived by Pettitte's move. Unlike Buhner, Tino made little attempt to engage in a rundown, instead surrendering himself to Mattingly's tag for the inning's final out. In the Mariner's dugout, Lou Piniella paced back and forth, hurling obscenities into the night air as he seethed about another Mariner runner getting picked off.

It had taken the Mariners only four hitters to regain the lead in the top of the sixth inning. In the bottom of the inning, it took them only four pitches to give it right back. Benes threw a 2–1 slider that limped over the plate, and Sierra drilled the ball to deep right field. It was a high, looping shot, unlike the line drive he had hit the night before. Sierra remained in the box for a moment before finally trotting several paces outside the first-base line as the ball landed into the right-field bleachers. Sierra's second home run of the series was a big one, tying Game 2 at two a piece and reinstilling the electric buzz that had pulsed through the crowd earlier in the game. Sierra's home run alarmed Piniella, who had Bill Risley begin warming up in the bullpen, even though Benes had thrown only eighty-two pitches.

The crowd remained abuzz as Don Mattingly strode to the plate. "The fans want a dinger out of him," commented NBC's Gary Thorne. Twenty seconds later, Mattingly drilled a changeup into the right-field bleachers, sending Yankee Stadium into a frenzy not seen since Chris Chambliss homered to end the 1976 ALCS. Unlike the slow, played-out trot of Ruben Sierra, Mattingly rounded the base paths at a brisk pace, the way the captain of the Yankees "would do it," pointed out commentator Tommy Hutton.[21] Yankees fans littered the field with objects of all shapes and sizes just as they had after Sierra's home run in Game 1.

Lou Piniella, tired of having things thrown at his players, rushed out of the dugout and immediately began waving the Mariners off the field. "I don't blame Lou. A Jack Daniels bottle came out of the upper deck and landed about twenty feet from me," said Yankees first-base coach Brian Butterfield.[22] Sitting behind the Mariner dugout, nine-year-old Chris Lumry, son of Mariners minority owner Rufus Lumry, was hit in the hand by a shot glass.[23] Bob Sheppard's voice came over the PA system, asking fans to refrain from throwing objects on the field, lest they be removed from the stadium. As they had in Game 1, the fans ignored his directive. They eventually relented, but the celebration continued, as "Don-nie Base-ball!" chants sprung up everywhere. Mattingly displayed little emotion in the dugout, getting a drink of water and watching the grounds crew clear the field of debris. In the owner's box, George Steinbrenner was more concerned about the stoppage in play than about his team's sudden 3–2 lead. "The only things that were thrown were some toilet paper and a Frisbee," Steinbrenner told reporters, either unaware of or ignoring the various accounts from players and his own security guards about "plastic cups . . . souvenir bats, stereo headphones, tomatoes, grapefruit, golf balls, bottles, batteries, and an assortment of coins."[24] "I know Lou," continued The Boss. "He's a brinksman. He did that to slow our momentum. But the rules say you can pull your team only if there are fans on the field. That didn't happen. It should be a forfeit."[25]

The game was not forfeited, and Seattle finally retook the field, albeit to a loud chorus of booing from the crowd. Andy Benes began throwing warm-up pitches, but much to his surprise, Piniella emerged and removed him from the game. Benes had pitched well in his first playoff start, but the back-to-back home runs signified the end of his night. He now stood to get the loss.

Order was finally restored, the Yankees were ahead 3–2, and Bill Risley entered the game. After Dion James grounded out, Risley's first pitch to Jim Leyritz nailed the Yankees catcher squarely in the back. Leyritz absorbed the blow, flung his bat toward the Yankees' dugout, then glared disapprovingly at Risley. Well aware of the history between Leyritz and the Mariners, the fans let out a load groan of disapproval. In the heat of the moment, Leyritz had little doubt that Risley intentionally hit him. "There were still some feelings [from the Randy Johnson incident]. At the time I thought it was on purpose, but I thought otherwise later," said Leyritz.[26] Generally, every hometown crowd looks upon a hit batter with suspicion and disapproval. Considering the confrontation between Leyritz and Johnson in May, there was certainly reason to think Risley might have hit Leyritz intentionally. But emotion is often the enemy of truth, and this case was no different. With his team down by a run and facing a two-games-to-none deficit, Risley had no reason to put a runner on base simply to settle any lingering tensions from a regular-season dustup. More likely, Risley was trying to throw him inside because Leyritz dove into pitches and had great power to the opposite field.

After tensions dissipated, Risley retired Fernandez and Velarde to end the sixth inning. Game 2 had seen controversial calls, lead changes, great defensive plays, back-to-back home runs, objects thrown on the field, and beanball incidents, all in just the first six innings. More thrilling moments were still to come.

• • • • • • • •

Like the Mariners in the sixth inning, the Yankees did not take long
to blow their newly found lead in the top of the seventh inning.
Pettitte retired Wilson, but Cora then doubled over the head of
O'Neill in a rare display of opposite-field power. Pettitte quickly
jumped ahead of Coleman, 0–2, and the crowd rose in anticipation of
the lefty's first strikeout of the game. Instead, Coleman drove a hard
ground ball down the third-base line. Boggs dove to his right, snared
the grounder on a high-bounding hop, rose quickly, and fired the
ball across the diamond. Like the Cora ground ball in the fifth inning,
the ball and Coleman seemed to arrive at first base almost simultaneously. Coleman lunged for first base so strongly that his momentum
caused him to trip over the bag, and he went tumbling to the ground.
Mattingly, assuming Coleman would be called out, briefly came
off the bag to check on Cora, who had remained on second base.
Jim McKeon, however, surprised Mattingly and just about everyone
else by calling Coleman safe. Mattingly, who rarely if ever argued
with umpires, immediately shot both arms in the air, exclaiming
"What?" in shocked disbelief. He called time-out, turned, and began
vigorously shouting in McKeon's face, violently pointing his left
index finger repeatedly toward the ground. The players in the
Yankees' dugout, led by David Cone, Darryl Strawberry, and Jack
McDowell, erupted, with McDowell climbing to the top step of the
dugout screaming in McKeon's direction. Most vocal, however, was
Buck Showalter, who according to Gary Thorne "came out of that
dugout as though he were ejected from a jet plane cockpit." Showalter
let loose on McKeon, shouting so loudly that his obscenities were
picked up by NBC microphones and relayed to the TV audience. "I
didn't want to stay out too long because I didn't want to incite the
fans even further," recalled Showalter.[27] McKeon simply stood and
took the abuse.

Meanwhile, George Steinbrenner had had enough. He had jumped
out of his seat screaming, "Out, out," and could not believe that McKeon
signaled safe.[28] Replays again showed that the call had incorrectly
gone against the Yankees, and The Boss wanted someone to be held
accountable for it. He held another impromptu press conference, this
time dragging reporters to the video replay room, where he blasted

American League president Gene Budig.[29] "This is awful. The first-base umpire blew both those calls. I've talked to our league president, Gene Budig, and demanded to know why we can't get the best umpires for these games. I asked for [supervisor of umpires] Marty Springstead to come up and look at the videotapes."[30] Springstead wisely declined Steinbrenner's invite, which surely was just an attempt by The Boss to berate the man in front of the press. Steinbrenner's rants were becoming so incessant and ridiculous, even the reporters couldn't take much more of it. "It got to the point where members of the media and Yankee personnel were scattering to avoid him," said one member of the Yankees' staff.

When play resumed, Cora stood at second base and Coleman at first base with just one out. Luis Sojo then slapped a single into center field. Cora scored to tie the game at three. More important, Coleman moved all the way to third base with just one out, meaning a fly ball could give the Mariners the lead back. The stadium was quiet as Ken Griffey Jr. strode to the plate. Junior's Game 1 performance was still fresh in people's minds, and they knew that with one swing, he could easily put the Yankees in a two-run hole. But he swung under a first-pitch fastball and sent a high fly ball to shallow left field. At the beginning of the inning, Showalter had replaced his left fielder, Dion James, with Gerald Williams. It was something he had been doing for the last few weeks of the season. James was a better hitter, but Williams had more range in the field and a far better throwing arm, which he was fond of showing off. As Griffey's fly ball slowly drifted down to Williams, Showalter looked like a genius. The ball was so shallow and Williams's arm so strong that it was uncertain if Coleman would even tag up. But Coleman did tag, and Williams caught the ball flat-footed with nearly no momentum behind his throw. Instead of unleashing a laser to home plate, Williams's throw barely made it to the infield on the fly. Boggs cut off the throw and, realizing he had no chance of getting Coleman at home, spun and fired toward second base. Sojo had tagged from first and was trying to advance, but Velarde caught Boggs's throw and immediately slapped down a tag. Umpire Larry McCoy called Sojo out, though Sojo vociferously argued the call, flailing his arms in a move reminiscent of his bases-clearing double dance. Sojo had a right to be angry, as finally a call had incorrectly gone against Seattle. As Sojo argued, Coleman pointed down toward home plate, making sure everyone knew that he had scored the go-ahead run before the third out had been recorded.

The Mariners were now ahead 4–3, and Piniella did not want this lead or this game to slip away from him. Although it was just the seventh inning, he called upon his closer, Norm Charlton, for a three-inning save. Charlton retired the first two batters, then had to stare ahead at the familiar face of Paul O'Neill. Having been on the same team only three years earlier, O'Neill came to bat looking to tie the game against his old teammate.

· · · · · · · · ·

The lean, six-foot-five O'Neill had made his way to the major leagues with the Cincinnati Reds. It was a great fit for the man who grew up a Reds fan in Columbus, Ohio. Blessed with a strong throwing arm, O'Neill was a pitcher in high school but converted to being a full-time outfielder when the Reds drafted him in 1981.[31] By 1988, he was the team's starting right fielder. In 1990 he played an integral role in the Reds' World Championship, batting .471 with a home run in the NLCS against the Pirates. The following season, he burst out offensively, hitting a career-high twenty-eight home runs. The jump in offensive numbers created large expectations for O'Neill going into the 1992 season. He faltered, hitting only fourteen home runs and batting .246.

That off-season, Yankees general manager Gene Michael was looking to trade outfielder Roberto Kelly. Kelly had never materialized into the player the Yankees thought he might be, and Michael abhorred the way Kelly seemingly gave up at-bats with his poor pitch selection.[32] When the Reds called offering O'Neill for Kelly, Michael initially hesitated. Uncertain whether he should make the deal, he reached out to a former confidant, Lou Piniella. Piniella had just taken the Seattle Mariners managerial position, but he'd been O'Neill's manager for three years in Cincinnati and knew the player well. Their relationship had been an odd one. Piniella felt that a guy like O'Neill should be drilling balls over the fence, but O'Neill did not want to push himself into being a power hitter. He preferred to use his natural swing and let the ball go where it may, whether that be over the fence or in the gap. In order to please his manager, though, O'Neill tinkered with his swing to generate more power and the results weren't pretty. Piniella became especially harsh toward his right fielder, mocking how someone of his size couldn't hit the ball with power all the time.[33] It was a lingering tension some felt still existed even years after both had left Cincinnati and enjoyed success in different cities. Despite this tension, Piniella knew O'Neill's potential. "Stick, what the hell are you waiting for? Paul is a good outfielder, a good hitter, and solid fielder," Piniella told his friend.[34] Michael listened and followed through on one of the greatest trades in Yankees history.

On November 3, 1992, O'Neill was outside his house, tending to his lawn. When he came inside, there were two messages on his answering machine. One was from Reds GM Jim Bowden, informing him that he'd been traded to the Yankees. The other was from Yankees GM Gene Michael, asking O'Neill to call him right away.[35] O'Neill and his wife were devastated. He'd spent nearly his whole life in Ohio and feared big-city life, especially a city as big as New York. But after meeting with Yankees officials and finding a home in New Jersey, O'Neill quickly adjusted. Little was expected of him upon his arrival, so he didn't face the normal pressure of a new player in New York. His trade was not viewed as a major acquisition but merely as a swap of semi-decent outfielders, neither of whom had achieved his full potential. But O'Neill worked with Yankees hitting coach Rick Down on establishing a timing mechanism whereby he would tap his right foot before the pitch.[36] As a result of his improved batting stance, O'Neill exceeded those limited expectations by hitting .311 in his first season in New York. Yankees fans fell in love with their new right fielder. Just weeks into the 1993 season, signs in the right-field stands began appearing with O'Neill's name, with the O drawn as a bull's-eye. In 1994, O'Neill hit over .400 for the first two and a half months of the season and became the first Yankee in a decade to win the American League batting title. He had another solid year in 1995, leading the team with twenty-two home runs and ninety-six RBIs and achieving notoriety for hitting three home runs in a single game against the Angels in September. O'Neill also became the Yankees' permanent number-three hitter, a position that had been Don Mattingly's for years.

O'Neill's offensive and defensive abilities went hand in hand with two other endearing qualities: humility and intensity. Extremely humble, O'Neill despised talking about his own accomplishments, preferring to focus on team achievements. His humility was surpassed only by his intensity, as no one on the Yankees was more driven to succeed than O'Neill. A fierce competitor, he abhorred making even a single out during the course of a game. If he went three for four, his focus after the game would be on the one at-bat in which he didn't get a hit. O'Neill was his own worst critic, constantly questioning his own performance and verbally lashing out at himself. Occasionally, he would lash out at umpires as well. In fact, his constant questioning of umpires' calls did not endear him to the men in blue or to opposing fans, who likened O'Neill to a crybaby who pouted if things didn't go his way. His constant slamming of bats, helmets, water coolers, and other inanimate objects after making an out led opposing fans to hate him only more. O'Neill's teammates and Yankees fans, however, adored him for it. To them, his temper tantrums were merely a sign of his intense desire to win all the time. It even got to the point where his outbursts became comical. Teammates began strategically placing objects around the Yankees' dugout, such as paper cups, in order to see which ones O'Neill might attack should he make an out. "Chummin' for Paulie," as it was known, provided teammates with a good laugh, though none of them would dare get in his sights once he finally did explode. Yet O'Neill never yelled at his teammates, never took his anger out on them, and never made excuses for himself. He played hard, all-out baseball, prompting Steinbrenner to call him "the Warrior."

As he stepped to the plate in the bottom of the seventh inning of Game 2, the Warrior needed a big hit. His team was down a run and would have to face Norm Charlton's screwball for another two innings. After a first-pitch ball, Charlton delivered a fastball low. Dale Scott called it a strike, and true to form, O'Neill lashed out at the home-plate umpire, incredulous over the call. When Scott called Charlton's next pitch low for a ball, the crowd rewarded him with mock applause. Ahead with a 2–1 count, O'Neill sat on a Charlton fastball and drilled it to right field. "I knew it was gone when I hit it," said O'Neill,[37] whose blast sailed nearly halfway up the right-field bleachers, where it bounced through the crowd before finally dropping into the old Yankees bullpen. The stadium erupted as beer cups, most still with beer in them, began hurtling through the air. O'Neill's home run tied the game at four, as the Mariners had blown their third lead of the game. On the mound, Charlton was livid with himself for having made such a bad pitch. "I left a ball up for him to hit. You don't want to give up a home run to a friend, especially in a close situation," said Charlton.[38] He struck out Sierra to end the inning, but it did not quell his disappointment. Charlton would stew over that pitch for innings.

· · · · · · · · ·

Andy Pettitte's night ended after seven innings. He hadn't dominated the Mariners, nor had they dominated him. If a few calls had gone his way, perhaps Pettitte would be leaving with a lead. Instead, the game was tied at four in the top of the eighth inning. Showalter called upon Bob Wickman to keep the game tied. Wickman was the "Iron Man" out of the Yankees' bullpen all year, leading the team with sixty-three appearances. Known for his bullpen pranks and big appetite, Wickman lost the tip of his right index finger in a compressor accident when he was two.[39] As a result, his pitches had extra drop to them, particularly his sinker. Some of his teammates thought Wickman had a golden horseshoe in a certain part of his anatomy, because he always picked up wins when he pitched. "We'd be down three, he would come in and get two outs, then we'd score four runs and he would get the win," recalled one teammate. Upon entering his first postseason game ever, Wickman succeeded where so many Yankees pitchers had failed: he struck out Edgar Martinez. Buhner followed with a single to right field, but Blowers popped out, and Tino Martinez grounded out to end the inning.

Charlton returned for the bottom of the eighth inning. After getting the first out, Gerald Williams drilled a breaking ball deep down the left-field line. The ball sailed foul at the last second and missed being a go-ahead home run by mere feet. Williams, so close to becoming a postseason hero, grounded out on the next pitch. The crowd mockingly cheered McKeon for making the correct call. A two-out error by Sojo became harmless when Charlton induced Tony Fernandez to ground out. The game moved on to the ninth inning.

· · · · · · · · ·

Looking for an offensive spark, Piniella called on Alex Diaz to pinch-hit for Wilson to start off the ninth inning. The move left the Mariners with just a single catcher in Chris Widger for what could potentially be a long game. Piniella took his chances, and it paid off when Diaz slashed a single into left field. Cora then bunted him to second, forcing Showalter to counter Piniella's move. Though it was not a save situation, Showalter called on John Wetteland. Considering his performance the previous night, as well as in the August 24 game at the Kingdome, there was tension in the air as Wetteland came trotting out of the bullpen. Fans wondered whether he would finally be able to hold down the Mariners. Wetteland responded by striking out Coleman on a devastating twelve-to-six curve, then blew away Sojo on a high fastball, ending the inning. It was a commanding performance by Wetteland: two hitters, seven pitches, all strikes, and two strikeouts. Now, if the Yankees could just get one run, Wetteland would get the win.

· · · · · · · · ·

One run was all that separated the Yankees from a commanding 2–0 lead in the series. Norm Charlton, however, stood defiantly in their way. Beginning his third inning of relief work, he quickly retired the first two hitters, leaving it to Bernie Williams to end the game. Williams had nearly homered off Charlton in the seventh inning, flying out to the warning track down the right-field line just before O'Neill tied the game. Now, he went down anticlimactically, striking out on a forkball. Game 2 moved into extra innings.

· · · · · · · · ·

Extra innings meant fans watching at home could continue to enjoy the commercials they had been forced to endure for hours. This included dozens of promotions for NBC shows. Oliver North was making a guest appearance on that week's *JAG*. The Thursday night lineup featured special guest stars on both *Friends* and the *Single Guy*, while on *Seinfeld*, Kramer sued a company for serving him coffee that was too hot. *ER* still featured George Clooney and Anthony Edwards. Regis Philbin and White Sox first baseman Frank Thomas were going to be that night's guests on the *Tonight Show*. *The John Larroquette Show* and *The Home Court* would be all new that Saturday night. The Dolphins, the only undefeated team left in the

NFL, were playing the Colts on Sunday. There were advertisements for movies such as *Strange Days* with Ralph Fiennes, *Assassins* with Sylvester Stallone and Antonio Banderas, and *Get Shorty* with John Travolta. A few advertisements were lighthearted, including one for Major League Baseball that featured Randy Johnson discussing new off-speed pitches he was working on. One pitch he called his "crazy ball." Another one he called "Mr. Snappy." "Mr. Snappy has a mind of his own," says Johnson as the TV shows a picture of the Big Unit hitting a batter. "There are a lot of guys that don't like Mr. Snappy," he adds. The Baseball Network ran an ad showing Game 1 highlights from the Division Series. At the end, the screen went dark and the words "You Saw It All Here" flashed on the screen. The problem, of course, was that fans hadn't seen it all there, since the broadcasts of the games were regionalized.

· · · · · · · · ·

Wetteland emerged for the tenth inning to encounter his arch nemesis. So far, Ken Griffey Jr. had faced Wetteland twice in his career, hitting the home run on August 24 and singling in Game 1. There was a weary feeling in the stadium as Griffey came to bat, almost as if the fans expected something bad to happen. To remind them of the history between these two, NBC showed the August 24 home run just as Junior stepped in. Griffey got under a curveball, though, and popped up to second base. The crowd collectively exhaled, and Wetteland proceeded to retire Edgar Martinez for the second out. Buhner then lined a double down the left-field line, putting the go-ahead run in scoring position. Piniella now made another strategic move. Blowers was due up, but including his at-bat against him in Game 1, he was 0–4 in his career against Wetteland, with three strikeouts. So Piniella called on Doug Strange to pinch-hit. The Mariners' all-purpose player was no stranger to big moments, having hit the ninth-inning game-tying home run against the Rangers just two weeks ago at the Kingdome. Strange jumped ahead of Wetteland, 3–0, but the closer fought back and induced Strange to ground out, ending the inning.

· · · · · · · · ·

Charlton was on fire. Excluding Sojo's eighth-inning error, he hadn't allowed a base runner since O'Neill's home run in the seventh, mainly because his forkball was flustering the Yankees. O'Neill led off the bottom of the tenth inning. Charlton was not going to make the same mistake with his fastball as he had in the seventh inning. Instead, he used his forkball, and O'Neill couldn't touch it, striking out. Cora then booted a ground ball by Sierra, allowing the designated hitter to reach base. Few fans could have imagined a better scenario than Don Mattingly, now batting, ending the game with a hit. But Mattingly lined a hard shot directly to Tino Martinez, who quickly turned a 3–6–3 double play. The game moved to the eleventh inning, still tied at four.

Buck Showalter saw no need to remove Wetteland, especially not after he pitched so effectively in the ninth and tenth innings. Wetteland took the mound for the top of the eleventh inning and again delivered for his team, retiring the side in order.

Charlton had thrown four innings, his longest outing in more than three years, and that was enough for Lou Piniella.[40] The Mariners manager opted to have Jeff Nelson pitch the bottom of the eleventh inning. Nelson was big, burly, and loud. He never hesitated to show emotion on the mound, often reacting to a big strikeout by gesturing wildly with his hands. He was just as emotional off the field, rarely hesitating to share his usually blunt opinion with the media. Standing at six-foot-six, with buzz-cut hair and short mustache, Nelson looked more like a state trooper than a baseball player. He threw with a unique three-quarter delivery. It wasn't completely sidearm, nor was it over the top, but right in between. His large stature and sweeping motion made him especially difficult on right-handed hitters, as his breaking ball appeared to move from the right-handed batter's box to the edge of the left-handed batter's box. After initially struggling with his control, Nelson became a deadly asset out of the bullpen. Like many Mariners, he enjoyed a breakthrough season in 1995, going 7–3, striking out ninety-six hitters in $78 \frac{2}{3}$ innings and limiting right-handed hitters to just a .191 batting average. Nelson, saddled with the loss in Game 1, now needed to keep the Yankees scoreless and allow the Mariners to get to the heart of the order in the twelfth inning.

Showalter sought to counter Nelson's effectiveness on right-handed hitters by sending Darryl Strawberry to hit for Gerald Williams.

Strawberry, once one of the game's perennial power hitters, had shifted around with three different teams in five seasons and served a suspension for violating MLB's drug policy before he signed with the Yankees in 1995. He worked out in the minors before finally joining the team in August during a road trip in Detroit. Despite not having been a full-time player in years, Strawberry was still in peak physical condition. "The first day he took batting practice in Detroit, he was hitting bombs," said Jack McDowell.[41] "That BP session in Detroit was ridiculous," said Mattingly. "In the first round, he hit six of eight into the seats. I sat in the outfield thinking 'This is unbelievable.'"[42] Despite that power, Strawberry was joining a team already steeped in outfielders and designated hitters. It made Showalter's job exceedingly difficult as he tried to find a role for Strawberry and determine who would play and who would sit. Strawberry got his at-bats here and there, but he'd been out of the game too long, was a defensive liability, and simply was unknown to Buck Showalter. In two months with the team, he drew only seventy-six at-bats. In a series between two big offensive teams, Showalter went with players he knew best and felt he could depend upon, such as Dion James and Gerald Williams, which meant Strawberry rode the bench. But hoping to counter Nelson and end Game 2 with one swing of the bat, Showalter sent the former All-Star to the plate. It was the first time Strawberry faced Nelson, and even for a lefty, the sweeping breaking ball could be difficult to hit. Strawberry flailed at a slider for strike three. Leyritz then flied out, and Fernandez struck out on another sweeping breaking ball. Still tied at four, the game progressed to the twelfth inning.

• • • • • • • • •

As the game went on, both sides were forced to make defensive changes. For the Mariners, Chris Widger was now catching and Doug Strange was playing third base. For the Yankees, Randy Velarde moved to left field and Pat Kelly now manned second base. The Yankees' pitcher, however, remained the same. John Wetteland emerged for his fourth inning of relief work. Only once during the regular season had Wetteland pitched three innings, but his Game 2 performance indicated that that he had gotten past his trouble with the Mariners, as he was holding them scoreless for $2\,2/_3$ innings. He quickly retired the first two hitters in the twelfth inning before facing Ken Griffey Jr. with no one on. The crowd, as always, grew tense. Give Junior enough at-bats, some were thinking, and eventually he was going to burn you. When Wetteland fell behind three balls and a strike, the stadium was still. Even with two out and no one on, Wetteland could ill afford to walk Griffey with the ever-dangerous Edgar Martinez on deck. So the Yankees' closer delivered a fastball down the heart of the plate. The mere crack of the bat as Griffey made contact sent a shiver down the spine of 57,000 people at the stadium. Wetteland immediately lowered his head, then turned briefly toward right center field to verify what he already knew: Griffey had beaten him once again. As the ball sailed over the right-center-field fence, a haunting silence filled the stadium air. Griffey's shot bounced among the Bleacher Creatures before finally being snagged bare-handed by a fan. The Mariners now led 5–4, and the players in their dugout exploded. As the ball dropped into the bleachers, Wetteland bent over, hands on knees, and dropped his head again. His three innings of solid relief, his seemingly turning the corner against Seattle, had been shattered in just one swing.

Inside Yankee Stadium, it felt like a funeral had broken out. Shocked, ashen faces were everywhere. These people had watched Griffey beat their team for years, but this was by far the biggest kick in the stomach. The Yankees still had to hit in the bottom of the inning, and it was only one run, but the mood around the ballpark emanated a feeling that this game was over. When Edgar Martinez followed the home run with a single, Wetteland's night was over. Like Charlton, Wetteland had pitched exceptionally well but made one crucial mistake. Twenty-five-year-old Mariano Rivera strode in from the Yankees' bullpen. "I got grief for putting him on the postseason roster," said Buck Showalter. "I can't say I knew Rivera would be great. But if I knew then what I know now. . . ."[43]

Showalter wasn't the only one who didn't know what Rivera would become. Rivera grew up in Panama and signed with the Yankees when he was twenty. Initially, he possessed a good fastball with decent movement, but nothing that indicated how he would dominate hitters in the future.[44] In 1992, Rivera had surgery to fix nerve damage in his elbow, which further clouded whether he would ever become a major-league pitcher.[45] He recovered and, as a starter, excelled in the minor leagues, pitching well enough that the Yankees promoted him in May 1995. Rivera made his debut as a starting pitcher against the Angels and got hit hard. He won his next start but then got hit hard again against the A's and the Mariners. "He didn't have it early in '95," recalled Jim Leyritz. "His fastball and slider were the same speed."[46] Rivera was demoted to the minors, where during the next three weeks something miraculous happened. He gained nearly four miles per hour on his fastball. How this occurred no one could explain, but the difference in speed was immediately noticeable to both his teammates and opposing hitters. The Yankees called Rivera back up, and on July 4, he pitched eight innings and struck out eleven White Sox at Comiskey Park.[47] He pitched well over the next few weeks, but eventually was regulated to bullpen duty. He made the postseason roster, but no one imagined that Rivera would play any pivotal role in the series.

Now, Rivera came into the twelfth inning of Game 2 needing to hold the Mariners to just the single run they had scored off Wetteland. Despite being a rookie and pitching in front of a full house, Rivera never displayed any signs of nervousness. Calm and collected, he dominated Jay Buhner, striking him out on four pitches to end the inning. Three outs now separated the Mariners from their first playoff victory.

• • • • • • • • •

Jeff Nelson's slider broke far to the outside, and Velarde swung right over it for strike three to begin the bottom of the twelfth inning. Yankees fans sat glumly in their seats, disappointed at the prospect of having Junior beat them yet again. Their slumped shoulders rose slightly when Wade Boggs used his keen eye to draw a seven-pitch walk. "With a one-run lead, I didn't need to walk Boggs," said Nelson. "[Dale Scott] had been calling the outside corner all night. I thought maybe I had struck him out."[48] Boggs, even without the bad hamstring, was no speedster on the base paths. In fact, Boggs was so slow that Showalter lifted him and used as a pinch runner his third-string catcher, Jorge Posada. Posada trotted in from the bullpen and quickly took his spot at first base. Up to that point, he had appeared in just one major-league game, as a ninth-inning defensive replacement against the Mariners in September. He had yet to run the bases as a major leaguer. Now he represented the crucial tying run in the twelfth inning of Game 2.

• • • • • • • • •

Lou Piniella saw something about the way Nelson threw to Boggs that he didn't like. When Nelson threw a first-pitch ball to the next hitter, Bernie Williams, Piniella quickly emerged from the dugout and removed his tall righty reliever. Out came the Mariners' fifth pitcher of the night, Tim Belcher. Unlike most of his teammates, Belcher had been here before. He had started Game 1 of the 1988 World Series for the Dodgers, getting a no-decision in the infamous Kirk Gibson game. Belcher was a stable starting pitcher for the Dodgers, Reds, White Sox, and Tigers, but he endured a rough 1994 season. When the strike was resolved, he ended up in the Homestead Camp. The Mariners expressed an interest in signing him, but Belcher wanted to remain in the National League. He went back to the Reds and pitched in the minor leagues, but two weeks later, Cincinnati traded him to Seattle. Though no fan of the Kingdome, Belcher pitched well there. He earned ten victories in twenty-eight starts and was on the mound the final day of the season in Texas when a win could have propelled the Mariners into the playoffs. But Belcher gave up five runs and was reduced to sitting in the clubhouse, hoping the Angels would lose their game.[49]

• • • • • • • • •

Though emotionless on the mound, Belcher was a fierce competitor who lived and breathed pitching. He hadn't pitched in relief since 1993, but Piniella trusted the veteran to record the last two outs and send his team back to Seattle tied at a game apiece. Belcher was going to be the Mariners' starter for Game 3 had they won this night. But the prolonged affair that was Game 2 forced Piniella into this move, meaning Randy Johnson was now going to pitch Game 3 no matter what. Belcher spent Game 2 in the bullpen, and like most Mariners, he had various objects thrown at him throughout the course of night. He entered Game 2 and proceeded to walk Bernie Williams on five pitches, placing himself in a precarious situation. The tying run was now on second base, the winning run was on first, and Belcher had to face Paul O'Neill. Few hitters had tagged Belcher like O'Neill, who in fifty-five career at-bats had homered off him five times. Belcher quickly fell behind two balls and no strikes, allowing the crowd to get back in the game. The tension was gut wrenching. In all the growing excitement, few people noticed that Mariners left fielder Alex Diaz was playing exceptionally far from the left-field line. Diaz fully expected O'Neill to pull the ball off Belcher, especially up in the count, 2–0. When Belcher delivered a fastball, O'Neill hit a seemingly weak fly ball down the line in shallow left field. At first glance, it appeared an easy play. Convinced he had made the second out of the inning and therefore wasted a golden opportunity to be a postseason hero, O'Neill slammed his bat down and began slowly trotting toward first base. Then, O'Neill suddenly saw what the rest of the crowd was noticing. This was not a routine fly ball at all. In fact, Diaz was running full speed from deep left-center field. This ball just might drop in. Diaz had made diving—some would even say outlandish—plays all year. "There wasn't a ball Alex couldn't dive for," teammate Norm Charlton playfully recalled.[50] This pop fly was no exception. Approaching the strip of dirt that runs along the left-field line, Diaz lunged and dove, snaring the ball in fair territory. The stadium again went silent.

Ruben Sierra, batting lefty, quickly took a strike and then a ball. A sense of extreme disappointment hung in the air at Yankee Stadium. After all the comebacks, close calls, and hours of baseball, the Yankees appeared on their way to defeat. Belcher, on the cusp of getting his first save since 1989, reared back and fired a 1–1 split-fingered fastball. It was supposed to dip toward the outer half of the plate, Sierra's well-known weak spot. "You didn't want to let Ruben extend his arms. He was a good bad-ball hitter," said Belcher.[51] Instead of the outer half of the plate, the pitch stayed up in the strike zone. Awkwardly swinging because he had been fooled, Sierra swatted at the pitch and sent it deep to left field. It was immediately clear that Alex Diaz was not going to catch this one. The only question was whether the ball had enough height to clear the eight-foot left-field fence. Everyone held his breath as the ball descended and smacked the very top of the wall. Another inch higher and Sierra would have had himself a game-winning postseason home run. Instead, the crowd let out an exasperated gasp of disbelief that the ball had not left the yard. Then they immediately turned their attention to the base runners. Jorge Posada easily crossed home plate, tying the game. Meanwhile, in left field, luck befell the Mariners. Though Sierra's shot had been heading right to left when it struck the wall, strangely it bounced off the wall in the opposite direction, heading left to right. Diaz had been chasing Sierra's shot at full speed. After hitting the fence and bounding in the opposite direction, the ball hit him in midair in the leg. Had Diaz arrived a second later or sooner at that exact spot, the ball would have bounded away from him and Williams would have easily scored the winning run. Instead, the ball hit Diaz and fell directly in front of him. He immediately picked it up and fired to Luis Sojo, who had moved out to short left field. With two outs, Williams was running on contact from first base and was in a full-out sprint toward home plate. The crowd was going crazy. Most of the Yankees left the bench and congregated near home plate in anticipation of the winning run's scoring. In the meantime, Sojo caught Diaz's throw, spun around, and fired a strike to catcher Chris Widger. In one motion, Widger caught the ball and blocked home plate. Bernie Williams slid in between Widger's legs, but the catcher slapped the tag on him before he could reach home plate. Dale Scott signaled Williams was out, and the crowd again let out a collective moan. Sierra stood on second base shocked, his hands on his head. The Yankees returned to the dugout in disappointment. "We're halfway to home plate ready to greet Bernie, and then 25 guys turned around and looked at the crowd in disbelief," said David Cone. "It was like 'Wait a minute, we just tied the game. But we had a chance to win it. But we get to keep playing.' When we went back to the dugout and looked at the fans' faces, jaws were dropped and mouths were wide open."[52]

Tim Belcher calmly walked back to the dugout, but inside he seethed at having allowed the tying run to score. "If I get that splitter down to Sierra, we win the game and we're on our way home. I didn't and that prolonged the agony," said Belcher.[53] Nearly everything imaginable had happened during the course of Game 2. Still, it wasn't over. The two teams moved on to the thirteenth inning, now tied at five.

• • • • • • • • •

All the excitement did not overwhelm Mariano Rivera. He easily retired the Mariners in order in the top of the thirteenth. Don Mattingly led off the bottom of the inning for the Yankees. With no idea what would happen in the series, or even in Game 2, every

Mattingly at-bat now meant it was possibly the last time fans were seeing him hit at Yankee Stadium. When he singled to center field, the crowd went crazy. After Pat Kelly sacrificed Mattingly over to second base, Jim Leyritz had a chance to play postseason hero. Instead, Leyritz hit a ground ball right back to Belcher, who threw to first for the second out. Mattingly remained at second base. Leyritz was irate over his performance. He ran through the dugout and into the tunnel leading toward the Yankees' clubhouse, where he proceeded to smash his bat and beat up a chair. David Cone watched the entire incident. "He was tearing up the place," said Cone. "It was a humid night . . . he probably lost 10 pounds catching, he swings at a 2–0 slider and comes in and tears up the clubhouse. Basic stuff, water coolers, chairs, tables."[54] Cone was impressed by the type of energy Leyritz was displaying and told him so. Leyritz took the compliment in good stride and calmed down. "Don't worry," Cone told him. "You are gonna get another shot."[55] After Tony Fernandez was intentionally walked, Randy Velarde popped out and an exhausted crowd awaited the fourteenth inning.

Rivera dominated again in the top of the fourteenth inning. In a display of raw power, the rookie from Panama struck out Felix Fermin, Chris Widger, and Luis Sojo, all swinging. It was the type of overwhelming performance that players in the Yankees' dugout hoped would propel them to victory in the bottom of the inning. When Russ Davis led off with a single against Belcher, it looked like the Yankees might be on their way. Davis was a rookie who had replaced Wade Boggs at third base the previous inning. He hoped not to screw up the momentum of his first playoff base hit, but on the next play, it was exactly what he did. Bernie Williams lined a shot right to Fermin, who had taken over for Joey Cora at second base. Fermin gloved it, then fired to first base, doubling up Davis who had strayed too far off the bag. Mortified, Davis returned to the dugout hoping his gaffe would not end up costing the Yankees the game.[56] Paul O'Neill followed with a walk, but Ruben Sierra grounded out to end the inning. Belcher had worked out of trouble yet again.

• • • • • • • •

In the top of the fifteenth inning, Rivera finally showed signs of wear. After Griffey flied out, Rivera allowed a single to Edgar

Martinez and then another to Buhner, putting runners at first and second and creating the Mariners' first legitimate threat since the twelfth inning. But Doug Strange struck out looking. Tino Martinez then swung at a 3–0 pitch and lifted a lazy fly ball to center field, which Bernie Williams easily caught for the final out. Rivera handled his first crisis with relative ease. Now, he just needed his teammates to finally, mercifully, end the game.

· · · · · · · · ·

Fourteen-plus innings had seemingly brought out everything in Game 2. Then, in the fifteenth inning, it started raining. It had rained in the New York area all day. Miraculously the wet weather had avoided Yankee Stadium. But finally at 1:00 A.M. on what was now Thursday morning, the drops starting falling.[57] It was not a heavy rain, and the game continued as most fans either popped open an umbrella or chose to get wet. At this point, a little rain certainly wasn't enough to drive them from their seats. In fact, nearly all of the 57,126 fans still remained, even after 14 ½ innings, five hours of baseball, and now rain. They watched as Belcher reemerged for the bottom of the fifteenth inning to face Mattingly. Mattingly's sixth-inning home run, responsible for so much chaos, was hours old and seemed to have occurred in another lifetime. Though he hadn't had a multi-home-run game since June 1989, few endings would have been more dramatic than a Mattingly walk-off home run. Instead, Mattingly reached for an outside pitch and grounded out to short. No one knew at the time, but it was Mattingly's last at-bat ever in Yankee Stadium.

· · · · · · · · ·

With one out, Belcher walked Kelly, setting up a confrontation with Leyritz. For Leyritz, who had missed a chance to become a hero just two innings earlier, it was the type of moment he relished. No one on the Yankees wanted the spotlight more than Leyritz. He was loud, brash, in-your-face, and never afraid to tell anyone how talented he was. He also never hesitated to complain about a lack of playing time, always believing that, no matter what the facts might say, he should be in the starting lineup. "Jimmy would be hitting .180 and would say 'play me or trade me,'" said one former teammate. The attitude was more confidence than arrogance, but it still tended to come off as cockiness. Mattingly nicknamed him "the King," and others referred to him as "Jumbo."[58] Leyritz didn't mind. He loved any kind of attention.

A Yankee his entire career, Leyritz was one of several minor leaguers the team brought up during the 1990 season. Yankees fans quickly learned that he sported one of the oddest batting stances in the game. He kept his front left leg fully extended at a forty-five-degree angle while his back right leg was bent. This was the result of Leyritz having broken his leg just before the major-league draft during his senior year of high school. Needing to take batting practice in front of scouts, he did so wearing a cast on his left leg, which prevented him from bending or putting pressure on it. Leyritz never changed his stance. Additionally, he was known for twirling his bat in between pitches. He picked up this habit in college and continued to do it after once hitting a home run just after he had twirled his bat.[59] Leyritz emerged as a legitimate power threat in 1993 when he hit fourteen home runs in just 259 at-bats. He followed that up with another strong season in 1994. His numbers fell in 1995, but he still felt he should be getting more playing time.

Finally, after all his talk, Leyritz had his moment to grab the spotlight. He had caught fifteen innings, and Buck Showalter informed him that this would be his last at-bat of the game, so he figured he would go to the plate and take his cuts.[60] Belcher immediately fell behind him 3–1. To avoid putting two runners on with just one out, Belcher needed to throw a strike. It was the same situation that had cost John Wetteland and Norm Charlton dearly in previous innings. As Belcher wound up at 1:22 A.M. on Thursday morning, the raindrops continued to fall. Somewhere in the crowd, a fan was using a whistle to sound the first few chords of "Charge." Sitting directly behind the Mariners' dugout, a Yankees fan shot up and began enthusiastically pointing toward the outfield as if to indicate Leyritz would hit a home run. Belcher's 3–1 fastball was out over the plate, and Leyritz belted it to deep right-center field. Initially, no one could tell if he had hit the ball far enough. The Yankees left the bench and climbed to the top steps of the dugout, following the flight of the ball. Belcher turned and watched as well. He couldn't tell at first if his fastball had been a fatal mistake.[61] Leyritz followed the flight with the same question. He knew he'd hit it well but wasn't certain if it was well enough to get out of the ballpark.[62] Showalter was equally uncertain, wondering if the rain might some how hold up the ball.[63] Buhner charged toward right-center field at full speed. He climbed the wall and reached up with his glove, but the ball eluded it by several feet. It crashed down over the fence, dropping between the blue outfield wall and the white wall in front of the right-field bleachers, where a member of the NYPD picked it up and began proudly displaying it. After five hours and thirteen minutes, the longest playoff game in history was finally over.[64]

The crowd went ballistic. The Yankees exploded off the bench, led by Rivera, who, with jacket on, emphatically jumped up and down along the first-base line. Mattingly, towel draped around his neck, pumped his fist and headed toward home plate. Belcher watched Leyritz's home run fall behind the wall, then turned and quietly walked back to the dugout, descending the steps and heading into the clubhouse. Leyritz pumped his fist rounding the bases. Halfway between second and third base, he encountered a fan who had run onto the field. Leyritz high-fived him before security personnel tackled the fan to the ground. Leyritz moved on, high-fiving third-base coach Willie Randolph. Finally, he reached home plate. Darryl Strawberry was the first person to greet Leyritz, using both hands to high-five him. After Strawberry came Dion James, who jumped up to high-five his teammate but leapt too high, instead swinging his left arm above Leyritz's head. After crossing home plate, Leyritz was overwhelmed by his teammates, who knocked him to the ground in celebration.

" 'The King,' of all people," thought Jay Buhner as he walked off the field.[65] Over in the Mariners' dugout, Lou Piniella stood watching the celebration unfold in front of him. He didn't look stunned or even angry but, rather, just seemed to be taking it all in. On the opposite end of the dugout, Charlton sat on the bench staring at the field. He seethed inside, still mad over the fastball he'd delivered to O'Neill way back in the seventh inning. Charlton remained on the bench longer than any Mariner before finally returning to the clubhouse. Out on the field, Leyritz was still receiving kudos from his teammates and from the crowd. Exhausted after catching for fifteen full innings, he held his hand pumped in the air, appearing on the brink of celebratory tears. "With the things that have happened between them and us, especially them and me, it makes it an extra nice feeling to do this tonight," said Leyritz after the game.[66] Meanwhile, with rain still coming down, many in the crowd remained to sing Frank Sinatra's "New York, New York." The song always played at the end of Yankees home games, but this time, the crowd remained to sing it once, then twice, then a third time.[67]

In the clubhouse, George Steinbrenner was in a jovial mood. He approached Russ Davis, who was still upset at having been doubled off first base in the fourteenth inning, patted him on the shoulder, and told him not to worry about it.[68] The postgame talk focused on the incredible game that had just been played. The Yankees were the first team in postseason history to win a game in which they trailed four different times. "It was," said Buck Showalter, "the kind of game you wish you were sitting in the stands watching."[69]

"You see games like this in the highlight reels when they look back over the years," said Pat Kelly, who scored the winning run. "But you never think you'll be in the middle of one. It was a great, great win. We've been on the other side of something like this, like when Ken Griffey hit a game-winning home run off us in the Kingdome, so we kind of know what they're battling right now." Kelly paused before adding, "I can't really fathom what they're going through right now."[70]

"We saw a little bit of everything out there tonight," said Piniella. "They come back and tie us every time we went ahead. Give them credit. We're down but not out."[71] Some of the attention in the Mariners' clubhouse shifted to Tim Belcher. Belcher walked down the tunnel as soon as the game was over and immediately encountered several cameramen. Normally, players were allowed a few minutes after the game before being greeted by the press. But this didn't happen and an angry Belcher told them to get the "hell out of here." They did not comply, instead getting even closer. Still frustrated over the loss, he shoved the camera off a cameraman's shoulder and onto the ground before storming into the clubhouse. Belcher later apologized and took full responsibility for his actions.[72] But the incident was indicative of how the Mariners felt after such a heartbreaking loss. The Seattle players dressed and made their way toward the buses that would take them to the airport. There, they encountered thousands of Yankees fans, who taunted them as they boarded and even followed their bus to the airport.[73] During the ride, Jay Buhner stood up and yelled, "We are gonna go home and kick their ass."[74] John Ellis took the subway back to his hotel. Still wearing his Mariner gear, he thought he might get killed.[75] At 2:40 A.M. as the Yankees boarded the bus that would take them to the airport, the same crowd swarmed around them, chanting "Sweep! Sweep! Sweep!"[76]

The Mariners' flight back to Seattle was quiet. After fifteen draining innings, most players tried to get some rest. Others were contemplating what had just happened. "We knew we were in trouble. No one wants to get swept, and guys were pissed about making it this far just to get swept," said Jay Buhner.[77] "It was the longest 3,000-mile flight. I thought there was no way you beat the Yankees three in a row. It was over," said Dave Niehaus.[78] Others tried to be more positive. Joey Cora, Tino Martinez, and Edgar Martinez attempted to keep things upbeat, knowing that they were returning to the Kingdome, where they dominated.[79] Piniella approached Rick Rizzs and told him the Mariners were going to win this thing. Rizzs would never forget the look in Piniella's eyes as he said it.[80]

8

Game 3: Playoff
Baseball in Seattle

"25 Yanks Can't Beat Our Johnson."

—Sign held by a Mariner's fan in
the Kingdome during Game 3

Two days later, people were still talking about Game 2 and wondering if there was any way the rest of the series could possibly live up to what had occurred in New York. The first two games had been a war on the field. Now the war spilled into the front offices. George Steinbrenner, already in trouble for his remarks about the umpiring in Games 1 and 2, now took shots at a different target: Mariners team CEO John Ellis. "I have trouble with Seattle owner John Ellis," Steinbrenner told the *New York Daily News* before Game 3. "He's the one crying poverty and saying he has to have revenue sharing to survive out there. Then he goes and adds $5 million [Andy Benes and Vince Coleman] to a payroll. Who's he kidding? I'm supposed to help him when he has a payroll of $34 million?"[1]

"That's a classic," Ellis fired back. "George operates on emotion and spur of the moment. He can be a very charming guy, but when he puts on his game face, who knows what he'll say? He can say what he wants, but what I'm saying is 'Hey, look what's happening here.' We've been told Seattle would never make it because we aren't a baseball town. Look what happens when you put a competitive team on the field. But he's a guest in our city this week, so I'm not gonna fight with him."[2] Steinbrenner had never shied away from fights with players, managers, umpires, or even commissioners. But openly feuding with a fellow owner was a new element to his game. It's questionable whether The Boss would have ever said an unkind word about Ellis had their teams not been duking it out in the playoffs.

A tense relationship between the two management sides was only made worse by the actions of one Yankees employee. Mariners president Chuck Armstrong had reserved a suite for Steinbrenner and his entourage for Games 3, 4, and 5 at the Kingdome. Upon being informed of this, a Yankees executive allegedly replied, "That's OK—we'll just need the one night," meaning, of course, that he fully expected the Yankees to win Game 3 and sweep the series. It was a comment that quickly spread around the Mariners' clubhouse.[3]

The Seattle fans also did their best to stir up emotions. They had waited years for this moment and they flooded the Kingdome that Friday night still carrying the energy and enthusiasm from Monday's victory over the Angels. In less than a month, Seattle had gone from a Seahawks town to a baseball city. It was an amazing, stunning transformation, especially having occurred in so short a time. Just three weeks earlier, the Mariners had played a home game against the Twins before only 16,469 people. Now, they were the hottest ticket in the Pacific Northwest. "It's amazing how far we have come," said Mariners fan Terry Donalds, as he sat in his seat preparing for Game 3. "A couple of weeks or so ago, we were only talking about the wildcard."[4] "We're gonna be there for the World Series," said another Mariners fan Bob Zurbrugg. "They've proven themselves, and we're gonna build them a stadium too."[5] "Notre Dame is in town to play the Huskies [today] and no one is talking about it," said Dave Niehaus before Game 3. "Notre Dame and the Huskies are playing and everyone is talking about the Mariners. How amazing is that?"[6]

Yelling and screaming, 57,944 people were rocking inside the Kingdome. It was the largest crowd ever to see a Mariners game in Seattle.[7] Even being down 2–0 in the series could not dampen their spirits. The Kingdome, in fact, was laden with banners. "I will always remember that," said Mike Stanley. "There were just banners and signs everywhere."[8] Banners were in the lower level, they were in the middle level, they were in the upper deck, and they were taped to the concrete walls of the stadium. One of the dozens of signs appearing in the crowd that night summed it up in two words: "WE BELIEVE!" Fully aware of what their players had to endure in terms of taunts and projectiles in the Bronx, Mariner fans also hung banners saying "Welcome Back to Civilization" and "Here We Let Our Pitchers Do the Throwing." There was also one directed at the Yankees owner: "Hey George, We Have Fans, Not Animals in the Stands."[9] Jim Leyritz, now Public Enemy Number One in Seattle, left the visitors' clubhouse, walked down the tunnel leading to the dugout, and emerged to see a sign in left field staring him straight in the face: "LEYRITZ: 0–0, 4 HIT BY PITCHES."[10]

Like Yankee Stadium, the Kingdome was decked out with bunting. The division series logo was present along both the third- and first-base lines in foul territory. The banners, the bunting, and the fans all made the Kingdome an almost aesthetically pleasing place to watch a game.

Niehaus, the voice of the Mariners since the team's inception in 1977, threw out the first pitch, which he bounced in the dirt. "The Yankees have Joe DiMaggio and the Mariners have me. What does that tell you about the history of the franchise?" Niehaus later joked.[11]

The antics of the team owners, fans, and announcers still didn't change the facts. Seattle was on the brink of elimination. Fortunately for them, they had the game's most dominant pitcher starting Game 3. Randy Johnson would be pitching on three days' rest for the second consecutive start. For many pitchers, this would be a daunting task, but the Big Unit could not have cared less. "I had the weight of all Washington on me," he said after Game 3 was over. "[But] I thrive on that kind of competition. I hope that's obvious by now."[12] To Johnson, the Mariners had come too far and fought too hard to be swept out of the playoffs. Not only that, but a sweep could very well kill the chances of their getting a new stadium and send the team to Tampa.

In order to combat the intimidating Johnson, Buck Showalter made several key changes to his lineup. Showalter knew he had an opportunity to put this series away, and he also knew that Johnson was torture on left-handed hitters. Johnson's breaking slider was just too sharp for them. Wade Boggs and Paul O'Neill may have been .300 hitters, but they didn't accomplish that feat hitting against Johnson 600 times a year. Seeking any edge he could get, Showalter sat Boggs on the bench for Game 3, replacing him with righty Russ Davis. O'Neill sat as well, as righty Gerald Williams patrolled right field. Randy Velarde was moved to left field and righty Pat Kelly got his only start of the series at second base. Not only did Showalter stack the lineup with right-handed hitters, but he also inserted players like Davis and Williams, who, little used as they had been, were exceptional fastball hitters. Although they wished to play, O'Neill and Boggs both understood Showalter's strategy. "In that case, you have to play the law of averages, because lefties had no chance against [Johnson]," said Boggs.[13]

Jim Leyritz, however, was irate. Upon hearing that he would not be in the lineup, he phoned his wife from the clubhouse and told her "pack our shit, we are leaving."[14] Already upset about a lack of playing time during the regular season, Leyritz did not want people to think he was afraid to face Johnson after their run-in in May. He was also still coming off the emotional high of his Game 2 home run. His anger may have been justified, but the truth was that Showalter could not have both Stanley and Leyritz in that lineup without one of them acting as designated hitter. That would mean putting Ruben Sierra in the outfield, and Showalter was not about to sacrifice defense to mend any hurt feelings.

Showalter was fully aware that his decision might be unpopular with Boggs, O'Neill, and Leyritz. "Boggs wanted to play," he admitted after Game 3. "In fact Boggsie was champing at the bit to get at this guy [Johnson]. But we have had better luck going with other guys."[15] Showalter's last line was no doubt a reference to Boggs's 2–16 career performance against Johnson. Game 3 did not showcase his All-Star lineup, but Showalter would take his chances.

· · · · · · · · ·

Johnson stepped onto the rubber for the start of Game 3 as the first person ever to throw a postseason pitch in Seattle. The noise leading up to the first pitch was deafening. "Loud is loud and this was loud," said Vince Coleman. "You can't even hear yourself think."[16] The noise barely dissipated, even after Johnson's first-pitch fastball to leadoff hitter Randy Velarde sailed outside. With nowhere to escape, thanks to the dome, the noise simply reverberated off every inch of the stadium, bouncing from the artificial turf to the roof and from corner to corner. It was ear shattering. "Man, this place is loud," thought Don Mattingly.[17]

Velarde swung at Johnson's second pitch, and flied out softly to right field. Amazingly enough, the out somehow raised the noise level inside. Rarely over the course of the next three nights would there be anything even remotely close to silence under the Kingdome roof. With one out, Bernie Williams stepped into the right-handed batter's box. Williams, batting from the right side, exhibited patience against Johnson, who was having trouble controlling his fastball. It tailed outside for three out of four pitches before Williams finally drew a walk. Johnson's lack of control would be crucial to the Yankees. If Johnson couldn't get his fastball over for a strike, he would be in trouble. The Yankees were patient enough to repeatedly take the fastball for a ball. This would cause Johnson to fall behind in the count and make it more difficult for him to throw that devastating slider. Alternatively, if he could not throw his slider for a strike, the Yankees were also good-enough hitters to sit back on fastballs and drill them over the short fences of the Kingdome.

The chance to strike first against the game's best pitcher would put the pressure on Seattle and take the boisterous crowd out of the game by the first inning. Mike Stanley attempted to capitalize on this opportunity. Stanley, like most hitters, hated batting against Johnson. "Even if I knew what pitch was coming, I still couldn't hit him," said Stanley.[18] Batting third in the righty-dominated lineup, Stanley jumped ahead in the count, 2–0. Johnson was only nine pitches into the game, but his stuff already appeared to be off. Stanley sat on the next pitch, a fastball, and drilled it deep to center field. The players on the Yankees' bench jumped up in excitement while everyone else in the Kingdome held their breath. As Ken Griffey Jr. inched slowly toward the wall, it looked for a moment like the Yankees might take a 2–0 lead. Griffey went back to the fence, fully relaxed, almost as if chasing a batting practice fly ball. He blew a bubble with his gum, pressed his back against the wall, reached up slightly with his glove, and made the catch. The ball had been mere inches from going out. Instead of a two-run home run that could have crushed the Kingdome spirits, Griffey's catch only incited them further. Two pitches later, Ruben Sierra popped up to second, and the Yankees' opportunity was gone. Johnson may not have been sharp, but it was still a scoreless game. The question now was whether Jack McDowell's back would hold up.

• • • • • • • • •

When the strike ended in April 1995, McDowell was literally not sure which team he played for. Now, he was trying to pitch the Yankees into the ALCS. "Black Jack," as he was known, had been selected by the Chicago White Sox in first round of the 1987 draft after having been a star pitcher for Stanford. By 1991, he had established himself as one of baseball's top starting pitchers and enjoyed back-to-back twenty-win seasons in 1992 and 1993. McDowell won the 1993 American League Cy Young Award, and his twenty-two victories led the White Sox to their first division title in ten years. In the championship series against Toronto, however, he was hammered in two starts, and Chicago was eliminated in six games. In the 1994 off-season, while the strike was still in effect, White Sox owner Jerry Reinsdorf, with whom McDowell had openly feuded for years, was looking to lessen the team's payroll and dump salary.[19] He traded McDowell to the Yankees for two prospects, neither of whom made an impact in Chicago. At the time of the trade, however, the Major League Baseball Players Association notified McDowell that the deal was null and void due to the strike, causing McDowell to openly refer to the trade as "a Rotisserie move" because it did not seem real.[20] After the trade was announced in December 1994, the Yankees made an attempt to sign McDowell to a long-term deal, but McDowell rejected the offer as being too low, and the two sides did not speak again for months.[21] He sat around during the winter not knowing exactly whom he would be pitching for. When the strike finally did end, McDowell received a call from the Yankees telling him to report to spring training in two days. The Players Association had not gotten back to him, so McDowell reported for camp in Fort Lauderdale.

New York was a good situation for McDowell, because he was not brought over to be the staff ace. That role was taken by Jimmy Key. Instead, the Yankees needed to fill holes in their starting rotation after not retaining pitchers Jim Abbott and Terry Mulholland. McDowell, armed with a great fastball and a devastating splitter, was going to be the number-two starter. All was going to plan until mid-May, when it was apparent that something was not right with Jimmy Key. Key won on Opening Day, but went winless in his next three appearances.

He was then pummeled for eleven hits and seven runs by the Indians on May 16. Obviously, something was wrong. Shortly after his May 16 performance, Key shut down a throwing session after forty pitches, the pain in his arm too great to continue. It was diagnosed as tendonitis in his throwing arm, and he was placed on the disabled list.[22] Key later required rotator cuff surgery. His 1995 season was over after only five starts, and Jack McDowell now had to step in as the team's ace.

If anyone on the team could have handled that situation, McDowell appeared to be that person. His tough, gritty attitude was considered something of value in New York, where fans and the media could easily wear down a thin-skinned player. In an age where complete games were becoming extinct, McDowell ate up innings, always thinking he should be in the game until the very last out. With Key unavailable, "Black Jack" looked the perfect fit to fill in, but instead, McDowell struggled through an up-and-down beginning to his season. There were times when he showed flashes of brilliance, like the night of May 24, when he took a no-hitter into the bottom of the eighth inning against the Angels in Anaheim. Chili Davis, however, broke up the no-hitter that inning, and even worse, the Angels scored three runs, making McDowell the losing pitcher.[23] It was a microcosm for how his season would progress: good, but not good enough.

As the season went on, McDowell's starts fluctuated between great and subpar. On July 18, the frustration finally boiled over. The Yankees, hosting a day-night double header against the White Sox, lost the first game 9–4 to former Yankee Jim Abbott. In the nightcap, former Yankee closer and now Chicago starter Dave Righetti, who hadn't won a game in over two years, led the White Sox to victory in an 11–4 drubbing. McDowell had started the second game, and his former teammates blasted him for nine runs in just $4\frac{2}{3}$ innings. When Showalter removed him in the fifth inning, the Yankee Stadium crowd treated him to an extremely loud chorus of boos and jeers. It was not what the Yankee pitcher wanted to hear. To that point, McDowell had been doing his best to carry a decimated staff. Three-fifths of the Yankees' projected rotation in spring training was down with injuries. The bullpen had been a weak spot all year. McDowell had absorbed shellings for the sake of trying to keep the bullpen fresh, knowing they would probably have to come in the next day to relieve whatever starter could not get out of the fifth inning. Fans weren't picking up on that, and McDowell felt angry and unappreciated. As he approached the first-base line on his way to the dugout, he raised his right arm high above his head and extended his middle finger to the crowd of 21,188. So that he didn't miss anyone, McDowell twisted his arm in a circular motion, making sure every booing fan in every section of the stadium received the brunt of his frustration. Buck Showalter, who had been staring at the bullpen, heard the crowd suddenly start to stir. "What was that, Stano?" he asked catcher Mike Stanley. "It ain't good. You ain't gonna like it," Stanley replied. "Jack just flipped off New York."[24]

The reaction was swift and harsh. On the back page of the *New York Daily News* the following day appeared a photo of McDowell flashing his middle finger under the headline "JACK ASS." McDowell, instead of making excuses, owned up to his actions immediately, calling it stupid. Shortly afterward, Showalter called McDowell into his office. "We have a problem," Showalter told him and explained that with a few off days in the upcoming schedule, it would be possible to shift McDowell so that his next start would not be at Yankee Stadium. McDowell refused. "I'll take it [the backlash]," he told Showalter. "They [the fans] are waiting to embrace me, I just need to give them something to embrace."[25] It was the type of action that endeared him to Showalter. McDowell made his next scheduled start, which was at Yankee Stadium, and defeated the Texas Rangers. By his next start, the Yankees had acquired David Cone, and with the emergence of Andy Pettitte and the return of a healthy Scott Kamieniecki, the pressure eased off him. He won seven of his last nine decisions in the regular season.

In September, McDowell developed a problem in his back due to a rib muscle that had popped off a rib. It created a lump in his back and made it extremely painful for him to pitch. The back became enough of a problem that despite needing every win down the stretch, the Yankees decided to sit him for the last two weeks of the regular season. There would be no bullpen sessions, no soft tossing, just rest. McDowell searched out many ways to help solve the pain, going to different doctors and even trying Don Mattingly's acupuncturist, but nothing eased the pressure.[26] So when he stepped onto the Kingdome mound in the bottom of the first inning of Game 3, McDowell had not faced live Major League hitting since September 21. The only throwing he had done was some tossing the day before. Two weeks had provided some much-needed rest, but the back problem still persisted. Despite this predicament, there wasn't a chance McDowell wouldn't take the ball. Few had dominated Seattle hitters as he had: ten career wins against one loss and a 2.24 ERA. Just four weeks earlier, he had thrown a complete-game victory against them at Yankee Stadium. Bad back or not, the Yankees had to feel good going into Game 3 with someone of McDowell's track record against the Mariners on the mound.

In the first inning, McDowell did his best to squelch any doubts about the back. Leadoff hitter Vince Coleman struck out looking and Joey Cora flied out to right. Griffey came to the plate with two outs and no one on. As Mariners public address announcer Tom Hutyler introduced Griffey with his signature "Ken Griffeeeeeeeeeeeey Jun-ior!" call, the hometown crowd gave him a thunderous ovation. This was their golden boy, the face of the franchise for so many years, stepping up for his first postseason at-bat in Mariners home white. His postseason career was only two games old, but a banner was already hanging in the stands declaring "KEN GRIFFEY, JR.: MR. OCTOBER THE NEXT GENERATION."

The excitement of Junior's first postseason at-bat in the Kingdome was short lived. He swung at the first-pitch fastball, got the bat out just a bit too far, and flied out to Bernie Williams in right-center field. For the third straight game in the series, the teams moved on to the second inning scoreless.

· · · · · · · · ·

In 1995, Seattle was a city of 600,000 people with a developing downtown, thanks to an upturn in economic times.[27] Years earlier, the city spawned the birth of grunge rock with bands such as Nirvana, Pearl Jam, and Alice in Chains. But by 1995, the grunge scene started to recede, as bands like Hootie & the Blowfish and singer Alanis Morissette topped the *Billboard* charts. Microsoft's Bill Gates was having a new home constructed southeast of the city on Mercer Island.[28] John Stanford, who had taken over as Seattle's superintendent of schools on September 1, had just announced that he was interested in a special levy to buy library books.[29] That weekend, King County executive Gary Locke was preparing to deliver his proposed 1996 county budget to the Metropolitan King County Council on Monday. The budget would include a 10 percent bus-fare increase to help pay for bus operations.[30]

The day before Game 3, demonstrations were held across Seattle in protest of congressionally proposed cuts to Medicare and Medicaid. Thirty-one people were arrested outside of the King County Republican Party headquarters.[31] Still, it was the Mariners who eclipsed all other news occurring in Seattle. Norm Rice, the city's first African American mayor, was preoccupied trying to work out a new stadium deal with the governor and the legislature.

· · · · · · · · ·

Randy Johnson entered the second inning in better command of his pitches. He retired the first two hitters with a mix of fastballs, sliders, and changeups, all hitting their spots and breaking where needed. With two outs, Yankees third baseman Russ Davis stepped in. Though Davis was a highly touted prospect in the Yankees' minor-league system, Wade Boggs's presence on the team had blocked the possibility of his advancement to full-time third baseman. He made a handful of appearances in 1994 and appeared in forty games in 1995. The Yankees believed so strongly in his potential that rumors abounded that they would not re-sign Boggs after the season was over, finally allowing Davis to take over the "hot corner" permanently. If he could come through against Johnson now, it certainly would help his cause.

Davis had Gold Glove potential and was in the starting line for two reasons: he was right-handed, and he was an exceptional fastball hitter. Though happy to play, he certainly didn't relish whom he had to face. "It was intimidating to face Randy," said Davis. "He'd release the ball and it would be right in front of your face already." Despite his apprehension, the night before, as Davis slept in his Seattle hotel room, he had actually dreamed about hitting a home run off Johnson in this game.[32] The dream nearly came true. With the count even at 1–1, Johnson came in with a fastball that Davis turned on and sent soaring straight down the left-field line. As with Stanley's shot in the first inning, the crowd turned silent as everyone in the ballpark waited to see if the ball would stay fair. As it started to descend, the ball just barely twisted foul at the last moment. Two fastballs had put Johnson and the Mariners just feet away from a 3–0 deficit. The count went full before Johnson threw a slider that caught Davis looking for strike three. The Big Unit had survived another close call to keep the game scoreless.

• • • • • • • •

McDowell picked up in the second inning right where he left off in the first, retiring Edgar Martinez on one pitch. Tino Martinez then singled into right field, but he barely had time to catch his breath before Jay Buhner slapped a first-pitch fastball to shortstop. Tony Fernandez fielded it smoothly and began a 6–4–3 inning-ending double play. McDowell got through the inning throwing only seven pitches.

In the top of the third, Johnson nearly matched McDowell's efficiency. Using a combination of fastballs and sliders, he needed only eight pitches to get through the inning. The Yankees could muster only two harmless groundouts and another strikeout.

In contrast to the five-hour affair that Game 2 had been, Game 3 was moving along swiftly as both pitchers worked quickly and efficiently. But McDowell began the bottom of the third inning by walking leadoff hitter Mike Blowers on four straight fastballs. While it was no reason to panic, at least not at that point in the game, it was evident that when McDowell's pitches were off target, they missed badly. The back was not preventing him from throwing strikes, but it was causing him to throw the occasional erratic pitch. The Yankees had to hope that it would not affect McDowell's entire game. After walking Blowers, McDowell erased any doubts about his effectiveness by getting Luis Sojo to ground into a 6–4–3 double play. Despite being a fly-ball pitcher, McDowell had now gotten out of jams in the last two innings with ground-ball double plays.

• • • • • • • •

The game remained scoreless as Bernie Williams came to the plate to lead off the top of the fourth. To that point, Williams had been the only Yankee hitter to reach base against Johnson, drawing a walk in the first inning. With the count at 1–1, Johnson intended to go inside with a fastball, but his pitch tailed back over the plate and Williams drove it deep to right field. Bernie dropped his bat and immediately sprinted down the first-base line as his shot settled deep into the stands beyond the right-field wall. Finally, after two near misses, the Yankees broke through and got a Johnson fastball over the fence. As Williams trotted around the bases, the Seattle fan who grabbed the home run decided against keeping it as a souvenir. Instead, the ball came hurling back from the stands, bouncing in short right field and rolling back to the infield. Throwing back an opposing player's home run was a standard practice for fans at Wrigley Field in Chicago. Now, it was becoming an adopted Kingdome tradition. The home run temporarily silenced the crowd but did not rattle Randy Johnson, who retired the next three hitters without difficulty.

• • • • • • • • • •

Staked to a one-run lead, McDowell came out in the bottom of the fourth firing a series of fastballs. Coleman grounded out to first on what turned out to be a much closer play than necessary. The grounder dribbled toward the hole between first and second, causing Don Mattingly to field it while moving toward his right and heading away from first base. McDowell failed to get off the mound in time to cover first base, so Mattingly had to turn his body and race to the bag. Sliding feet first to avoid what could have been a nasty collision, Mattingly just beat Coleman to the bag.

It was a big out, because Cora grounded out to second base, bringing Griffey to the plate again with two outs and no one on base. Just as he had done in the first inning, Griffey was a fraction off on a fastball and popped up to short. McDowell's back may have caused him to throw an erratic pitch occasionally, but through the first four innings, he had faced the minimum twelve hitters. To that point, he was outpitching Randy Johnson.

• • • • • • • • •

In addition to throwing back an opposing player's home run, the Kingdome fans were engaging in another tradition. With every two-strike count Randy Johnson had on a hitter, fans were up on their feet, cheering as loud as they could, hoping for yet another strikeout. The two-strike chant is thought to have originated at Yankee Stadium in June 1978 during a game in which Ron Guidry struck out eighteen California Angels. Now, the Mariners fans were adopting it as their own, and with the way Johnson pitched in the fifth inning, they were obtaining a lot of practice performing it. Johnson struck out Gerald Williams, got Davis to pop out to first, and then struck out Fernandez on a sharp slider. Johnson's earlier control struggles were behind him. He was now doing his job. He needed the Mariners' lineup to start doing theirs.

· · · · · · · · ·

McDowell began the bottom of the fifth inning by walking Edgar Martinez. The Kingdome came back to attention as the Mariners' other Martinez approached the batter's box.

Constantino Martinez hailed from Tampa, Florida. He attended school at the University of Tampa and, early in his career, was best known for being a member of the USA baseball team that took home the gold medal in the 1988 Summer Olympic Games. Martinez was a hero that summer, hitting two home runs in the gold-medal game against Japan.[33] A right-handed first baseman who batted from the left side, Martinez had a smooth swing that involved a slight swirling of the bat as he anticipated the pitch. That bat had become a dangerous weapon in 1995.

The Mariners selected Tino Martinez as their first pick in the 1988 draft. His emergence to the big leagues was held up due to Pete O'Brien and Seattle hometown favorite Al Davis splitting time between first base and designated hitter. Davis left after 1991 and Martinez, who had spent limited time with the team in 1990 and 1991, was finally called up for good in 1992. He split time between first base and DH over the next two years before finally becoming the regular first baseman in 1994.

Defensively, Martinez would never gain the credit he deserved for his fielding abilities. He was particularly adept at turning 3–6–3 double plays, which many right-handed first basemen have difficulty with. Unlike lefties, righties must first field the ball; then turn their entire body toward second base in order to provide the strongest possible throw. It is a move that takes time, and in baseball, every second is precious. Martinez, however, pivoted his body with relative ease, making the throw to second and then returning to first base.

Offensively, Martinez's hitting progressed steadily over the years, as his home run totals increased in every season leading up to 1995. While not a physically dominating presence, Martinez possessed power, and his smooth left-handed swing was perfect for the short fences in the Kingdome. Most important, as he progressed, he began hitting balls up the middle and to the opposite field. Spraying the ball to all fields turned him from a good hitter to a great hitter and during the 1995 season, Martinez batted .293, thirty-two points higher than his previous career best. In addition to batting average, his power numbers shot up dramatically. His thirty-five doubles, thirty-one home runs, and 111 RBIs were all significantly higher than any previous numbers he had posted in those categories. "Tino had his coming-out party in '95," said teammate Tim Belcher.[34] Martinez's increased production began to draw the attention of fans and fellow players, and he made the 1995 American League All-Star team.

There was more to Martinez than just a smooth glove and impressive offensive numbers though. Inside him was a burning desire to win. He was a fierce competitor who could be as focused as any player. "He's got what I call controlled intensity," said Martinez's minor-league manager, Tommy Jones. "He's not a screamer. He's not a big rah-rah guy. But everybody who plays with him knows his competitive nature. You can just see it in his eyes."[35]

On June 7, in a game at Baltimore, Orioles rookie pitcher Armando Benitez drilled Martinez in the back following an Edgar Martinez grand slam. The incident nearly resulted in a brawl as both benches and bullpens emptied onto the field. Tino refused to back down, yelling at Benitez, who slowly approached home plate. "Normally, I would either charge the mound or say nothing and walk to first base, but I wasn't prepared so I did neither," said Tino after the incident. "I stood there and yelled at him. . . . Should I have charged the mound? No comment."[36] Martinez was not going to instigate, but he certainly wasn't going to back down either. (Three years later, while he was with the Yankees, he would again be drilled in the back by a Benitez fastball following a big home run. One of the nastier brawls in baseball history ensued as Martinez stared down Benitez, flashed two fingers, and yelled at him "That's twice!" It had been three years, but Tino had not forgotten the beaning in Baltimore in June of 1995.)

Few teams were better aware of Martinez's abilities than the Yankees. In 1995, he torched them with a .319 batting average—and that actually lowered his career average against them to .322.[37] In addition, he also displayed power, hitting five home runs and driving in thirteen RBIs in thirteen games against New York during the regular season. The Yankees certainly knew what Martinez was capable of, and people in their front office took notice. Some thought his style would fit in with the Yankees. With the prospect of Don Mattingly not returning in 1996, the Yankees had their eyes on Martinez for more reasons than most people at the Kingdome that night realized.

Naturally, Martinez wasn't aware he was auditioning for the Yankees as he came to bat in the fifth inning with a runner on and no outs. To that point, the Mariners had managed only one hit off McDowell, but that hit belonged to Martinez. McDowell fell behind, 1–0, then delivered a fastball. Catcher Mike Stanley had set up on the outside corner, but as the pitch approached home, Stanley began reaching back toward the inner half of the plate, an ominous sign for any pitcher. Martinez reached down and sent the misplaced fastball high and deep to center field. Bernie Williams frantically raced toward the fence, but the ball crashed into the blue batter's-eye tarp, fifteen feet behind the center-field wall, for a two-run home run. "I thought [the home run] gave the team a little confidence to get back into the game and make everyone swing the bat," said Martinez, whose home run created bedlam.[38] The *Seattle Post-Intelligencer* was recording decibel levels in the Kingdome, and after Martinez's home run, the sound level on the meter jumped to 116, nearly the same level as a rock concert.[39] It was ear-shattering noise that shook the stadium to its foundation.

In celebration of the home run, some fans in the Kingdome decided to do their best Yankees fan impersonation. Shortly after Martinez crossed home plate and just after Seattle radio announcer Dave Niehaus was discussing how well Seattle fans were acting compared with the New York crowd, someone in the outfield stands threw a quarter at Gerald Williams, hitting him in the lip. "It's all part of the battle," said Williams after the game, a cut visible on his lip. "Those are some spirited fans out there."[40] Buck Showalter and Yankee trainee Gene Monahan ran out to right field to attend to Williams. Shortly after they arrived, Alfredo Castaneda-Valezuez, sitting in the stands above right field, threw a tomato at them, missing all three. Seattle fans, who were behaving themselves for the most part, quickly pointed out the tomato thrower, and Castaneda-Valezuez was escorted out of the building and arrested.[41] While it turned out to be an isolated incident for the Kingdome crowd, it was unsettling for the Yankee players on the field.

"My thoughts are, two wrongs don't make a right," said Showalter after the game. "We don't like it whether it's in New York or Seattle. The safety of your players is not something to be taken lightly."[42]

The quarter and tomato incidents were only temporary distractions from more important news: the lead had changed hands. "I kicked myself for giving up the home run," said McDowell, angrily referring to his first mistake of the night.[43] He recovered to strike out Jay Buhner but then drilled Mike Blowers with a fastball right in the middle of his back, just in between the shoulders. Although it was the ideal location to aim for any pitcher who intended to hit a batter, everyone there, except maybe Mariner fans, knew that it was not intentional. McDowell was not going to hit a batter now that his team was down a run. Immediately after plunking Blowers, McDowell turned away in disgust over letting the ball get away from him like that. McDowell had sprinkled in these types of wild pitches throughout the night, so it was only a matter of time before someone got hit.

Blowers took his base, and as he reached first, he was having noticeable trouble with the grip in his hands. The ball had hit him so squarely that numbness had shot through his body, causing him to lose the feeling in his fingers.[44] Blowers reached second base on a groundout by Luis Sojo and then advanced to third on a wild pitch, but he was stranded there after Dan Wilson struck out swinging. Despite the additional missed opportunity, the Mariners were now in the situation they had hoped for all day: a lead with baseball's best pitcher on the mound.

• • • • • • • • •

Randy Johnson responded to his new lead by striking out Pat Kelly to begin the sixth inning. Johnson then walked Randy Velarde on five pitches. Bernie Williams, the Yankees' only offensive production to that point, smacked a single into the hole between first and second. It appeared as though the Yankees were on the cusp of a big inning, but just as quickly, it disappeared. On Williams's single, Velarde had rounded second and thought about heading toward third base. Buhner had caught the ball in right field and looked as if he was going to throw the ball to third, so Velarde instead decided to stop and return to second base. By that point however, Velarde was already too far off the bag. Buhner, instead of throwing to third, threw a one-hop laser to second base. "I think Luis [Sojo, the shortstop] and I read each other's minds," said Buhner of the play. "As soon as Velarde slammed on the brakes, I knew we had a shot."[45] Sojo, covering the bag, fielded Buhner's throw and quickly applied a tag on Velarde, who made a desperate attempt to get back to the bag. Umpire Jim Evans immediately called Velarde out. It was "a play that doesn't work a whole lot," Buhner conceded. "It just happened to work in that situation. It was a big break for Randy Johnson."[46]

"A stupid base running mistake," Velarde admitted after the game. "There's no need at all to think about going to third. I thought I got in there, but it was a stupid mistake trying it. You've got to shut it down and let [Mike] Stanley [the next hitter] and all those guys come up."[47]

Replays showed that Velarde was safe, but he did not to argue the call. He made a mistake, and he knew it. The Yankees would have had two runners on with Stanley, who had already come within inches of homering off Johnson in the first, coming to bat. Instead, it was one on, two out, and a potential rally squelched. Velarde's gaffe was made more painful when Stanley singled up the middle and Johnson walked Ruben Sierra on four straight pitches to load the bases. Again, Johnson was in a precarious situation, and up next was Don Mattingly, one of the few left-handed hitters in baseball who had given him trouble. Coming into Game 3, Mattingly was a career .381 hitter against Johnson, a high average for any hitter, much less a left-handed one.[48] Even more impressive was that Mattingly had only struck out twice against him in forty-two at-bats. The numbers, however, were from previous years, when both Mattingly and Johnson were far different players. Showalter had hesitated to play Mattingly against Johnson during the 1995 season because of the eye infection, so the Yankee captain had not faced the lefty in over a year. That year meant quite a difference, as Johnson had pitched on another level in 1995. Mattingly would not be facing the same pitcher he had seen before.

Mattingly had displayed his rustiness during his first at-bat when, leading off in the second inning, he couldn't touch Johnson's slider, flailing hopelessly at it until he struck out swinging. In the fourth inning, Johnson threw him three straight sliders, the last of which Mattingly just got a piece of, fouling it off. Then, down in the count, 1–2, Mattingly again looked for the slider, but Johnson came back with a fastball, catching Mattingly off guard. He struck out for the second straight at-bat. The situation in the sixth inning was different than Mattingly's first two at-bats, because the bases loaded were now loaded. Regardless of what had transpired in the second and fourth innings, the pressure was now on Johnson. One mistake could easily erase the euphoria of Martinez's fifth-inning home run.

Johnson threw two sliders, both for strikes. With the count at 0–2, the Kingdome crowd engulfed the field with an exuberance of sound and enthusiasm, praying for a third strike. Johnson, bent down, picked up the signal from Wilson, then delivered his most devastating slider of the night. Mattingly chased after it, reaching as far to the outside corner of the plate as his arms could stretch, but he still didn't come close to touching the pitch.

The crowd erupted after the inning-ending strikeout, and Johnson shouted out in excitement. He had escaped the greatest threat of the night and had done so in dominating fashion. In the span of three consecutive at-bats, he had struck Mattingly out more times than he had done previously in his entire career. "Johnson [was] like a knuckleballer," said Mattingly after the game. "He's different than everybody else in the league. He threw me three straight sliders and when he gets that pitch over it makes it awful tough for me."[49] Despite Johnson's heroics, it was still just a one-run game. Seattle was going to have to come up with more runs before it could feel secure in its lead. There were few people better to begin a much-needed Mariners rally than the team's leadoff hitter, Vince Coleman. It was something Coleman had been doing since he joined Seattle on August 15. Although he had been a key ingredient in the Mariner's miracle comeback and was basking in the results, for Coleman, 1995 wasn't just about winning baseball games. It was also about redemption. More than just accumulating hits or stolen bases, Coleman was trying to reestablish himself off the field as well.

• • • • • • • •

Coleman literally raced his way to National League Rookie of the Year for the NL champion St. Louis Cardinals in 1985. Though he struck out too much and walked too little for a leadoff hitter, Coleman was blessed with amazing speed, stealing 110 bases in his rookie season and wreaking havoc on opposing pitchers once he got on base. A walk or a single to Coleman might just as well have been a double, as he was nearly guaranteed to steal second. "I hated Vince when he was on the other team," recalled Norm Charlton, referring to Coleman's habit of driving pitchers crazy on the bases.[50]

During the 1985 National League Championship Series, Coleman was run over by the tarpaulin machine at Busch Stadium.[51] The freak injury prevented him from doing any damage that postseason, but he returned in 1986 to steal 107 bases and then stole 109 more in 1987 as he led the Cardinals to another NL championship. By 1990, Coleman was a two-time All-Star and had led the National League in steals every single season since his rookie year. In 1991, he signed a large multiyear deal with the Mets, who hoped his speed could lead them back to the top of the NL East. The deal became a mess for both sides. Coleman was frequently hampered by a bad hamstring, missing large parts of the 1991, 1992, and 1993 seasons. After leading the league in steals every year during his career with the Cardinals, Coleman failed to finish higher than seventh in any year with the Mets.

Any shortcomings that Coleman had on the field paled in comparison to two incidents that occurred off the field in 1993. On April 26, Coleman was practicing his golf swing in the Mets' clubhouse when he accidentally struck Dwight Gooden in his pitching arm, causing Gooden to miss his start that night.[52] The golf club incident was strange, but it was an accident. What happened on July 24 of that year was just bizarre and inexplicable. The Mets were in Los Angeles for a weekend series against the Dodgers. After the Saturday game, Coleman and teammate Bobby Bonilla were riding in the Jeep of their friend, Dodger outfielder Eric Davis. As they drove out of the Dodger Stadium players' parking lot, Coleman lit a large firecracker known as an M-100 and dropped it outside the Jeep window. Just how far Coleman threw it is a matter of dispute. What could not be disputed, however, was the result. Three fans, including two-and-half-year-old Amanda Santos, suffered injuries as a result of the explosion.[53]

The incident brought a firestorm of criticism against Coleman, whose action afterward only made matters worse, because he initially refused to apologize. In fact, he said that he saw it as no big deal, merely something he had done before as a gag. When finally addressing the issue, Coleman admitted, "I haven't slept, nor have I been able to concentrate on anything else," but the lack of his actually saying he was sorry caused many to feel his "apology" was nothing more than a public relations move.[54] The fans and the press were all over him. Immediately after the incident surfaced, the Mets announced that

Coleman would be put on leave and would never play another game for the team again. The *New York Times*' Style section used Coleman as an example of America's fraying sense of civility.[55] Coleman eventually faced criminal charges for his actions, pleading guilty to a misdemeanor, and was sentenced to a one-year suspended jail term, three years' probation, a $1,000 fine, and 200 hours of community service.[56]

In January 1994, the Mets traded him to the Royals for outfielder Kevin McReynolds. Believing Coleman to be healthy and capable of putting up the numbers he had with the Cardinals, the Royals were willing to take a chance on him. While he did not return to his 1980s form, he did put up respectable numbers, stealing fifty bases and hitting .284 in the strike-shortened season. The Royals were in contention for first place in the American League Central when the strike hit, but once the work stoppage was over, they decided to dump many of their higher-priced older players. Coleman actually made it through most of the 1995 season with the team, but he had to endure some deep personal shots on the way. Despite his being seventh on the all-time stolen-base list, the Royals made him play two weeks in the minor leagues.[57] In August, Kansas City surprised both Coleman and his teammates by placing him on waivers. "That was very hard to digest," said Coleman of his release from the team. "That's the worst feeling I've ever had in 13 years."[58] With ten days to trade, release, or send him to the minors, the Royals took an offer from Seattle and shipped him to the Pacific Northwest.

For the Mariners, it was a much-needed and much-heralded move. They had tried different leadoff hitters without success all year long. Now, with the wild-card race heating up, they had someone in Coleman who could ignite the top of the order. "[Vince] is an excellent get-on-base guy with experience," said Lou Piniella at the time of the trade. "When you have a chance to get a player who has been through these types of wars, you take your shot. And that's what we have done."[59]

Coleman's impact was felt immediately. The Mariners went 26–14 after he joined the team, as he provided the spark at the top of the lineup the team needed. Almost as important as the Mariners' success was Coleman's ability to redeem himself for the mistakes of 1993. Although he did not need to prove anything to himself, he was out to show that he was not just a good ballplayer but a good human being too. It worked, as his teammates and Seattle fans showed nothing but acceptance. His teammates loved him for what he brought to the lineup and the way he affected opposing teams once on base. "He just makes their [the other team's] defense and pitcher work harder," said Griffey after Coleman's first day with the team. "I've never seen so many first pitch fastballs," Griffey added, referring to how Coleman's speed forced pitchers to throw more fastballs to hitters like himself and Edgar Martinez.[60]

Fans especially loved Coleman for the hustle he brought to the field. A sign in the Kingdome read: "Who is this man? ~~Shaft~~ Vince Coleman!" In just a month and a half, Coleman had won the support of his teammates and fans, and he received a generous ovation as he led off the sixth inning of Game 3. He had had a tough time against McDowell up until that point, striking out in the first inning and hitting a routine ground ball to first base in the fourth. This time up, Coleman hit nearly the same type of ground ball, only he managed to pull it a few more feet toward the line. The ball just escaped the reach of a diving Mattingly and shot down the right-field line, skidding across the turf and bouncing into the corner. Gerald Williams fielded it, but by that time, Coleman was already rounding second base. He made it to third with a headfirst slide, bringing yet another round of thunderous applause from the crowd. "The stolen base is my favorite play," said Coleman, "but the triple ranks second. Sometimes it rattles a pitcher, even a veteran like Jack [McDowell]."[61]

Joey Cora followed Coleman's triple with a walk, putting runners on the corners with no outs for Ken Griffey Jr. With the count full at 3–2, McDowell relieved some of the tension emanating from the Kingdome by faking a throw toward third base but then quickly turning and firing to first. The "fake to third, go to first" move is done by pitchers hoping to catch the runner on first not paying attention. McDowell had actually done it successfully twice during the regular season, but nearly every time a pitcher attempted it, it didn't work. In fact, it was generally such a fruitless move that any pitcher who attempted it on the road was guaranteed to get booed by the home crowd. Mariner fans did not disappoint, booing McDowell loudly when his attempt failed on Cora. Making it worse for McDowell, Cora stole second base easily on the next pitch as Junior struck out swinging.

The strikeout of Griffey was huge for McDowell, and Cora's steal of second, while putting another runner in scoring position, did leave an open base at first. This allowed McDowell to pitch around Edgar Martinez, throwing three straight pitches out of the strike zone. With the count at 3–0 and a base open, Buck Showalter began screaming over the crowd for catcher Mike Stanley's attention. He flashed four fingers, meaning McDowell was to intentionally walk Martinez with his next pitch. Showalter wanted to avoid any chance of Martinez swinging away at a 3–0 fastball down the middle of the plate. McDowell and Stanley complied, setting up the bases loaded with one out for Tino Martinez.

McDowell's intentional ball four was his last pitch of the night, as Showalter was not going to allow him to pitch to this Martinez. Tino had already touched McDowell for a single and a two-run home run. He was only a .083 career hitter against Steve Howe, who was warming up in the bullpen.[62] After Edgar reached first, Showalter went to the mound and signaled for Howe to come into the game. McDowell was not pleased. "I thought I'd get to go after Tino," he said, "but I know I created the jam, and that's probably why I didn't stay in there."[63] McDowell had seen the way Johnson was pitching and knew, like everyone else, that he did not have his best stuff. He felt the Yankees were on the brink of breaking through, and if he could just stay in the game, McDowell could limit the damage to one run and keep it close enough for the Yankees to complete the comeback he felt was inevitable.[64] Showalter did not have the same feeling, and so Steve Howe came into Game 3, his first appearance of the series.

Most hitters might be insulted when a team intentionally walks someone to get to them, but Tino knew the other Martinez was the stronger hitter. "Walking Edgar to get to me is something teams have been doing all season," said Tino. "You have to walk him. He's the best hitter in the league. That's common sense."[65] While he did not mind the intentional walk, he wasn't that crazy about the pitching change, admitting that Howe was "one of the toughest lefties I've ever faced."[66]

Howe's appearance must have tied a record for the shortest performance in postseason history. Martinez, with just one career hit against Howe, swung at a first-pitch fastball, driving it the other way for a single to left field. He hit the ball so hard that Cora had to hold at third, and only one run scored. Coleman had barely dented home plate before Showalter emerged from the Yankees' dugout to remove Howe after just one pitch. With the bases still loaded and Jay Buhner coming up, Showalter signaled for Bob Wickman, hoping the right-hander's sinker could induce Buhner to hit into an inning-ending double play.

Wickman used the sinker on his first pitch to Buhner, but instead of a double play, the ball was lined into right field for a single. Like Tino's single, the ball was hit too hard for the runner from second to score, so the bases remained loaded for Mike Blowers. Falling behind in the count, Wickman threw a sinker that Blowers grounded to third. For a moment, it looked as though Yankees had gotten what they needed, but Russ Davis bobbled the grounder and then threw the ball wide of first base, drawing Mattingly off the bag. Everyone was safe and another run scored. It was 5–1 Mariners, and the wheels were falling off for the Yankees.

Luis Sojo drove in another run on a sacrifice fly, making it 6–1. Wickman struck out Dan Wilson to mercifully end the inning, but the damage was done. Jump-started by Coleman's triple, the Mariners scored four runs in a span of just six pitches and had seemingly broken the game open.

• • • • • • • • •

Randy Johnson finally had some breathing room, so when he walked Gerald Williams to start off the top of the seventh inning, there was no need for the Mariners to panic. Johnson managed to strike out Davis, who, upset over his performance, walked back to the dugout and slammed his helmet into the bat rack. A piece of wood splintered off the rack and cut him near his wrist. He would need seven stitches to close the wound.[67] Johnson then gave up a single to Fernandez, sending Williams to third. Kelly drove in Williams with a sacrifice fly, but Velarde struck out looking on a slider, ending any threat of a Yankee comeback. Despite not having his best fastball, Johnson still held the Yankees to four hits, and he struck out ten batters through seven innings.

Jump-started yet again by Coleman, the Mariners added another run in the bottom of the seventh inning. Hitting against the Yankees' new pitcher, left-hander Sterling Hitchcock, Coleman singled to center field and moved to second on Cora's sacrifice bunt. Next, Griffey walked on four pitches. He and Coleman then executed a double steal, putting two runners in scoring position with one out for Edgar Martinez. As had happened in the sixth inning, the open base allowed the Yankees to walk Martinez and set up lefty against lefty with Tino Martinez.

Tino, already 3–3 with three RBIs, lifted a fly ball into shallow left field. Coleman, the runner on third, went back to the bag as if he were going to tag up and run home, but he faked going home, instead halting a few feet down the line from third base. Left fielder Randy Velarde initially just saw Coleman head home and did not realize that Coleman was in fact merely faking his tag up. Velarde unleashed a throw to home plate that sailed over catcher Mike Stanley's head. "Once it came out of my hand, I could tell by the fan reaction," recalled Velarde. "The only thing that would have brought [the throw] down is if I'd been on the warning track."[68] Coleman, who originally had no intention of trying to score, easily made his way home, and it was now 7–2 Mariners. Seattle had their five-run lead back, and Hitchcock's night was over. Mariano Rivera, the star pitcher of Game 2, came in and retired Jay Buhner for the inning's last out.

Staked to a five-run lead late in the game, Lou Piniella decided it was safe to remove Johnson. Piniella felt no need for Johnson, pitching on three days' rest for the second consecutive start, to expend any more energy on his pitching arm. There was also another reason to remove him. It would leave open the possibility, however remote it may have seemed at the time, that Johnson would be available to pitch if the series came to a Game 5. To get to that point, however, the Mariners would first have to nail down what seemed like a certain victory in Game 3. Wishing to give closer Norm Charlton a rest, Piniella called on Bill Risley to pitch in the eighth inning. The first Yankee to face Risley in the eighth inning was Bernie Williams, the only Yankee hitter that Johnson had failed to retire at least once during Game 3. Williams's performance that night should not have come as a surprise to anyone, because the Yankees' center fielder was a rising star.

· · · · · · · · ·

Bernie Williams had been a highly touted prospect in the Yankees' minor-league system for years. The Yankees first noticed him as a sixteen-year-old kid playing in the Mickey Mantle League in Puerto Rico. A skinny outfielder, who at the time only hit from the right side, Williams was signed by the Yankees in 1985.[69] Although his skills did not blow people away at first, scouts in the Yankee organization could see great potential in him. He remained in the minors for nearly half a decade before finally making the big-league club in 1991.

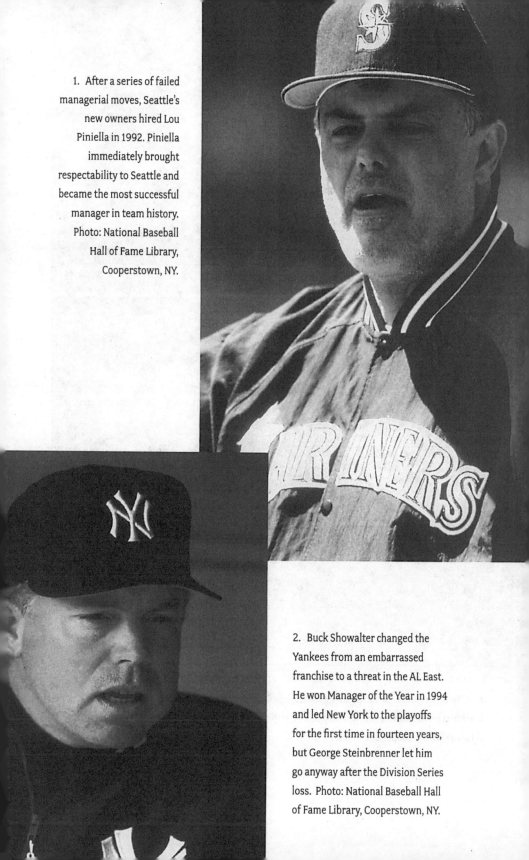

1. After a series of failed managerial moves, Seattle's new owners hired Lou Piniella in 1992. Piniella immediately brought respectability to Seattle and became the most successful manager in team history. Photo: National Baseball Hall of Fame Library, Cooperstown, NY.

2. Buck Showalter changed the Yankees from an embarrassed franchise to a threat in the AL East. He won Manager of the Year in 1994 and led New York to the playoffs for the first time in fourteen years, but George Steinbrenner let him go anyway after the Division Series loss. Photo: National Baseball Hall of Fame Library, Cooperstown, NY.

3. With his bright smile and amazing ability, Ken Griffey Jr. was the face of the Mariners for a decade. In his first postseason series, he tied a record by hitting five home runs. Photo: National Baseball Hall of Fame Library, Cooperstown, NY.

4. After thirteen years, Don Mattingly finally made the postseason in 1995. Beloved by fans, teammates, and opponents, Mattingly struggled throughout much of 1995, but the Captain hit .417 with 6 RBIs in his only postseason appearance. Photo: National Baseball Hall of Fame Library, Cooperstown, NY.

5. Armed with a blazing fastball and devastating slider, Randy Johnson dominated baseball in 1995, winning the AL Cy Young award. In one week, Johnson won Seattle's one-game playoff against the Angels and two games against the Yankees in the series. Photo: National Baseball Hall of Fame Library, Cooperstown, NY.

6. Despite a bad hamstring, Wade Boggs was the hero of Game 1, collecting three hits, including a two-run home run, and making a diving catch that saved a run. Photo: National Baseball Hall of Fame Library, Cooperstown, NY.

7. Jim Leyritz, "The King," talked a big game, and usually backed it up. His two-run game-winning home run in the rain during the fifteenth inning of Game 2 began a string of clutch postseason hits that would last years. Photo: National Baseball Hall of Fame Library, Cooperstown, NY.

8. The game's least-known superstar, Edgar Martinez, killed the Yankees throughout 1995. The assault continued into the Division Series, where his grand slam in the eighth inning of Game 4 broke a 6–6 tie. It was the biggest home run in Mariners' history. Photo: National Baseball Hall of Fame Library, Cooperstown, NY.

9. Randy Velarde's eleventh-inning single in Game 5 scored Pat Kelly with the go-ahead run. The base hit silenced a stunned Kingdome as the Yankees appeared to be on their way to the American League Championship Series. It was not to be. Photo: Ben VanHouten.

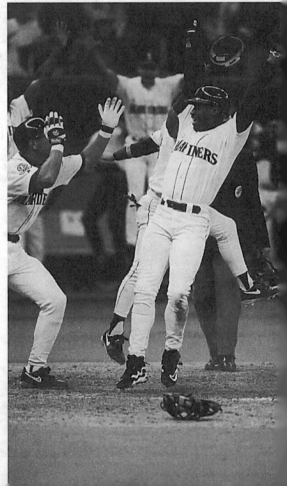

10. An ecstatic Ken Griffey Jr. is greeted by Alex Rodriguez after the scoring the series-winning run on Edgar Martinez's two-run, eleventh-inning double in Game 5. Martinez's hit, forever known as "The Double," was the biggest in Mariners' history and incited a euphoric celebration that lasted into the next day. Griffey's slide into home plate with the winning run became the signature moment of Seattle baseball, and helped create Safeco Field. Photo: Ben VanHouten.

Williams's early years with the Yankees were not easy. At the time, the team was playing poorly, and the atmosphere in the dugout was not conducive to mentoring a rookie. His presence on the roster meant reduced playing time for certain Yankee players, and those players did not react kindly to the new, skinny kid who wore big-rimmed glasses. Williams endured merciless taunting from the Yankees' senior outfielders, particularly Mel Hall, who one day drove the rookie to tears.[70] Attempting to show that Williams meant nothing to the team, Hall took to referring to him as "Mr. Zero."[71] Williams, quiet and shy, was mild mannered by nature, often visible in the clubhouse playing guitar, perhaps his favorite activity, even above baseball. It simply was not in his style to fight back. That did not mean, however, that he was weak or lacked a competitive drive. Much like Tino Martinez, once Williams got onto the field, he could be as intense as anyone. While not the showboat that Sierra was, he did not have a problem displaying emotion after a big hit or play in the field. He persevered through those early years, and Gene Michael had such faith in the outfielder that he called Williams up during the 1992 season to be the team's center fielder, actually pushing Roberto Kelly, the team's lone representative to the All-Star Game that year, from center field to left field. By 1993, Kelly, Hall, and Jesse Barfield, the Yankees' regular outfielders from 1990 to 1992, were all gone, eliminating Williams's biggest tormentors from the scene. Williams emerged from spring training in 1993 as the Yankees' everyday center fielder, perhaps the most cherished and sacred position in all of sports.

After earning that slot, Williams broke out statistically. While his offensive numbers did not progress as fast as George Steinbrenner may have liked,[72] his production increased every year from 1993 to 1995. He was a major part of the 1993 team that made a surprising run for first place, contributing big hits and making numerous sliding and home-run saving catches in the field. He drew the attention of other teams in baseball, including the Montreal Expos, who offered their star outfielder Larry Walker in exchange for Williams in 1994. Gene Michael, despite Steinbrenner's insistence, turned down the offer.[73]

Having filled out physically, finally becoming a power threat capable of driving in runs, Williams had a career turning point in 1995. Like many Yankees, he got off to an incredibly slow start to the season. Steinbrenner demanded that Gene Michael trade Williams for another center fielder after he hit just .198 through the Yankees' first thirty-one games. Michael refused.[74] It was fortunate for the Yankees. After the All-Star break, Williams hit .348. When Luis Polonia was designated for assignment on August 4, Boggs and Williams officially became the team's one–two hitters. They were the most potent leadoff tandem in the Major Leagues from that point on, becoming a driving force at the beginning of the lineup. Williams posted then–career highs in home runs and RBIs. Although he had poor base-stealing instincts, he possessed great speed, which benefited him as he tracked down fly balls hit into the spacious power alleys of Yankee Stadium. His performance gained him recognition throughout the league, and he emerged as a fan favorite in the Bronx.

Williams's hot bat continued into the postseason. He had homered off Randy Johnson from the right side of the plate in the fourth inning. Now, he stepped in against Risley from the left side of the plate and drilled the second pitch he saw deep into the right-field stands and into baseball history. "I went 1–0 on Williams, so I figured he'd take a strike," said Risley. "He took it all right and deposited it into the seats."[75]

Just as had happened in the fourth inning, the fan who caught Bernie's second home run decided to throw the ball back onto the field. It was an unfortunate decision, because the home run marked the first time in postseason history a player had hit a home run from both sides of the plate in the same game. Mickey Mantle, Eddie Murray, Chili Davis were all power-hitting switch hitters with postseason experience, yet all had failed to accomplish what Bernie Williams had just done. Most likely the fan who threw the ball back had no idea the piece of history he or she was relinquishing (or did not care) but the ball was historic, and even in the days before eBay, that souvenir probably could have netted a considerable amount of money.

Williams's home run, though historic, seemed insignificant in its impact on Game 3 because the Mariners still had a 7–3 lead. That changed instantly when Risley's first pitch after Williams's home run was driven deep into the right-field stands by Mike Stanley. Two pitches, two home runs, and suddenly what looked like a laugher for Seattle was turning into a potential nail biter.

Risley fought back to retire Sierra, bringing Don Mattingly to the plate. During the pregame introduction ceremonies, Mariners fans had actually been courteous to the Yankee captain, applauding him as he was introduced. Now, with three strikeouts in three at-bats, the hospitality toward Mattingly ceased. Suddenly, a murmur began to grow in the crowd. The chanting started off small at first, beginning in one section of the Kingdome, but it then spread quickly and began to echo from turf to roof before it became abundantly clear what the fans were saying: "DON-NIE STRIKE-OUT! DON-NIE STRIKE-OUT!" It was a new, creative twist to the adoring chant of "Don-nie Base-ball" that Yankee fans had developed and lavished upon their captain for years. As Mattingly stepped in, the chant began picking up momentum across the Kingdome. Trying to avoid striking out for the fourth time in the game, which would have been a career first, he fouled off five pitches before finally flying out to deep left-center field. The flyout was the tiniest of victories for Mattingly. Although he had not reached base, Mariners fans appeared disappointed that he had not struck out again. But they would store away the memory of his earlier three strikeouts and the "Don-nie Strike-out" chant would continue at various intervals throughout the rest of the series.

After Mattingly's flyout, Showalter decided to play strategy, pinch-hitting for Gerald Williams with Paul O'Neill. It was more than just the offensive move of putting in a better hitter. The switch forced Piniella, much to his unhappiness, to bring in Norm Charlton. Piniella wanted to give Charlton some rest, but now, with the game in a save situation and the lefty O'Neill capable of reducing Seattle's lead to just two runs, Piniella had to go for the lefty-lefty matchup.

Unfortunately for those watching the game at home, they never saw what happened next. The Baseball Network began using a double screen during the end of Don Mattingly's eighth inning at-bat in order to show the ninth inning of Game 3 of the Rockies–Braves series. Once Mattingly flied out and Piniella made the pitching change, ABC completely left Seattle to show the action in Atlanta exclusively. While the ninth inning in Atlanta was exciting, those with a vested interest in what was occurring under the Kingdome roof were outraged. Charlton wound up striking out O'Neill, but the only people who saw it were those in attendance in Seattle that night.

• • • • • • • • •

Mariano Rivera continued to dominate the Seattle lineup, blowing through them in the eighth inning on just ten pitches and keeping it a three-run game. Rivera's performance proved irrelevant, though. Charlton had his best stuff working, and the Yankees quickly went down in order in the top of the ninth inning, barely able to touch Charlton's fastball or forkball. When Pat Kelly struck out to end the game, the crowd let loose with a sound equal to, if not greater than anything ever heard in the Kingdome to that point.

• • • • • • • • •

Despite the mental mistakes and missed opportunities, the Yankees' clubhouse maintained a relative calm after the game. "Look at the attitude around the clubhouse," said Randy Velarde at the time. "We still feel confident we can win one of three."[76] Showalter had nothing but praise for the opposing team's tall left-handed starter. "Even when [Johnson's] not on top of his game, he's still better than the majority," he conceded, referring to Johnson's struggles to find the plate at various parts of the game.[77]

In the other clubhouse, the Mariners were basking in the performance of their starting pitcher. "He really wore Donnie down tonight," said Piniella, referring to Johnson's three strikeouts of the Yankees first baseman.[78] Charlton also heaped praise upon Johnson. "We had to have this win tonight, and Randy didn't have his best stuff early and [he] still ended up striking out 10," said Charlton. "He comes on real strong late and wins the ballgame for us."[79] "We've been riding [Johnson's] shoulders so long, man, I hope he can pitch tomorrow," joked Coleman.[80] "I didn't have my good stuff today," said Johnson, "[but] this shows that I can pitch without it. I kept them off balance, and that's the biggest thing you have do against a team like the Yankees."[81]

It was an enormous victory for the Mariners, as they had fended off elimination and lived to see another day. In the process they used their best pitcher and may have gotten a little lucky. "I was obviously physically and mentally drained," said Johnson. "I was mostly pitching on adrenaline and the importance of the game."[82] Johnson's performance had been great, but the Mariners were still looking uphill, and it would take yet another series of comebacks and miracles to get them past Game 4.

9

Game 4: Saint Edgar

"Nobody in the United States had any idea how good Edgar Martinez is. . . . If he played in New York, he'd be a household name." —Norm Charlton, after Game 4 of the Division Series

Despite the euphoria in Seattle on the morning of October 7, the fact remained that the Mariners were on the brink of elimination heading into Game 4. The odds once again were stacked against them, at least on paper. Chris Bosio would take the mound on only three days' rest. Bosio had pitched respectably in Game 1, but it did not change the fact that nearly every player in the Yankees' lineup had better-than-average career numbers against him. Moreover, Lou Piniella admitted he could hope for Bosio to go no more than six innings.[1] Piniella was going to have to go to his bullpen earlier than he would like to. Worse yet, the Mariners' bullpen had already pitched 13 2/3 innings in the series and given up eleven runs. Even with the day off between Games 2 and 3, the bullpen had been used excessively (out of necessity). Not leaving New York until three in the morning after Game 2 was yet another cruel twist of fate in a long line of problems that put Piniella in a tough situation. Using Randy Johnson in the playoff game against the Angels, thereby ensuring that the Big Unit could only start one game in the Division Series, was the first issue. To make matters worse, Piniella had to use

Tim Belcher in extra innings for Game 2, thus depriving the team of its only other bona fide starter to pitch either Game 3 or 4. Then, in Game 3, Piniella had to use Norm Charlton again, preventing the lefty from getting a much-needed extra day off after throwing four innings in Game 2. The fact that Piniella had to use Charlton to save Game 3 after having a five-run lead going into the eighth inning also goaded the Seattle manager.

While the Mariners' own pitching was stretched to the limits, the Yankees were able to throw the well-rested Scott Kamieniecki. If any pitcher on the Yankees' staff could have challenged Jack McDowell for the title of Mariner killer, it was thirty-one-year-old Kamieniecki. He had overwhelmed the Seattle hitters at both Yankee Stadium and the Kingdome. In fact, he was responsible for the Yankees' only regular-season win in Seattle that year.[2] The Game 4 start meant a lot to the Yankee pitcher, as he had come a long way to get to the postseason.

• • • • • • • • •

Scott Kamieniecki grew up in Flint, Michigan, and twice passed up a chance to play baseball after graduating high school. In 1982, he was drafted by his hometown team, the Detroit Tigers, but he opted instead to go to college. Two years later, the Milwaukee Brewers drafted him during his junior year at the University of Michigan, but Kamieniecki again passed up the opportunity, instead completing his degree in physical education.[3] After graduating, he was drafted by the Yankees in 1986 and spent nearly half a decade lingering in the minors. In 1991, the Yankees pitching staff's subpar performance forced Gene Michael to bring up several minor-league pitchers to fill out the rotation, namely Wade Taylor, Jeff Johnson, and Scott Kamieniecki. Of the three, Kamieniecki was the only one to enjoy any type of success for an extended period of time in the Major Leagues, as both Taylor and Johnson were out of baseball by 1994.

Kamieniecki made his debut on June 19, 1991, against the eventual American League East division champion Blue Jays and picked up the win. In his next start, he beat the eventual world champion Twins. His performance was impressive enough that he made the starting rotation in 1992. The offensively challenged Yankees failed to provide adequate run support during many of his starts that year, and Kamieniecki finished 6–14, pitching better than his record indicated.

As the Yankees began to improve after the 1992 season, so too did Kamieniecki, and he became a stable force in the team's rotation. Though he didn't possess dominating stuff, Kamieniecki was able to utilize his talents to the best of his ability. His fastball was not overpowering and he had an average curve, but Kamieniecki picked at corners and tried to establish the inner half of the plate as his own property. In 1995, he was to be the team's number-four starter, but just two weeks into the season, he sprained his elbow attempting to throw a curve to the Milwaukee Brewers' Greg Vaughn.[4] Kamieniecki missed nearly two months of the season before finally rejoining the team at a time when they desperately needed pitching. He performed solidly down the stretch drive and with the Yankees unable to afford a loss, Kamieniecki pitched his only complete game of the season on the second-to-last day of the year in Toronto, winning the game 6–1.

In the Division Series, Showalter held off on using Kamieniecki until Game 4. Some questioned whether it would have made more sense though to use him in Game 3. In their view, the Yankees were not going to beat Randy Johnson, especially in the Kingdome, so why waste Jack McDowell in what would most likely be a losing effort no matter how well he pitched. There was some merit to the idea, but Buck Showalter did not agree. "I don't buy the theory that you take the pitcher you perceive as having the best opportunity to win and push him back," said Showalter.[5] The Yankees' manager had looked for the kill in Game 3, holding out hope that McDowell could keep the Yankees in the game long enough to eventually wear out Johnson and get the lead late in the game. Don Mattingly agreed. "We came to beat Johnson," said Mattingly. "That's why you throw Jack [in Game 3]."[6] It did not work as planned, and now Showalter was asking Kamieniecki to advance the Yankees to the ALCS.

• • • • • • • • •

As they had the previous night, Mariners fans filled the Kingdome with an exorbitant amount of sound and energy for Game 4. Even before the game's first pitch, they stood on their feet, cheering as loudly as they had the night before. It was a fantastic display of energy that continued to dispel the myth that Seattle was not a baseball town. The Kingdome again was littered with banners and signs. They ranged from the popular manufactured "Refuse to Lose" signs to homemade ones that declared "BRING ON CLEVELAND" and "THIS IS WHAT IT'S ALL ABOUT MAN." Another sign played off the popular "I Love New York" signs, but, in this case, the heart had a diagonal line through it.[7] Thirteen-year-old Keith Whigham, a Make-a-Wish youth, threw out the ceremonial first pitch, with Ken Griffey Jr. receiving the throw.[8]

As the fans prepared themselves for Game 4, Randy Johnson sat in storage on the Mariners' bench, so Buck Showalter penciled in his normal lineup. That meant Wade Boggs, who had homered off Chris Bosio in Game 1, stepped into the batter's box to lead off Game 4.

Despite the Kingdome's reputation as a hitter's park, Bosio had performed well there during his career, mostly due to his sinker-ball. Other than that, he had little in his favor as he stepped onto the mound to begin Game 4. He was working off of three days' rest and faced a lineup full of hitters who had faired well against him throughout his career. Bosio stared in at Dan Wilson and fired a first-pitch fastball. Home-plate umpire Rocky Roe, who looked more like an NFL linebacker than like a Major League umpire, shouted his trademark "STRRRRRIIIIIIKE!" Roe was known for his boisterous strike calls because they were always audible through out the ballpark. But, tonight, even Roe's exceptionally loud strike call was drowned out by the Kingdome crowd. The noise continued even after Bosio threw his next pitch for a ball. The crowd went quiet, though, when Boggs lined a 1–1 sinker into the right-center-field gap for an easy double. Bosio had now failed to retire the side in order in the first inning for the seventeenth time in his last eighteen starts.[9]

Bernie Williams followed Boggs's double by ripping an 0–1 fastball into right field for a single. Williams hit the ball so hard that Boggs, still nursing the tight hamstring, had to hold at third base. Already stuck in a precarious situation, Bosio made matters worse by walking Paul O'Neill, thus loading the bases with no outs. In a matter of five minutes, the Yankees had silenced the boisterous Kingdome crowd and were on the verge of an explosive first inning.

Facing Ruben Sierra, Bosio caught a minor break. Sierra, overly anxious after jumping ahead in the count, swung at an outside fastball and lifted a high pop-up in foul territory off third base. The ball began drifting farther away from Mike Blowers, but the third baseman kept his eye on it. Sprinting full out, Blowers was able to track down the pop-up and make an over-the-shoulder catch, à la Willie Mays, in deep foul territory, halfway between the foul line and the stands. Though Blowers caught the ball, it was still deep enough down the line that Wade Boggs tagged up from third base and headed home. Blowers, after making the catch, immediately spun and launched a throw toward home plate. Boggs, one of the slowest runners on the Yankees, with or without the bad hamstring, came charging down the third base line, shoulders up and arms pumping in his signature running style. The ball and Boggs arrived at home at the same time, but Boggs snuck his leg underneath catcher Dan Wilson, touching home plate before Wilson could apply the tag. Rocky Roe emphatically signaled safe, and a loud roar of disapproval arose from the Kingdome. Bosio and Wilson both screamed in anger, disputing the call, while Boggs shot up and screamed in excitement at having scored the game's first run. The Mariners' argument lasted mere seconds as both Bosio and Wilson conceded that Boggs had been safe.

Overlooked in all the arguing, both Williams and O'Neill had tagged up and each advanced one base on Blowers's throw. This meant that Don Mattingly came to the plate with two runners in scoring position and only one out. Coming off what might have been the worst offensive performance of his career, Mattingly had shown up early to the Kingdome that day to get in extra batting practice before any of the other players arrived at the stadium.[10] No amount of extra hitting, however, was going to erase in the minds of Mariner fans what had happened the night before. The chants of "DON-NIE STRIKE-OUT" began as soon as Tom Hutyler announced Mattingly's name. It grew even louder when, after a first-pitch ball, Mattingly took a Bosio fastball down the middle for a called strike. The chanting, however, was silenced when Mattingly drove a ground ball up the middle just off the tip of second baseman Joey Cora's glove and into center field for a single. Williams and O'Neill both scored and the Yankees jumped out to a 3–0 lead. As Williams and O'Neill were greeted by high-fiving teammates, a hush fell over the Kingdome crowd. It was the quietest the stadium had been in weeks.

With only one out in the first, Piniella already had Jeff Nelson and Bobby Ayala warming up in the bullpen. It was his worst nightmare come true: down 3–0 to a known Mariners killer and possibly having to go to a tired bullpen as early as the first inning. Bosio eased some of the tension by retiring Dion James and Mike Stanley, but with three runs in, the damage was done. The Yankees hoped it would be enough for Scott Kamieniecki.

• • • • • • • • •

Scott Kamieniecki was a notoriously bad first-inning pitcher. He brought with him into Game 4 a 5.08 career first-inning ERA.[11] There was no rhyme or reason to it. He just couldn't get through that inning without encountering some sort of difficulty. But Kamieniecki couldn't afford to let those first-inning jitters affect his performance. His offense had provided him with three runs, and the last thing he needed to do was to give it all back or allow the Mariners even a run or two to swing the momentum in their favor. For Kamieniecki, success was a matter of throwing strikes. It sounded simple, but throwing strikes was sometimes quite difficult for him. In fact, only two pitchers in the American League had walked more hitters per nine innings that year than Kamieniecki.[12] After Vince Coleman grounded out to second base, Kamieniecki came in high and tight to Joey Cora on a fastball. The pitch took Cora by surprise, nearly grazing him in the head, and he immediately dropped to the ground and lay flat on his back. A huge roar of disapproval immediately showered Kamieniecki. To the fans, there was no doubt about what had just occurred. But the count was 2–2 and with a three-run lead, it was doubtful that Kamieniecki had been attempting to hit Cora. The pitch itself had actually gone over the plate, though too high to be a strike. The closeness of the pitch had more to do with Cora's batting stance, because he leaned over the inner half of the plate.

Even so, Lou Piniella, sitting on the Mariners' bench, immediately shot up and rushed toward Wilson and Bosio. "You gonna let that motherfucker do that to our guy?" yelled Piniella as he pointed toward the mound.[13] He then turned toward the Yankees' dugout. "You're going down and when you do, remember, I ordered it!"[14] Piniella was hopping mad. To him, Kamieniecki had made a career of coming in tight to hitters, especially those on the Mariners. Piniella refused to be intimidated, and he demanded that a warning be issued to the Yankees pitcher. This was more than just the move of an angry manager, though. Always the showman, Piniella didn't just want to incite his players. He also wanted to take away the inner half of the plate from Kamieniecki. If the umpires would issue a warning, then Kamieniecki would have to avoid that inner half or risk being ejected from the game. Without being able to pick at that part of the plate, Kamieniecki would be vulnerable, and Piniella wanted exploit that. After the inning was over, Piniella approached the umpiring crew.

Buck Showalter was well aware of Piniella's mind games and felt he was completely overblowing the situation. After Piniella was allowed to have his say, Showalter then got in his two cents. The whole situation was ridiculous, he told them. "There is no way Kamie is throwing at this guy," Showalter informed them. The umpiring crew did not concur and warnings were issued to both Kamieniecki and Bosio.[15]

Play resumed and Kamieniecki walked Cora on the next pitch. The crowd, silenced by Mattingly's single but now awakened by the close pitch to Cora, became fully reimmersed as Ken Griffey Jr. came to the plate. Griffey, however, had little success against Kamieniecki in his career, going only 4–24 with no home runs.[16] Though not totally undisciplined at the plate, Griffey was not above chasing pitches outside the strike zone, and Kamieniecki had used this to his advantage throughout their encounters. He did it again in the first inning, when he jumped ahead in the count, 1–2, and then got Griffey to swing and miss at an inside curve ball. The strikeout of Griffey was big, made even bigger when Kamieniecki walked Edgar Martinez, bringing up Game 3 hero Tino Martinez as the potential tying run. But Tino grounded out to shortstop, ending the threat. Kamieniecki survived a shaky first inning unscathed.

· · · · · · · · ·

Bosio made it through the second inning with little trouble, erasing a walk to Velarde when Boggs hit into an inning-ending double play. Kamieniecki again worked himself into trouble in the bottom of the second inning only to escape. He retired Jay Buhner to start the inning, but Mike Blowers then sent a long drive to deep right field. Paul O'Neill went back gingerly, knowing that with each step he was getting closer and closer to the short right-field wall. He also knew that if he misjudged the fly ball and it bounced off the twenty-three-foot fence, it could roll forever and Blowers would have a triple or possibly an inside-the-park home run. With one step left before reaching the fence, O'Neill leapt and made a one-handed catch as he smashed his back into the wall. O'Neill's play was fortunate for Kamieniecki, because Luis Sojo and Dan Wilson each singled following the catch. Forced to pitch with two runners on and two outs for a second consecutive inning, Kamieniecki again got out of it, getting Coleman to ground out to end the inning. Kamieniecki had escaped two jams, but the Mariners' offense was simply too good to continually get runners on base and not score. If he kept putting runners on, eventually he was going to pay a price for it.

· · · · · · · · · ·

The Yankees were well aware of the Mariners' offensive capabilities and knew that a three-run lead was probably not enough. The King-dome was a hitter's park, the Mariners were an offensive juggernaut, and Kamieniecki looked shaky through two innings. They needed to deliver a knockout punch to Chris Bosio, whom they had on the ropes in the first two innings. Another rally would put Bosio out of the game and force Piniella to go to an already tired and mostly ineffective bullpen. With that in mind, Bernie Williams led off the top of the third inning with a walk, and O'Neill looked to be the one to deliver the KO.

Like many lefties, O'Neill was a great low-ball hitter, making Bosio's sinking fastball an especially appetizing pitch. As he stepped to the plate in the third inning, he boasted a career .600 batting average against the Seattle pitcher, having gotten hits off Bosio in six of ten at-bats.[17] Down by three runs, Bosio attempted to keep the ball away from the hitter, but in the fourth pitch of the at-bat, he left a fastball over the plate and O'Neill crushed it, sending the ball deep into the right-field stands. O'Neill dropped his bat and began trotting toward first base, but not before sneaking a peak at the mound. "He looked at me right after he hit it with a look like 'I got you fucker,'" said Bosio.[18] O'Neill's second home run of the series deadened the crowd. The silence was broken when the home run ball came hurtling back to the field. It was a minor victory, and the applause for the fan's action was less enthusiastic than what had occurred the previous night because the gravity of the situation sunk in. Seattle was now down by five runs. Yes, they had made an entire season out of coming from behind and beating the odds, and yes, "Refuse to Lose" was the team's mantra, but at some point, people had to wonder if it could really go on forever. Whether they would later admit it or not, most Mariners fans and players had to wonder whether another comeback was possible.

Chris Bosio would not be involved in any such comeback. "I couldn't get the ball down, and I couldn't finish, and Lou knew it," said Bosio.[19] By the time O'Neill crossed home plate, Piniella was making his way to the mound for a pitching change. "You gave me everything you had," he told his pitcher.[20] Disappointed, Bosio walked off the mound and headed toward the dugout, hoping this would not be his last memory of the 1995 season.

Jeff Nelson entered the game with a simple mission: "Just hold them there," Nelson thought to himself. "Just give them [Mariner hitters] a chance to come back."[21] Not having pitched in Game 3, Nelson had gotten a much-needed two-day break. He allowed a one-out double to Mattingly but escaped the inning without any further damage.

Ideally, any team facing a large deficit attempts to come back gradually. Score one or two runs an inning, hope your pitching can prevent the other team from extending its lead, and eventually you win the game. Down 5–0 in the bottom of the third, the Mariners attempted this approach, and who was better to start it off than the American League batting champion?

· · · · · · · · · ·

"He's the best hitter in the league," said Lou Piniella, referring to Edgar Martinez. "He's a professional at the plate. He has no particular weakness."[22]

"He's just Edgar," said Ken Griffey Jr., "I just get on base and run. He's been over .350 all year. In fact, we get upset when he's under .350."[23]

"I haven't seen anybody throw past Edgar," said Norm Charlton. "His hands are too quick."[24]

"By far Edgar is the best right-handed hitter I have ever played with," said Tim Belcher.[25]

"Edgar is one of the greatest hitters in the game," said Buck Showalter. "The only way to pitch him is to try and keep the ball in the yard and hope that he lines out somewhere."[26]

Teammates, opposing players, and opposing managers could not say enough about the hitting abilities of Edgar Martinez. Martinez's swing was simple and compact. He held the bat at a forty-five-degree angle slightly elevated above and to the right of his head and used a small leg kick to generate power. When stepping to the plate, Martinez placed his back foot, the right foot, on the very edge of the batter's box, sometimes almost out of it entirely. This gave him the maximum amount of time possible to determine the type of pitch he was about to receive.

Part of Martinez's skill as a hitter was his amazing ability to decipher one pitch from another. It was an exceptional gift that separated him from other Major League hitters. Wade Boggs, himself a five-time batting champion, marveled at Edgar's ability to distinguish between pitches.[27]

In addition to his pitch-deciphering ability, Martinez seemed to have a sixth sense at the plate. "Edgar would come up to you before an at-bat and say 'This guy is gonna throw the ball here, and I'm gonna hit the ball here,'" recalled Norm Charlton. "Then he'd get up to the plate, the pitcher would throw him exactly what he said he would, and Edgar would hit it exactly where he said he would."[28]

His unique abilities had turned Martinez into the game's greatest all-around hitter by 1995. Unfortunately for Edgar, few outside the Seattle area knew it. Until the Division Series, Martinez had been playing in relative obscurity in the Pacific Northwest, where he had spent his whole career. He was drafted by the Mariners in 1982 and spent several years in the minor leagues being groomed as the team's new third baseman. Unfortunately for Martinez, at the time the Mariners had an extremely productive third baseman in Jim Pressley. Edgar made brief appearances with the team in 1987, 1988, and 1989. By the end of the 1989 season, Pressley's playing time had been cut and his production dropped. He was traded to the Braves that off-season, in a move that seemingly opened the door to Martinez. But when the 1990 season started, it was Darnell Coles, not Martinez, who became the team's new third baseman. Coles, however, got off to a horrific start at third base, committing five errors in just six games. That performance finally led to Martinez's officially becoming the team's third baseman.

After finally achieving full-time status, Martinez responded by hitting .302 in 1990 and .307 the next year. In 1992, he became the first

Mariners player to lead the American League in batting average, hitting .343. But even a batting title did not bring Martinez the recognition he deserved. His obscurity grew worse when, in the final weekend of spring training in 1993, he tore his hamstring.[29] He missed nearly three-fourths of the 1993 season. When he did play that year, he was clearly hampered by the hamstring and, thus, not the same hitter. The injury allowed Mike Blowers to become the team's everyday third baseman. Blowers and Martinez split time there in 1994, but by 1995, Edgar was reduced to being the team's full-time designated hitter. Such a move did not faze the Mariners or Martinez. Blowers showed that he was quite capable of playing full time, and Martinez was now baseball's best all-around hitter, regardless of whether he played the field or not. He won the American League batting crown again in 1995, becoming only the second right-handed hitter since 1943 to win two batting titles. In addition to batting average, Edgar was also among the league leaders in nearly every single offensive category that year, including on-base percentage, walks, total bases, runs, hits, doubles, RBIs, and slugging percentage. It was the greatest offensive year any Mariner player had ever had.

Despite the staggering offensive numbers, fans across the country were still barely acquainted with Edgar Martinez. For all his obscurity, however, Mariners fans absolutely adored him. Many of the numerous banners in the Kingdome in Game 4 were devoted to him, including one made to look like a Washington state license plate that read "EDGRRR8." Another simply said "Saint Edgar" and another, paying homage to both of the Martinezes, contained a picture of the two and read "We'll Take The Yankees to the Cleaners with Our 24 Hour Martinizing."[30]

Unlike much of the country, the Yankees were well aware of Edgar's abilities. While Griffey, Buhner, and Tino Martinez all had taken turns crushing New York throughout the last few years, Martinez was the greatest Yankees killer of them all. His regular-season numbers against them in 1995 were staggering: .391 batting average, seven home runs, and twenty RBIs in thirteen games.[31] None of the Yankees pitchers were safe from him—not Cone, not Pettitte, not Rivera, not Wetteland. He had touched them all and continued his tear into the postseason, hitting .556 through the first three games. "I have no clue why I do so well against them," said the always modest Martinez.[32]

Kamieniecki had avoided Edgar in the first inning, throwing him breaking balls out of the strike zone and walking him on five pitches. Now, in the third inning, he didn't have the option of avoiding him. Trying to climb back from a five-run deficit, Cora led off the bottom of the third inning with a first-pitch bunt single. Griffey followed with a first-pitch single to right field, putting two runners on with no outs for the Mariners' designated hitter. Kamieniecki could not pitch around Martinez this time, but he also couldn't give in to him either, for one mistake would put the Mariners right back in the game. He began with a well-placed fastball, which Edgar took for a strike. Looking to bust him inside, Kamieniecki then followed with a fastball that was up and in. The pitch hit its intended spot, yet somehow, Martinez got the bat around and sent a screaming line drive down the left-field line. He hit it so hard that the ball did not have enough time to hook foul. It took mere seconds for it to land beyond the left-field wall, only a few feet away from the foul pole, elating the crowd of 57,180.

Kamieniecki stared in disbelief. "I can't begin to tell you how he hit it out," he said.[33] He had pitched Edgar exactly as he wanted to and still yielded a three-run home run. "To hit that pitch is one thing," said Kamieniecki. "But to keep it fair is another. And to hit it out of the ballpark."[34] "[The Kingdome's] gotta be haunted," said Brian Butterfield. "Edgar's home run actually sliced fair, so that place has got to be haunted."[35]

The Mariners, left for dead ten minutes earlier, were now right back in the game. Martinez's home run not only made it a two-run game, it reenergized a crowd that to that point had little to cheer about. The noise grew even louder when Tino Martinez followed Edgar's home run with a line-drive single up the middle that nearly decapitated Kamieniecki. Buhner then walked. Next up, Blowers, who had only three sacrifice bunts all season, laid down a perfect bunt toward the third base line to Boggs, moving both runners up to second and third. Sojo further charged up the crowd by lining an 0–2 pitch to right-center field. The ball seemed destined for the gap and a tie ballgame, but it remained in the air just long enough for Bernie Williams to track it down. Tino Martinez tagged up and scored easily from third base, making it a one-run game. The turnaround was amazing. In a matter of minutes, the Mariners had gone from five runs down and perhaps closing up their season to now having the tying run in scoring position. Kamieniecki continued to make things interesting by walking Wilson and therefore putting the go-ahead run on first. Watching from above, George Steinbrenner was not pleased. He felt Kamieniecki "looked like a deer in headlights" and didn't miss the chance to point out that Showalter should have started McDowell in Game 4 instead. Kamieniecki fought back and struck out Vince Coleman looking, on a sharp breaking ball, to end the inning. Even the inning-ending strikeout could not dampen the spirits of the Mariner faithful. As they made their way out to the field to begin the top of the fourth inning, the Kingdome crowd gave the Mariners a standing ovation.

• • • • • • • • •

One of the worst things a pitcher can do after his team has a big inning is to return to the mound and immediately give up runs. Jeff Nelson was trying to prevent that. His funky, three-quarter motion, delivering fastballs and sliders at all sorts of odd angles, induced Randy Velarde to ground out to begin the fourth inning. Boggs followed with a walk, but Nelson struck out Williams on three sharp breaking balls. O'Neill then singled up the middle, sending Boggs to third. Ruben Sierra now came to bat in a huge spot because the Yankees' one-run lead was clearly not going to hold up. The Mariners' offense had put pressure on Kamieniecki in each of the first three innings and would most likely continue to do so. If it did, the Yankees were going to need more runs.

Nelson pitched Sierra carefully, focusing on the outside corner that was Sierra's known weak spot. Sierra had driven managers and coaches crazy with his stubborn refusal to move closer to the plate and take away that advantage for the pitcher. Nelson sought to exploit that. The count went full before Sierra struck out swinging at a breaking ball. Nelson, never afraid to show emotions on the field, pumped his fist before sprinting off the mound toward the dugout.

Kamieniecki pitched through minor trouble in the bottom of the fourth inning. After getting the first two outs, Edgar Martinez lined a single into center field. Tino Martinez, who nearly drilled a ball off Kamieniecki's head the previous inning, lined a shot into center field. Bernie Williams was able to run it down and end the inning. It had been Kamieniecki's best inning so far, yet it had still required him to escape trouble. Four tense innings were over and the Yankees were desperately clinging to a one-run lead.

• • • • • • • • • •

Heading into the top of the fifth inning, the Yankees were still winning, but the pressure was mounting on them and not on the Mariners. Kamieniecki was struggling through each inning, and his pitch count was steadily rising. He would not be long for the game, and Showalter was going to have to go to a bullpen that had been less than spectacular. Looking to add to the Yankees' lead, Don Mattingly led off the top of the fifth inning against Nelson and hit a checked-swing double. Only twenty-four hours after he could do no right, it now seemed the Yankees captain could do no wrong. In the first inning, his single had narrowly avoided the reach of a diving Joey Cora at second base, tipping off his glove and shooting into center field. In the third inning, Mattingly had lined a shot down the right-field line that quickly bounded off the wall directly to Buhner. Buhner gunned the ball in to Sojo, and the throw appeared to beat Mattingly to the bag, but he slid around the tag and was called safe. Now, in the fifth inning, he had caught a break again. Mattingly had been fooled by a Nelson slider and attempted to check his swing. Instead, he accidentally tapped the ball straight down the third-base line for an easy double.

The Yankees were set up with a runner on second and no outs with Dion James coming to the plate. The left-handed hitter's goal would be to pull the ball and get Mattingly over to third with fewer than two outs. James nearly did himself one better, drilling a Nelson fastball deep into right field. Buhner made the catch on the warning track. James, with only two home runs all year, had come within a few feet of giving the Yankees a three-run lead. As the crowd exhaled, Buhner, standing on the warning track, launched a throw toward third base that nearly got Mattingly, who had tagged up. With a runner on third and just one out, Piniella brought his infield in against Mike Stanley. It was only the fifth inning and the Mariners still had opportunities to tie the game or take the lead, but Piniella took a chance. Nelson, however, put himself into a dangerous position by falling behind with two straight balls. Stanley, who had singled against Nelson in Game 1, did not enjoy hitting against the six-foot-six righty and his sweeping breaking ball and swatted weakly at a 2–0 fastball. The ball dribbled to Cora who easily threw out Stanley. Piniella's gamble worked, as Mattingly was forced to hold at third base. Two pitches later, Tony Fernandez flied out to left field, ending the inning. Nelson had pitched himself out of a jam for the third straight inning.

Kamieniecki would not be so lucky, as Buhner led off the bottom of the fifth inning with a sharp single to center field. Because of the play of Griffey, Edgar Martinez, and Tino Martinez, Buhner's performance was going largely unnoticed. Though known primarily for his power and not his batting average, Buhner was now hitting .352 in the series.

After Mike Blowers struck out looking, Sojo punched a seeing-eye single between third base and shortstop. Dan Wilson now batted. The Kingdome was ecstatic as the Mariners had yet again put the tying and go-ahead runs on base. But Seattle's momentum nearly came to a screeching halt when Wilson hit a ground ball right to Velarde at second base for what appeared to be a tailor-made double play. However, instead of flipping the ball to Fernandez, who was covering second base, Velarde attempted to tag Sojo as he came running down the line. Sojo alertly dropped to the ground, avoiding the tag, and Velarde then rushed his throw to first base, narrowly getting Dan Wilson for the second out of the inning. "It's a mental mistake you can't afford," said Velarde, referring to his attempt to tag Sojo instead of throwing to second base. "No reason I shouldn't have gone for two on that. It was just a brain lock."[36] Sojo, who was still a live base runner, immediately got off the ground and rushed to second base. Don Mattingly, believing for a split second he had a chance to get Sojo out, threw to second. The throw was on line, but Sojo blocked Tony Fernandez's view of the ball. Fernandez caught sight of it at the last second, but it was too late and Mattingly's throw sailed into left field. "I've got to be thinking better there," said Mattingly, referring to the play, "It was such a bad play, a bad decision on my part. It was too risky, and I tried for it anyway, when I should have held the damn ball."[37] Buhner, who had been on second base when the play began, easily came home with the tying run. Sojo moved on to third, and just like that, the Yankees' lead was gone.

Kamieniecki escaped further trouble when Coleman popped out to third base to end the inning. The game was far from over, but the Yankees walked off the field visibly stung but what had just occurred.

• • • • • • • • •

Trying to atone for his mental mistake in the field, Velarde led off the top of the sixth inning with a single. For the fourth time in six innings, the Yankees had the leadoff hitter on base. Trying to capitalize, Buck Showalter decided to take a chance. Velarde had stolen only five bases all year, but that total was due more to Showalter's lack of enthusiasm for stealing bases. Velarde had better-than-average speed, and Wade Boggs, now hitting against Nelson, was a contact hitter who rarely struck out. When Boggs worked the count full, Showalter gambled. As Nelson delivered the 3–2 pitch, Velarde broke from first, only the second time a Yankees base runner had attempted to steal a base in the series. Boggs, however, struck out on a checked swing, and Dan Wilson fired a strike to second base, nailing Velarde. Showalter's gamble had failed, and the "strike 'em out, throw 'em out" double play only further incited the crowd. Throwing salt on Showalter's wound, Bernie Williams followed the double play by singling to center field. With the pressure on him yet again, Nelson struck out Paul O'Neill to end the inning. It was the fourth time in four innings of work that Nelson had "Houdinied" himself out of a jam.

• • • • • • • • •

After 101 pitches, Scott Kamieniecki's night was over. Showalter signaled for lefty Sterling Hitchcock. It was not the first time Showalter had called on the young pitcher in a big-game situation. Just the previous Sunday, with David Cone available to him, Showalter had asked Hitchcock to pitch the season's final game against the Blue Jays in Toronto. With a chance to clinch the wild card, it was the biggest game for the Yankees in fourteen years, and there was intense pressure on Hitchcock. He responded by getting the victory and sending the Yankees into the postseason. It was his eleventh win of the year against ten losses. Though not particularly impressive, the record betrayed an underrated performance. While Cone, McDowell, and Pettitte received most of the credit for reviving the Yankees' pitching staff that year, Hitchcock also played a significant role. Only Jack McDowell had started more games for the Yankees that season.

Hitchcock had entered the 1995 season as an afterthought. The Yankees' top four starting pitchers were set, meaning he would have to fight Andy Pettitte for the fifth spot in the rotation. Pettitte was a rookie and Hitchcock was not, but there was no guarantee who would get the assignment. The Yankees were very favorable toward Pettitte's ability, and Hitchcock had yet to establish himself as a Major League pitcher. He had made a handful of starts for the Yankees in 1992 and 1993 and spent a significant amount of time with the team in 1994. A few of his starts that year were impressive, but the team had used him primarily out of the bullpen. Hitchcock pitched well enough during spring training in 1995 that he beat out Pettitte for the fifth spot. His stuff, though not overwhelming, including a ninety-one MPH fastball, a curve, a changeup, and a forkball/split-fingered fastball that few left-handed pitchers threw.[38] As was the case with many other Yankees, his 1995 season began with a series of rough and disappointing performances. Through his first fourteen starts, Hitchcock's ERA hovered at 5.23, and he had posted only a 3–6 record. He was getting hammered, yet the Yankees, devastated by injuries, had no choice but to continue putting him on the mound every five days. Gene Michael and Buck Showalter both felt it was a matter of when with Hitchcock, not if.[39] Down the stretch, Hitchcock won four of his last five starts, none bigger than the wild-card-clinching victory in Toronto. In that situation, Showalter had resisted constant pressure from Steinbrenner to start Cone that weekend. Showalter would not relent, believing that at worst, Cone would be pitching a one-game playoff at Yankee Stadium and, at best, he would be pitching Game 1 of the Division Series at Yankee Stadium. Besides, Hitchcock had pitched his best game of the year, a 2–1 complete game victory, against the Blue Jays two weeks earlier at Yankee Stadium.

Hitchcock had handled the pressure in Toronto, but Game 4 was a different scenario. The Blue Jays did not have the quality of hitters that Seattle had. Hitchcock, working from the stretch even without runners on base, retired Joey Cora with ease to begin the inning, bringing up Ken Griffey Jr. With no one on base and Edgar Martinez looming on deck, Hitchcock directly challenged Griffey, throwing a first-pitch fastball that sailed a bit too far outside for a ball. Hitchcock's second pitch, also a fastball, did not sail far enough, and Junior sent the ball high and deep to left-center field. Dion James made a futile effort to track it down, even climbing the wall, but the ball landed over the fence into the first row of seats. As fans scrambled for the ball, the rest of the Kingdome let loose with yet another display of exuberance. Their hometown hero, the face of this franchise, had just hit his first postseason home run in Seattle. The applause was another cathartic reaction from a fan base that had suffered through years of mediocrity. A sign in the Kingdome that night read: "Griffey: That's Our Boy."[40] It was an appropriate summation of how 57,000 screaming fans felt. The home run could have easily rattled Hitchcock, but he recovered to retire both Martinezes to end the inning.

· · · · · · · · · ·

Jeff Nelson had entered the game down five runs, and now he stood in line for the victory. As he had done in the three previous innings, however, he created another tightrope situation for himself. Ruben Sierra, who had ceased to be a factor in the series since his twelfth-inning double in Game 2, led off the top of the seventh inning with a line-drive shot down the left-field line that bounced into the stands for a ground-rule double. The Yankees had gotten the leadoff hitter on yet again. They wanted to prevent it from being the third straight inning they had done so and failed to score.

After four gutsy innings—the longest performance of Nelson's career—Sierra's hit knocked him out of the game. Future events would fade the memory of this performance, but he had kept the Mariners in the game long enough to take the lead. It was one of the truly underrated performances of the Division Series. "Without Nellie, we go home," said Norm Charlton after the game.[41]

Replacing Nelson was Tim Belcher, who had not thrown a pitch since Jim Leyritz ended Game 2 at 1:15 Wednesday morning. Don Mattingly, already three for three, came to bat, and like Dion James in the fourth, he just needed to pull the ball and ensure that Sierra made it to the third base with fewer than two outs. More important, Mattingly sought to recover from his throwing error, which had allowed Seattle to tie the game two innings earlier. But Mattingly tried to pull an outside fastball from Belcher and instead popped the ball up to Sojo at shortstop for an easy out. Sierra had to stay at second base. James moved Sierra to third base with a ground ball to second, but the opportunity was gone. Mike Stanley flied out to center field and the inning was over. The Yankees had wasted yet another chance.

After Hitchcock pitched only one inning, Showalter took him out of the game. He had made only one daring mistake, but now Hitchcock was saddled with being the potential losing pitcher. With the bottom half of the Mariners' lineup scheduled to hit and all of them being right-handed, Showalter turned to Bob Wickman. Jay Buhner greeted the reliever by sending a ground-ball single into left field. But Wickman retired Blowers, Sojo, and Wilson with little trouble. It had been the easiest inning so far for any Yankees pitcher. The game moved on to the eighth inning.

• • • • • • • • •

Belcher retired Tony Fernandez to start the eighth inning, but when he walked Velarde, Piniella decided to make a move. Norm Charlton had pitched in Games 2 and 3, but this was a save situation, and Piniella was going with this closer. Though Charlton had been used extensively, it was strategic move that on the surface made sense. Three of the next five Yankees hitters were lefties, and Sierra was weaker from the right side of the plate than from the left. To try to stave off the Mariners' elimination and allow them to live to fight another day, Charlton came in from the bullpen. For Charlton, it was a far cry from where he had been only a few months earlier.

Charlton had come up through the Cincinnati Reds organization as a starting pitcher but was moved to the bullpen in 1989. While he did make sixteen starts for the Reds in 1990, Charlton's fame came from being part of the Reds relief trio known as "the Nasty Boys," which also included Randy Myers and Rob Dibble. Under the leadership of manager Lou Piniella, the Nasty Boys helped lead the Reds to a shocking upset in the 1990 World Series over the heavily favored Oakland A's. During that time, Piniella took a liking to Charlton, and when Lou moved on to the Mariners in 1993, he helped push for a trade with the Reds that brought the lefty over to the Pacific Northwest.

Charlton pitched well for Seattle in 1993, but he blew out his elbow and had to undergo "Tommy John" surgery in 1994, causing him to miss the entire season. He returned to the majors in 1995 with the Philadelphia Phillies, but he had missed the entire previous season and did not have enough time to adequately regain his arm strength. As a result, he was pounded by National League hitters, averaging nearly two base runners per inning. His situation presented a catch-22 for Phillies manager Jim Fergosi. Charlton needed more work to gain back his arm strength and become the pitcher he had been, but his performances were so poor that he could only be used sparingly. By July, the Phillies decided they could no longer keep him and issued his release. Even Charlton admitted that he would have released himself, with the way he had been pitching.[42]

Upon learning of his release, Charlton's agent reached out to the Mariners. Charlton had enjoyed his time there, he liked playing for Piniella, and he was actually one of the few pitchers who enjoyed throwing in the Kingdome. The Mariners agreed to have him come to audition by throwing off the mound in the Seattle bullpen. Piniella saw Charlton throw for a while then approached him. "Are you healthy? You ready to go?" Piniella asked. Charlton replied that he was. "Then go upstairs and sign a contract."[43]

Just like that, Norm Charlton had a second lease on baseball life. In a season when so many different things went right for the Mariners, perhaps no move was more remarkable or miraculous than signing Charlton, who returned to Seattle and became the complete opposite of what fans in Philadelphia had seen. His forkball began devastating American League hitters and he averaged more than one strikeout per inning. Whereas he was averaging almost two base runners an inning with Philadelphia, he was averaging less than one with Seattle. "I could do no wrong," recalled Charlton, who earned the nickname "the Sheriff." "It was the best half[-season] of baseball I've ever thrown. Every pitch was the right one. Even when I made mistakes, they ended up being outs."[44]

Although Charlton had not been signed with the intention that he would be the team's closer, he moved into that role after only a few appearances due to the continuing struggles of Bobby Ayala. The result was not just Charlton's fourteen saves but also a sense of security with a late-inning lead the team had not had all season. Charlton was not a one-inning closer either, but a workhorse, entering games in the eighth and sometimes the seventh inning.

In addition to late-game security, Charlton brought to the Mariners one of the games more unorthodox warm-up routines. By his own admission, he "could not take the ups and downs of the game."[45] Fans were emotionally involved from the first pitch, standing on their feet, clapping, yelling, and cheering. Charlton couldn't handle the constant emotional roller coaster, so early in his career he decided that after the first two innings of a game, he would return to the clubhouse.[46] Once there, he would take a nap for the third and fourth innings. After napping, he would have a cup of coffee to wake himself up, then return to the bullpen by the sixth inning and begin his daily stretching routines. Yes, it was unorthodox, but considering his performance so far, no one in Seattle was complaining about it.

Even Charlton would have had trouble sleeping through the noise that was reverberating around the Kingdome as he entered Game 4. With a one-run lead to protect, Charlton went to work on Wade Boggs, who ripped a 2–0 fastball back up the middle for a single. The ball had been hit too hard for Velarde to advance to third, but the Yankees still had two runners on and only one out for Bernie Williams. Up in the count, 2–1, Williams again drove a fastball to right field. It was not particularly deep, but with the short right-field fence, it appeared for a second it might have a chance to leave the ballpark. Jay Buhner tracked it down on the warning track in nearly the same manner he had caught Williams's drive during the seventh inning of Game 2. Given how close the game had just come to turning into a two-run Yankees lead, most fans might not have noticed that Velarde had tagged up from second and advanced to third. With two outs, it seemed a relatively unimportant move.

• • • • • • • • •

Paul O'Neill stepped to the plate for round three of O'Neill versus Charlton. So far, the fights had been a draw, with O'Neill having homered off Charlton in Game 2 but having struck out against him in Game 3. Charlton jumped ahead in round three when O'Neill fell behind in the count, 1–2. Trying to close out the inning, Charlton went with his bread-and-butter pitch, the forkball. But this time, the pitch broke too much. Dan Wilson, who had became adept at stopping these types of pitches, could not block this one. It took an awkward bounce off the dirt in front of home plate, skimming past Wilson and bouncing to the backstop. Velarde alertly broke for home plate. Wilson broke for the ball, recovering it near the backstop, and flipped it to Charlton who had rushed in to cover home plate. Wilson's throw bounced off Velarde, who scored without a play. Luckily for the Mariners, after hitting off Velarde, the ball deflected off home plate umpire Rocky Roe and stopped dead. Had it not hit Roe, the ball would have headed toward the Yankees' dugout and allowed Boggs, who had already moved to second, to take third.

Charlton had been burned by his best pitch, but with two strikes on O'Neill, he stayed with the forkball. "You gotta go with the one that got you there," said Charlton, looking back on the at-bat.[47] His next two forkballs both bounced in the dirt, earning O'Neill a walk. Ruben Sierra now had a chance to put the Yankees ahead. The Kingdome, already shaken from the wild pitch, turned to despair when Charlton fell behind, 3–0, to Sierra. Charlton could have given up and thrown the next pitch out of the strike zone, walking Sierra and setting up a lefty-against-lefty matchup with Don Mattingly, but Mattingly was 3–4 in the game. His Game 3 performance notwithstanding, he had been crushing the ball in the series. Plus, Mattingly was the only lefty to have hit a home run against Charlton all season. Instead of relenting, Charlton came right back at Sierra, firing a fastball for a strike. He fired another one, which Sierra fouled off. The crowd got back into it, rising to their feet and howling their newly adopted two-strike chant. Charlton delivered a sharp breaking ball, and Sierra swung hard but over the pitch for strike three. Inning over. Even having relinquished the lead, the crowd still gave a boisterous yell as Charlton walked off the mound. Charlton was seething inside at having given up the tying run and visibly cursed at himself. He could take solace in knowing that the top of the Mariners' order was starting off the bottom of the eighth inning and that the Mariners' favorite punching bag was coming in to pitch.

• • • • • • • •

John Wetteland was, in the words of one former teammate "out there." Wetteland had lived the stereotypical ballplayer's lifestyle earlier in his career. He stayed out late, partied hard, and enjoyed all the frills of a major leaguer out for a night out on the town. Then he became a born-again Christian and deeply devoted religious man who gave up his hard-living ways.[48]

Wetteland's religious devotion did not, however, cause him to change other parts of his personality, such as his free spirit. A rabid Rollerblade enthusiast, he once showed up to a teammate's apartment unannounced decked out in full roller-hockey regalia and then proceeded to skate around the apartment complex, body-checking doors and hallway walls. As the Yankees' closer, he had nothing but time to kill for the first seven innings of a game and generally would initiate a series of pranks and practical jokes.

For all the jokes and "out there" behavior, there was no mistaking Wetteland's ability. He had a large physique for a pitcher, including an especially thick lower body. Though armed with an effective fastball, Wetteland's best pitch was a devastating curveball that gave hitters what is referred to as "the jelly legs."

Wetteland began his career with Dodgers in 1989, primarily as a reliever, though he did make a handful of starts. He did not become a full-time closer until his first season with the Montreal Expos in 1992. At the time, the Expos were a team on the rise and had made surprising runs for the National League East title in 1992 and 1993. Both runs fell short, but the Expos emerged as baseball's best team in 1994. Wetteland played a major role in the team's emergence, consistently posting ERAs under 3.00, averaging a strikeout per inning and thirty-five saves a season. The players' strike, however, crippled the franchise. Even before the strike and despite their success in the standings, the Expos had remained near the bottom in attendance figures throughout the early nineties. Facing ever-increasing difficulties that were made only harder by the work stoppage, team ownership issued a fire sale before the 1995 season, shipping out several big-name players. Wetteland was included in the purge, going to the Yankees in exchange for the long-since-forgotten Fernando Seguignol.[49]

Wetteland became the closer the Yankees had not had since Dave Righetti entered games in the 1980s. Yankees fans soon learned to adjust to Wetteland's often stomach-churning performances, as he became known for pitching himself into difficult situations in the ninth inning, only to escape unharmed. Any questions about his ability to adjust to the American League were silenced by his thirty-one saves.

Wetteland's domination in both leagues was what made his problems with the Seattle Mariners so vexing. He had saved two games against them during the regular season, but the result of the August 24 game at the Kingdome was still fresh in people's minds entering the playoffs. In Game 1, Seattle had continued to hit Wetteland, scoring two runs off him in the ninth inning of what was supposed to be a mop-up role. The next night, Wetteland appeared to have recovered, pitching 3 1/3 scoreless innings until Griffey took him deep in the twelfth inning. Now with a tied game in the bottom of the eighth inning of Game 4, Showalter called on his battered closer. This was not to save the game but to hold off the Mariners until the Yankees could score in the ninth inning and take the lead. Some may have questioned bringing Wetteland into a tied game, especially given his track record against Seattle, but Showalter did not have faith in his other options in the bullpen, including Mariano Rivera, who had dominated the Mariners to that point. As Charlton had said about sticking with his forkball, Showalter went with the one that got him there. It proved disastrous for the Yankees.

Vince Coleman again played the role of sparkplug for the Mariners' lineup. Though well built, Coleman was not an especially large player. This allowed him to shrink his strike zone, which drove opposing pitchers crazy. Leading off the bottom of the eighth inning, he walked when Wetteland could not find the strike zone With the go-ahead run on first, it was assumed that Joey Cora would bunt to advance Coleman to second. It would take the bat out of Ken Griffey Jr.'s hands, as the Yankees would most likely intentionally walk him, but it would also mean Edgar Martinez coming up with two runners on. It was a chance the Mariners would take.

Cora did in fact bunt, but it was not to sacrifice Coleman over to second. The ball scurried along the turf to Mattingly, who fielded the ball, but instead of flipping it to Randy Velarde at first base, he attempted to tag Cora. Cora dove headfirst into the bag, avoiding the tag in the process and reaching first base safely. Before Cora could dust himself off, Buck Showalter shot out of the dugout toward first-base umpire Jim Evans.

"He ran out of the line," Showalter screamed at Evans. "He was out of the line, Jim."[50] Showalter had to scream. It was so loud in the Kingdome that Evans could not hear him otherwise. Showalter argued that Cora had run out of the baseline in his attempt to avoid the tag. Approximately halfway down the first base line there is a separate line that runs parallel and three feet to the right of the first-base line. This additional line represented the boundary in which a player has to remain when running down the first base line for a hit. If a player runs outside that boundary, he can be called out (this does not apply to runners who are attempting to round first base after a "clean" base hit). Evans disagreed with Showalter, maintaining that, while Cora's feet were outside the line, his upper body had remained inside the plane and therefore, he had done nothing wrong. Attempts by Showalter to have Evans appeal to home-plate umpire Rocky Roe were in vain.

The umpiring had been questionable throughout the series. Some players thought the umpires were intimidated by the scenes created in New York and Seattle, but they agreed that calls went for or against teams at an even rate. But the call on Cora's play, more than any, stuck in the craw of some Yankees even years after it had occurred. Not only did it result in two runners on and no one out for Griffey, but it set a precedent that Cora would again test the next night in an even more crucial situation.

Regardless of opinions, Cora was safe and now standing on first base and Coleman was on second. Wetteland now encountered a living nightmare. Griffey had faced Wetteland only three times in his career so far, and he had homered in two of those at-bats. Wetteland attempted to regain his demeanor after the Cora bunt and worked Junior to a 1–1 count, but as Wetteland delivered his next pitch, Griffey surprised everyone by positioning his bat as if he were going to bunt. Considering Griffey's career numbers against Wetteland and the Yankees in general, it was a bold move that no one on defense anticipated. But Wetteland's curveball, his first of the inning, dipped too far inside. Griffey made a less-than-valiant attempt to move out of the ball's path and it struck him in the foot. Mike Stanley argued in vain that Junior had not moved and in fact had attempted to bunt, so he should not be awarded first base. He failed to persuade Rocky Roe.

A loud roar went up as Seattle's cleanup hitter placed his right foot on the back line of the batter's box. The Kingdome faithful, as they had been for a large part of the last two nights, were on their feet, waiting for "Saint Edgar" to deliver yet another miracle. The bases were loaded, there were no outs, and the American League's batting champion stood in against the team he had crippled and crushed his entire career. But, amazingly, Martinez was only a .197 career hitter with the bases loaded.[51]

Wetteland, working cautiously, threw two straight breaking balls, both outside. It was impossible to pitch to Martinez, regardless of the situation, but Wetteland wanted to keep the ball outside, hoping Martinez would end up hitting the ball hard somewhere for an out and keep the damage to a minimum. Wetteland's breaking ball was not working, and he could not afford to walk Martinez. Down 2–0 in the count, he delivered a fastball straight down the middle. Martinez swung under the pitch, sending a high pop down the first-base line in foul territory and the Yankees almost caught a break. Randy Velarde made a mad dash for the ball, nearly tripping over the visiting team bullpen mounds in the process. Stretching as far as he could, he stabbed at the ball, but it dropped just out of his reach in foul territory. Had Velarde caught it, Coleman would most likely have scored from third base, giving the Mariners the lead, but considering how the Mariners' bullpen had pitched in the series, a one-run lead would not have assured victory. Instead of an out, Martinez was presented with a second chance.

Wetteland fired two more fastballs and Martinez fouled off each of them. The tension and anticipation inside the Kingdome on each pitch was utterly nerve-racking. The count now 2–2, Wetteland got the sign from Stanley, brought his hands to his belt, checked the runners, and delivered a fastball straight down the middle. "I wanted to get just one good slider over to Edgar [but] I had to come in with [a fastball]. When you do that you have to live with the consequences," said Wetteland.[52] Martinez, following through with a lightning-fast swing, sent the ball screaming to straightaway center field. It was hit so hard that fans didn't have enough time to contemplate whether it may or may not go over the fence. The ball quickly sailed over the centerfield wall just to the right of the 405-foot mark and crashed into the batter's-eye tarp for a grand slam. Mariners announcer Dave Niehaus, sounding like he might blow a vocal chord, could barely contemplate what he was seeing. "Get out the rye bread and the mustard . . . a graaaaand salaaami," the overly excited broadcaster screamed into his microphone. "I don't believe it, my oh my!"[53] In the Mariners' dugout, Lou Piniella high-fived Lee Elia with both hands. The crowd reaction surpassed anything that had taken place inside the Kingdome to that point. It was ear-shattering, painful, and unreal. A mix of elation and pure pandemonium.

Martinez, mild-mannered and rarely one to wear emotions on his sleeve, raised his right arm in triumph after seeing the ball clear the fence. The emotional display was certainly justified. Edgar Martinez had just hit the biggest home run in the history of the Mariners' franchise. "I was only trying to make contact," said Martinez. "I was surprised it went out. I was so excited. As a kid you always dream of hitting a home run like that, and here it is in the playoffs."[54] His team, once down 5–0 and looking at the end of their season, was now leading 10–6. Just two hours ago they had been thinking about spring training in 1996. Now they were starting to think about Game 5 the next night.

John Wetteland stood dejected on the mound. Things had collapsed so rapidly it was hard to contemplate what had just happened. "It was just a poor, ugly, non-inning," said Wetteland after the game. "I started off bad and things caved in on me from there. The walk, the ball off Griffey's foot . . . it was just ugly all around."[55] Seconds after Martinez's shot had crashed behind the center-field wall, Buck Showalter was already making his way toward the mound. Chaos ensued all around him as "Shout" blasted from the loudspeakers and 57,000 people sang along. Just a minute after giving up the home run, Wetteland sat on the bench in stunned silence.

Steve Howe trotted in from the bullpen and got Tino Martinez to line out sharply to left field for the first out of the inning. Showalter kept Howe in the game to face Buhner, who responded by sending an 0–1 fastball deep to right-center field. Bernie Williams kept pace with the ball and trotted toward the fence. As he reached the wall, Williams leapt and the ball ricocheted off the tip of his glove and landed behind the fence for another home run. Williams stood stunned on the warning track. Since leading 5–0 in the top of the third inning, the Yankees had now been outscored 11–1. With a seemingly secure four-run lead, Buhner's home run simply added insult to injury, but the next play was like kicking someone when he was already down. Mike

Blowers sent a ground ball up the middle that Tony Fernandez fielded and, throwing across his body, sent a one-hopper to Don Mattingly who gloved it cleanly. Blowers looked out by at least a step, but first-base umpire Jim Evans called him safe. Mattingly, upon seeing Evans's call, stood incredulous at first base with an expression that cried, "What else could go wrong?" Blowers had been out, and perhaps at a different point in the game, the Yankees would have put up more of an argument. Down by five runs, arguing a call now seemed trivial to them. Showalter held a mild discussion with Evans before returning to the dugout. Luis Sojo then singled into right field. ABC, certain now that there would be another game, posted the Game 5 pitching matchups on the television screen. The rally finally died when Dan Wilson grounded into a double play. The Yankees walked off the field looking mentally beaten and shell shocked.

The Kingdome had always been a hell on earth for the New York Yankees, but no one could have imagined what had just transpired. A leadoff walk, questionable calls, a hit batsman, barely missed fly balls, and a meltdown by their closer. It was a five-run disaster of an inning. Seattle now stood three outs away from a winner-take-all Game 5. The Mariners and their fans had to feel good going into the top of the ninth inning. Even the Mariners' bullpen couldn't blow a five-run lead, could they?

• • • • • • • • •

Mattingly started the ninth inning off by lining a single down the right-field line, his fourth hit of the game. It was an impressive response to the three-strikeout performance the night before. With right-handed batters coming up and a five-run lead, Piniella took Charlton out and brought in Bobby Ayala. Piniella wanted the righty-righty matchup, but he also saw a psychological opportunity, because the Mariners needed Ayala. He had to pitch well, otherwise it was merely a wasted spot on the playoff roster, and Piniella wanted to give Ayala an opportunity to boost his confidence. It was needed, since Ayala was the only Mariner booed during pregame introductions by the home crowd.[56] Piniella felt there was enough breathing room to allow Ayala to give up a hit or two. Even if he got touched up for a run, it was still a large enough lead not to place the game in jeopardy.

Ayala quickly retired the pinch-hitting Darryl Strawberry, but Mike Stanley then singled up the middle. Mattingly, who had moved to second on Strawberry's groundout, scored easily. It was now a four-run game, and Ayala's room for error got smaller. Stanley's single began a stir in the Kingdome crowd. They were not in full-blown panic mode yet, but they had seen this type of performance before and were already becoming impatient with Ayala. The groans grew even louder when Fernandez singled up the middle, putting runners on first and second and the tying run in the on-deck circle.

Piniella emerged from the dugout unpleased. He stared at Ayala and asked him if he was all right. Ayala said he was. So let's go then, Piniella responded. Piniella's talk did not work. Ayala walked Randy Velarde, loading the bases and bringing the tying run to the plate in Wade Boggs. Considering how things had played out in the series, it was not implausible to those watching that Boggs might put the ball into the right-field stands and tie the game. Piniella certainly knew it was possible, and he had seen enough of Ayala.

It was another less-than-ideal situation Piniella was faced with. Nelson, Belcher, Charlton, and Ayala were gone, so he was left with few options. He went with Bill Risley. It wasn't that Risley was not capable—he had been a steady force in the Mariners' bullpen all year, posting career highs in games, innings pitched, strikeouts, and a career-best 3.13 ERA, but Risley was not a closer. He had only one save in his career, and he had appeared the night before and quickly given up two home runs, turning a laugher into a save situation. The moment did not faze the Seattle reliever, though. "I was probably the most composed of anyone, except maybe Junior [Griffey] out there in centerfield," said Risley. "I was not nervous at all, no butterflies, nothing. Lou [Piniella] told me to 'relax like you've never relaxed before.' That really helped me because he knows I'm an intense guy and I try to overdo it."[57]

Piniella's telling Risley to be relaxed was a difficult request, considering that Boggs came to bat as a career .371 hitter with the bases loaded, including three grand slams. Though known more as a batting champion, Boggs did have power and could tie the game with just a deep fly ball to right field. Despite all that had happened in the eighth inning, the Yankees were now putting the pressure on the Mariners. One pitch, one mistake, and all of Edgar Martinez's heroics would be moot.

Risley had little room for error and quickly jumped ahead of Boggs, 1–2. Looking to jam him, Risley came inside with a hard fastball. Boggs, fooled and jammed by the pitch, attempted a half-swing reminiscent of the kind of one might take in cricket. He accidentally made contact and sent a ground ball toward the hole between first and second base. The ball was not hit especially hard, but it quickly shot across the thin turf. Tino Martinez, reaching to his right, stabbed at the ball and knocked it down. For a split second, it looked like he might not recover in time, but Martinez picked up the ball and fired it to second base for one out. The momentary bobble had allowed Boggs time to get down the first-base line, so shortstop Felix Fermin decided not to attempt to complete the double play. The crowd was relieved, but the tying run was still coming up to the plate in the form of Bernie Williams.

By now, there was no hitter in the Yankees' lineup that the Mariners wanted to see less than Bernie Williams. He was the Yankees' equivalent of Edgar Martinez. Stepping in with a .500 batting average in the series, Bernie was much more of a threat to tie the game than Boggs was. He had had two home runs the night before; he was two for two in the series against Risley, including a home run and a double; and he had nearly homered in two separate at-bats against Charlton. If the Kingdome was filled with nervous energy during Boggs's at-bat, the energy doubled as Williams hit.

Risley, remaining calm, blocked out Williams's home run from the night before. "I'm not thinking about that, I'm thinking I've got to get that out," said Risley.[58] The count went full and the tension mounted. Risley did not want to walk Bernie and put the tying run on base, especially with Paul O'Neill lurking on deck. On 3–2, Williams swung hard and sent a high fly ball to deep center field. The entire ballpark held its breath for a moment. It couldn't be? The Yankees bench leapt to their feet. Ken Griffey Jr., in his usual, graceful manner, slowly backpedaled toward the wall in center field. Other center fielders might have been nervous, frantically using their throwing hand to find the wall, but Junior displayed no such signs of despair. While thousands of fans were suffering anxiety attacks, he calmly settled in the middle of the warning track, reached up with his glove hand and caught the ball. Five more feet and the game would have been tied. The crowd erupted, more out of relief than from excitement, and the Mariners rushed out of the dugout. Fireworks exploded as the home team congratulated themselves on a come-from-behind victory. "I am so excited," said Edgar Martinez in the clubhouse afterward. "I am so excited we get to be back here tomorrow."[59] "All we wanted to do was get back to another one-game playoff," said Mike Blowers. "And that's where we are at. Now, they're up against the wall tomorrow as well."[60]

The Yankees had made an admirable comeback attempt in the ninth inning but the fact that they were mere feet from tying the game would long be forgotten. What would be remembered was that they had blown a five-run lead and collapsed in the eighth inning. They left the field dejected. "It's hard to swallow," said Wetteland after the game. "The only thing that can ease my pain is a win tomorrow."[61] "It doesn't mean much now," said Mattingly, referring to his four-hit performance. "I hurt us in the field."[62] Their two games-to-none lead had evaporated, as had all the good feelings and excitement that had come with them on the plane from New York. "Whatever edge we had coming out of New York is gone now," said Buck Showalter.[63] Four heart-stopping, gut-wrenching games had merely rendered the two teams equal. It was going to come down to one game on a Sunday afternoon in Seattle. "It seems like going to the last game is the way it should be," said Mattingly. "We'll tee it up tomorrow and see what happens."[64]

10

Game 5: Warriors, Heroes, and Heartbreak

"Who is going to forget the sight of the ball off Jim Leyritz' bat in
the bottom of the 15th as it cut a triumphant path through the
Bronx night and sent everybody home? How can you not marvel
at the way the Mariners took the 5–0 Yankees' lead in Game 4
and turned it into chopped liver, and the way they came back
to win it—or, for that matter, the way they almost lost control
at the finish? And who is going to forget Sunday night?"

—Jerry Izenberg, *Trenton Times*, October 9, 1995

On Sunday, October 8, 1995, the city of Seattle woke up in a
frenzy. Edgar Martinez's seven-RBI performance was the talk
of the town, eclipsing even Seahawks football. He had nearly single-
handedly propelled his team to victory in Game 4. Left for dead at
1:15 A.M. the previous Wednesday morning, the Mariners had tied the
series in the most dramatic of ways. It was only fitting that after four
games of high drama on the East and West coasts, it now came down
to one final game. After weeks in which both teams could truly not
afford to lose a single game, their respective seasons would now be
determined in one winner-take-all showdown.

Though the players may have had their fill of drama and heart-
pumping intensity, baseball fans were crying for more. The first

212

four games had been just the remedy baseball needed to remind everyone—owners, players, and fans alike—of why baseball was America's pastime. Unfortunately, because of the Baseball Network, only those in select regions of the country had witnessed the amazing events that had transpired over the last five days. Now that the other three divisional series had concluded, Game 5 was going to be shown on primetime television across the entire country. Thus, the television schedule that was undoubtedly clunky and worked against creating the largest national viewership for each playoff team actually helped spotlight the Yankees and the Mariners in the end. While only local fans watched the Indians sweep the Red Sox, the Reds sweep the Dodgers, and the Braves beat the Rockies, all baseball eyes were peeled on this final, undecided matchup. Everyone was going to have the chance to witness the conclusion of the greatest postseason series in baseball history.

Buck Showalter was a man with a sense of history. It was one of the many characteristics that had helped him rebuild the team he inherited in 1992. His sense of what it meant to be a Yankee—and more important, what it meant to play in the postseason—was especially strong. He was well aware of what had occurred over the previous five days. He knew that what these two teams were doing was magical and that baseball didn't always play out this way. Showalter wanted to make sure his players were aware as well. However, he was not one to give Knute Rockne "win one for the Gipper"-type speeches or what he referred to as "no shit" speeches. If players needed a reminder of what they had to do to win a big game, then they didn't deserve to be there. Instead, Showalter told his players to remember that no matter what happened after this game was over, they had been part of something special, something that would be remembered for years. Win or lose, they should take it all in tonight and remember what they had been a part of.[1]

To those who had feuded with Showalter in the past, it was an out-of-place speech that only reinforced their belief that he was losing grasp of the team as the pressure to win mounted. To them a "win or lose, it's still okay" speech was not acceptable. This was just part of an underlying tension that existed for the Yankees heading into Game 5. That morning, Yankees adviser and George Steinbrenner confidant Arthur Richman derided the team in front of Rick Down, saying they didn't have the intestinal fortitude of Yankees teams of the past. Down told Richman to "fuck off." Historically, the Yankees prided themselves on giving off an aura of professionalism. But before Game 5, the tension was apparent enough that Brent Musburger made mention of it during ABC's pregame opening analysis. The feeling could certainly be understood. The Yankees, Buck Showalter especially, were not stupid. The team knew that certain contracts, most notably those of Showalter, Gene Michael, and Don Mattingly, were up after this season. They knew that Steinbrenner would be irate over the thought of not just blowing a two-games-to-none lead but of blowing it to Lou Piniella and a Mariners ownership that he had come to revile. They knew this game was not just about advancing to the American League Championship Series. This game was about people's careers. How could there not be tension with that thought lingering over them?

For the Seattle Mariners, Game 5 was the proverbial icing on the cake. No one had expected them to come this far. Not in April, not in August, not even three days ago. Yet here they were, loosening up in the clubhouse for the biggest game of their lives without a sign of tension anywhere. Piniella, like Showalter, did not feel the need to give his players a rah-rah pep talk. If they had come this far and needed their manager to motivate them, they didn't deserve to be here.[2] Everyone recognized the stakes. Now, it was a matter of going out and just playing ball.

On paper, the Game 5 matchup appeared to favor the Yankees. David Cone was starting with a complete four days' rest. He hadn't been brilliant in Game 1, but the majority of the damage had been caused by Ken Griffey Jr.'s bat, so Cone had shown the ability at least to tame the rest of the lineup. Additionally, Cone had been in these pressure situations before. Down three games to two in the best-of-seven NLCS in 1988, Cone had pitched a complete-game victory for the Mets against the Dodgers at Dodger Stadium, forcing a Game 7. He had also pitched the deciding sixth game of the 1992 World Series for the Blue Jays. Pressure was certainly nothing new to David Cone. The same could not be said for Mariners starter Andy Benes. Benes had pitched well in Game 2 but had never been in a spot like this before. While Cone had a successful track record in elimination games, Benes had no track record at all. Edge: Yankees. Additionally, including Cone, half of the

Yankees' Game 5 starting lineup had previous postseason experience. Sixty-eight games' worth to be exact, and that didn't include the first four games of this series. Only two members of the Mariners' lineup had any previous postseason experience—Vince Coleman and Joey Cora—and their total was just twenty-three games. Again, edge: Yankees. The offenses were a draw, leaving only one more factor: the bullpens. While neither team's bullpen had been particularly good in the series, going into Game 5 the Yankees appeared to have the edge here as well. Chris Bosio had only gone two innings the night before, forcing Piniella to use Jeff Nelson for a career-long four innings and an already fatigued Norm Charlton for a third straight game. Piniella's bullpen was tired and, with scant exceptions, had been largely ineffective. Though not especially good either, the Yankees' bullpen at least had some rest. Showalter, thanks largely to some bad performances, had used his relief pitchers for only an inning or two per appearance. Additionally, because everyone was available tonight, Showalter now had a third left-handed option out of the bullpen with Andy Pettitte. The biggest problem for Showalter remained John Wetteland. Could Showalter afford to bring Wetteland out in the bottom of the ninth inning, considering his struggles against the Mariners?

Overshadowing all Game 5 possible scenarios, however, was an X factor that would be sitting in the Mariners' dugout. Piniella made it clear that Randy Johnson, even on one day's rest, would be available to pitch in Game 5. It was a thought that put fear into the hearts of Yankees fans and players. But how effective could Johnson be out of the bullpen? He had pitched two consecutive starts on three days' rest, and it had been only one day since his Game 3 start. Did he still have enough in his arm to come in and preserve a ninth-inning lead if called upon?

• • • • • • • •

Buck Showalter filled out his lineup card with the normal names and positions. The one name that stood out was Dion James in left field. While there had been an offensive explosion during the first four games, Showalter decided to stay with James despite the outfielder's lack of power. The decision was questionable to those who wanted to see Darryl Strawberry up at the plate taking shots at the Kingdome's short right-field wall. Steinbrenner, who had personally gone about signing Strawberry, was extremely unhappy with the decision, according to one Yankees official. But Showalter didn't care what these people thought. Strawberry had not played a full season in four years and could not be trusted defensively in left field. He remained on the bench.

Piniella also filled out his lineup with the same names and positions, but he made one minor change. The struggling Mike Blowers was put in the ninth spot and Luis Sojo and Dan Wilson were each moved up one position in the batting order.

For the third straight night, Mariners faithful decked out the Kingdome with banners of all shapes, sizes, and colors. "It's Too Late for You NY" read one, while another declared, "Today's Menu: Yankee Noodles." An especially daunting sign was unfurled over the overhang in the upper deck: "Yanks Are Sweepless in Seattle." Among the hundreds of thousands in the Seattle area watching that night would be the state's lawmakers, many of whom were still not convinced that a new stadium was required. They were going to need something special to change their minds

After the extra-inning home runs, blown saves, grand slams, errors, mental mistakes, controversial calls, and hit batters, it all came down to this one game. The winner would advance; the loser would go home. The Mariners took the field to an explosion of applause and fireworks. Andy Benes threw his warm-up pitches, then as he did before every start, knelt behind the mound to ask, "Please let me do the best I can with the ability I have been given." Just three months earlier, he had been pitching a string of meaningless games a thousand miles down the coast in San Diego. Now, he was pitching in the most important game in Mariners history.

For Yankees leadoff hitter Wade Boggs, this was not a new experience. It was the third winner-take-all postseason game he had played in. As a member of the Red Sox, he was part of an amazing comeback against the Angels in the 1986 ALCS. Just a week later, he sat on the visitors' bench in Shea Stadium with tears in his eyes as the Mets celebrated their Game 7 World Series–clinching victory. Boggs had already established himself as a Hall of Famer, but he certainly did not want to be in the subsection of Hall of Famers consisting of those who had never won a World Series. It included Ted Williams,

Ernie Banks, and Harmon Killebrew—all among the greatest to have played baseball, yet all had never won a championship. Boggs would be damned if he joined that group and he certainly did not want to see yet another team celebrating a postseason-series victory in front of him. He strolled to the plate and dug in. Benes readied himself and delivered a first-pitch fastball right down the middle. Home-plate umpire Jim Evans immediately signaled strike one. While not nearly as vocal as the Game 4 home-plate umpire, Evans was clear in his calls, immediately signaling with his right arm if the pitch was a strike. Benes eventually got two strikes, and the crowd became excruciatingly loud. The fans were so boisterous that the center-field camera visibly shook. After Benes tried to fool Boggs with an inside fastball for a ball, he came back with a fastball again. Boggs cut right through it, his timing off, his swing late. Strike three! Dan Wilson shot up and fired the ball to Mike Blowers at third to start the around-the-horn. The crowd began to chant, "Andy! Andy!"

Bernie Williams swung right over a breaking ball for strike three. Two hitters, two strikeouts. Paul O'Neill then flied out weakly to Vince Coleman. Benes had overpowered the Yankees in the first inning.

• • • • • • • • •

David Cone stepped onto the Kingdome mound to begin the bottom of the first. Twenty-three hours earlier, it appeared that his next start would be at Jacob's Field. Leading 5–0 in Game 4, the Yankees were on their way to Cleveland with their ace pitcher starting the first game of the ALCS. But Edgar Martinez's seven RBIs squelched that possibility. The previous night, Cone had tried to reassure his teammates by telling them not to worry, he would "take care of everything."[3] Now he was pitching with the weight of New York on his shoulders. He was a free agent after the season, so he didn't want his possibly last performance in New York to be remembered as one that cost the Yankees a chance to play for the pennant. On this night, Cone, as gritty and determined as he would ever be, was on a mission. He was going to win this game. If it meant throwing 200 pitches, if it meant throwing till his arm came off, he was going to win this game.

Cone normally toyed with hitters, but in the first inning, he went right after the Mariners. He fired fastballs to Vince Coleman, getting him to fly out to left field with little effort. Joey Cora then sent a short fly to center field on the first pitch he saw for the second out. The two quick outs did not dampen the anticipation of Ken Griffey Jr.'s coming to bat. Griffey had homered twice off Cone in Game 1, both times on pitches that were left out over the plate. Cone did not want a repeat performance so he worked Junior inside, preventing him from extending his arms. Cone fell behind but came back with a fastball that Griffey swung under and popped up to Tony Fernandez. Cone had a tendency to labor through innings, running up his pitch count and expending tons of energy in the process. But he'd gotten through the first inning on only eight pitches. He had reaped the rewards of directly challenging the Mariners hitters and now, for the fifth time in the series, Seattle had failed to score in the first inning. Both the Yankees and the Mariners had been retired in order. It was the second and last time in the series where a full inning didn't see at least one base runner.[4]

Picking up in the second inning where he'd left off in the first, Benes fired fastball after fastball to Ruben Sierra, getting the DH to fly out to left field. Benes had gotten burned by Sierra in Game 2. In fact, it was his pitches to Sierra and Don Mattingly that led to his departure in the sixth inning of that game. In Mattingly's case, Benes had left a changeup over the plate. This time, he tried a breaking ball for a strike to start things. By now, any time Mattingly had even one strike on him, the crowd grew giddy anticipating another strikeout. Mattingly's four-hit performance the previous night had tempered some of that enthusiasm, as the fans were not chanting "Donnie Strikeout" by the end of Game 4. But this was a new day and as the count went full to Mattingly, thoughts of "Donnie Strikeout" still lingered in the air. Mattingly disappointed slightly them by flying out to left field. Dion James followed by grounding out weakly to first base. It was now six up and six down for Benes. For the first time in the series, the Yankees had failed to get a base runner on in the first two innings of a game.

· · · · · · · · ·

Things did not go so easily for David Cone in the second inning. Fresh off his record-setting seven-RBI performance in Game 4, Edgar

Martinez led off the bottom of the inning to thunderous applause. "Saint Edgar," as some were now referring to him, had destroyed Yankees pitching all year. The Yankees had talked about just throwing the ball to Martinez down the middle, the theory being that he would not expect it.[5] In counts that called for breaking balls, throw a fastball down the middle. Make him think, because, as Leyritz put it, "[At the plate] when you think, you are wrong."[6] But Cone had a habit of changing the game plan once he got the mound. "He shook me off 90 percent of the time," recalled Mike Stanley.[7] Instead of down the middle, Cone tried to stay away from Edgar with a combination of fastballs, sliders, and splitters. After the count went full, Edgar slapped a splitter in center field for a leadoff single. Cone then went full again to the other Martinez, before Tino knocked a fastball into left field for another opposite-field single. Cone was in trouble. No outs and two runners on for Jay Buhner. Though this type of situation normally called for a sacrifice bunt, there was no chance of that occurring. Buhner had not only homered off Cone that year, but he had laid down only two sacrifice bunts all season. Additionally, the Mariners were looking for more than just one run. They wanted to extend this rally into a much larger inning and get the Yankees out of the game early. The series had been all offense, so no matter how well Benes might be pitching, the Yankees could certainly overcome a one- or two-run deficit. The Mariners aimed for something more.

Quickly, Buhner fell down in the count, 1–2, before Cone fired a splitter in the dirt. Buhner flailed at it haplessly for strike three. Not only did Buhner strike out, but the runners remained on first and second. But Cone then threw a breaking ball in the dirt to Luis Sojo that bounded away from Stanley, allowing the runners to advance. With runners now on second and third and just one out, virtually any contact by Sojo would give the Mariners the lead. But after falling behind in the count, Cone regained his composure and struck out Sojo. Dan Wilson, whose checked swing against Cone had set George Steinbrenner off in Game 1, fouled off a few fastballs, took a ball, and then fell victim to a devious splitter. The ball dropped out of the zone, leaving Wilson to swing drastically over it for the third out. Cone had worked out of a jam by striking out the side. It was a Jekyll-and-Hyde show that he would put on throughout the rest of the night. The Martinezes had been able to smack Cone's pitches for line-drive hits, but the others could only reach out helplessly at the same pitches and go down swinging. At one point, Cone looked vulnerable; then a second later, he was dominating. The downside was that he had expended twenty-five pitches in the process. Another inning like that, and he might not be long for this game.

• • • • • • • • •

Mike Stanley led off the third inning with a seeing-eye single to left field, but Tony Fernandez quickly grounded into a 6–3 double play. It was the first ground-ball double play Benes had induced since joining the Mariners.[8] Randy Velarde's struggles continued as he looked at called strike three to end the inning. Benes walked slowly back to the bench, having held the Yankees scoreless through the first three innings.

Much like Velarde, Mike Blowers had struggled throughout the series. He had mustered only two hits through the first four games and had to endure being drilled in the back by a Jack McDowell fastball in Game 3. Piniella had batted Blowers seventh in Game 1. Now, because of his struggles, Blowers was moved down to the last spot in the lineup. The change did not help, as Blowers flied out to right field. But Blowers had made Cone throw seven pitches, and deep hitting counts were now becoming a theme for the Mariners. Coleman made Cone throw another five pitches before flying out to short center field. With two out and no one on, Cone eased back as Cora came to bat. Cora was one of many unsung heroes for the 1995 Mariners. His numbers were not overwhelming, and he was not considered an all-star second baseman. But Cora was the type of player who slowly wore away the opposition. Unimposing at five-foot-eight and 150 pounds, he used the so-called old-school fundamentals of the game to drive teams crazy.

Cora started his career with the San Diego Padres before being traded to the White Sox. It was on Chicago's South Side that people took notice of his style of play. He led the American League in sacrifice bunts in 1993 and stole twenty bases as the White Sox made the playoffs for the first time in a decade. But the White Sox wanted highly touted prospect Ray Durham to play second base, and they allowed Cora to walk during the strike off-season. Lou Piniella had made it known to the higher-ups in the Seattle organization that he wanted a veteran middle infielder. Cora, who had gone months without finding a team since he was granted free agency, signed with Seattle for $425,000 for the year. It was a $200,000 cut from what he had made in 1994.

Cora's style and all-out hustle quickly endeared him to Seattle fans and teammates, who came to refer to him as "Little" Joey Cora. "He was a little warrior. He never stopped talking since the day he came over," said Chris Bosio with a laugh.[9] "He would get in guy's faces. 'Buhner, you struck out three times. You suck.' But he would do it on purpose to get them fired up," said team trainer Rick Griffin.[10] When Vince Coleman joined the team in August, the combination of Coleman and Cora at the top of the lineup became a sparkplug that ignited the Mariners. Cora could bunt with the best of them, and only two hitters in the American League struck out with less frequency than he. Though not a prolific base stealer, he could swipe a bag when needed and had a knack for clutch hitting, including a .333 batting average with runners in scoring position. In fact, it was Cora's ninth-inning single that had started the August 24 rally that changed the Mariners' season.

If there was one category where Cora was lacking, it was power. As he stepped in against Cone in the third inning, the second baseman had hit just seven home runs in 2,028 regular season at-bats. He hadn't hit his first big-league home run until his sixth season, and he'd averaged just two home runs a year since then. So when Cone fell behind to Cora, 1–0, he did not think he was in any danger by throwing a fastball down the heart of the plate. In response, Cora belted the pitch to deep right field. Paul O'Neill tracked it a few steps, stopped, peered up, then saw the ball land just over the railing atop the right-field fence, where it bounded off a fan and bounced back onto the field. People could not believe it. Did Little Joey Cora just hit a home run? Yes he had, and more important, he had given the Mariners a 1–0 lead. Seattle had not lost a game all year in which Cora homered.[11] "I think the homer against Cone really started the game. Both sides started to get loose. [They thought] if Joey can hit a home run . . . anyone could," said Cora.[12] Cora would have sixty-one more postseason at-bats in his career, and he would never hit another home run. In fact, he would never drive in another run in the playoffs.

The crowd was still abuzz over Cora's shot when Griffey flied out to right field. Cone had thrown another twenty-one pitches. His pitch count was mounting, and now the Yankees were down a run. After three innings, the veteran hired gun was being outdueled by the new hired gun.

• • • • • • • • •

Wade Boggs flied out to begin the top of the fourth inning. Andy Benes was keeping the Yankees off balance through an assortment of fastballs and sliders they normally wouldn't chase. That changed when he couldn't locate his fastball against Bernie Williams and walked him. Benes's first walk of the night immediately became a distraction to him. Though an average stealer at best, Williams had great speed. He had stolen the only base of the series for the Yankees and, down a run, there was a chance he would try and swipe second and get himself into scoring position. Benes twice fired over to first. Neither attempt was particularly close. But that was not the point. Benes was not necessarily trying to pick off Williams as much as he was trying to keep him close to first base. He wanted Bernie to know he was paying attention, so he could scare him into not venturing too far off the bag. But in his attempt to do this, Benes ignored O'Neill at home plate. It was a dangerous move. Unlike many of his teammates, O'Neill was not facing the righty for just the second or third time. He was well acquainted with his style from having faced him in the National League. O'Neill also knew that Benes had, with the exception of one breaking ball, gone exclusively to the fastball against him in the first inning. Now, with a runner possibly trying to steal second, O'Neill was even more certain Benes would throw a first-pitch fastball. Benes did, and O'Neill crushed it. O'Neill immediately dropped his head and began circling the bases. The ball landed in nearly the same spot as O'Neill's third-inning home run the night before. Just as it had then, the crush of his bat and the thump of the ball dropping into the right-field stands sent a stunning silence across the Kingdome. The howls of his teammates could be heard everywhere as O'Neill rounded the bases and crossed home plate. In the blink of eye, one misplaced pitch had put Seattle down 2–1. They had now trailed at least once in every single game in the series.

O'Neill's home run rattled and shocked the crowd. Even the sight of the home-run ball being thrown back onto the field did not draw the normal applause. But Benes went right back to attacking the

Yankees hitters. Three pitches after O'Neill's blast, the inning was over after Sierra and Mattingly both flied out. Benes's ignoring of O'Neill had cost him dearly and put his team in a hole. It was time for yet another Mariners comeback.

• • • • • • • • •

Edgar Martinez just got under a Cone fastball, popping up to Mattingly for the first out of the inning. Handed a lead, Cone went back to going straight after the Mariners hitters, throwing Edgar fastballs down the middle. But that strategy changed again when Tino Martinez lined a fastball into left-center field for a hit. Though not driven far, the ball carried all the way to the fence, allowing even the slow-footed Tino to stroll easily into second base with a double. The Kingdome again grew loud as Jay Buhner stepped in. Returning to his pattern from the second inning, Cone tried using a series of sliders and splitters to make Buhner chase pitches out of the strike zone. This time, Buhner did not bite. The count went to 3–1 when Buhner swung at a fastball, making contact and shattering his bat in two. The upper portion landed just in front of third base, and Buhner was left holding a nub of wood at home plate. The ball sailed above Fernandez's head and dropped softly into short left center field. Tino scored easily to the tie game. The sting of O'Neill's home run, so shocking just minutes before, was gone.

Cone retired Sojo, but Dan Wilson singled into center field. It was only Wilson's second hit of the series, but it was a big one. Now, Blowers had his turn at putting the Mariners ahead. Blowers could easily make it a 5–2 Mariners lead with one swing, but Cone was a strikeout pitcher, and he had gotten Blowers twice in Game 1. Cone quickly jumped ahead in the count, 0–2. Ignoring the runners he had been so occupied with only moments earlier, Cone threw a slider that Blowers grounded directly to Fernandez, who moved quickly to second base, stepped on the bag and ended the inning. Cone had allowed the Mariners to tie the game, but he escaped further damage. His pitch count, however, continued to balloon. He had needed another twenty-five tosses to get out of the fourth.

• • • • • • • • •

While Cone was toiling endlessly inning after inning, Benes was quickly working through Yankees hitters with ease. O'Neill's home run aside, the Yankees were having difficulty with the righty and assisting him in ways the Mariners hitters were not helping Cone. Normally patient, the Yankees were cutting at first pitches and failing to go deep into counts. Dion James began the fifth inning by grounding out on three pitches. Mike Stanley then grounded out on the first pitch he saw. Tony Fernandez, dealing with his share of offensive struggles, swung at the second pitch he saw, drilling it to right-center field where it bounced in between Griffey and Buhner. Fernandez moved into second with a stand-up double. Now the Yankees needed a big two-out hit to get the lead back. Instead, Velarde popped up to Wilson, ending the inning. Benes, despite the double, had strolled through the fifth inning, this time throwing only seven pitches. It brought his pitch count to fifty-seven for the game. Through five innings, Benes had thrown only slightly more pitches than it had taken Cone to get out of the just the third and fourth innings combined. The game remained tied as Benes continued to outpitch his counterpart.

Cone responded with a solid and, more important, efficient fifth inning. Coleman lined out to Fernandez on only two pitches. Cora, the hero just two innings ago, popped up to second on just four pitches. Griffey swung over a splitter, striking out. Needing a quick inning, Cone had delivered, throwing only twelve pitches. The game moved on to the sixth inning tied.

· · · · · · · · ·

"Strike three!" yelled home-plate umpire Jim Evans, his fists pumping in the air. The call was barely audible above the crowd reaction, but Wade Boggs certainly heard it. Boggs had been expecting a fastball and instead watched a slider drop over the plate for strike three. It was the second time he had struck out in the game, something he had done only six times the entire season. Knowing the pitch was a strike, he turned and headed back to the dugout without arguing.

Bernie Williams then walked on five pitches, and the faint detection of moans and groans could be heard throughout the Kingdome. Fans had seen this already. Two innings earlier, Benes had walked

Williams with one out, become preoccupied with him at first base,. and subsequently given up a two-run home run to O'Neill. Benes knew this, of course. He gave a courtesy throw to first, just to let Williams know he was aware of his presence, then set about retiring O'Neill. Benes lost control of the strike zone. His fastballs sailed outside, and he walked O'Neill on four pitches. It wasn't just his fastball, either, that was failing to find the plate. His slider began to break outside, and he walked Ruben Sierra on five pitches to load the bases with just one out for Don Mattingly.

Had this been 1987, Benes might just as well have placed the ball on a tee for Don Mattingly to hit out of the ballpark. That year, Mattingly set a Major League record by hitting six grand slams. But this was not 1987, and amazingly, those six grand slams were the only ones Mattingly hit in his entire career. Still, Mattingly had turned back the clock for the first four games of the series, showing shades of the younger, healthier player who had dominated American League pitching. It was not inconceivable to imagine Mattingly's sending a shot over the right-field wall and giving the Yankees a four-run lead. In this series, anything was possible. Despite the tension of the moment, the fans in the Kingdome rose in support of their pitcher, begging for a pop-up, strikeout, or double play, just anything that would keep this game tied.

A day earlier, Mattingly had grabbed Benes so the two could take a few pictures together. "I just thought it would be nice for both of us to have a photograph to remember all this," said Mattingly, referring to the fact that he and Benes were from the same hometown.[13] The memory of those pleasantries now ceased to exist. Benes stared in at the Yankees captain. It was the biggest confrontation either of them experienced in their careers, regardless of the differences in age. Mattingly was fully expecting a first-pitch fastball, which is exactly what Benes delivered. It was just off the plate, and Mattingly ripped the ball deep down the left-field line, where it landed fair just before the warning track. There the ball took a bounce that changed history. Smacking hard against the Kingdome's turf, the ball skipped high in the air, hurdled the left-field fence, and bounced off the stands, then fell back into the field of play. Left-field umpire Joe Brinkman immediately signaled a ground-rule double. Sierra, running on contact, was forced to halt at third base. Two runs scored and the Yankees now led 4–2, but it could have been 5–2 if not for that bounce. There was no guarantee that Sierra would have scored had the ball not bounced over the fence, but the odds were in his favor. He had been running on contact, and Vince Coleman had a below-average arm in the outfield. Still, such talk seemed pointless at the time, because the Yankees still had runners on second and third with fewer than two outs. And that bounce was not overshadowing the fact that Mattingly, in what would be the last hit of his career, had given his team a two-run lead. The enormity of that bounce would not be realized until later in the game.

Mattingly's double jolted the Kingdome crowd into silence, and the Yankees were still threatening. Dion James, with just one hit in the series, was intentionally walked. Strategically, it was the right move by Lou Piniella. It set up a double play and created a force-out at every base. But because of who was coming to the plate, some people were shaking their heads wondering: "Doesn't Lou know what Mike Stanley does with the bases loaded?"

• • • • • • • • •

Gene Michael received his share of kudos for such acquisitions as Paul O'Neill, Jimmy Key, Wade Boggs, and John Wetteland, but there was one player he'd signed for whom no one ever seemed to thank him. That was Mike Stanley. Stanley was drafted by the Texas Rangers in 1985, debuting with the team the next season. While given a handful of starts at third base, first base, and even two appearances in the outfield, Stanley was primarily used in a platoon situation at catcher. His numbers, both offensively and defensively, were not overly impressive. Gene Michael, however, noticed one element of his game: his on-base percentage. Though Stanley never generated a batting average above .249 with Texas, his on-base percentage tended to be nearly 100 points higher. That was the type of player Gene Michael looked for. Stanley signed with the Yankees in January 1992 and became their backup catcher behind Matt Nokes. For a time, it seemed Stanley was destined to be in New York just what he was in Texas: a part-time catcher. But early in the 1993 season, Stanley began to explode offensively. His batting average shot up, and he became a legitimate power threat at the plate. Shortly thereafter,

Buck Showalter called Stanley into his office to inform him that his playing time would increase.[14] Essentially, Showalter was handing him the full-time catcher's position. Stano, as Showalter referred to him, responded with the greatest offensive season of his career, hitting .305 with twenty-six home runs and eighty-four RBIs. The numbers instantly turned him into a fan favorite in New York.

Stanley proved the numbers were not a fluke by hitting .300 with seventeen home runs the next year. In 1995, while his average dropped, his offensive production remained steady, as he finished second on the team in both home runs and RBIs. During the season, Stanley hit three home runs in a game against the Indians on August 10, the first time in eighteen years a Yankee had done so. For the first and only time in his career, he made the All-Star team. Known in the clubhouse as "Tools," after the popular Stanley Tools brand, he was widely regarded as one of the nicest, most sincere people in baseball. Stanley was shy, but he had an easygoing manner and determined work ethic that endeared him to fans, teammates, and especially manager Buck Showalter. "He always seemed to be getting hit with foul tips, always," recalled former Yankees bullpen coach Glen Sherlock.[15] But Stanley played through the pain. Another endearing trait, perhaps the most so about him, was his uncanny ability for big hits. He hit .308 with runners in scoring position in 1994 and .320 in 1995. With the bases loaded, though, Mike Stanley wasn't just great, he was phenomenal. During the '95 regular season, he had gone 9–11 with two grand slams and twenty-seven RBIs when the bags were full. For his career coming into Game 5, Stanley was a .373 hitter with the bases loaded, including eight grand slams, one of which he hit against Randy Johnson.

Some Mariners fans had to be shaking their head when Piniella had Benes intentionally walk Dion James to set up the bases loaded for Stanley with one out in the sixth inning of the deciding Game 5. Only five days earlier, Gary Thorne had referred to Stanley as "the new Mr. Bases Loaded."[16] Now, Stanley brought his .818 regular-season batting average with three runners on into the biggest at-bat of his career. Not only was Piniella's intentional walk to James surprising, but so was his decision to keep Benes in the game. By now Benes had lost control of his fastball and off-speed pitches. Additionally, Stanley had one of the three Yankees hits off him. But Piniella had few options. The Mariners' bullpen had been unreliable and overused due to Bosio's early exit in

Game 4. Seattle's season and maybe the future of the franchise now rested on Benes's right arm.

The tension inside the Kingdome was nerve-racking. A base hit could kill baseball in the Pacific Northwest. "There are very few hitters in baseball that have had the production with the bases loaded like Mike Stanley," Jim Kaat reminded viewers as Stanley stepped into the box.[17] Benes quickly jumped ahead of Stanley, putting him in a 0–2 hole. But Stanley fought back and the count went full. With no room for error and no place to put Stanley, Benes was forced to throw a fastball. It was a dangerous option, as Stanley was of the best fastball hitters in the game. Benes shook his head in agreement at the sign from Wilson, set himself, and then delivered the most important pitch of his life. It was a fastball that started rising as it headed over the plate. It was destined to be ball four, but with two strikes, Stanley had to swing at anything reasonably close. Instead of driving the fastball, Stanley swung under it, popping it straight up behind home plate. The crowd exhaled as Wilson settled under the ball in foul territory and squeezed it for the second out. In a series where the angle of deflection off a wall had temporarily saved the Mariners in Game 2 and Don Mattingly struck out more times against a pitcher in a single game than he had in his entire career, this twist of fate seemed inevitable. Stanley had made only two outs all year with the bases loaded, yet in the biggest bases-loaded at-bat of the season, he popped up.

Still needing one more out to escape the jam he had created, Benes fell behind Tony Fernandez, 3–1, but recovered to eventually induce the shortstop to fly out to left field. "I just got a little too careful with my pitches and got into trouble," said Benes. "But getting out of that inning allowing only two runs. That wasn't bad."[18] The crowd, on an endless supply of energy, gave their team another loud ovation as they left the field. But the euphoria of having escaped that bases-loaded jam was temporary. The Mariners were now two runs down and had just twelve outs remaining in their season to get them back. Still, the Yankees knew it was too early to start celebrating. "Four-two in the sixth is too early in this ball park. The way things have been going, runs have been going up like crazy, no one felt comfortable [at] 4–2," said Don Mattingly.[19]

• • • • • • • • •

As Edgar Martinez strolled into second base, the Yankees could hardly have been surprised. A Martinez base hit was predestined at this point. It was the sun rising in the east and setting in the west. Edgar's sixth-inning leadoff double put yet another charge into the Kingdome and did little to shock anyone. In fact, the shock now came when the Yankees actually retired Martinez. Cone had his lead back, but he was already getting himself into trouble. With the leadoff hitter now on second, the Mariners could get a run without the benefit of a hit. That was assuming they did not get any more hits, which was a big assumption, since Tino Martinez was now batting. Tino was already two for two and had driven Cone crazy by taking his pitches to the opposite field. But he quickly fell behind 0–2 and eventually chased a slider, striking out. It prevented Edgar Martinez from advancing to third with fewer than two outs. The crowd, quieted by Tino's strikeout, grew quieter when Buhner struck out on three straight pitches, the last of which was a devastating splitter that dropped out of the strike zone at the last second. Needing a base hit and looking for some added punch, Piniella sent up left-handed hitting Warren Newson to pinch-hit for Sojo. The move was purely offensive-minded, as Newson was not a shortstop and Piniella had at least two shortstops sitting on his bench. Piniella wanted the lefty–righty matchup. But Cone was too much for even the lefties. Newson, in his first appearance of the series, was easily overmatched, striking out on four pitches. The last one was another splitter that fell completely out of the strike zone, causing him to swing right over it. Cone had been digging holes for himself all game and then leaping out of them with split-fingered pitches that the Mariners could not touch. He was now at 104 pitches and slowly putting in a playoff performance for the ages.

• • • • • • • • •

Andy Benes had labored through the sixth inning, but he returned in the seventh and promptly retired the first two hitters. But another walk to Bernie Williams derailed his night. The left-handed Paul O'Neill was coming up and Piniella decided it was finally time to remove his starting pitcher. Benes headed toward the dugout, receiving a rousing ovation from the hometown crowd. Benes was a free agent come the off-season, and there was a good chance that this would be his last appearance as a Mariner. Even though he left down two runs, the fans appreciated the effort. Then they welcomed the familiar face of Norm Charlton. The Mariners closer had pitched in three straight games and shown signs of fatigue in Game 4, but Piniella wanted a lefty–lefty matchup. This was the fourth time the two faced each other in the series, so the drama of the Charlton–O'Neill confrontations had been sapped already. The fourth confrontation proved anticlimactic anyway, as O'Neill flied out to left field to end the inning. As the fly ball settled into Vince Coleman's glove, people had to wonder: did Norm Charlton have another two innings left in his arm? Sitting in the Mariners' dugout, Randy Johnson might just have been one of those people.

By the bottom of the seventh inning, David Cone's arm could have fallen off and he would not have cared. Given a two-run lead, he was dead set on getting the Yankees to the ALCS. Showing no sign of predictability, he went right after hitters, firing fastball after fastball past Wilson, striking him out to start the inning. Blowers went down just easily, staring at a called strike-three slider. Coleman lined out to Mattingly, ending the inning. The Mariners were down to six outs, and Cone looked like he was getting better as the game went on.

· · · · · · · · · ·

The Yankees went down with little fanfare in the top of the eighth inning. Knowing his team could not afford to fall behind any further, Charlton held the Yankees in check despite a two-out walk to Gerald Williams, now playing left field in place of Dion James. The biggest commotion came during the half inning from the Seattle bullpen. To some, Piniella may have sounded like he was bluffing when he said that Randy Johnson was available for Game 5. Now, he showed he was dead serious because the six-foot-ten long-haired lefty began warming up in the bullpen. Within seconds, everyone, especially the Yankees, took notice. It was a move as strategic as it was psychological. His team two runs down, Piniella knew he needed the crowd back in the game. With Cone firing strikes and keeping the Mariners at bay, having Johnson walk to the bullpen was just the way to do it. Piniella also knew that the mere sight of

Johnson and the idea that he might appear on the mound would be imprinted on the minds of the Yankees as they played the remaining few innings of the series. The message to New York was clear: if you do not hold this lead, you will have to face this guy to keep your season alive.

But the Yankees were still holding the lead. They were up by two runs with just six outs to go, and Cone was coming off his most effective inning of the game. But few could have guessed that as Cone headed to the mound in the bottom of the eighth inning, the next few minutes would drastically alter the course of history for dozens of players, coaches, managers, and even owners. And it all started so simply.

· · · · · · · · ·

Memories of his third-inning home run were still fresh in people's minds when Joey Cora gave the crowd a jolt by sending a Cone slider to right field. But it was just an ordinary fly ball out to Paul O'Neill. Only five outs remained for another Mariners miracle. With no one on base, Cone directly challenged Ken Griffey Jr. with a fastball right over the plate. Junior extended his arms, ripped the bat through the zone, and sent the pitch high and deep to right field. O'Neill barely moved as the ball disappeared far into the right-field seats. It was Griffey's third home run off Cone and his fifth of the series. As Junior slowly rounded the bases in his signature trot, ABC cameras panned to Reggie Jackson. Previously, only two men had ever hit five home runs in one postseason series. One was Babe Ruth. The other was sitting in the Yankees' box in the Kingdome, one row in front of George Steinbrenner. As if on cue, "Mr. October" held up his hand and flashed five fingers, acknowledging that Junior had just matched his feat. Additionally, it was the twenty-second and final home run of the series, setting a postseason record for combined home runs by both teams.[20]

The crowd went berserk over Griffey's home run. David Cone was not pleased with himself for having left the ball over the plate, but he still had a one-run lead and he still had outs to record. He refocused and induced the ever-dangerous Edgar Martinez to ground out to short. As the out was recorded, Derek Jeter, a rookie who was not on the Yankees' postseason roster but still dressed and traveled with the team at the behest of Buck Showalter, enthusiastically leapt off the bench, pumping his fists. His Yankees were now just four outs away from a flight to Cleveland. Then, it all fell apart.

· · · · · · · · ·

During the course of Game 5, Baseball Network analyst Jim Kaat had repeatedly remarked that David Cone had yet to issue a walk, despite all his troubles. This was an accomplishment for Cone, as walks tended to be the bane of his existence. It wasn't because he had control issues that he walked so many hitters; rather, his personality would simply not allow it. When ahead on a hitter 0–2, he had no problem pushing the count full, as long as it did not mean giving in and delivering a hittable pitch. Confident in his abilities, Cone wanted to make the perfect pitch to get every hitter out. It was a style that resulted in large numbers of walks per game and bloated pitch counts. So it was fortunate for the Yankees and somewhat odd, when Tino Martinez came to bat with two out in the eighth inning, that no Mariner had yet to draw four balls from Cone. But in an instant, Cone began missing the strike zone. Aware that he had lost considerable arm strength during the course of the game, Cone shied away from his fastball, now going almost exclusively with off-speed pitches. But his sliders and splitters were breaking low, and Martinez was not chasing them. Tino walked on five pitches. The crowd, silenced by Edgar's groundout, reversed course and got back on its feet, cheering as loud as it could.

With the tying run now on first, Cone fell behind Jay Buhner, two balls and one strike. His off-speed stuff not working, Cone finally reared back and fired a fastball. Buhner, swinging late, slashed the ball toward second base. Randy Velarde quickly ran three steps to his right and leapt. There were to be so many "what ifs" to take out of the series. In this case, it was what if Velarde had been two inches taller? Buhner's line drive narrowly escaped the reach of Velarde, who had stretched his glove hand as long and high as possible. Another two inches and the ball would have slammed into Velarde's glove, ending the inning. Instead, it sailed into right-center field for a single. Martinez held at second base.

Cone was in serious trouble, and his arm had almost nothing left. Sensing the danger Cone was in, Showalter had a pitcher begin warming up in the bullpen. But it was not John Wetteland. Showalter had lost faith in his closer, and for good reason. Wetteland had collapsed in the last few days, losing Game 4, nearly losing Game 2, and almost blowing a five-run lead in Game 1. In what was shaping up to be the biggest save situation of the season, Wetteland sat on the bench. Instead, Showalter had twenty-five-year-old rookie Mariano Rivera warming up down the right-field line.

Lou Piniella also sensed Cone was running out of gas. Opting for speed on the bases, he pinch-ran the speedier rookie, Alex Rodriguez, for Tino Martinez, now in scoring position. Felix Fermin, who had replaced Luis Sojo at shortstop, was scheduled to hit, but Piniella sought a bat off his bench. While many expected Doug Strange, Piniella instead went with Alex Diaz. Cone, now at 136 pitches and his strength almost gone, hesitated to throw fastballs to Diaz. He instead went strictly with off-speed pitches, throwing to Diaz as if he were Babe Ruth. The result was a five-pitch walk that loaded the bases. Cone's breaking pitches were not fooling hitters, as they had earlier in the game. The Kingdome now resembled a rock concert, as ear-shattering noise reverberated from every crevice of the building.

Lou Piniella again went to his bench, this time sending up his professional pinch-hitter Doug Strange in place of Dan Wilson. For Strange, it was the chance of a lifetime. The Mariners were his fourth team in just six seasons. With the exception of one year in Texas, he had never been a full-time Major League player, generally being relegated to platoon or pinch-hitting duties. Strange had watched mostly from the bench all year as the Mariners made history. But he made sure to soak it all in. To him, what was occurring that season was the most incredible thing he had ever seen.[21] On September 19, as voters were deciding the future of the Mariners in Seattle, Strange played no small part in the team's run when he drilled a game-tying ninth-inning home run against his former team, the Texas Rangers. He also assisted in winning the game in extra innings. It was the biggest moment of his career. That was until he came to the plate with the bases loaded and two outs in the eighth inning of Game 5, his team down a run. This was the type of situation ball players dreamed about and role-played in their backyards when they were kids. The moment was Doug Strange's for the taking.

The tying run was just ninety feet from home plate, and all after two were out. Showalter had a decision to make. Admitting later that he was not completely aware of what he had in Mariano Rivera, he felt his best option was to stick with Cone.[22] Cone, exhausted and dripping sweat through his uniform, still refused to throw a fastball. Instead, he threw a first-pitch slider to an overanxious Strange, who checked his swing but went too far. Strike one. Ahead of the hitter, Cone still chose breaking pitches, and the next three were all out of the strike zone. Strange patiently refused to chase them. Three balls, one strike. The tension inside the Kingdome reached a boiling point. The sound was so deafening that Strange had to step out of the box to regain his composure.[23] Now a pitch away from giving up the lead, Cone gave in. "I got the take sign and I think they [the Yankees] saw it. [Fernandez] went to the mound to talk to Cone, who must have known I wasn't going to swing because he threw me a fastball right down the middle," said Strange.[24] Strike two. The count was full, and despite his pitching pattern, Strange believed that Cone would now come back with another fastball. How could he not? He couldn't afford to miss the strike zone. Cone, however, had other ideas. He had nothing left on his fastball. Absolutely nothing. He had never followed pitching patterns before, and he was not going to start now. Cone pitched by feel, not pattern, and at this point, he felt the splitter was the best way to go. Catcher Mike Stanley yielded to the pitcher who threw by feel and readied himself for a splitter. Cone went into his delivery and all runners broke from their bases. As the splitter came out of Cone's hand, it began to break too early. Strange, perhaps taken aback by the off-speed pitch, held off and watched as the ball bounced into the dirt just behind home plate. Ball four. "Ninety percent of the time, I am going to swing at that pitch because I'm aggressive," said Strange. "This time I didn't, for some reason."[25] The Mariners, led by cheerleaders Andy Benes and Chris Bosio, exploded from the bench, running onto the field to greet Alex Rodriguez after he crossed the plate to tie the game. Strange tossed his bat back to the dugout and headed toward first base. It was a euphoric moment for his teammates and the city, but for Strange it was bittersweet. "Like kissing your sister," he later described it.[26] Strange didn't want to the tie game. He had wanted to win the game for Seattle.

David Cone did not empathize with Strange. Once his ball-four splitter bounced into the dirt, Cone's upper body hunched down, almost as if it could no longer sustain itself. He remained in that position momentarily, staring at the thin green turf. It was half out of disappointment and half out of sheer exhaustion. He was physically and emotionally drained. Showalter immediately left the dugout, approached the mound, and signaled for Rivera. Cone, dejected, handed Showalter the ball and walked very slowly toward the dugout, carrying his glove in his hand. Willie Randolph and Derek Jeter jumped out to offer him their solace, but Cone walked past them in a straight line through the dugout and into the tunnel. "I rolled the dice. I gambled it. It wasn't a good pitch. It wasn't even close enough for him to swing at. I really tried to rear back and throw the best splitter I had left," said Cone.[27] He had thrown 147 pitches in one of the gutsiest, grittiest performances by a pitcher in postseason history. He had constantly created, then worked his way out of danger until he finally ran out of steam with two outs in the eighth inning. Now, after all that, the only thing keeping him from being the losing pitcher in Game 5 was a showdown between Mike Blowers and Mariano Rivera.

· · · · · · · · ·

Mariano Rivera jogged in from the bullpen and began his warm-up tosses. He had delivered three solid innings in Game 2, picking up the victory in a pressure-packed situation. But how would he react now? He had 57,000 people screaming against him, not for him, and his margin for error was zero. The go-ahead run stood at third base in Jay Buhner, and Mike Blowers was hitting. Yes, Blowers had struggled throughout the series, but he was not a hitter to be taken lightly, especially when the bases were loaded. This excitement was all the Kingdome needed to be on their feet, yelling, screaming and chanting.

Rivera, who had been crushed in start after start at the beginning of the season, delivered a first-pitch fastball that screamed by Blowers for strike one. He fired another fastball that Blowers was able to foul back for strike two. Rivera then fired a fastball that captivated Blowers. "Strike three," yelled Jim Evans. What had been set up as a dramatic finish was reduced to an anticlimactic three-pitch strikeout. "I didn't want to have that picture in my mind all winter long, and I would have if we had lost," said Blowers.[28] Rivera strolled calmly back to the dugout to receive congratulations from his teammates. In the Yankees' box, Gene Michael stood up and said, "I think we found something here."[29]

Randy Johnson was still warming up in the Mariners' bullpen when Norm Charlton came back out to the mound to begin the ninth inning. The series of pinch hitters had forced Piniella to completely redesign his infield. Doug Strange was now playing third. Alex Rodriguez, who had yet to play defensively in the series, now manned short-stop. Blowers moved from third base to first base, and Chris Widger crouched behind home plate as the new catcher. The only infield position that remained the same was Joey Cora at second base. Charlton, fatigued from working in four straight games, finished his warm-up and stared in at the Yankees' shortstop, Tony Fernandez.

• • • • • • • • • •

The year 1995 was not an easy one for Tony Fernandez. Injuries had placed him on the disabled list and hindered his overall performance throughout the year. The result was a subpar season that made him a target for fans who were thoroughly disappointed by the team's play. What Yankees fans saw that year was a far cry from the player that fans in Toronto and San Diego had enjoyed throughout the 1980s and early 1990s. Fernandez had come up with the Blue Jays as they became a powerhouse in the American League East in the 1980s. His long, lanky frame betrayed his extreme athleticism, specifically his defensive abilities at shortstop. Fernandez possessed excellent range and had a soft, easy throwing motion that was accurate and deceptively strong. His natural fielding ability was so smooth that those who did not know him better might have mistaken his style as lazy and carefree. It was hardly anything of the sort. His colleagues recognized this and awarded him the Gold Glove at shortstop for four consecutive seasons between 1986 and 1989. Fernandez had a hitting style similar to his fielding style in that it gave off an appearance of effortlessness, even laziness. A switch-hitter, Fernandez didn't swing so much as chop and swat at the ball in a manner that could easily have been seen as apathetic, though it certainly was not.

After reaching the postseason twice with Toronto, Fernandez was involved in a blockbuster trade in 1990 that sent him and teammate Fred McGriff to the San Diego Padres for Roberto Alomar and Joe Carter. He enjoyed moderate success in San Diego before being traded to the New York Mets in 1993. Fernandez's first stint in New York was a disaster, as he batted just .225 for a Mets team that was the worst in baseball. He was given a reprieve in June when he was traded back to the Blue Jays. At the time, they were fending off a pesky challenge by the Yankees for first place, and the trade rejuvenated Fernandez. North of the border again, he hit over .300 and played in the World Series for the first time in his career. In the Fall Classic, he batted .333 and drove in nine runs as the Blue Jays defeated the Philadelphia Phillies in six games. Despite his postseason heroics, Fernandez moved on to Cincinnati in 1994, playing third base for the Reds. During the strike, he agreed to a two-year contract to play shortstop in the Bronx. The Yankees already had two Gold Glovers in their infield with Don Mattingly and Wade Boggs. A potential third was at second base in Pat Kelly. The addition of Fernandez gave the team possibly the best defensive infield in their history. But injuries limited Fernandez's effectiveness, and he slumped badly at the plate. The lone highlight of his season came against the A's on September 3 when he became the first Yankee in twenty-three years to hit for the cycle.

Fernandez's numbers had not endeared him to Yankees fans, but his teammates respected his natural ability and enjoyed his rather dry sense of humor. Not outwardly funny or prankish like John Wetteland or Bob Wickman, Fernandez had a different style that greatly amused his teammates. During his first start in Chicago after having left the White Sox, Jack McDowell gave up a three-run home run to John Kruk in the first inning on a high fastball. When Kruk came up for his second at-bat, Fernandez called time just as McDowell was about to go into the windup. McDowell expected some prolific words of wisdom from his shortstop. Instead, Fernandez merely said, "Hey, this guy [Kruk] . . . he like the high one," and then returned to his position. McDowell, befuddled at first, simply laughed it off.[30] Fernandez was also a fitness fanatic. "I called him Inspector Gadget, because he had all these gadgets to do pregame warm-ups. He would be in the batting cage with tapes doing yoga and doing his mantra: 'See the ball,'" said Rick Down.[31]

Leading off in the top of the ninth inning of Game 5, Fernandez wanted to erase his sluggish season. Despite some terrific defensive plays, his offensive struggles had continued into October. The beauty of the postseason, however, was that one swing could erase all bad memories from any season. Fernandez nearly did just that. Hitting from the right side against the left-handed Charlton, Fernandez drilled a 1–0 fastball high and deep to right-center field. In an instant, the Kingdome became silent, outside of the screams from the Yankees' dugout. Ken Griffey Jr. tracked the ball but had no chance of catching it. Norm Charlton stared it down too, hoping the ball would stay to the right and crash into the wall. Fernandez thought he had gotten all of it and given the Yankees the lead. But just as he rounded first base, he saw the ball smack off the right-center-field wall. Fifteen feet off the ground, the ball smashed into the scoreboard in nearly the identical spot where Junior had broken his wrist months earlier. Griffey retrieved the ball and fired into second, where Fernandez was already standing with a double. Despite the clutch hit, Fernandez was not pleased. He stood on second base flustered and visibly annoyed that the ball had not carried out. A few feet to the left and he would have hit the go-ahead home run. So close was his shot to being a home run that Brent Musburger mistakenly gave false hope to millions of Yankees fans when he incorrectly claimed on air that Fernandez's drive had left the playing field. Seeing his error, he immediately corrected himself, but in turn drew the ire and scorn of many suddenly disappointed Yankees fans.

The game now turned into a chess match, with Showalter and Piniella matching wit against wit, move against move. The first move belonged to Showalter, who called for Randy Velarde to lay down a sacrifice bunt and get Fernandez to third base. Velarde twice attempted to bunt. Both times he was unsuccessful. Charlton, however, was mixing fastballs and forkballs and missing the plate with both. Instead of allowing Velarde to bunt, he ended up walking him, putting two runners on with no one out. Piniella, in turn, went to the mound and made a move. "I tried to convince him I was fine and to let me stay in, but Lou always knew when I was lying," said Charlton. "Lou told me, 'You did a great job. Now I'm gonna get you some help.'"[32] Piniella lifted his worn-out closer from the game. Charlton, naturally disappointed at the situation he created, walked solemnly back to the bench. He received a warm ovation from a crowd that showed its gratitude for everything he had done that year. But Charlton's ovation was nothing compared to what greeted the new pitcher. As "Welcome to the Jungle" blared over the PA system, Randy Johnson walked across foul territory, past third, and to the mound. It was only his third career relief appearance, and he had just pitched seven innings only two nights ago. None of that mattered. Johnson would take the ball under any condition, and he would pitch all night if it meant winning the game.

Few if any Yankees were pleased to see Johnson stroll in from the bullpen. None could have been less thrilled than the man due to hit, Wade Boggs. Boggs was a five-time batting champion, a career .300 hitter, and a future Hall of Famer. Few pitchers put any fear into him. Randy Johnson was a different story. To Boggs, Johnson was the toughest pitcher he had ever or would ever encounter. "It was not a fun day at the office facing him," said Boggs.[33] Making the upcoming at-bat more difficult for Boggs was that he hadn't actually faced Johnson since 1992, when he was still a member of the Red Sox. It would be difficult to expect even Boggs to single against the Big Unit, and regardless, the situation screamed for a bunt. But Boggs had not sacrificed once all season and had done so only three times in the last six years. Now, he would have to bunt against the most dominant pitcher in baseball.

The crowd was loud and on its feet, but it was also on edge. One misplay or wrong throw and the season could be ruined. The rust on Boggs's bunting skills was immediately apparent when he bunted Johnson's first-pitch fastball foul. Showing bunt again, Boggs instead held up, but took a called strike two. Showalter was now forced to remove the bunt. It didn't matter. Boggs's vulnerability was evident to all, even when he was just trying to bunt against Johnson. The Big Unit delivered a 0–2 fastball that ripped through the air and right past Boggs's bat for strike three. It was a huge out. Johnson, so focused on retiring Boggs, actually had not realized that there were two runners on.[34] Now, the Yankees would need a hit or some sort of large misplay on the part of the Mariners to take the lead. Bernie Williams, who homered off Johnson in Game 3, tried to deliver that big hit, but instead popped up a fastball to Cora. O'Neill then popped out to Widger. Inning over. As quickly and loudly as the Yankees had begun the inning, they just as quickly went out with a whimper against the Big Unit. The lack of fundamentals had cost them dearly. The Mariners had the top of the order coming up in the bottom of the ninth inning. Soon, it would be Showalter's chance to counter Piniella's latest move.

• • • • • • • • •

Before the start of Game 5, both Piniella and Showalter made it known to their players that everyone was available. Having used nearly all his bench players and bringing in Randy Johnson on just one day's rest, Piniella was showing he clearly meant it. With rookie Mariano Rivera facing the top of the Mariners' order, Showalter decided it was his turn to show he meant it too. The rookie left-hander Andy Pettitte had been warming up in the Yankees' bullpen, but now he was joined by Game 3 starter Jack McDowell. McDowell's appearance down the line did not cause nearly the stir that Johnson's had. Still, it was quite a sight. Rarely did you see a starting pitcher come into a game in relief on just one day's rest. Even more rarely did you see the opposing team's starter also come into the same game in relief. Before Game 5, only four times in the history of league championship play had pitchers started and relieved in the same series.[35] Now, it might happen twice in the same game.

A single run separated the Seattle Mariners from the American League Championship Series. The Kingdome was rocking as the theme to *Rocky* played over the PA system, and Mariner Moose did the worm on top of Seattle's dugout. Vince Coleman singled to center field to start the ninth inning, and knots grew in the pit of every Yankees fan's stomach. The way things had gone since the series moved to Seattle, and with Junior and Edgar waiting in the wings, it seemed a foregone conclusion that Coleman would eventually come around to score the series-winning run. With Rivera still in the game, Joey Cora laid down a perfect sacrifice bunt that allowed Coleman to get to second. Rivera intentionally walked Junior, and Showalter immediately made his next move. The Kingdome was so loud that bullpen coach Glen Sherlock couldn't hear the bullpen phone ringing, even though he was sitting right in front of it. Instead, he had his hands on it to feel for the vibration when Showalter called to tell him that Jack McDowell was now coming in.[36] Even though it was the ninth inning of Game 5, the series was in the hands of Game 3's starting pitchers. The 1993 American League Cy Young Award winner now battled the soon-to-be-announced 1995 American League Cy Young Award winner. And the game had been started by the 1994 American League Cy Young Award winner. Could this series offer anymore strange twists?

The second-guessing that Showalter faced for possibly leaving Cone in too long would pale compared to the criticism that resulted from his bringing in McDowell. There were those who felt he had done so merely to go move for move with Piniella. Piniella had brought in his Game 3 starter, so Showalter was going to use his. Critics thought it resembled an "anything you can do I can do better" scenario, one in which Buck was outmaneuvered. Allegedly, George Steinbrenner was one of these critics. Showalter did not agree with any of this. "Jack was our best option. He's throwing the ball well and John [Wetteland] has struggled against these guys," he told reporters after the game.[37] Showalter also admits that he still didn't realize what he had in Rivera at the time. Regardless of whether people agreed or not, McDowell was now in the game. "At that point, adrenaline takes you through. I didn't feel anything. I felt I had my stuff. It was just a matter of executing pitches," said McDowell.[38]

McDowell's task was far from easy. Pitching on just one day's rest and still feeling the effects of the bulging muscle in his back, he was called upon to get out Edgar Martinez with just one out and two runners on. Whereas David Cone may have attempted to outwit Martinez in this type of situation, McDowell went right after him. The rock concert loudness of the Kingdome did not affect "Black Jack" as he fired fastball after fastball at the American League batting champion. Finally, with the count at 2–2, McDowell threw a splitter that broke forcefully halfway toward home plate. The break was too much for Edgar, who swung underneath the ball for strike three. With that strikeout, the biggest of his career, McDowell just might have single-handedly saved the Yankees' season. As it turns out, fate would ensure that almost no one would ever remember that it happened.

Martinez was frustrated with himself as he returned to the dugout. Norm Charlton knew something about that feeling. He had been especially unhappy with some of his own actions during the series and saw that his teammate needed a pick-me-up. He told Edgar not to worry, he would get another chance.[39] The strikeout, while huge, did not end the inning. Rookie shortstop Alex Rodriguez stood in the batter's box with no desire to allow Martinez that second chance. Rodriguez, or

A-Rod, as he would popularly become known as in succeeding years, had pinch-run for Tino Martinez in the fateful eighth inning, scoring the tying run on Doug Strange's two-out walk. The rookie swung at a first-pitch fastball, sending it skidding across the turf to short. It was a routine play, but the crowd, probably as overanxious as the rookie, screamed in excitement. Tony Fernandez shifted quickly to his right and, with his trademark smooth side arm toss, threw the ball to second base, forcing out Griffey and ending the inning.

After six pitchers, three home runs, a huge two-out rally, and the constant sitting and standing of 50,000 people, nine innings were not enough to decide the final game of this already classic series. For only the fifth time in baseball history, the deciding game of a playoff series would move into extra innings.

• • • • • • • • •

"Only one inning," Lou Piniella had told Jim Kaat before the start of Game 5.[40] That's how long he felt he could use Randy Johnson. Piniella had lied. Johnson emerged in the tenth inning and showed he could pitch all night if need be. Ruben Sierra led off and struck out on a slider. Don Mattingly then faced Johnson for the first time since striking out against him with the bases loaded in the sixth inning of Game 3. This confrontation would be no different. Johnson threw nothing but sharp breaking sliders, the last of which broke over the plate for a called strike three. Mattingly remained at home plate, staring ahead at no one in particular, in total disbelief at the called third strike. He did not know it at the time—no one did—but it was his last at-bat ever. Known as one of the toughest hitters to strike out, Mattingly had struck out in his last career at-bat.

With two outs in the inning, Gerald Williams came to bat. "If there's one hitter on their roster who can turn on a Randy Johnson fastball . . . it is Gerald Williams," Jim Kaat told viewers.[41] Williams failed to prove a hero, though, striking out looking on a Johnson fastball. The Big Unit, who Piniella said would only pitch one inning if needed for Game 5, had now pitched two innings and struck out four hitters. To those witnessing this spectacle, he seemed more machine than man.

Unlike Piniella, Showalter had made no mention of how long Jack McDowell could pitch. Even if Showalter had set a limit, McDowell would have ignored it. As far as Black Jack was concerned, this was now his game, and he was in it for the long haul. The long haul, however, may not have seemed long when Jay Buhner led off the bottom of the tenth inning with a single to left field. Chris Widger, the backup catcher, came to the plate with just one goal in mind: get Buhner over to second base. But Widger hadn't sacrifice-bunted once all season, and now he was being asked to lay down the biggest bunt in Seattle history. His first attempt was botched as he missed the ball. After a called strike two, Widger peeked down at third-base coach Sam Perlazzo to see if the bunt was still on. Perlazzo ran through the signs. Yes, it was still on. Awaiting McDowell's pitch, Wilson squared, lunged at a curveball, and bunted it foul for strike three. The pressure lessened, and the crowd mildly deflated. McDowell induced eighth-inning hero Doug Strange to hit into a fielder's choice. The struggling Mike Blowers came to bat and hit a seeing-eye ground ball to short. Tony Fernandez fielded it and threw to second base, but Strange beat the throw. Like that, the winning run was in scoring position, and the pressure was back on McDowell.

The noise was unbearable. Yankees fans across the country cringed. Hoping to capitalize on the tension was the man who had been on the road to redemption since joining the Mariners that August. One swing could catapult Vince Coleman into a baseball legend: It would be a fitting conclusion for someone who had been stuck in the Homestead Camp, unsigned and seemingly unwanted, just six months earlier. But Coleman slammed a ground ball hard into the Kingdome turf right to Don Mattingly, who easily stabbed the ball and threw to second base for the out, ending the inning.

• • • • • • • • •

The Big Unit glared at Mike Stanley as the eleventh inning began. Talk of just pitching one inning was long gone. Johnson knew full well that Stanley had nearly homered off him in the first inning of Game 3, so he pitched him very carefully. But Johnson pitched too carefully. Stanley watched four straight balls sail high and wide of the strike zone. He took first base and was immediately replaced by a pinch runner. The agonizingly slow Stanley would have trouble scoring on any extra-base hit or from second base on a single. His run could mean the difference between going to the ALCS and going home. Showalter inserted late-season hero and much-faster base runner Pat Kelly. Tony Fernandez laid down a sacrifice bunt, the first time in three tries that either team was able to actually do so, and Kelly moved to second base. Randy Velarde now came to bat. If anyone in a Yankees uniform needed a hit in this situation, it was Velarde. He had toiled for years in the Yankees' system, being shuffled back and forth between the minors and majors before permanently joining the club. Velarde had been a member of some the worst Yankees teams in recent memory and even then, he was forced to split his playing time with other players. After all that, he had finally made the postseason. Yet here he was, hitting just .125 in five games. Even worse, he'd had a disastrous Game 3, committing a costly base-running gaffe and a throwing error. Blowers, Boggs, Rodriguez, and Coleman had all had this opportunity in the last three innings. It was a chance to have one's name forever etched into baseball's history book as a hero. They had all failed.

The scene for Velarde could not have been better. While most people dreaded facing Johnson, Velarde did not mind. He was one of the few players who had had success against the tall lefty, batting a career .500 against him in the regular season. As Johnson set to deliver, the Kingdome settled down with nervous anticipation. Kelly, as was his custom, held a batting glove in each hand to prevent breaking a finger if he had to slide. He took his lead off second, peeking over his shoulder to get a sense of where the outfielders were positioned. It was small but crucial. Any single hit too hard might mean he would have to hold up.

After a first-pitch ball, Johnson briefly peeked at Kelly, then delivered a fastball. Velarde, ahead of the pitch, swung and bounced the ball hard off the turf toward left field, just out of the reach of both Strange and Rodriguez, for a seeing-eye single. Willie Randolph frantically waved his arm in a windmill pattern, sending Kelly home. Coleman charged in from left field, grabbed the ball and unleashed as strong a throw as he could muster toward home plate. On-deck hitter Jim Leyritz began motioning with both arms and screaming "Down! Down!" as Kelly raced toward home. Coleman's throw hit the turf a little more than halfway between third base and home plate and bounded high in the air toward Widger. Kelly, gloves in hand, dove head first into home plate ahead of the throw and scored easily without a play. The Yankees had retaken the lead, 5–4.

The Yankees exploded from the bench, rushing out to greet Kelly almost before he could shake the dirt off his uniform. First among them, with a towel draped around his neck, was Don Mattingly. A level above the field, Gene Michael stood clapping vigorously, grinning from ear to ear. Seated behind him, Steinbrenner also glared approvingly down at the field. The tension in that box for ten-plus innings had been palpable. Steinbrenner had spent the game continually belittling Showalter, saying he was being outmanaged by Piniella. Velarde's single had lightened the mood beyond description. Velarde stood on second not letting his emotions show. Inside, though, he was elated. He could picture the reporters gathered around him after the game, asking questions about his game-winning hit.[42]

Showalter's move to pinch-run Kelly for Stanley had paid great dividends. Although Coleman had a below-average throwing arm, Stanley would not have been able to score on Velarde's single, and he might very well have ended up stranded on third base.

Johnson tried to forge ahead. Velarde had made his way to second on Coleman's throw, so the Big Unit had to buckle down and prevent that run from scoring. The deadening silence of the Kingdome was finally broken by the announcement of Jim Leyritz being inserted as a pinch-hitter for Boggs. It was Leyritz's first at-bat of the series in Seattle and the first time he had hit since ending Game 2 at 1:15 Wednesday morning. The announcement of Leyritz's name allowed the fans to let loose their animosity. Though more restrained than what a visiting player might expect in the Bronx, their dislike for the Yankees catcher was clear. To their delight, Leyritz stuck out looking on a fastball. As the fans howled in his misfortune, Leyritz screamed at home-plate umpire Jim Evans. "No way! That's fuckin' bullshit," yelled Leyritz, arms raised and flailing in disgust. The emotion of the moment had gotten to him, because he did not realize how careful he needed to be. Mike Stanley was out of the game, meaning the Yankees' only remaining catcher, should Evans eject Leyritz, was rookie Jorge Posada. Posada had just one Major League at-bat to his credit and had been used in the series only once, as a pinch runner in Game 2. Showalter could ill afford to go into the eleventh inning needing the biggest three outs of his life with a rookie behind the plate. He rocketed out of the dugout, jumping in front of Leyritz, trying to shield him from ejection. Evans, showing remarkable composure, allowed both Leyritz and Showalter to have their say before they returned to the dugout.

The strikeout brought Bernie Williams up with two outs, but Piniella was back to playing chess. Williams had homered off Johnson in Game 3, and the Seattle manager did not want his team falling behind further. One run was doable, but three runs down was perhaps asking too much of his team. Piniella went out to the mound. "I said, 'Randy, you get O'Neill and we'll win the ballgame for you in the bottom of the inning.'"[43] He had Johnson walk Williams, allowing him to face the left-handed Paul O'Neill instead. O'Neill had no desire to hit against Johnson. Excluding his ninth-inning at-bat, he had faced him only three times in his career, and those three at-bats had all come in the same game in May 1989, when Johnson was a rookie. O'Neill did as best a left-handed batter could do, fouling off a few pitches. Finally, he succumbed to a slider for a called strike three. O'Neill, known for arguing nearly every call that did not go his way, gave a glance at Jim Evans but put up no fight. Johnson walked off the mound slowly and silently. Tim Belcher was warming up in the bullpen, which meant that if Seattle tied the game in the bottom of the inning, Johnson was done. After all he had accomplished during the year, including losing only twice, it was possible that he would be the losing pitcher in the Mariners' biggest game of the season, nay, the biggest game in their history. He needed some more magic from his teammates. He needed yet another "Refuse to Lose" moment.

• • • • • • • • •

"Refuse to Lose" had become a mantra in the Pacific Northwest in the weeks and days leading up to the eleventh inning of Game 5. Once just a catchy phrase, it had taken on a life of its own. People had truly begun to believe that it was something real, an essence or aura that surrounded this Mariners team. After years of mediocrity and disappointment, the Mariners' 1995 surge had instilled in fans a sense that their team would always come back, no matter what the odds or gravity of the situation. So when Joey Cora led off the bottom of the eleventh inning, his team down a run, the Kingdome was as vibrant as it had ever been. In another time, the Mariners being down a run in the last inning would have caused most fans to go home and beat the traffic. Or maybe they would have remained at the park, sitting on their hands, believing any effort to cheer on their team was futile. But this time, it was different. Fans just knew deep down in their heart that the Mariners were going to come back. The players knew it too. For most of them, 1995 was the experience of a lifetime. They would never see anything like it again in their careers, whether they remained in Seattle or moved on to another team. It was a constant attitude of there being no deficit being too great to keep them from coming back. As Cora dug in, the hometown fans and players fully expected the Yankees lead to crumble.

Jack McDowell sought to stifle any thoughts of a glorious comeback. His reemergence to the mound had surprised some people, but Showalter's confidence in John Wetteland had eroded completely. He didn't even have his closer warming up in the bullpen. Instead, he had rookie Andy Pettitte warming up. As far as Showalter was concerned, this was McDowell's game. The Yankees infield had been completely reworked. Leyritz was now catching. Velarde shifted from second base to third base and Kelly was now playing second. It turned out, however, that the most important infield spot was first base.

"When the inning started, I kind of looked at the situation and thought maybe I would bunt . . . because Mattingly was playing back. I know Jack [McDowell] had a little trouble getting out there, so if I laid down a good bunt, maybe I would have a chance," said Cora.[44] Mattingly had come up on the short end of Cora's bunt in Game 4. Now, as McDowell fell behind Cora, 2–1, to start the bottom of the eleventh, Yankees third-base coach Willie Randolph noticed that Mattingly was a step too far back from home plate. Before McDowell could deliver his next pitch, Randolph tried motioning to the first baseman, screaming for him to move in.[45] But Mattingly could not hear him over the screaming of 57,000 people. McDowell delivered a fastball and Cora lowered the bat, squared, and laid down a perfect bunt that dribbled along the first-base line. Mattingly charged, fielded the ball with his glove hand, and in one motion reached across his body to swipe-tag Cora. He exuded such force in doing so that he actually knocked himself off his own feet. Cora dipped his left shoulder, avoided the tag, and dove headfirst toward first base, reaching out and touching the bag with his left hand.

As the crowd roared with delight over the leadoff single, Showalter sprinted toward first base. As in Game 4, Buck felt Cora had gone out of the baseline. He begged first-base umpire Dan Morrison to appeal to home-plate umpire Jim Evans, but Morrison refused. Replays showed that Cora's feet had clearly left the allotted space for a base runner down the first-base line. Whether Cora's entire body had left the space was debatable, though. In a situation this large, there was little to no chance that the call would be overturned. Knowing his argument was headed nowhere, Showalter gave up and returned to the dugout. Years later, both Showalter and Leyritz would still contend that Cora had absolutely been out of the line and should have been called out.

Mattingly, who thought he had tagged Cora but had really missed him, walked toward Jack McDowell. "I got 'em Jack," Mattingly said as he handed McDowell the ball, "but we gotta keep going."[46]

It was a nightmare for the Yankees. Cora was on first base, there with no outs, and Ken Griffey Jr. was now hitting. Showalter stuck with McDowell instead of bringing in lefty Andy Pettitte. It was a choice some players would question, but Showalter had faith in the lanky starter-turned-reliever, and McDowell had had success against the next two hitters in the lineup: Griffey and Edgar Martinez. To Buck, it was a matter of going with his best option, which he believed was McDowell. Not Pettitte, not Wetteland, not anyone else. With the season on the line, McDowell wanted nothing to do with the inner part of the plate against Griffey. His first-pitch fastball outside for a ball was followed by another fastball high and outside. Griffey swung, grinding the ball up the middle. Pat Kelly dove and stretched as far as he could, but the ball was moving too fast and bounded past him into center field. Cora easily moved to third base. McDowell couldn't believe it. "This guy never hits a ground ball off me," he thought, "and he hits one now?"[47]

The season hung in the balance. The tying run was on third, and the series-winning run was on first base with no outs. The Yankees kept the infield back. They would give up the tying run if it meant getting a double play. In fact, considering the situation, they would be grateful for a double play and just having the game tied.

Edgar Martinez had struck out against McDowell in a crucial situation in the ninth inning. Afterward, Charlton had told him that he would get another chance. Edgar remembered that conversation as he came to bat.[48] In the Mariners' dugout, Chris Bosio turned to Andy Benes. "Dude, we are one pitch away," he told him.[49] Everyone was on his feet, except perhaps those sitting in the box with George Steinbrenner. "Game 5 was the most excruciating experience of my life," said David Sussman, a member of the Yankees staff who sat with the Boss that night. "It went beyond the usual sense of claustrophobia and intensity you normally had when sitting with Steinbrenner. There were long stretches where there was silence, and it was only broken by Steinbrenner bad-mouthing Buck."[50] The tension that seemingly had been erased on Randy Velarde's single minutes earlier had now returned with a vengeance.

Edgar Martinez took a first-pitch fastball down the middle for a strike. Ahead in the count, McDowell got his sign from Leyritz, who signaled for a splitter. McDowell nodded in agreement. Coming set, he briefly peered over his shoulder to catch a glance of Griffey at first base. Then he wound up and delivered. The splitter broke too early, but it was still up and in as planned. Edgar adjusted. Realizing this was the same pitch he had stuck out on in the ninth inning, he quickly turned and lashed the ball down the left-field line.[51] "I was amazed that he turned on the ball. It should have hit him in the neck," recalled Wade Boggs.[52] The crowd had gone silent on delivery of the pitch, but the line drive got them instantly screaming. It was an unbelievable sound of exuberance. A loud, deafening roar, the kind that sends chills down your spine when heard on replay.

Martinez's line drive bounced all the way to the left-field wall. Cora scored easily, tying the game. Though there were no outs, Griffey had no desire to stop. "I saw that [Gerald Williams] was playing toward left-center and when I saw the ball land near the line, I ran as fast as I could for as long as I could," said Griffey.[53] Third-base coach Sam Perlozzo had a decision to make. "When Edgar hit the ball, I noticed Williams was more toward center. I never saw Junior run so fast. It wasn't an easy call," said Perlozzo.[54] Williams rushed into the corner to retrieve the ball. He momentarily hesitated in fielding it, waiting to see which way the ball would deflect off the wall. Tony Fernandez rushed out to short-left field waiting for the relay throw. Griffey charged full steam around second base and kept running past third. Perlozzo was waving him home. Mattingly ran to the middle of the infield diamond, screaming, "Home! Home!" though no one could hear him. The Mariners all emerged from the bench, eyeing the ball down the left-field line and then turning to watch Junior. "Seriously, every guy on the bench was out on the field, not just the mat [warning track], either. They were almost on the turf. They were waving and screaming," said Jay Buhner.[55] Piniella tried to watch the ball in the corner and Griffey rounding the bases at the same time.[56] To Leyritz, the play unraveled in slow motion. He thought initially they had a shot at Griffey, but the ball seemed like it would never get to him at home plate.[57] The reality that his season was about to end hit him as Junior raced toward home. Williams got the ball in to Fernandez, who spun around and fired to home plate. Velarde, who wanted to clothesline Griffey as he came around third to keep him from scoring, squatted down so he wouldn't be hit by the throw.[58] It didn't matter. "Mariners win it! Mariners win it!" screamed Brent Musburger as Griffey slid home just as Leyritz received the relay throw. Griffey's left leg partially knocked Leyritz off balance, but at that point, it no longer mattered. Junior popped up immediately only to be knocked right back down by a stampede of teammates who charged him. Coleman, Rodriguez, and others leapt onto the center fielder and created a pile of frenzied major leaguers right behind home plate. Others focused their attention toward the game's greatest hitter who had just doubled in the game's greatest player, giving the game's greatest pitcher the victory. The greatest playoff series in baseball history ended on a come-from-behind, extra-inning, game-ending double. After all that had occurred over the entire five-game series, it couldn't have finished any other way.

11

Deconstructing the Yankees

"I would not wish that flight on anyone."

—Buck Showalter, referring to the flight
home from Seattle after Game 5

Paul O'Neill stood dazed in right field. He'd been the only Yankee not involved when Edgar Martinez doubled, and he'd helplessly watched as the entire season collapsed before his eyes. His blank expression conveyed a feeling of incredulity. How could this have happened? Slowly he made his way back to the dugout, staring at the celebrating Mariners as he went. Eventually he sat down on a bench outside the dugout, his back slumped, looking straight at the ground as he rubbed his left hand through his hair. "Everything we've been working for since last March comes down to one play in the eleventh inning. It just doesn't seem fair," O'Neill later told reporters.[1] Jack McDowell had been backing up home plate after Martinez doubled. Once Griffey scored, he immediately turned away and proceeded directly to the dugout, where he walked into the tunnel and straight down to the visitors' clubhouse. Once there, McDowell sat down in a metal chair facing his locker, buried his head in his hands, and began to cry. "I feel like I let a lot of people down in here," he said after the game. "I didn't do the job. I didn't close it out for the team."[2] Tony Fernandez stayed on the field after unleashing his relay throw, almost as if remaining there might erase what just occurred. Finally, he left the field and sat at the end of the dugout, watching the celebration.[3] Jim Leyritz slowly walked away from home plate, the ball still in his glove. He took off his catcher's gear and remained in the dugout, wanting to take in all that was happening before him.[4] First-base coach Brian Butterfield left the bench and was headed down the tunnel before Griffey even crossed home plate.[5] Some players, like Mike Stanley, Randy Velarde, and Scott Kamieniecki remained in the dugout, staring blankly at the Mariners celebrating in front of them. Don Mattingly was in the middle of the diamond when Griffey scored, and he immediately turned and walked off the field, not watching the celebration. He headed back to the dugout where he quietly gathered his bats and glove, muttered a few words to himself, and then exited the dugout and headed for the clubhouse for the last time as a big-league player. He stopped just before the entrance so he could greet and console his teammates as they came in.[6] Overlooking the field and watching the celebration, George Steinbrenner remained quiet.[7]

Inside the Yankees' clubhouse, an eerie silence hung in the air. Buck Showalter had the clubhouse doors closed so he could address his players. "I want to thank you all for everything you did for me," Buck told his players. "I appreciate your support. Who knows where we'll be next year? Maybe some of us will be together again. I don't know for sure I'll be here, either."[8] Wade Boggs sneaked into the trainer's room, a place where the media was not allowed. For Boggs, the moment was all too reminiscent of what he'd been through with the 1986 Red Sox. He'd played his fourteenth season in 1995. Now it was his fourteenth straight season without a championship. He was also a free agent, and there had been much talk of Russ Davis finally taking over at third, which would end Boggs's career in New York. Alone in the trainer's room, Boggs sat down at a table and began to cry. "You know you go around hugging guys and you don't know if you're ever going to see them again. You walk out the door and you might never see them again," said Boggs.[9] In the clubhouse, other players began crying as well. Leyritz ran into Mattingly's wife, Kim, who was in tears. "It was an experience," she remarked to him. "I know this is Donnie's last shot."[10] Mattingly was talking to Steinbrenner when the media entered the clubhouse. The two were facing each other, seated in folding chairs, talking privately. As reporters approached, "Steinbrenner got up to leave. The owner grabbed [Mattingly] around the neck with both hands and squeezed. It was the closest Mattingly came to tears."[11] Red-eyed and speaking in a voice filled with emotion, Mattingly fielded questions from the media. "I really don't have any plans," he said in response to a question of what he would do now. "I was sort of counting on a trip to Cleveland."[12] Despite the situation, Mattingly calmly remained in front of his locker, fielding question after question. "It's obviously painful," he told them. "This team worked awfully hard to get here. But I'm very proud, in a sense, of this ballclub, the way we played down the stretch. We walked off that field not leaving anything out there. Every guy, from top to bottom, was totally in it."[13] Gene Michael then approached Mattingly and the two hugged. "Thank you for everything, Donnie," Michael told him.[14]

David Cone was heartbroken. He believed he had blown the game for his team and let down all of New York. "Everybody will come to realize how great this series was for baseball and the fans. Right now, for us, it hurts too much," said Cone, who acknowledged it was the toughest loss of his career.[15] "I'm going to need some time to get over this one."[16] Cone made his way over to the Mariners' clubhouse where he offered his congratulations to several players. Showalter did the same, wishing Lou Piniella good luck in the championship series. "That was really classy of Buck," said Piniella. "I know how hard that was for him. I'll tell you, he managed the hell out of that game."[17] Showalter also congratulated Luis Sojo, Jay Buhner, Tim Belcher, and Ken Griffey Jr. before returning to his office in the visitors' clubhouse.[18] For the past four years, Showalter had lived his dream as manager of the Yankees. Though he had handled his share of angry phone calls, no manager had lasted as long or gotten along so well, at least publicly, with Steinbrenner. Buck restored a winning attitude and dignity to the greatest franchise in sports history. With his contract up at the end of the month and no World Series ring—in fact, not even a World Series appearance—he was well aware that he stood to lose it all. Now seated at his desk, he laid his arms across it, buried his head into them and began to cry heavily into his Yankees windbreaker. Butterfield put his hand on Showalter's shoulder trying to console his friend, then closed the door to the office.[19] Later, while shaving in preparation for the flight home, O'Neill ran into Showalter. "The tone of [Buck's] voice indicated that he seemed to think he would not be back," said O'Neill.[20]

Eventually, the players packed up their belongings and headed to the airport. Suzyn Waldman, then covering the Yankees for WFAN radio, ran into Mariano Rivera on the way out. "I put my arm around him and said, 'Let's go to the bus.' He looked at me and said: 'You know, Suzyn, I didn't know it would hurt this much. It just hurts.'"[21] George Steinbrenner was solemn but praised his team. When asked if any changes would occur, he refused to speculate.[22] Without the reporters around, however, he told a different story. Yankees radio announcer John Sterling ran into Steinbrenner while waiting for the team bus to the airport. "You and Mike [Sterling's radio partner, Michael Kay] do great," Steinbrenner told him. "You're staying. But there will be changes."[23] Once at the airport, the Yankees boarded a plane for the nearly six-hour flight back to the East Coast. For many, it seemed like the longest flight of their lives. "It was like a funeral," said Rick Down.[24]

"It was just horrible," said David Sussman. "It felt like we went around the globe twice."[25] McDowell and Cone, who had become good friends during the last two months, sat in the back of the plane discussing whether or not they would remain with the Yankees. "We said 'let's be a package deal,'" recalled McDowell.[26] Cone remained upset throughout the course of the flight, particularly about the 3–2 splitter to Strange. Mike Stanley approached him. "You are one of the best pitchers I have ever caught," Stanley told him, trying to cheer him up.[27] "Mike . . . kept telling me it was his fault for calling the pitch, but I wouldn't let him get away with it," said Cone.[28] Mattingly made his way up and down the aisles. He hadn't publicly announced his retirement, but he knew he would not be returning. Mattingly went from seat to seat, stopping to talk to individual teammates. "It was depressing. Tough knowing that that was it. I was kinda saying good-bye," said Mattingly.[29] He informed Boggs that he wouldn't be returning. Boggs did his best to talk him out of it but without success.[30] In the front of the plane, Buck Showalter sat quietly with his coaching staff. It was the last time they would all be together. "I never, ever, ever, ever cry about sports," said Michael Kay on observing the coaches, "but I was choked up."[31] Mattingly eventually made his way up to the coaches, who were discussing the positives of the club and the future of the organization.[32] Showalter told Mattingly how proud he was of him.[33] The plane finally landed at Newark Airport in New Jersey at 6 A.M., Monday, October 9.[34] The players returned to Yankee Stadium, where they packed their bags and headed home for the winter.

Cone returned home still haunted by the 3–2 splitter in the dirt to Doug Strange. "I couldn't sleep. I almost didn't go out of my house for a couple of weeks after," said Cone.[35] Mattingly was equally depressed. "I remember getting back to New York and not leaving home for three days. When I did, everyone I ran into was bummed," said Mattingly.[36]

While the players tried to recover, George Steinbrenner spent the next four months on a tear the likes of which no one had ever seen during his time as owner. He began completely dismantling the 1995 Yankees nearly the moment the plane landed on the runway in Newark. The first victim of The Boss's purge was Gene Michael. The general manager, who was more responsible for the Yankees' resurgence than anyone, had made his way onto Steinbrenner's hit list through his constant disagreements with The Boss. It was not personal, because Steinbrenner liked Michael and valued his expertise. Still, he became the first casualty. Michael, who made $550,000 in 1995, had an option on his contract for 1996, which the Yankees could pick up for $600,000. Instead, The Boss offered Michael a 33 percent pay cut to remain as general manager.[37] Michael refused. Steinbrenner, not wanting to lose Michael completely, especially once it became known that the rival Orioles were interested in his services, allowed him to devise his own position, director of scouting, for a $150,000 yearly salary.[38] Though the offer was clearly insulting, Michael put a positive public spin on it. "It's a chance to do what I really enjoy and have more time off," said Michael. "Instead of being in the office 15 hours a day, I'll be in the field, watching games." Still he couldn't resist adding, "I thought I should have been back [as GM]."[39] The announcement of Michael's demotion was made on October 19, just eleven days after Edgar Martinez ended the Yankees' season. Four days later, Bob Watson, the last Yankee player to have hit in a World Series game, was named general manager.[40]

With Michael now demoted, the focus shifted to Showalter and whether he would return. For days after the Division Series loss,

George Steinbrenner played coy. "I will," said Steinbrenner on October 15, when asked if he was going to call Showalter. "Just as soon as I have time, and he has time. There's a number of things we have to look into. He's right at the top."[41] Eventually, the two did talk, and what occurred is shrouded in mystery. Steinbrenner offered Showalter a two-year, $1.05 million contract but informed the Yankees manager that two of his coaches, Brian Butterfield and Rick Down, would not be allowed to return.[42] The reasons why Steinbrenner had selected these two individuals were never known, not even to Butterfield or Down. "I don't know why," said Down when asked. "I don't think I've had more than 10 words with the man since I've been here."[43] According to Showalter, he refused to allow these two to be terminated. The Boss partially acquiesced, saying that Butterfield could stay but Down definitely could not return.[44] Showalter would not agree to this either. According to Showalter, he refused Steinbrenner's initial offer on this basis, but believed that Steinbrenner would come back with another offer or desist from replacing Down. Instead, Steinbrenner, claiming to believe that Buck's rejection of the contract was his way of resigning from the Yankees, issued a press release an hour before the start of Game 5 of the World Series stating that Showalter would not return. "We tried but were unable to dissuade Buck [from leaving]," said the release, written on behalf of Steinbrenner. "I have nothing but praise for Buck and the job he did for us and I told him I am very upset by his leaving. I wish Buck and his fine little family nothing but the best. There will be no criticism of Buck in any way from me."[45] Showalter claimed to have known nothing of his "resignation" until his wife Angela called him while he was on his way back from playing golf.[46] "She read [the statement] to me. I couldn't believe it," said Showalter. "I felt we were negotiating. I thought there might be a counteroffer."[47] He also could not explain a statement in the release stating that he and Steinbrenner had discussed "lengthening" his contract. "Mr. Steinbrenner never told me anything about a third year," said Showalter.[48]

Whether Buck Showalter resigned, was fired, or some odd combination of both depends on who is telling the story. Showalter maintains that he was unwilling to sacrifice his coaching staff, was merely awaiting a counteroffer, and was heartbroken by Steinbrenner's decision. But there were those who felt that Buck was simply using his coaches as an excuse to leave since he knew he had potential offers from other teams. One former Yankee felt Showalter knew as early as September 1995 that he would be moving on once the season was over. Others, however, contend that The Boss had no intention of bringing Showalter back. Showalter had been hired by Gene Michael and therefore was never truly a Steinbrenner guy. Showalter had also committed the unforgivable sin of attaining popularity greater than that of the owner, as evidenced by the rousing ovation Buck received before Game 1. Steinbrenner abhorred anyone getting more credit for the Yankees' success than him. Two of Steinbrenner's closest confidants, Yankees advisers Arthur Richman and Billy Connors, were leading an anti-Showalter campaign by bad-mouthing him day in and day out to The Boss.[49] Connors was especially unfavorable toward Buck. He had been Showalter's pitching coach until being fired in the middle of the 1995 season. Rumors swirled that Showalter may have played a hand in Connors's removal because he considered him a spy for Steinbrenner. "I remember Buck said he'd stand behind his coaches. That he'd quit for them. He didn't quit for me," said Connors shortly after Buck's "resignation" was announced.[50] Additionally, Steinbrenner had constantly questioned Showalter's decisions during the series, saying Lou Piniella was outmanaging him. All of these factors led some to believe that Buck's fate had been decided the moment Ken Griffey Jr. slid into home plate to end Game 5. Steinbrenner just needed an excuse to rid himself of his manager, and he found that excuse when Showalter rejected his initial contract offer.

Though the exact story of what occurred may never be known, it seems highly unlikely that Showalter would willingly give up his dream job, especially after having just led the Yankees to the postseason. Steinbrenner's behavior during and after the series gave every indication that he was looking to make major changes and that he was unhappy with Buck's performance. Surely Steinbrenner knew that his traditional tactic of attacking a manager's coaches would be enough to make Showalter question whether he wished to return. The demotion of Gene Michael certainly could not have been well received by Showalter, either. Regardless of who was to blame, the Buck Showalter era that saw the Yankees go 313–268 was over, and the New York media and fans lambasted Steinbrenner for it. Thousands of angry faxes flooded Yankee Stadium. "You're just being the typical ignorant, arrogant fool that most Yankee fans always thought you were," wrote one fan in a letter to The Boss. "This is just George Steinbrenner slapping the face of another guy who has given his whole career to the Yankees," said another.[51] The press decried Steinbrenner for trying to divert attention away from the World Series with his pre–Game 5 press release. "Baseball interrupts George Steinbrenner's management seminar to present the sixth game of the 1995 World Series," New York Newsday's Joe Gergen wrote sarcastically. "The Indians and the Braves apologize for the intrusion and promise to relinquish the spotlight as quickly and quietly as possible. This is, after all, The Boss' favorite month of the year."[52] They also questioned Steinbrenner's version of events and wondered how he could let such a successful manager go. "George Steinbrenner does not just act like a fraud a lot of the time. Sometimes he acts like a gutless one as well. Now he wants it to look for all the world as if Buck Showalter resigned his job as manager of the Yankees when he did nothing of the kind. Steinbrenner is the one who wrote the letter of resignation . . . not Showalter," wrote Mike Lupica in the New York Daily News.[53] "He still doesn't know what he had," Dave Anderson wrote in the New York Times. "George Steinbrenner never understood that Buck Showalter was not only a good manager but also the best possible person for the most difficult job description of any Yankees employee: coexisting with the principal owner himself."[54] Seven days after the press release announcing Showalter's "resignation," the Yankees announced their new manager would be Joe Torre. Perhaps aware of the blistering questions that would come from the media, George Steinbrenner did not attend the press conference. Torre's hiring was widely panned. The Daily News printed a back-page headline referring to him as "Clueless Joe." "Torre was the favored choice by the confederacy of dunces running the Yankees' office in Tampa," wrote Lupica. "Joe Torre is a sweetheart of a guy, but there is about the same demand for his services as a manager as there was for Darryl Strawberry's as a player."[55] Though regarded by many as one of the nicest people in baseball, Torre had few accomplishments as a skipper. He had gone 286–420 as manager of the Mets from 1977 to 1978, 257–229 as manager of the Braves from 1982 to 1984, and 351–354 as manager of the Cardinals from 1990 to 1995. Only once had he managed a team to the postseason: the 1982 Braves, who were promptly swept by the Cardinals in the NLCS. In fact, Torre was perhaps best known for having played and managed a combined 4,106 games without ever having made it to the World Series. Additionally, the only Yankees coach to return was third-base coach Willie Randolph. Gone were Brian Butterfield, Nardi Contreas, Rick Down, and Glen Sherlock, men who were loyal to Showalter. They were replaced by Jose Cardinal, Mel Stottlemeyre, Chris Chambliss, and Don Zimmer. "If we had just won against the Mariners, we all would have been fine," said Gene Michael.[56]

• • • • • • • • •

With a new general manager, manager, and coaches now in place, the deconstructing of the 1995 Yankees turned to the players. The first to go was Mike Stanley. Torre and his new staff brought with them a National League idealism, one that emphasized strong pitching and defense over offense. This new emphasis led them to acquire catcher Joe Girardi from the Rockies on November 20. Stanley had become a free agent once the season ended, and the trade for Girardi meant he would not be returning to the Yankees in 1996. "I'm disappointed they didn't even talk to me," said Stanley of the Yankees upon hearing of the trade. "I thought I had played well enough to at least get an offer, or even consideration."[57] Stanley had not been completely surprised by the deal. Once Showalter left, Billy Connors, who had never been a fan of Stanley's, had much more influence on the decision-making process. "Billy didn't like Mike," said a member of the Yankees, who added that it was Connors who told Steinbrenner that Stanley should not return.[58] Torre and bench coach Don Zimmer had both seen and been impressed with Girardi's style of play. "Joe Girardi is one of the best catchers in the game. I like the way he takes charge. . . . I'll feel comfortable having Joe behind the plate," Torre told reporters after the trade was announced. To fans, however, and even some in the media, Girardi's supposed defensive capabilities didn't outweigh the offensive loss of Stanley.[59] It was quickly and repeatedly pointed out that Girardi had hit only eight home runs in hitter-friendly Coors Field during 1995 and had never hit .300 in a season. Meanwhile, Stanley had hit over .300 twice and had averaged twenty home runs over the last three seasons. That offense was now gone, and fans were irate over it.

The next player to leave was Don Mattingly. The Captain had informed several teammates he wouldn't be returning, but he made no public statement on the matter for weeks. Though it would have most likely been in a diminished capacity, the Yankees did offer Mattingly an open-ended deal, essentially saying he could name the price and length of his contract.[60] But Mattingly did not allow negotiations to get that far. He issued a statement on November 21, the day after the Girardi trade, stating that he informed the Yankees he was "unable to commit, at this time, to playing major-league baseball next year."[61] Mattingly did not say he was retiring. Instead, the statement was his way of informing the Yankees they had his blessing to seek out other options at first base. He acknowledged that Steinbrenner had been trying to bring him back and had in no way forced him into this decision. His announcement, though heartbreaking for fans, allowed the Yankees to seek an offensive upgrade at first base without seeming callous to their former leader. The idea of the Yankees without Don Mattingly, though, seemed unreal to many, regardless of his statistics.

The day after Mattingly's announcement, the Yankees lost another key player. Randy Velarde, second on the team in seniority, signed with the California Angels. Velarde had sought a three-year deal from New York, but the Yankees would only offer him two years with a club option for a third.[62] Velarde might have taken that offer, but the Yankees wouldn't guarantee he'd return as anything more than a utility player. The man who had been a utility player his whole career was tired of it. "The Yankees indicated to us . . . he wasn't going to play every day. At thirty-two, Randy wants a chance to play every day," explained Velarde's agent Adam Katz.[63] Velarde rejected the Yankees' offer, and the Angels swooped in with a guaranteed three-year deal and a promise that he would play full-time. "I'm not bitter," Velarde told the media. "I just wish we'd won that series with the Mariners. Then Buck would probably still be here, and maybe Donnie and Mike and myself too. We had a good thing going."[64] Velarde's decision shocked New York, who in just three days lost three of the most important pieces of the 1995 team.

On November 30, the Yankees declined to pick up the $1.8 million option on Darryl Strawberry's contract, instead buying him out for $175,000. The move mystified Strawberry, who was playing winter ball in Puerto Rico, essentially for the Yankees' benefit, when he heard the news. "I don't understand, I didn't do anything wrong. I did everything they [the Yankees] asked me to do," said Strawberry.[65] That same day, Tim McCleary, who had been the Yankees' assistant general manager and was sitting with George Steinbrenner during Game 5, was hired as assistant general manager for the Blue Jays.[66]

On December 7, the Yankees traded Sterling Hitchcock and Russ Davis to the Mariners for Tino Martinez, Jeff Nelson, and Jim Mecir. For the Yankees, the trade for Martinez became necessary once Don Mattingly announced he wouldn't be returning. George Steinbrenner was so concerned over acquiring Martinez and keeping him long term that he personally handled negotiations regarding a contract extension.[67] Tino, who had worn number 23 in Seattle, was going to have to relinquish it in New York, as that had been the Captain's number. "You can't replace a Don Mattingly, so I'm not even going to try," said Martinez.[68] But Tino, who had unknowingly been auditioning for the Yankees during the Division Series, *was* replacing Mattingly, whether he liked it or not. Even though many Yankees fans knew Mattingly had made the decision on his own not to return, they were not going to allow Martinez much slack. He was going to have to produce immediately and prove he was worthy of the Captain's spot. Davis, once considered the third baseman of the future, became expendable when Wade Boggs signed a two-year contract on December 5 to return at third base for New York. Nelson, meanwhile, would provide much-needed stability in the Yankees' bullpen, something the team hadn't had during the series.

On December 14, Jack McDowell signed with the Cleveland Indians, a team that had won 100 games during the strike-shortened season. The Yankees had concerns about a hip condition of McDowell's and decided not to offer him arbitration or even to try to sign him.[69] That same day, Mike Stanley signed with Boston, bolstering a lineup that already featured Mo Vaughn and Jose Canseco. Additionally, on that day the Yankees lost out on second baseman Craig Biggio, who re-signed with the Houston Astros, and pitcher Al Leiter, who signed with the Florida Marlins. "If the Yankees find themselves in their living rooms instead of their locker room next October," John Giannone wrote in the *Daily News*, "they can legitimately point to Dec. 14, 1995, as the day they were left in the dust by the American League powers-that-be."[70]

By New Year's Day 1996, the Yankees had parted with seven of the twenty-five players from the Division Series roster, not to mention their manager, almost every member of the coaching staff, the assistant general manager, and the general manager. With the exception of Tino Martinez, few of the players the Yankees brought in, Girardi, Dwight Gooden, Mariano Duncan, Tim Raines, and Kenny Rogers, seemed like improvements over the players they were replacing. While the Yankees appeared to be falling apart, the division-rival Orioles had signed All-Star second baseman Roberto Alomar and pitcher David Wells. George Steinbrenner's purging of the team appeared to be setting the Yankees on a course for disappointment in 1996. During spring training, they announced that rookie Derek Jeter would be the full-time shortstop, a risky move that meant Gold Glover Tony Fernandez would have to shift to second base. Fernandez was not pleased with the decision, but it became a moot point when he fractured his ulna diving for a ball late that spring.[71] The injury cost him the entire 1996 season—yet another member of the 1995 team gone. When the season began in Cleveland on April 2, Wade Boggs was the only infielder in the starting lineup who had played in the 1995 Division Series. The Yankees won that day, but the drastic overturning of the roster during the off-season had few people believing that the team would be making its way back to the postseason in 1996.

• • • • • • • • •

Whether it was pure luck or sheer genius, nearly all the moves made by George Steinbrenner after the Yankees were eliminated from the 1995 Division Series paid dividends. After struggling early and being lustily booed by the fans, Tino Martinez rebounded to lead the Yankees in home runs and RBIs. Joe Girardi, also initially booed by the fans, hit .292 for the year, played stellar defense, established great rapport with the Yankees' staff, and even added an element of speed, stealing twelve bases. Mariano Duncan became the full-time second baseman and hit a career-high .340. Dwight Gooden, who had returned from a suspension for violating the game's drug policy, also had early struggles. But he eventually became an anchor for the pitching staff, particularly during the middle of the year when injuries hampered the team. Tim Raines, who had been acquired merely because Steinbrenner was good friends with his agent,[72] hit .292 and was an ideal teammate in the clubhouse. Derek Jeter batted over .300 and was named Rookie of the Year. Only Steinbrenner's signing of Kenny Rogers turned out to be a flop, as the pitcher struggled throughout his initial season in New York.

During the course of the 1996 season, Dion James, Steve Howe, Ruben Sierra, Bob Wickman, and Gerald Williams, all participants in the 1995 Division Series, were either traded or let go. Scott Kamieniecki, the Game 4 starter during the Division Series, was plagued by injuries and pitched only 22 $2/3$ innings in 1996. Pat Kelly was also felled by injuries and limited to only twenty-one at-bats. Despite the off-season upheaval, the 1996 Yankees did the 1995 Yankees one better by winning the AL East division title over the Orioles. It was not just Steinbrenner's player acquisitions that led to this. Joe Torre, the man dubbed "Clueless Joe," turned out to be the perfect successor for Buck Showalter. Torre was a laid-back manager who rarely let pressure get to him and, in turn, rarely put pressure on his players. Whereas Buck was a micromanager obsessed with the most minute of details, Torre had little problem allowing his coaches to handle issues or even allowing players to police themselves. Torre's National League style of play, which including hitting and running and double stealing to a degree rarely seen under Showalter, proved extremely successful. Torre also had a compelling personal story. He was a native New Yorker who, during the course of the 1996 season, lost one brother to a heart attack and had another, Frank, who was in desperate need of a heart transplant. These types of human-interest stories made it easy for fans to like and accept Torre. When the Yankees won the American League championship to advance to the 1996 World Series, Torre sat in the dugout with tears in his eyes. And it all made George Steinbrenner look like an absolute genius. As the Yankees prepared to play in the World Series, few fans recalled that just a year earlier, they had been ready to hang Steinbrenner in Times Square for his handling of Buck Showalter.

The Yankees wound up winning the 1996 World Series in six dramatic games over the Atlanta Braves. It was their first championship in eighteen years, the longest drought in their history. The series' final out was made by Mark Lemke, who popped up to third baseman Charlie Hayes. Hayes had been a member of the Philadelphia

Phillies as the Yankees were battling it out with the Mariners a year earlier. In fact, of the twenty-five players on the Yankees' 1996 World Series roster, only nine had been on the Yankees' roster against the Mariners a year earlier: Wade Boggs, Paul O'Neill, Bernie Williams, Jim Leyritz, Darryl Strawberry, David Cone, Andy Pettitte, Mariano Rivera, and John Wetteland. As Hayes caught the final out, only two players on the field, Williams and O'Neill, had been on the Kingdome turf when Edgar Martinez doubled to end the Yankees' 1995 season. At the clubhouse celebration afterward, George Steinbrenner fought back tears as he described the efforts of his 1996 team. It was a surreal moment, considering only months earlier no one, absolutely no one, thought that what Steinbrenner had done to the team would result in this kind of success. They were all wrong. The Yankees went on to win the World Series in 1998, 1999, and 2000, and only a ninth-inning rally by Arizona in Game 7 prevented them from winning yet another championship in 2001. Between 1996 and 2003, only two teams other than the Yankees represented the American League in the World Series. Attendance figures continuously shot up as the team's performance brought back fans who had turned bitter over the strike. In 1996, the Yankees drew over 2.2 million people. In 1998, they drew 2.9 million. In 2001, just six years after drawing only 1.7 million fans, they broke the 3 million attendance mark. Joe Torre became one of the most successful managers in history, possibly cementing a spot in the Hall of Fame. Derek Jeter eventually became the Yankees captain and established a Hall of Fame career based on phenomenal regular-season numbers and even better postseason statistics. Joe Girardi, booed by Yankees fans when he replaced their beloved Mike Stanley, succeeded Joe Torre as manager in 2008. Out of the heartbreak of the 1995 Division Series, the Yankees and George Steinbrenner ended up creating one of the greatest dynasties in baseball history. This dynasty and all that came with it would never have happened had Edgar Martinez not broken the hearts of the Yankees and their fans on that Sunday night in October 1995.

12

Safeco Is Born

"Nobody cared about the Mariners, but then they kept winning and winning. If they had not been in the playoffs, the job of getting a new stadium would have been impossible."

—Washington State Representative Steve Van Luven

It was pandemonium inside the Kingdome. The stands shook, the walls vibrated, and the press box swayed back and forth. "We won, and all hell broke loose," said Lou Piniella.[1] Beneath a pile of teammates at home plate lay Ken Griffey Jr., smiling from ear to ear. Many of his former teammates said they had never seen Griffey run faster than he did on that play. Other Mariners scattered across the field, some so excited they didn't know where to go. Tim Belcher, who had been warming up in the bullpen, ran toward the infield still carrying his glove and ball.[2] Chris Bosio headed toward home plate, pushing and shaking Andy Benes along the way. Then he switched courses and headed toward second base.[3] Fireworks went off, and "Shout" blasted from the PA system. Fans danced in the aisles, hugging and kissing one another. One held up a sign reading "Start Spreading the News—Yankees Lose." Radio announcer Dave Niehaus stood in the broadcast booth with his arms raised in triumph.[4] ABC tried to interview Griffey and Edgar Martinez on the field, but it was so loud that both could barely be heard. "I thought that last night was the greatest game I ever played," said Edgar. "Now I'll tell you, this is the best game I've ever played."[5]

The players made their way into the clubhouse where beer and champagne awaited them. There, they put into context what had happened. "This whole series was unbelievable and I can't imagine any series ever being played that was more exciting than this one," said Mike Blowers.[6] "What these two teams did in this series was act as ambassadors of baseball," said Piniella. "The game lost fans with the strike last year because there was so much anger, so much pain surrounding the game. This series ought to remind fans of what they love about baseball."[7] The fans, agreeing wholeheartedly with Blowers's and Piniella's assessments, would not leave the Kingdome. "Look at this," said Griffey. "They're there and it's 20 minutes after the game."[8] Eventually, many players made their way back to the field to continue the celebration with the crowd. "I made a point of going back out to be with the fans, drinking beer and champagne with them," recalled Jay Buhner.[9]

Inside the clubhouse, Edgar Martinez celebrated with his children. He then joined Griffey, Buhner, Blowers, Randy Johnson, Rick Griffin, and Norm Charlton in the team's whirlpool. All seven were still fully clothed, some drinking beers and smoking cigars. Joey Cora stood on a sofa taking pictures with an instamatic camera.[10] "I got through this with the help of all my teammates, for no individual stands out in our room . . . or if anyone does, it should be Edgar Martinez for his game-winning hit," said Johnson. "Now, I'm going to have to go out and find a gas station for a fill-up."[11] Johnson was not kidding. He had pitched nineteen innings in over three appearances in just six days. Johnson's performance did not stand alone in terms of Division Series achievements. The series, remarkable just for its intensity, also set or tied an amazing sixteen postseason records. Among them were most combined home runs in one series (22), most combined runs in a five-game series (68), and the highest combined batting average in a five-game series (.288).[12]

As Johnson celebrated inside, another celebration ensued outdoors as thousands of fans poured out of the Kingdome and headed north to Seattle's Pioneer Square. Although it was a Sunday, and many of these people had work or school the next morning, the party continued for hours into the night. Car horns honked up and down Seattle's First Avenue. Police officer Tim Pugell complained of a sore shoulder because so many people were high-fiving him.[13] Many in the crowd were chanting "Ed-gar! Ed-gar!"[14] "Jim Kaat drove me back to the hotel and we could hardly move, with the fans celebrating and horns honking," said Brent Musburger.[15]

The city was hysterical over the Mariners. In western Washington, 78 percent of all televisions had Game 5 on that Sunday night, among the highest for any television event in that area's history.[16] On Monday, nearly five thousand people attended a team rally held at Westlake Park.[17] Dave Niehaus spoke and revealed a T-shirt that read, "My Oh My," a reference to his popular call, known throughout the area.[18] The special legislative session was taking place in three days, and the rally was a clear indication of how the locals felt. "We want a stadium and we want the Mariners here," Seattle mayor Norm Rice told the crowd.[19] "Are we a baseball town?" King County executive Gary Locke asked the crowd. "Yes!" they yelled back. "Are we gonna save the Mariners?" "Yes!"[20] The stadium package was assembled, but would Game 5 and the series win be enough? "We'll see if we can handle the pressure as well as the Mariners have handled it," said State Senate majority leader Marc Gaspard.[21]

The team's future was still in doubt the next day, October 10, when 57,065 filed into the Kingdome for Game 1 of the American League Championship Series. Facing a Cleveland team that went 100–44 during the regular season and had an offense just as potent as if not better than Seattle's, Lou Piniella's pitching staff was expended and exhausted. Randy Johnson could not start Game 1. Neither could Andy Benes or Chris Bosio. Tim Belcher had thrown in Game 4 and would need at least another day's rest. The bullpen was spent, so no one could make a spot start. The lack of pitching forced Piniella to call upon twenty-two-year-old Bob Wolcott to start Game 1. Wolcott hadn't been on the Division Series roster. In fact, he had made only six starts his entire career and would be facing 231-game winner Dennis Martinez. Piniella's choice seemed a mistake when Wolcott walked the first three hitters of the game, loading the bases with no outs for the slugger Albert Belle, the league's most dangerous hitter. Wolcott, admittedly nervous, bore down and struck out Belle. The crowd went crazy. "[The noise] got me pumped up after I struck out Belle," said Wolcott.[22] Eddie Murray then fouled out, and Joey Cora made a diving stop of a Jim Thome ground ball, throwing out the Cleveland first baseman. Wolcott got out of the jam without allowing a run. Mike Blowers's first home run of the postseason, a two-run shot, gave the Mariners an early lead. Later, with the score tied at two in the bottom of the seventh, Luis Sojo doubled in Jay Buhner to give Seattle a 3–2 lead they would not relinquish. Norm Charlton, pitching in a fifth straight game, recorded the save, and the Mariners took Game 1 of the series.

The next night, Orel Hershiser handcuffed the Mariners through eight innings, allowing only one run. Tim Belcher gave up four runs in his first start of the postseason, and Cleveland took Game 2, 5–2. The series shifted to Cleveland. No one knew what might happen there. Should the Indians win all three games, and thus the series, not only would the Mariners' miracle season be finished, but so might baseball in Seattle once and for all. As 58,144 fans left the Kingdome that night, many of them wondered if they had seen their last baseball game.

• • • • • • • • •

On Thursday, October 12, with just eighteen days left to the Mariners' ultimatum date, Washington State lawmakers gathered in Olympia for a special session called by Governor Mike Lowry. Their purpose was simple: save the Seattle Mariners. Governor Lowry had met with the top legislative leaders throughout the course of the Division Series to formulate a financing package. Now they had one. The plan would raise $250 million for a retractable-roof stadium, with the Mariners chipping in $45 million of their own money. The funds would be raised through a variety of ways, including new sports lottery games, special stadium license plates, and a 2 percent admissions tax on events at the new stadium. Additionally, taxes and fees would be raised, but only in King County. This included a 1 percent additional sales tax on food and beverages at all King County restaurants and bars, a 2 percent additional tax on rental cars, and a 5 percent additional tax on events at the Kingdome and the new ballpark.[23] Many legislators had come around to the cause of the Mariners, thanks in no small part to Edgar Martinez's series-winning hit. They included both Democrats, such as Marlin Appelwick and Marc Gaspard, and Republicans, such as Steve Van Luven. Still, the plan was not without its detractors. "I've had a chance to study this for a while," said Representative Steve Hargrove, who was originally against the idea. "Now, I'm even a stronger no."[24] "It's King County's problem and they ought to deal with it," said Senator Alex Deccio.[25]

These anti-Mariners lawmakers were chastised in the Seattle area. A legislative hotline set up after October 1 received 27,000 telephone calls in favor of keeping the Mariners in Seattle.[26] The local media also took shots at them, particularly the *Seattle Post-Intelligencer*. "Having major-league baseball in Seattle, in King County, in the state of Washington, is clearly of economic benefit to the entire state. And unless the usually pro-business, pro-economic development members of the conservative contingent realize that . . . we'll need more than prayers," wrote the paper in an editorial.[27] Additionally, as the lawmakers assembled that Thursday, nearly 200 Mariners fans gathered on the steps of the Capitol to rally for legislative support. They wore "Refuse to Lose" T-shirts and loudly booed a state employee who held up a sign opposing the proposed package.[28] They loudly cheered Governor Lowry and various legislators who supported the stadium plan. Inside, the special session began "with a roll call, a flag salute and prayers calling for divine intervention on behalf of the Seattle Mariners."[29] Then the lawmakers quibbled over details of the package. Nothing was resolved, and what was supposed to be a one-day session stretched into Friday. The main point of contention was the Kingdome. Members of the House refused to fund any bill that would help pay off the Kingdome's debt. "They said they came to Olympia to save the Mariners, and any bill should address only that problem," reported the *Seattle Times*.[30] Instead, the House passed a bill supporting the package only and leaving out any funds for the Kingdome. As they did so, members of both the House and Senate watched Game 3 of the ALCS from the nearest available televisions.[31] In fact, the vote was delayed because the game went into extra innings, and members didn't want to miss any of the action.[32] By that time, members of the Senate had already gone home, so the session continued into Saturday. In order to win over Senate votes, top legislative leaders and Governor Lowry agreed that the package would not include any funding for the Kingdome. That was enough to satisfy the senators who held out.

On Saturday, October 14, in what George Armstrong later referred to as its finest hour, the legislature officially approved the stadium package.[33] It dealt solely with a new, retractable-roof stadium for the Mariners and omitted any issues dealing with the Kingdome.[34] The

Mariners would contribute $45 million to the estimated $320 million cost. The state would start new sports-themed scratch-off lottery games and give approximately $4 million a year in sales tax revenue to King County. King County would institute the necessary sales tax increases in food and beverages, rental cars, and ballpark admissions.[35] Because King County had to institute tax increases, the King County Council would also have to approve the package. But the issue of no funding for the Kingdome was a problem for the council. They were facing intense pressure from the Seahawks, who felt a legislative package without Kingdome funding, "create[d] an unlevel economic playing field for different major-league franchises in Seattle."[36] Still, the council's ultimate decision seemed obvious to many. "The County Council's duty is now clear and simple—save baseball by quickly implementing the plan approved by the Legislature, then get busy finding other means of financing Kingdome needs," wrote the *Seattle Post-Intelligencer*.[37] Members of the council hinted that they could not dare vote against the package. "None of us wants to be the group that says, 'We lost baseball,'" said council member Ron Sims.[38] Some also didn't see the sense in letting the Kingdome issues hold up the Mariners. "We still won't have funding to cover the [Kingdome] roof," said council member Chris Vance, referring to what would happen if they voted against the proposal. "We still won't have funding for the Kingdome renovations. We'll lose the Mariners, and we probably will have so infuriated the Legislature they will never help us."[39] On Wednesday, October 18, Governor Lowry signed the bill authorizing the stadium funding at a public ceremony held at West Seattle Elementary School.[40] Even as he signed, the King County Council had not taken action. There were just twelve days left to save the Mariners.

On October 23, with just a week left, the council voted 10–3 to adopt the state's financing plan. The new stadium was tentatively set to open in 1999. Various groups would be assembled to study how to resolve issues with the Kingdome as well as to oversee the construction and funding of the new ballpark.[41] After eighteen tumultuous years that saw various ownerships, mediocre teams, a miracle season, a lethargic then revitalized fan base, and an ultimatum that had just six days left to termination, the Seattle Mariners were finally, *finally* saved for good.

• • • • • • • • •

The Mariners' miracle season had concluded by the time the King County Council approved a new stadium. Nine days earlier, tied at one game apiece in the ALCS, the Mariners and Indians headed to Cleveland. That city was exemplary of the type of enthusiasm and public support the Mariners were seeking for their new stadium. The Indians had long been a sad story, going for decades without reaching the playoffs or even fielding a competitive team. Their home ballpark, Municipal Stadium, was an old, antiquated, dull place for baseball that was descriptively referred to as "the Mistake by the Lake." Its cavernous seating capacity of over 70,000 made the stadium look even emptier when only a few thousand fans were showing up for games during the 1970s and 1980s. But in the early 1990s, the Indians rejuvenated themselves around a core of homegrown talent and veteran pickups. By 1994, they were a force to be reckoned with in the American League Central. That same year they opened a brand new ballpark, Jacobs Field, in the heart of downtown Cleveland. Sparked by a successful ballclub and one of the game's best playing venues, fans flocked to Jacobs, selling out game after game. If it could happen in Cleveland, it could certainly happen in Seattle.

The Indians' faithful tried their best to intimidate the Mariners. They chanted on every two-strike count and bore signs reading "Hey Seattle: Refuse This!" and "Bring on the Big Eunuch."[42] Still, they proved far less hostile than those of New York, and the Mariners battled through Game 3. Randy Johnson, making his first ALCS appearance, dominated the potent Indians lineup through seven innings, taking a 2–1 lead into the bottom of the eighth inning. But then Jay Buhner misplayed a fly ball to deep right field, allowing the Indians to tie the game. In the top of the eleventh inning, Buhner redeemed himself by drilling an Eric Plunk breaking ball into the right-field seats for a three-run home run. It proved the difference, as the Mariners took Game 3 by a score of 5–2 and took a 2–1 lead in the series. Buhner's home run, however, represented the last of the Mariners' magical moments in 1995.

The next night, in a rainy, cold Cleveland, the Indians offense exploded against Andy Benes. A first-inning home run by Eddie Murray gave Cleveland a 3–0 lead. In the second inning, they added three more runs. Benes did not make it through the third inning. "The game got out of hand and that was my responsibility," said

Benes.[43] The Mariners' offense turned stagnant against Ken Hill, and the Indians evened the series with a 7–0 victory. In Game 5, Chris Bosio turned in another gritty performance, but with the Mariners leading, 2–1, in the bottom of the sixth inning, he made a crucial mistake to Jim Thome. "With the count 2-and-0 in a close game, I thought he'd be taking a pitch," said Bosio. "But he is a very aggressive hitter and swings hard. He got an off-speed pitch to his liking and smoked it."[44] The result was a two-run home run that gave the Indians a 3–2 lead. Afterward, the Mariners went hitless against the Indians' bullpen, and Cleveland won the game and took a 3–2 lead in the series. Seattle tried to remain upbeat afterward. "There's still a lot of fight left in this team," said Dan Wilson. "We've been here before and I still like our chances."[45] It was not to be for the Mariners.

● ● ● ● ● ● ● ● ●

At the Kingdome for Game 6, Randy Johnson reared back and fired to the Indians' Omar Vizquel, but the ball got away from Wilson. It made its way to the backstop and rolled along the wall. Enough time passed to allow Ruben Amaro to score from third base and Kenny Lofton to score all the way from second base. Just like that, the Mariners were down, 3–0, in the eighth inning of Game 6. The game had been tense from the start, but this moment shattered the heart of the Mariners' faithful. One hitter later, Carlos Baerga homered to make it 4–0. The Big Unit, having pitched in four games over the course of sixteen days, was officially out of gas. Lou Piniella removed him, and the tall lefty received a rousing ovation from the Kingdome crowd. Though he left down by four runs, the applause let him know how appreciative the fans were of his effort all season long. Johnson was the losing pitcher, but the fans certainly didn't blame him for the loss. In the bottom of the ninth, the fans hoped for one last miracle comeback, but Buhner grounded out to third base to end the series. The Indians were going to Atlanta to play in the World Series. The Mariners were going home for the winter. It had been their most incredible season ever, a roller-coaster ride that had seen them transform Seattle into a baseball town. In the Mariners' dugout, Joey Cora sat crying inconsolably. Teammate Alex Rodriguez draped his arm around the second baseman. It was a touching moment that summed up what this season meant to the men in uniform and to those in the crowd.

Minutes after the series ended, the crowd still stood applauding their team. Though the Indians were still celebrating, many fans ignored them and instead turned their attention to the players who had given them their greatest sports experience ever. "God, I'm going to miss this. What an incredibly amazing year this has been. People really had a love affair with this team, and I think that's going to continue," said fan Sally Cammerton.[46] Realizing that these people were not leaving, Lou Piniella had his team go back out on the field to acknowledge them. It was a surreal moment. Just a month after the Mariners could barely draw 15,000 fans, 58,489 people stood and cheered their team, even though they had just lost. Chants of "Ed-gar! Ed-gar!" went up as did chants of "Lou! Lou! Lou!"[47] "They showed that, win or lose, they're behind us 100 percent," Ken Griffey Jr. said afterward. "It was great, and it was something we never had before. I have to take my hat off for them. They made a difference in this town and in this ballpark."[48] At that point, the stadium proposal was still in doubt, meaning many of the fans were uncertain if they would ever see this team again, at least in a Seattle uniform. If this was it though, the last few weeks had been one hell of a ride. "We have a lot of wonderful memories to think about this winter," said fan Leon Masters.[49]

Less than a week after the Mariners' postseason ended, the King County Council approved the stadium-financing plan. The new stadium plan endured a bumpy ride afterward. Local groups protested the use of taxpayer funds, and the Seahawks remained upset regarding the lack of funding for the Kingdome. In September 1996, the site of the new stadium was selected directly south of the Kingdome. But later that year, the Mariners ownership announced it was fed up with delays and public opposition to the ballpark. They were going to put the team up for sale. In time, however, the issues were resolved, and the team was not put up for sale (eventually the Seahawks would also get a new stadium).[50] In March 1997, nearly 8,000 fans turned out to see Ken Griffey Jr. break ground for the new ballpark.[51] A year later, the Seattle-based Safeco Corporation bought the naming rights to the stadium. Safeco would pay $1.8 million a year for twenty years, adjusted for inflation, for these rights.[52] The purchase immediately brought out the sharp wit of Seattle's talk radio hosts and newspaper writers, who wondered "whether the team might become one of the insurance company's liabilities" or if "Safeco promise[d] double indemnity for the M's bullpen."[53]

· · · · · · · · ·

On July 15, 1999, the Mariners played their first game at the new ballpark, known as Safeco Field. Dave Niehaus, dressed in a tuxedo, threw out the first pitch of the game, an interleague matchup against the San Diego Padres. The stadium cost nearly $518 million to construct, much higher than the original estimated cost, including $372 million in public funding, also much higher than expected.[54] The costs were among the highest of any stadium built in the history of sports in the United States.

Regardless of the price tag, Safeco Field was a beautiful facility. The ballpark loomed over the Kingdome, a clear contrast between the dark, gloomy, domed stadium and the new, state-of-the-art retractable-roof stadium. Safeco seated just over 47,000, nearly 10,000 fewer than the Kingdome. Unlike the hitter-friendly dimensions of the Kingdome, Safeco was a pitcher's park, featuring power alleys of 390 feet in left field and 387 feet in right center. Gone was the large wall in right field, replaced by eight-foot fences all around. More important, however, the hard concrete-and-steel views at the Kingdome were replaced with the more aesthetically pleasing sights at Safeco. With the retractable roof open, fans could catch a glimpse of Seattle's skyline over the left-field wall. Out behind right field, a train could be seen and heard running through the east side of the city every few innings. Other sections of the ballpark allowed fans sweeping views of Puget Sound. The press box was perhaps the biggest and nicest in the Major Leagues. In the main concourse of the left-field entrance was a mural depicting Ken Griffey Jr. sliding into home plate to end the 1995 Division Series. The mural, complete with Jim Leyritz lunging for the throw and Joey Cora leaping in celebration, was dubbed simply "The Double." Some referred to Safeco as "the House That Griffey Built" a play on the "House That Ruth Built" nickname that had been given to Yankee Stadium.[55]

Fans' reviews of Safeco were overwhelmingly positive. "Incredible," said Joe Cox of West Seattle, the first patron to enter the ballpark.[56] "This is like something no one has even seen before in Seattle. This is great. Outside baseball at last," said Rocky Ruddy.[57] Fan Cathy Engrissei referred to it as "a magical place."[58] It was hard to believe they were describing a baseball stadium in Seattle after so many years at the dreary Kingdome. The players offered glowing praise as well. "In the long run it's going to pay big dividends for a lot of guys because the turf definitely had taken its toll," said Jay Buhner, comparing the new ballpark to the old one.[59] "This is just gorgeous . . . really . . . this is really impressive," said the Padres' Phil Nevin.[60]

Perhaps no one enjoyed Safeco's opening more than the owners and state leaders who had fought so hard for its construction. "This is an absolutely great day for the franchise, for the fans and for the Pacific Northwest," said Mariners CEO Howard Lincoln. "Back in 1994, it was such a difficult struggle to save this for Seattle and keep it from going to Tampa Bay. The other side of it was in 1995 when we had that wonderful playoff experience. Then you say to yourself that every minute the ownership spent on this was worth it because it was so exciting."[61] Gary Locke, the former King County executive who was then Washington governor, agreed that the struggle was worth it. "The owners have gone through a lot. They stepped in to rescue baseball for us and [the opening of Safeco] is the fruition of that with an awesome, gorgeous stadium that is going to make the people of the Pacific Northwest love baseball."[62]

The optimism from fans, players, owners, and politicians was enough to lessen the impact of minor protests that occurred outside the stadium gates from those still upset over Safeco's public financing. The good feelings surrounding the opening momentarily erased the politics and cost overruns that had been a problem for the last few years. On that night, the majority of people were happy just to have the Mariners around. That kind of thought simply wasn't possible in Seattle a mere ten years earlier.

Over the course of the 1999 season at Safeco, the Mariners never drew fewer than 33,000 fans and usually saw crowds in excess of 40,000. The following year, over 2.9 million people came to Safeco. Then in 2001, the Mariners drew over 3.5 million people and led the league in attendance. It was truly remarkable. The city that Jim Bouton had said would never be a baseball town was drawing more fans than any other team.

· · · · · · · · ·

At 8:32 A.M., on Sunday, March 26, 2000, several loud pops were heard in Seattle. The reverberations echoed across downtown. Then, 16.8 seconds later, the Kingdome came crashing down in a fantastic demolition. The impact, which equaled the magnitude of a 2.3 earthquake, shattered windows of nearby buildings and created a giant cloud of dust.[63] It took more than 4,450 pounds of dynamite to bring down the ballpark, which was just one day shy of its twenty-fourth birthday. Thousands of onlookers where there, creating a party atmosphere in south Seattle that day. People "whooped it up from balconies, barbecues, and brunches. They also cheered from the King County Jail, where prisoners had a terrific view," reported the *Seattle Post-Intelligencer*.[64] Though most people rejoiced, some felt melancholic. "I look at it as a funeral," said Mark Dale of West Seattle. "It's part of the skyline. It's kind of ugly, but it's like the ugly cousin you've always liked."[65] Others felt that way, as well. Former Washington governor John Spellman, who had played a role in the Kingdome's bonding and construction, refused to watch the building come down.[66] Most, however, celebrated the event. The dark and dreary Kingdome, the site of so much of the Mariners' misery over the years, was finally gone.

Three thousand miles away, dozens of New Yorkers took in the scene while watching in Times Square. Most of them were more than happy to see the Kingdome disappear forever. "It's just too bad the Seattle Mariners weren't in there when it went down—after what they did to the Yankees in the 1995 playoffs," said Yankees fan Adam Lusk.[67] Five years later, the hard feelings still had not subsided in the Big Apple.

Epilogue

"The first three games of the 2000 American League Championship Series between the New York Yankees and the Seattle Mariners were acceptable big league games. . . . But what happened five years ago when these same teams met in the first post-strike playoff series was more than just an exciting baseball confrontation. It was a transcendent athletic experience."

—Bob Ryan, *Boston Globe*, October 15, 2000

Buck Showalter found a job just four months after his "resignation." The expansion Arizona Diamondbacks hired him as manager, even though they didn't begin play until 1998. In 1999, they won the National League West. Showalter, however, endured heartache again when the Mets' Todd Pratt homered in the tenth inning of Game 4 to end the Diamondbacks' season. Showalter was fired a year later. The following season, the Diamondbacks won the World Series. Showalter managed the Texas Rangers from 2003 to 2006 and later worked for the Cleveland Indians and as an analyst for ESPN's *Baseball Tonight*.

• • • • • • • • •

Gene Michael remained with the Yankees after his demotion and is among one of the top and most trusted advisors in the team's hierarchy.

• • • • • • • • •

Don Mattingly officially retired in January 1997. His number 23 was
retired by the Yankees in August of that year. The Captain stayed
away from baseball for almost a decade before returning to the
Yankees in 2004 as the team's hitting coach. He served as bench
coach in 2007 before leaving the team and joining Joe Torre on the
staff of the Los Angeles Dodgers.

• • • • • • • • •

Jim Leyritz's postseason dramatics continued for years. In 1996,
his eighth-inning three-run home run tied Game 4 of the World
Series, pushing the momentum of the series toward New York. With
the Padres in 1998, he hit four home runs during the postseason.
Leyritz returned to the Yankees in 1999 and hit the last home run
of the twentieth century when he connected in the eighth inning of
Game 4 of the World Series against the Braves. He ended his career
with eight home runs in just sixty-one postseason at-bats.

• • • • • • • • •

Wade Boggs stayed with the Yankees through the 1997 season, then
joined the expansion Tampa Bay Devil Rays. There Boggs achieved
his goal of 3,000 hits, becoming the only person to do so by hitting
a home run. He retired after the 1999 season and was voted into the
Hall of Fame in 2005.

• • • • • • • • •

Tony Fernandez returned to the postseason in 1997 with the Cleveland Indians. His eleventh-inning home run in Game 6 of the ALCS
against the Orioles broke a scoreless tie and sent Cleveland to the
World Series. But in the Fall Classic, Fernandez made a crucial error
in the deciding Game 7, helping the Florida Marlins win their first
championship. He returned to the Blue Jays in 1998, where he hit over
.300 and made the 1999 All-Star Team. After a brief stint with the
Brewers, he joined the Blue Jays for a fourth time and retired after
the 2001 season.

· · · · · · · · ·

Pat Kelly never overcame the numerous injuries he incurred on a constant basis. Between 1996 and 1999, he never had more than 153 at-bats in a season. Kelly retired after the 1999 season and eventually became a scout, evaluating talent overseas.

· · · · · · · · ·

Dion James began the 1996 season with the Yankees but was released on May 1 of that year after only twelve at-bats. He never played in the majors again.

· · · · · · · · ·

Darryl Strawberry ended up back with the Yankees in 1996 after playing half the year for the St. Paul Saints of the Independent League. Strawberry became an integral part of the Yankees' dynasty teams, but late in the 1998 season he was diagnosed with colon cancer. He recovered but was suspended from baseball in 1999 for violating the league's drug policy. Strawberry was suspended once more in 2000 and never played baseball again. He eventually became an advisor for the New York Mets.

· · · · · · · · ·

Bernie Williams followed his breakout 1995 season with one of the greatest careers in Yankees history. By the time he retired after the 2006 season, Williams had four championship rings, four Gold Gloves, and a batting title and was among the team's all-time leaders in runs scored, hits, doubles, home runs, and RBIs.

· · · · · · · · ·

Paul O'Neill continued his success in New York, hitting over .300 every year until 1999 and driving in over 100 runs every year from 1997 until 2001. During Game 5 of the 2001 World Series, O'Neill's last game at Yankee Stadium, the fans showed their appreciation by chanting his name continuously throughout the top of the ninth inning.

• • • • • • • • •

Ruben Sierra's production declined in 1996, and he wore out his welcome with Joe Torre. He was traded to the Tigers that July, and by 1999, he was out of the game altogether. But Sierra underwent a resurrection and returned to baseball in 2000 as an offensive force again. He was traded in 2003 to the Yankees, where he became a model teammate and key player off the bench. He retired with 306 home runs and over 2,200 hits.

• • • • • • • • •

David Cone's career nearly ended when an aneurism in his arm was discovered in May 1996. But Cone underwent successful surgery and recovered in time to lead the Yankees through the 1996 playoffs. In 1998, Cone won twenty games for the second time in his career. In 1999, he threw a perfect game at Yankee Stadium. After a season with the Red Sox in 2001 and five appearances with the Mets in 2003, Cone retired with 194 career wins.

• • • • • • • • •

Andy Pettitte became one of the game's premier left-handed pitchers, winning 137 games between 1996 and 2003. He also became known for his clutch postseason performances, including being the starting pitcher in the 1998 and 2000 World Series–clinching games. Pettitte left the Yankees after 2003, spent three seasons with the Astros, then returned to New York in 2007. He was the starting and winning pitcher in the last game played at the original Yankee Stadium.

• • • • • • • • •

Jack McDowell won thirteen games for Cleveland in 1996 but injuries took their toll, and by 1999, he was out of baseball. He continued, however, to play with his rock band, Stickfigure.

• • • • • • • • •

Scott Kamieniecki left the Yankees for Baltimore in 1997. There he pitched well, winning ten games and pitching eight shutout innings in the 1997 ALCS. He retired after the 2000 season.

• • • • • • • • •

Bob Wickman was traded to the Brewers during the 1996 season. In Milwaukee, he was converted into a closer and enjoyed success in that position with the Brewers, Indians, and Braves. He retired to his native Wisconsin after the 2007 season.

• • • • • • • • •

Steve Howe's struggles on the field continued in 1996, as he posted a 6.35 ERA. He was released by the Yankees and retired shortly thereafter. Howe was killed in a car accident in April 2006.

• • • • • • • • •

Mariano Rivera became the Yankees' setup man in 1996 and their closer in 1997. In the latter role, he became the greatest relief pitcher in history. Rivera won the 1999 World Series MVP and the 2003 ALCS MVP, and he made twenty-three consecutive appearances in the postseason between 1997 and 2000 without giving up a run.

• • • • • • • •

John Wetteland put the memory of 1995 behind him, saving seven games during the 1996 playoffs, including all four victories for the Yankees in the World Series. That effort earned him the series MVP. He left New York that off-season and signed with the Rangers. He retired after the 2000 season with 330 saves. He eventually became a coach with the Seattle Mariners.

• • • • • • • • •

For Mike Stanley, Randy Velarde, Gerald Williams, and Sterling Hitchcock, fate was especially cruel. All four left the Yankees between

November 1995 and August 1996. All four would at some point return to the Yankees during the team's 1996–2001 dynasty run. Yet none of them ended up winning a championship. Mike Stanley was traded back to the Yankees in August 1997. He had three hits in four at-bats in the ALDS, but the Indians eliminated the Yankees in five games. Stanley did not return to New York in 1998. In 1999, Stanley's Red Sox were eliminated from the ALCS in five games by the Yankees. In 2000, Stanley's A's were eliminated from the ALDS in five games by the Yankees. He retired that off-season and later gained notoriety when he coached his son's team to the Little League World Series.

Randy Velarde became a successful full-time player on the West Coast. In 1999, he had a career-best 200 hits for the A's, and in 2000, he was a major part of the Oakland team that surprisingly won the American League West. In 2001, Velarde was traded back to the Yankees late in the season. There he joined Gerald Williams, who had also been reacquired by the Yankees earlier that year. Williams had been a successful leadoff hitter with both Atlanta and Tampa Bay before his return to New York. Joining Velarde and Williams was Sterling Hitchcock, whom the Yankees had reacquired that July. Hitchcock had pitched well for the Mariners and had won the 1998 NLCS MVP with the Padres.

Velarde, Williams, and Hitchcock all watched from the dugout in Arizona as the Yankees failed to protect a 2–1 lead in the bottom of the ninth inning of Game 7 of the World Series. All three were retired by 2006.

· · · · · · · · ·

Coincidentally, the man credited with the victory in that Game 7 in Arizona was none other than Randy Johnson. The Big Unit had been traded from Seattle to Houston in 1998, where he led the Astros to the playoffs. In 1999, Johnson signed with the Diamondbacks. That year, he won the first of four consecutive Cy Young Awards. In 2001, Johnson had already won Games 2 and 6 of the World Series against the Yankees when he came out of the bullpen in the eighth inning of Game 7. He held the Yankees scoreless the rest of the game, and Arizona scored two runs in the ninth to take the game and the series. In 2005, Johnson was traded to the Yankees, where he spent two turbulent years before heading back to the National League.

• • • • • • • • •

Chris Bosio pitched one more year in the Major Leagues, retiring after the 1996 season. He eventually became a college and minor-league pitching coach.

• • • • • • • • •

Andy Benes left Seattle after 1995 and continued a successful career with the Cardinals and Diamondbacks. He retired with 155 career victories and 2,000 strikeouts.

• • • • • • • • •

Norm Charlton remained in baseball until 2001, though he never duplicated the success of his 1995 season. He left Seattle for Baltimore in 1998 and spent parts of the next three seasons with the Orioles, Braves, Devil Rays, and Reds. He returned to Seattle in 2001 and became an effective lefty out of the bullpen as the team won 116 games. In 2008, Charlton was named the Mariners' bullpen coach.

• • • • • • • • •

Jeff Nelson became a key setup reliever for the Yankees' bullpen during their championship run. In 55 postseason appearances, Nelson posted a 2.65 ERA, with 62 strikeouts in $54\frac{1}{3}$ innings. He rejoined the Mariners in 2001, was traded back to the Yankees in 2003, and eventually ended up back with Seattle in 2005. He retired in 2006 and began doing a sports radio program in the Seattle area.

• • • • • • • • •

Tim Belcher signed with the Kansas City Royals after 1995 and averaged fourteen wins a year between 1996 and 1998. He retired after 2000 and eventually became a scout.

• • • • • • • •

Dan Wilson had his best season in 1996, hitting eighteen home runs, driving in eighty-three runs, and making the All-Star Team. He played the rest of his career with Seattle, becoming a fan favorite and key player of the Mariners playoff teams of 1997, 2000, and 2001. He retired after the 2005 season.

• • • • • • • •

Tino Martinez became a beloved member of the Yankee championship teams. He drove in over 100 runs for five consecutive seasons and hit two of the biggest home runs in World Series history, the first coming in the seventh inning of Game 1 in 1998 and the second coming in the bottom of the ninth inning of Game 4 in 2001. Tino retired with 339 career home runs and two All-Star Game appearances.

• • • • • • • •

Edgar Martinez remained the game's best designated hitter for years, driving in 100 runs or more in six of seven seasons. At age thirty-seven, Edgar had his best year, hitting thirty-seven home runs and driving in 145 runs. He retired with a .312 lifetime average and is one of the most beloved figures in Seattle sport's history. He remained in the Seattle area and began a business called Branded Solutions.

• • • • • • • •

"Little" Joey Cora continued to ride teammates for three more seasons. In 1997, he had the best year of his career, earning his only All-Star team selection. He retired after 1998 and eventually became a coach.

• • • • • • • •

Luis Sojo was claimed off waivers by the Yankees in August 1996. He was playing second base when the Yankees won the World Series that year. Sojo achieved cult hero status in New York because, while his numbers were never overwhelming, he continued his knack for clutch hits. In 2000, his two-out ninth-inning single against the Mets in Game 5 drove in the World Series–winning runs. After retiring in 2002, Sojo played in the Yankees Old Timers' game in 2003, then came out of retirement to bat four times during that season.

• • • • • • • •

Mike Blowers was traded to the Dodgers after the 1995 season, but he returned for two different stints with Seattle before retiring. Blowers eventually became a color commentator for the Mariners and remained in the Seattle area.

• • • • • • • •

Vince Coleman left Seattle after 1995 and played two more seasons. He retired with 752 stolen bases, one of the highest totals in baseball history.

• • • • • • • •

Jay Buhner followed his forty-home-run season in 1995 by hitting forty-four in 1996 and forty in 1997. The Bone continued to patrol right field for the Mariners until injuries finally caught up to him. He retired after the 2001 season. Fittingly, Buhner's last act as a major leaguer was scoring a run against the Yankees at Yankee Stadium in Game 5 of the 2001 ALCS. To the very end, Buhner was still sticking it to the Yankees.

• • • • • • • •

Ken Griffey Jr. remained the game's most dominant player throughout the nineties, averaging fifty-two home runs a year between 1996 and 1999. He won a Gold Glove and was selected to the All-Star team in each of those seasons. But the man who helped build Safeco Field didn't enjoy it for long. Junior was traded to the Reds in 2000. In Cincinnati, injuries hampered his pursuit of the all-time home-run record. Still, he remained a threat when healthy. In June 2007, Griffey returned to Seattle during interleague play for the first time as a visiting player and was warmly received by the hometown crowd. He then went 5–13 with two home runs in the three-game series, bringing back great memories for so many Seattleites. In 2009, Junior returned to Seattle and homered in his first game back in a Mariners uniform. As of this writing, he is fifth on the all-time home run list.

• • • • • • • • •

Lou Piniella managed the Mariners to the playoffs three more times after 1995. He left Seattle after 2002 with 840 wins and a .542 winning percentage, by the far the best-ever totals for a Seattle manager. He moved closer to home, managing the Tampa Bay Devil Rays for three seasons before being named manager of the Cubs in 2007.

• • • • • • • • •

Almost two decades after purchasing the team, Hiroshi Yamauchi, John Ellis, and Howard Lincoln were still with the Mariners, as was Chuck Armstrong. Amazingly, the team that couldn't find a permanent owner ended up with one of the longest active ownerships in baseball as of this writing.

• • • • • • • • •

The 1995 Division Series spawned one of baseball's best rivalries of the late 1990s. Throughout that period, the Mariners and Yankees played a series of tense, electric games that always invoked, but never quite matched, the drama of 1995. It began with the first post–Division Series meeting between the two teams in May 1996 when Dwight Gooden no-hit the Mariners at Yankee Stadium. It was a small measure of revenge for New York, though neither Gooden nor the man who caught him, Joe Girardi, had played in the 1995 Series. Later in the year, Paul O'Neill and Mariners catcher John Marzano had an altercation at home plate that led to a bench-clearing brawl in the Kingdome. In 1999, the two teams engaged in another brawl, this time at Safeco Field.

The following year, both teams met in the ALCS, their first post-season encounter since 1995. There were efforts by the media to rehash the spirit of the 1995 series and perhaps an effort on the Yankees' part to seek revenge. But it wasn't the same. Unlike 1995, both teams had been successful for years, and there was no tension regarding new stadiums or returning fan bases. Don Mattingly had retired, as had many others from the series. Ken Griffey Jr. and Randy Johnson had been traded from Seattle, and various other players had moved on from both Seattle and New York. The Yankees took the series in six games. Fittingly, Edgar Martinez made the last out of the series, though to some it was five years too late.

The following year, the two teams met again in the ALCS. In Game 4, the Yankees' Alfonso Soriano hit a game-winning ninth-inning home run to right field that was eerily reminiscent of Jim Leyritz's shot in the rain six years earlier. The Yankees won the series in five games, and it marked the end of the rivalry. By 2002, Edgar Martinez and Dan Wilson were the only Mariners left from the magical 1995 team. For the Yankees, only Mariano Rivera, Andy Pettitte, Bernie Williams, and Jorge Posada remained. But the memory of the 1995 series and its implications lived on, even a decade and a half after Edgar Martinez's line drive down the left line got Seattle a new ballpark and gave birth to a new Yankees dynasty.

NOTES

Interviews

The following people were interviewed exclusively for this book and their cooperation and stories were much appreciated: Jim Abbott, Randy Adamack, Rich Amaral, Marty Appel, Ambassador George Argyros, Chuck Armstrong, Steve Balboni, Jesse Barfield, Craig Beatty, Tim Belcher, Andy Benes, Wade Boggs, Chris Bosio, Phil Bradley, Darren Bragg, Jay Buhner, Brian Butterfield, Mike Cameron, Norm Charlton, Dave Cohen, Joey Cora, Russ Davis, Rick Down, Lee Elia, John Ellis, Jim Evans, Steve Farr, Tony Fernandez, Senator Slade Gorton, Rick Griffin, Lee Guetterman, John Hirschbeck, Tom Hutyler, Dion James, Jim Leyritz, Howard Lincoln, Governor Gary Locke, Governor Mike Lowry, Edgar Martinez, Don Mattingly, Jack McDowell, John McLaren, Dave Niehaus, Paul O'Neill, Lee Pelekoudas, Sam Perlozzo, Ken Phelps, Lou Piniella, Harold Reynolds, Mayor Norm Rice, Rick Rizzs, Scott Sanderson, Herman Sarkowsky, Steve Sax, Glen Sherlock, Buck Showalter, Luis Sojo, Mike Stanley, John Sterling, Doug Strange, David Sussman, Honorable Steve Van Luven, Randy Velarde, Chris Widger, and Dan Wilson.

Approximately a dozen people, including Randy Johnson and Ken Griffey Jr., either directly or through a representative, declined or did not respond to requests to be interviewed.

1. Don-nie Base-ball

1. Phone interview with Velarde, 7/23/08; e-mail interview with Abbott, 4/27/07; phone interview with Leyritz, 2/28/07; phone interview with Guetterman, 1/24/08; phone interview with Down, 6/5/08.
2. Phone interview with Mattingly, 4/2/08.

3. Baseballreference.com; Jeff Bradley, "Red-Hot Mattingly Now Captain Video," *New York Daily News*, 7/27/95, 74; Bob Raissman, "Mattingly Stirs Media War," *Daily News*, 7/21/95, 24.
4. Phone interview with Showalter, 2/24/07.
5. Baseballreference.com.
6. Showalter interview; phone interview with O'Neill, 3/7/07; phone interview with Benes, 1/12/08.

2. Winless in Seattle

1. David Wilma, "From Cranks to Fans: Seattle's Long Love Affair with Baseball," *HistoryLink*, 7/10/01, 1. Kenneth Hogan, *The 1969 Seattle Pilots: Major League Baseball's One-Year Team* (Jefferson, NC: McFarland, 2007), 10.
2. Hogan, *The 1969 Seattle Pilots*, 11–12, 15.
3. Russ Dille, "Play Ball! A Slide Show History of Early Baseball in Washington," *HistoryLink*, 01/01/03, 8.
4. Hogan, *The 1969 Seattle Pilots*, 15.
5. John Reeves, "Seattle Angels," Seattle Mariners Dugout, geocities.com/colosseum/field (2000).
6. Jim Bouton, *Ball Four* (New York, NY: Wiley Publishing, 1970), 15.
7. Philip Lowry, *Green Cathedrals* (Reading, MA: Addison Wesley Publishing, 1993), 217.
8. Hy Zimmerman, "Finley Asks for Kindly Approach to Expansion," *Seattle Times*, 1/16/76.
9. Lowery, *Green Cathedrals*, 217.
10. Wilma, "From Cranks to Fans," 3.
11. Bouton, *Ball Four*, 103.
12. Hogan, *The 1969 Seattle Pilots*, 128.
13. "Expected Shift of Pilots: High Hopes to a Disaster," *Seattle Post-Intelligencer*, 3/16/70.
14. Hogan, *The 1969 Seattle Pilots*, 128.
15. "Wanna 'Play Ball' with the Pilots?" *Seattle Post-Intelligencer*, 3/1/70.
16. Lenny Anderson, "Seattle Could Still Lose Pilots, P-I Writer Says," *Seattle Post-Intelligencer*, 3/8/70; Larry McCarten, "It's Off to Milwaukee for Pilots," *Seattle Post-Intelligencer*, 4/1/70.
17. In-person interview with Gorton, 11/07/07.
18. Dick Rockne, "A.L. 'Doctored' Resolution," *Seattle Times*, 1/22/76.
19. Art Thiel, *Out of Leftfield: How the Mariners Made Baseball Fly in Seattle* (Seattle: Sasquatch Books, 2003), 13.
20. J. Michael Kenyon, "57,000 Cheer Mariners," *Seattle Post-Intelligencer*, 4/7/77.

21. Thiel, *Out of Leftfield*, 14.
22. Baseballreference.com.
23. Dick Rockne, "The Way It Was," *Seattle Times*, 3/26/97, F8.
24. Gordon Wittenmyer, "The Gory Years," *Seattle Times*, 10/6/95, E3.
25. Thiel, *Out of Leftfield*, 272
26. In-person interview with Adamack, 11/9/07.
27. Byron Rosen, *Washington Post*, 7/15/77, D3.
28. "Pitching Improbables," *Seattle Post-Intelligencer*, 5/12/06, C2.
29. Wittenmyer, "The Gory Years," E3.
30. Thiel, *Out of Leftfield*, 7.
31. Kirby Arnold, *Tales from the Seattle Dugout* (Champaign, IL: Sports Publishing, 2007), 19.
32. Barry Horstman, "Field of Play: New Owner of the Padres Liked Trip around Bases on Way to Business Success," *Los Angeles Times*, 4/12/87, Metro pt. 2, p. 1.
33. United Press International, 1/8/81.
34. Phone interview with Argyros, 3/5/08.
35. "A.L. Owners Approve Two Sales," *New York Times*, 1/30/81, A20.
36. Horstman, "Field of Play," 1; Arthur Lingle, "George Argyros: Sportsman, Developer, Philanthropist," *Orange County Business Journal* 10, no. 8, 4/27/87, 12.
37. "Orioles' Pitching, Royals' Hitting Are the Key Factors; Eastern Division," *New York Times*, 4/5/81, sec. 5, p. 10.
38. Argyros interview.
39. Baseballreference.com.
40. Thiel, *Out of Leftfield*, 5.
41. Arnold, *Tales*, 65.
42. Maury Wills and Mike Celizic, *On the Run: The Never Dull and Often Shocking Life of Maury Wills* (New York, NY: Carroll & Graf Publishers, 1991), 126.
43. Arnold, *Tales*, 65.
44. Thiel, *Out of Leftfield*, 6.
45. Wills and Celizic, *On the Run*, 126.
46. Thiel, *Out of Leftfield*, 7.
47. Baseballreference.com.
48. Jim Street, "Hindsight on a Funny Anniversary," MLB.com, 5/8/03; Baseballreference.com.
49. Thiel, *Out of Leftfield*, 7.
50. United Press International, 6/26/83.
51. Wittenmyer, "The Gory Years," E3.
52. G. S. Khalsa, United Press International, 6/25/83.

53. Jim Cour, "BBA: Mariners-Williams," Associated Press, 5/9/86.
54. *Los Angeles Times*, 7/11/85, part 3, p. 16.
55. United Press International, 5/9/86.
56. Cour, "BBA."
57. Brian Mottaz, United Press International, 5/9/86.
58. Jim Cour, Associated Press, 5/16/88.
59. Dennis Anstine, United Press International, 6/6/88.
60. Bob Slocum, "Williams' Exit Repeats Old Pattern," *San Diego Union-Tribune*, 6/7/88, C5.
61. Anstine, United Press International.
62. "Mariners, Astros Hire Managers," *Washington Post*, 11/8/88.
63. Arnold, *Tales*, 53.
64. Argyros interview.
65. Thiel, *Out of Leftfield*, 16.
66. Phone interview with Phelps, 5/27/07.
67. Arnold, *Tales*, 53.
68. Phone interview with Bradley, 11/15/07.
69. "Pitching Improbables," C2.
70. Thiel, *Out of Leftfield*, 16.
71. "Baseball," *Washington Post*, 3/27/87, D2.
72. Dennis Georgatos, Associated Press, 3/26/87.
73. Thiel, *Out of Leftfield*, 17.
74. Dave Distel, "San Diego Sportscene: Next Time, Argyros May Just Send Flowers, *Los Angeles Times*, 4/22/87, part 3, p. 1.
75. Distel, "San Diego Sportscene," 1.
76. Jim Street, "Indianapolis Ownership for M's," *Sporting News*, 9/4/89, 16.
77. In-person interview with Armstrong, 11/8/07.
78. Larry LaRue, "Kingdome, Like Mariners, May Get a Facelift," *Los Angeles Times*, 11/12/89, C4.
79. LaRue, "Kingdome," 4.
80. Arnold, *Tales*, 89.
81. Thiel, *Out of Leftfield*, 18, 49.
82. Ibid.
83. Phone interview with Sarkowsky, 10/29/07.
84. Gorton interview.
85. Ibid.
86. In-person interview with Lincoln, 11/08/07.
87. Thiel, *Out of Leftfield*, 50.
88. Lincoln interview.
89. Gorton interview.
90. Thiel, *Out of Leftfield*, 51.
91. Lincoln interview.

92. In-person interview with Ellis, 11/08/07.
93. Phone interview with Rice, 11/07/07.
94. Thiel, *Out of Leftfield*, 66.
95. Lincoln interview.
96. Thiel, *Out of Leftfield*, 73.
97. Lincoln interview.
98. Ibid.
99. Ellis interview; Armstrong interview.
100. Thiel, *Out of Leftfield*, 88.
101. Phone interview with Piniella, 2/23/07.
102. Ibid.
103. Ellis interview.
104. Piniella interview.
105. Ellis interview.
106. Buhner interview.
107. Phone interview with Bosio, 10/03/07.
108. Thiel, *Out of Leftfield*, 79.
109. Bosio interview.
110. In-person interview with Griffin, 11/08/07.
111. Thiel, *Out of Leftfield*, 80.
112. Griffin interview.
113. Ronald Blum, Associated Press, 6/3/87.
114. Phone interview with Cameron, 2/12/08.
115. Thiel, *Out of Leftfield*, 25.
116. Armstrong interview.
117. Ibid.
118. Thiel, *Out of Leftfield*, 30.
119. Ibid., 36.
120. Bosio interview.
121. Phone interview with Bragg, 2/12/08.

3. Bronx Bummers

1. Kenneth Hogan, *The 1969 Seattle Pilots: Major League Baseball's One-Year Team* (Jefferson, NC: McFarland, 2007), 27.
2. Murray Chass, "Mets and Yankees Are Eliminated as Cards and Blue Jays Win Titles; Alexander Triumphs, 5–1," *New York Times*, 10/6/85, sec. 5, p. 1.
3. Buster Olney, *The Last Night of the Yankee Dynasty: The Game, the Team, and the Cost of Greatness* (New York, NY: HarperCollins, 2004), 25.
4. Ibid., 26.
5. William Ladson, "Boss Talk: George Steinbrenner Reflects on His Twenty-five Years as Owner of the Yankees," *Sporting News*, special

edition, *The Yankees: Steinbrenner's 25 Years of Triumph and Turmoil* (1998), 22.

6. Dave Kindred, "That Damn Yankee," *Sporting News*, special edition, *The Yankees: Steinbrenner's 25 Years of Triumph and Turmoil* (1998), 18.

7. Mark Basch, "Hockey's Fire a Lot Brighter in Jacksonville," Albany *Times-Union*, 11/8/04, FB-12.

8. Baseballreference.com.

9. Kindred, "That Damn Yankee," 18.

10. Art Thiel, *Out of Left Field: How the Mariners Made Baseball Fly in Seattle* (Seattle: Sasquatch Books, 2003), 278.

11. "George Speaks," *USA Today*, 8/20/90.

12. Ladson, "Boss Talk," 23.

13. Kindred, "That Damn Yankee," 19.

14. Pat Calabria, "18 Years of Chaos and Championships," *Newsday*, 7/31/90, 89.

15. Kindred, "That Damn Yankee," 19.

16. Michael Martinez, "Decision on Steinbrenner: Spira Case Just One Chapter in Stormy, 17fi-Year Adventure," *New York Times*, 7/31/90, B9.

17. Bill Madden and Moss Klein, *Damned Yankees: A No-Holds-Barred Account of Life with "Boss" Steinbrenner* (New York: Warner Books, 1990), 18.

18. Moss Klein, "Minaya's Got Nothing on Steinbrenner," *Newark Star-Ledger*, 6/18/08.

19. Madden and Klein, *Damned Yankees*, 56.

20. Klein, "Minaya's Got Nothing."

21. Madden and Klein, *Damned Yankees*, 281.

22. Barry Bloom, "The Team That Never Won," *Sporting News* special edition, *The Yankees: Steinbrenner's 25 Years of Triumph and Turmoil* (1998), 67.

23. Madden and Klein, *Damned Yankees*, 281.

24. Thiel, *Out of Left Field*, 84.

25. Madden and Klein, *Damned Yankees*, 82.

26. Ibid., 254.

27. "Sports News," Associated Press, 8/22/89.

28. Olney, *The Last Night*, 30.

29. Steve Marantz, "Donnie Baseball," *Sporting News* special edition, *The Yankees: Steinbrenner's 25 Years of Triumph and Turmoil* (1998), 78.

30. Jane Gross, "Steinbrenner Issues an Apology to Fans," *New York Times*, 10/29/81, B13.

31. Madden and Klein, *Damned Yankees*, 112.

32. Olney, *The Last Night*, 32.

33. Joel Sherman, *Birth of a Dynasty: Behind the Pinstripes with the 1996 Yankees* (Holtzbrinck Publishers, 2006), 53.

34. Madden and Klein, *Damned Yankees*, 98.

35. Murray Chass, "Martin Jokes after Brawl," *New York Times*, 9/23/85, C1.

36. Madden and Klein, *Damned Yankees*, 104.

37. Michael Martinez, "2 Dates Hawkins Won't Forget," *New York Times*, 7/2/90, C4.

38. Jim Donagy, "Sports News Wire," Associated Press, 12/24/88.

39. Moss Klein, "Motown Slowdown Has Even Sparky Gloomy," *Sporting News*, 1/1/90, 48.

40. Rick Hummel, "Cards Send Sykes to Yankees for AA Player Willie McGee," *St. Louis Post-Dispatch*, 10/22/81.

41. Murray Chass, "Kemp Signed by Yanks, Morgan Traded," *New York Times*, 12/10/82: B5.

42. "Sports News," United Press International, 2/9/84.

43. Murray Chass, "Yanks Get Rhoden for $1.35 Million," *New York Times*, 11/27/86, D15.

44. Madden and Klein, *Damned Yankees*, 9.

45. Baseballreference.com.

46. Ed Sherman, "Sox Only Warming Up?" *Chicago Tribune*, 11/14/87, C1.

47. Baseballreference.com.

48. Ronald Blum, "Sports News Wire," *Associated Press*, 12/13/89.

49. Ibid.

50. Joe Donnelly, "Yanks Acquire Phelps: Mattingly to Play OF?" *Newsday*, 7/22/88, 174.

51. Tom Verducci, "Plod Thickens in AL East," *Newsday*, 8/31/88, 122.

52. Joe Sexton, "Yanks Stumble after a Big Lift," *New York Times*, 8/20/88, sec. 1, p. 47.

53. Phone interview with Phelps, 5/29/07.

54. Thiel, *Out of Leftfield*, 82.

55. Ibid., 83.

56. Donnelly, "Yanks Acquire Phelps," 174.

57. Phelps interview.

58. Donnelly, "Yanks Acquire Phelps," 174.

59. Phelps interview.

60. Ibid.

61. Madden and Klein, *Damned Yankees*, 9.

62. Olney, *The Last Night*, 32.

63. Murray Chass, "Steinbrenner Turns to Wooing Jackson," *New York Times*, 12/17/80, B7.

64. Joe Gergen, "Boss Talk: The Feud," *Sporting News* special edition, *The Yankees: Steinbrenner's 25 Years of Triumph and Turmoil* (1998), 74.

65. "George Speaks," *USA Today*, 8/20/90.

66. Michael Martinez, "Winfield Ties R.B.I. Mark as Yankees Roll," *New York Times*, 5/1/88, sec. 8, p. 2.

67. Gergen, "Boss Talk," 74.

68. Ronald Blum, "Sports News Wire," Associated Press, 7/31/90,.

69. Gergen, "Boss Talk," 75.

70. Steve Fainaru, "Steinbrenner Ordered to Relinquish Control of Yankees," *Boston Globe*, 7/31/90, sports sec., p. 1.

71. Murray Chass, "Steinbrenner's Control of the Yanks Severed," *New York Times*, 7/31/90, A1.

72. John Heyman, "George Is Out as Yanks Boss: Players in Shock," *New York Newsday*, 7/31/90, 90.

73. Ibid.

74. Malcolm Moran, "No Joy for Yanks, Despite a Victory," *New York Times*, 7/31/90, B7.

75. Editorial, "Yogi Come Home," *New York Newsday*, 8/1/90, 54.

76. "Decision on Steinbrenner," *New York Times*, 7/31/90, B9.

77. Ibid.

78. Olney, *The Last Night*, 54.

79. Klein, "Minaya's Got Nothing."

80. Sherman, *Birth of a Dynasty*, 81.

81. Steve Jacobson, "Who's Minding Yanks' Store?" *Newsday*, 8/19/90, 2.

82. Shaun Powell, "Life without George," *Sporting News* special edition, *The Yankees: Steinbrenner's 25 Years of Triumph and Turmoil* (1998), 92.

83. Joe Sexton, "Michael Is Named Yanks' General Manager," *New York Times*, 8/21/90, D23.

84. Powell, "Life without George," 92.

85. Ibid.

86. Sherman, *Birth of a Dynasty*, 76.

87. Olney, *The Last Night*, 60.

88. Tom Verducci, "For Now, Buck Looks Just Fine," *Newsday*, 10/30/91, 149.

89. Jack Curry, "Yankees to Name Showalter Manager at End of Series," *New York Times*, 10/24/91, B11.

90. Dave Anderson, "Sports of the Times," *New York Times*, 10/30/91, B9.

91. Ibid.

92. Verducci, "For Now, Buck Looks Just Fine," 149.

93. Curry, "Yankees to Name Showalter," B11.

94. Jon Heyman, "It's Official: The Buck Stops Here," *Newsday*, 10/30/91, 150.

95. Phone interview with Showalter, 2/24/07.

96. Phone interview with Barfield, 1/21/08.

97. Sherman, *Birth of a Dynasty*, 77.

98. Phone interview with Butterfield, 2/25/07.

99. Olney, *The Last Night*, 61–62.
100. Tom Verducci, "Buck's Belle of the Brawl," *Newsday*, 5/18/92, 102.
101. E-mail interview with Abbott, 4/27/07.
102. Sherman, *Birth of a Dynasty*, 144.
103. Phone interview with Stanley, 2/24/07.
104. Murray Chass, "When It Comes to Stealing, Yankees Can't Get Past First Base," *New York Times*, 5/16/93, sec. 8, p. 8.

4. Strike

1. Murray Chass, "No Runs, No Hits, No Errors: Baseball Goes on Strike," *New York Times*, 8/12/94, A1.
2. Howard Bryant, *Juicing the Game* (New York: Penguin, 2005), 7.
3. George Will, "Tribe Fans Might Share Baseball Labor Pains," *Cleveland Plain Dealer*, 7/10/94, 2C.
4. Bryant, *Juicing the Game*, 7.
5. Tom Yantz, "When We Last Left the Game . . . ," *Hartford Courant*, 4/25/95, G1.
6. Ronald Blum, "No Joy in Mudville: The Players Have Struck," Associated Press, 8/12/94.
7. Will, "Tribe Fans," 2C.
8. Murray Chass, "Players Association Sets Strike Date of Aug. 12," *New York Times*, 7/29/94, B9.
9. Chass, "No Runs," A1.
10. Ibid.
11. Blum, "No Joy."
12. Ronald Blum, "Game Moves Indoors," Associated Press, 8/12/94.
13. Street, "Baseball's Over," A1.
14. Bryant, *Juicing*, 46.
15. Robert McG. Thomas Jr., "If It's Over, '94 Season Had Tight Races and Individual Accomplishments," *New York Times*, 8/12/94, B11.
16. "Belle Denies Corking: AL Reduces Suspension," *Seattle Post-Intelligencer*, 7/30/94, D5.
17. Steve Marantz, "Partners in Time," *Sporting News*, 11/14/94.
18. Jeff Bradley, *New York Daily News*, 3/17/95, 87.
19. Jennifer Frey, "Mets vs. Yanks: Guy Named Bubba at 2d, Guy Named Sisk on the Mound," *New York Times*, 3/5/95, sec. 8, p. 2.
20. Murray Chass, "Throw a Bit? Hit a Little? Majors Want You," *New York Times*, 1/15/95, sec. 8, p. 4.
21. Phone interview with Guetterman, 1/24/08.
22. Dan Bickley, "Filling in the Blanks," *Chicago Sun-Times*, 3/1/95, 114; Frey, "Mets vs. Yanks," 2.

23. Phone interview with Cohen, 9/5/07.

24. Kellye Dubard, "Baseball Brouhaha," *Atlanta Journal-Constitution*, 3/5/95, 9J.

25. Ibid.

26. "Talks Close to Collapse as Owners Make Move," *Los Angeles Times*, 3/3/95, C1.

27. Frey, "Mets vs. Yanks," 2.

28. Chass, "Throw a Bit?" 4.

29. "Orioles Won't Budge; Spring Schedule Cancelled," *Chicago Sun-Times*, 3/2/95, 89.

30. Tim Kurkjian and Tom Verducci, "Time Is Running Out," *Sports Illustrated*, 3/20/95.

31. Phone interview with Butterfield, 2/25/07.

32. Phone interview with Down, 6/5/08.

33. Dubard, "Baseball Brouhaha," 9J.

34. "Orioles Won't Budge," 89.

35. John Lowe, "Klein Finally Finds Time to Enjoy Baseball Again," *Detroit Free Press*, 3/3/95, 8C.

36. Phone interview with Showalter, 2/24/07.

37. Greg B. Smith and Bill Madden with John Giannone, *New York Daily News*, 4/1/95, 5.

38. Phone interview with Niehaus, 2/27/08.

39. Murray Chass, "Backed by Court, Baseball Players Call Strike Over," *New York Times*, 4/1/95, sec. 1, p. 1.

40. John Harper and John Giannone, "Replacements Now in Lim-ball," *New York Daily News*, 4/1/95, 4.

41. Tom Yantz, "Baseball '95," *Hartford Courant*, 4/25/95, G1.

42. Tracy Ringolsby, "AL East," *Rocky Mountain News*, 4/26/95, special sec., 21R.

43. Andy Knobel, "AL East Preview," *Baltimore Sun*, 4/25/95, 5D.

44. Ringolsby, "AL East," 21R.

45. Peter Gammons, "Here Are the Favorites Entering Starting Gate," *Boston Globe*, 4/23/95, 88.

46. Dave Caldwell, "Baseball Goes after Lost Fans," *Philadelphia Inquirer*, 4/5/95, D1.

47. Lawrence Levy, "Reopening Day: Say You Won't Go Joe," *New York Newsday*, 4/5/95, A37.

48. Yantz, "Baseball '95," G1.

49. Martin Miller, "Angels, Padres Play to 63,000 Empty Seats," *Los Angeles Times*, 4/25/95, B1.

50. Chuck Johnson, "Strike Sours 69% of Fans on Majors," *USA Today*, 4/5/95, 1A.

51. Tom Lowry and Patricia Winters, "Baseball Loads Bases with Freebies for Fans," *New York Daily News*, 4/25/95, 25.

52. Tom Lowry, no title, *New York Daily News*, 4/25/95, 18.

53. Yantz, "Baseball '95," G1.

54. Miller, "*Angels*, Padres Play," 1.

55. Lowry, "Baseball Loads Bases," 25.

56. Yantz, "Baseball '95," G1.

5. Baseball Returns

1. Chris Sheridan, "Mets 10, Cardinals 8," Associated Press, 4/28/95; Bob Hunter, "If Reds Play Like That, They'll Drive Fans Crazy," *Columbus Dispatch*, 4/27/95, 1E; Paul Hoynes, "Tribe Hopes Fans Hang On to Posters," Cleveland *Plain Dealer*, 5/2/95, 6D.

2. Michael Kay, "A Season to Remember," *Yankees Magazine* 16, no. 10 (12/19/95), 9.

3. Phone interview with Showalter, 2/24/07.

4. "The 1995 Yankees Statistical Review," *Yankees Magazine* 16, no. 10 (12/19/95), 55–56.

5. Jim Street, "M's Win in 12th; Amaral's Home Run Caps Comeback against Yanks," *Seattle Post-Intelligencer*, 5/30/95, D1.

6. John Harper, "Yanks by a Whisker," *New York Daily News*, 6/3/95, 39.

7. George Willis, "The Hair Goes, and So Does Offense, for Slumping Yanks," *New York Times*, 6/3/95, sec. 1, p. 27.

8. In-person interview with Griffin, 11/8/07.

9. In-person interview with Perlozzo, 2/16/08.

10. In-person interview with Belcher, 3/14/07.

11. Phone interview with Bragg, 2/12/08.

12. E-mail interview with Evans, 3/9/08.

13. Phone interview with Guetterman, 1/24/08.

14. "Lawmakers OK Plan for Seattle Stadium," *Austin American-Statesman*, 10/15/95, C9.

15. "Probe, Repairs Begin at Dome," Seattle Times, 7/20/94, A1.

16. Art Thiel, *Out of Leftfield: How the Mariners Made Baseball Fly in Seattle* (Seattle: Sasquatch Books, 2003), 104.17. Jim Simon, "Front Porch Forum: Stadium Vote Is Bigger than Baseball, Panel Says," *Seattle Times*, 9/4/95, A1.

18. Mike DiGiovanna, "Angels Hold Off Yankees in 9th for 5–3 Victory," *Los Angeles Times*, 8/20/95, C1.

19. Griffin interview.

20. Phone interview with Buhner, 11/08/07.

21. Blaine Newnham, "Walk in August Launched Pennant Run That May Have Saved Baseball in Seattle," *Seattle Times*, 10/15/95, C4.

22. Jeff Bradley, "Whopper Jr. Cooks Yanks: 9th Inning Blast Kills a Dying Breed," *New York Daily News*, 8/25/95, 83.

23. John Giannone, "Starting Over Yanks Can Forget Poundings They Took in Regular Season," *New York Daily News*, 10/3/95, 58.

24. In-person interview with Adamack, 11/9/07.

25. Buhner interview.

26. In-person interview with Elia, 2/16/08.

27. Ellis Conklin, "Buy Oh Buy! 'Refuse to Lose' Is a Top Seller," *Seattle Post-Intelligencer*, 10/6/95, A1.

28. Phone interview with Widger, 1/13/08.

29. Phone interview with Rizzs, 11/9/07.

30. Rebecca Boren, "Supporters of New Ballpark Praise Survey," *Seattle Post-Intelligencer*, 9/1/95, B1.

31. Phone interview with Strange, 12/18/06.

32. In-person interview with Ellis, 11/8/07.

33. Giannone, "Starting Over," 58.

34. Ellis Conklin and Kathy George, "M's Owners Give 30-Day Reprieve on New Stadium," *Seattle Post-Intelligencer*, 9/29/95, A1.

35. Conklin, "M's Owners," A1.

36. Ellis interview.

37. Buhner interview.

38. Jim Street, "M's Alone at the Top," *Seattle Post-Intelligencer*, 9/23/95, D1.

39. Ian O'Connor, *New York Daily News*, 9/30/95, 41.

40. Jason Diamos, "Kelly's Blast Drives Yanks Closer to Post-Season," *New York Times*, 9/30/95, sec. 1, p. 27.

41. O'Connor, *New York Daily News*, 41.

42. Jon Heyman, "Everything Is Going Yanks' Way," *New York Newsday*, 10/3/95, A60.

43. Phone interview with Mattingly, 4/2/08.

44. George Vecsey, "George Used Buck's Pride to Ditch Him," *New York Times*, 10/27/95, B13.

45. Jim Street, "Happy 'Tails': Coin Flip Goes Mariners' Way," *Seattle Post-Intelligencer*, 10/3/95, D7.

46. Adamack interview.

47. In-person interview with Armstrong, 11/08/07.

48. Jim Moore, "Seattle Exit Still Gnaws at Langston," *Seattle Post-Intelligencer*, 8/29/07, D7.

49. Phone interview with Amaral, 1/22/08.

50. Phone interview with Charlton, 2/6/07; Belcher interview.

51. In-person interview with Pelekoudas, 2/17/08.

52. Phone interview with Sanderson, 4/25/07.

53. Phone interview with Bosio, 10/3/07.

54. Phone interview with Sojo, 2/25/08.

55. Phone interview with Wilson, 9/15/08.

56. Michael Paulson, "Owners Warn State Lawmakers They Won't Back Off Sale Threat," *Seattle Post-Intelligencer*, 10/3/95, A1.

57. Bob Sherwin, "Outta Here: M's Sweep, Team Hits Road on a Hot Streak," *Seattle Times*, 6/1/95, C1.

58. Phone interview with Leyritz, 2/28/07.

59. Marc Topkin, *St. Petersburg Times*, 10/3/95, 4C; *Portland Oregonian*, 10/3/95, D04; *Chicago Sun-Times*, 10/3/95, 87; *Chattanooga Free Press*, 10/3/95; Jerry Sullivan, "Postseason Should Be Special, But You Won't See Much," *Buffalo News*, 10/3/95, 1C; "Mariners vs. Yankees, AL Series," *Austin American-Statesman*, 10/3/95, C4.

6. Game 1: The Bronx, Baseball, and Beer Bottles

1. David Lennon, "Blasting Off: Yankees 4 Run 7th Is Crusher," *New York Newsday*, 10/4/95, A74.

2. Matthew Purdy, "For Fans, Yankees' Troubles Are Eclipsed by Playoff Joy," *New York Times*, 10/3/95, B3.

3. Michael O. Allen, "Yanks Do Dandy," *New York Daily News*, 10/4/95, 7.

4. Laura Vecsey, "Baseball Is Searching for a Brand New Mr. October," *Seattle Post-Intelligencer*, 10/4/95, C1; Ian O'Connor, "Stadium Turns Men into Boys," *New York Daily News*, 10/4/95, 49.

5. In-person interview with Ellis, 11/8/07.

6. John Eisenberg, "Grounding Not in Seattle Flight Plan," *Baltimore Sun*, 10/4/95, 1D.

7. Larry Whiteside, "Long Way to Go," *Boston Globe*, 10/4/95, 90.

8. Ryan Peck, "KGW Defends Delay of Mariners," *Portland Oregonian*, 10/4/95, E06.

9. In-person interview with Armstrong, 11/8/07.

10. Bob Finnigan and Bob Sherwin, "Junior in Pinstripes? Not as Long as George Is Around," *Seattle Times*, 10/5/95, D5.

11. Mike Wise, "Griffey Quiets the Stadium Twice, If Only Briefly," *New York Times*, 10/4/95, B12.

12. Phone interview with Mattingly, 4/2/08.

13. Stephen Borelli, " 'Voice of God' Presides over Yankees," *USA Today*, 10/25/00.

14. Ibid.

15. Phone interview with Bosio, 10/3/07.
16. Jim Street, "Lou Gets a Hearty Greeting from Yanks," *Seattle Post-Intelligencer*, 10/4/95, C4.
17. Mattingly interview.
18. Phone interview with Widger, 1/13/08.
19. Bosio interview.
20. In-person interview with Elia, 2/16/08
21. In-person interview with Griffin, 11/8/07.
22. Phone interview with Benes, 1/12/08.
23. Roger Angell, *A Pitcher's Story: Innings with David Cone* (New York: Warner Books, 2001), 181–182.
24. Phone interview with Showalter, 2/24/07.
25. Phone interview with McDowell, 11/20/06.
26. McDowell interview.
27. Phone interview with James, 6/17/08.
28. Mattingly interview.
29. Mike DiGiovanna, "Baseball Daily Report: American League," *Los Angeles Times*, 10/4/95, C4.
30. Wise, "Griffey Quiets the Stadium," 12.
31. Bob Finnigan, "Griffey's Opening Act a Big Hit," *Seattle Times*, 10/4/95, C8.
32. Bosio interview.
33. Phone interview with Buhner, 11/08/07.
34. Phone interview with Guetterman, 1/24/08.
35. Buhner interview.
36. Ibid.
37. Bill Knight, "Boggs Dismisses His Playoff Power Surge as Accidental; Yankee Veteran Says Homer Generally Means He's Fooled," *Seattle Post-Intelligencer*, 10/5/95, C7.
38. Buster Olney, *The Last Night of the Yankee Dynasty: The Game, the Team, and the Cost of Greatness* (New York: HarperCollins, 2004), 279.
39. Jon Heyman, "Boggs Adds Up as a Bigtown Fit," *New York Newsday*, 10/4/95, A75.
40. Stan Grossfeld, "Quirks of Fortune Superstitions the Norm among Baseball Players," *Boston Globe*, 3/29/07, C1.
41. "Boggs Isn't 100 Percent But He Plays Like It," *New York Times*, 10/4/95, B13.
42. Lennon, "Blasting Off," A74.
43. Knight, "Boggs Dismisses His Playoff Power," C7.
44. Wise, "Griffey Quiets the Stadium," 12.
45. John Harper, "Can't Fool Martinez," *New York Daily News*, 10/5/95, 107.

46. Art Thiel, "Ayala Takes Pratfall on National Stage," *Seattle Post-Intelligencer*, 10/4/95, C1.

47. Wilson interview.

48. Benes interview.

49. In-person interview with Cora, 2/18/08.

50. Wilson interview.

51. Bill Madden, "Wilson Fills M's Plate," *New York Daily News*, 10/4/95, 53.

52. O'Connor, "Stadium Turns Men into Boys," 49.

53. George Vecsey, "Sports of the Times: Mariners Don't Blame Red Eyes," *New York Times*, 10/4/95, B11.

54. " '95 Playoffs: Steinbrenner Blasts Umpire," *New York Times*, 10/4/95, B12.

55. Ian O'Connor, "Umpire Draws Boss' Ire," *Daily News*, 10/4/95, 49.

56. "Benes Ready to Pitch for M's Tonight: Short Outing vs. Rangers May Be Benefit," *Seattle Times*, 10/4/95, C3.

57. Bosio interview.

58. Jim Caple, "Tough Crowd Gets Mariners Pumped Up," *Saint Paul Pioneer Press*, 10/5/95, 5F.

59. "Boggs Recovers to Punish M's," *Seattle Post-Intelligencer*, 10/4/95, C5.

60. Don Burke, "Boggs, Cone Key Victory," *Trenton Times*, 10/5/95, B1.

61. Jack Curry, "Yankee Lights Sparkle Bright Amid Power Display," *New York Times*, 10/4/95, B11.

62. Jim Street, "Bronx Bombed: Two Griffey Home Runs Wasted as M's Stumble," *Seattle Post-Intelligencer*, 10/4/95, C1.

63. Tom Yantz, "Griffey Shows He'll Go a Long Way in Mariners' Behalf," *Hartford Courant*, 10/5/95, C4.

64. Bill Madden, "It's a Madd, Madd World: Notes, Quotes and Anecdotes from Baseball's Second Season," *Daily News*, 10/4/95, 52.

65. Mattingly interview.

66. In-person interview with Sherlock, 5/5/07.

67. Roger Angell, "The Game's the Thing," in *The Best American Sports Writing 1996*, edited by John Feinstein (New York: Houghton Mifflin, 1996), 169.

68. Steve Kelley, "Just Another Night in the Bronx Zoo," *Seattle Times*, 10/4/95, C1.

69. Jon Heyman, "Firing Back at Goons," *Newsday*, 10/5/95, A92.

70. Cora interview.

71. Kelley, "Just Another Night," C1.

72. Thiel, "Ayala Takes Pratfall," C1.

73. Street, "Lou Gets a Hearty Greeting," C4.

74. "Benes Ready to Pitch," *Seattle Times*, C3.

75. Bob Finnigan, "Ayala: Why, Oh Why?" *Seattle Times*, 10/4/95, C1.

76. Mike DiGiovanna, "It's October, So Yanks Win 9–6," *Los Angeles Times*, 10/4/95, C1.

77. Ibid.

78. Parker, "Just Like Old Times," A73.

79. Ken Wheeler, "Yankees Swing Away in Opener," *Portland Oregonian*, 10/4/95, E01.

7. Game 2: A Classic in the Bronx

1. Jack Curry, "Pettitte Has Nerves of Steel," *New York Times*, 10/4/95, B13.

2. Ibid.

3. Phone interview with Mattingly, 4/2/08.

4. Phone interview with Leyritz, 2/28/07.

5. Phone interview with Benes, 1/12/08.

6. Jim Street, "M's Players Approve of Benes Deal, Say Management Did Right Thing," *Seattle Post-Intelligencer*, 8/2/95, D6.

7. Phone interview with Charlton, 2/6/07.

8. Jim Street, "Benes Feeling Confident Despite Texas Tattooing," *Seattle Post-Intelligencer*, 10/4/95, C4.

9. Benes interview.

10. Bill Madden, "It's a Madd, Madd World: Notes, Quotes and Anecdotes from Baseball's Second Season," *New York Daily News*, 10/5/95, 106.

11. Benes interview.

12. Steven Lee Myers, "Giuliani and Board of Education at Odds Over Plan to Name Interim Chancellor," *New York Times*, 10/5/95, B14.

13. Harvy Lipman, "Health Hearings Closed," *Albany Times Union*, 10/5/95, A1.

14. Robert D. McFadden, "The Pope's Visit: Pope Arrives, Urging America to Live Its Ideals," *New York Times*, 10/5/95, A1.

15. Bob Keeler and Patricia Hurtado, "Hizzoner Meets His Holiness," *New York Newsday*, 10/5/95, A40.

16. *Chicago Sun-Times*, 10/6/95, 3.

17. Phone interview with Buhner, 11/8/07.

18. Phone interview with James, 6/17/08.

19. Art Thiel, "The Boss Calls for Forfeit," *Seattle Post-Intelligencer*, 10/5/95, C3.

20. Roger Angell, "The Game's the Thing," in *The Best American Sports Writing 1996*, edited by John Feinstein (New York: Houghton Mifflin, 1996), 169.

21. Referenced during NBC's broadcast of Game 1.

22. Phone interview with Butterfield, 2/25/07.

23. Thiel, "The Boss Calls," C3.

24. Ibid.; Randy Kennedy, "At Raucous Yankee Stadium, Cheers Cross Line to Jeers and Fear," *New York Times*, 10/6/95, B15.
25. Thiel, "The Boss Calls," C3.
26. Leyritz interview.
27. Phone interview with Showalter, 2/24/07.
28. Ian O'Connor, "Return of Bronx Zoo High-Drama Game Rattles Boss' Cage," *New York Daily News*, 10/5/95, 105.
29. John Eisenberg, "Leyritz Puts Cap on the Full NY Treatment," *Baltimore Sun*, 10/5/95, 1D.
30. Bill Madden, "George Goes Wild and Trashes Umps," *New York Daily News*, 10/5/95, 105.
31. Paul O'Neill with Burton Rocks, *Me and My Dad* (New York: HarperCollins, 2003), 57.
32. Joel Sherman, *Birth of a Dynasty: Behind the Pinstripes with the 1996 Yankees* (Holtzbrinck Publishers, 2006), 77.
33. Buster Olney, *The Last Night of the Yankee Dynasty: The Game, the Team, and the Cost of Greatness* (New York: HarperCollins, 2004) 40.
34. Sherman, *Birth of a Dynasty*, 78.
35. Phone interview with O'Neill, 3/7/07.
36. Phone interview with Down, 6/5/08.
37. O'Neill interview.
38. Charlton interview.
39. David Vecsey, Associated Press, 8/25/92.
40. Bob Finnigan, "Leyritz's Revenge: Hit a Second Time by M's, He Hits Back," *Seattle Times*, 10/5/95, D1.
41. Phone interview with McDowell, 11/20/06.
42. Mattingly interview.
43. Showalter interview.
44. Olney, *The Last Night*, 278.
45. Sherman, *Birth of a Dynasty*, 17.
46. Leyritz interview.
47. Sherman, *Birth of a Dynasty*, 19.
48. Steve Kelley, "Mariners Lost Playoff Game for the Ages," *Seattle Times*, 10/5/95, D1.
49. Phone interview with Belcher, 3/14/07.
50. Charlton interview.
51. Belcher interview.
52. Ian O'Connor, "Later Tater after Early Failures, Leyritz Has a Blast," *New York Daily News*, 10/6/95, 87.
53. Kelley, "Mariners Lost Playoff Game," D1.
54. O'Connor, "Later Tater," 87.

55. Leyritz interview.

56. Phone interview with Davis, 3/16/07.

57. Dave Anderson, "Sports of the Times: On Hearing the Echoes of a Chant," *New York Times*, 10/5/95, B19.

58. Sherman, *Birth of a Dynasty*, 273.

59. Leyritz interview.

60. Ibid.

61. Belcher interview.

62. Leyritz interview.

63. Showalter interview.

64. Chris Sheridan, "Yankees Sink Mariners in 15th Inning; Leyritz's Homer Ends Longest Game in AL Playoff History," *Austin American-Statesman*, 10/5/95, C1.

65. Buhner interview.

66. "Yanks Leave in Style after Drive into Night," *St. Petersburg Times*, 10/6/95, 4C.

67. Eisenberg, "Leyritz," 1D.

68. Davis interview.

69. Bill Madden, "Boss Stars in Late Show," *New York Daily News*, 10/6/95, 86.

70. Claire Smith, "Joy in the Yankee Clubhouse for an Improbable Hero," *New York Times*, 10/5/95, B19.

71. Bob Ford, "Yanks Win in 15th," *Philadelphia Inquirer*, 10/5/95, D01.

72. Belcher interview.

73. Charlton interview.

74. In-person interview with Griffin, 11/8/07.

75. In-person interview with Ellis, 11/8/07.

76. Chris Sheridan, "Yanks Full of Emotion; So Far, Mariners Have Been Turned Back," *Memphis Commercial Appeal*, 10/6/95, 5D.

77. Buhner interview.

78. Phone interview with Niehaus, 2/27/08.

79. In-person interview with Cora, 2/18/08.

80. Phone interview with Rizzs, 11/9/07.

8. Game 3: Playoff Baseball in Seattle

1. Larry Whiteside, "Duo Left Out: Boggs, O'Neill Miss Johnson," *Boston Globe*, 10/7/95, 77.

2. Bill Madden, "It's a Madd, Madd World: Notes, Quotes and Anecdotes from Baseball's Second Season," *Daily News*, 10/7/95, 39.

3. Art Thiel, *Out of Leftfield: How the Mariners Made Baseball Fly in Seattle* (Seattle: Sasquatch Books, 2003), 124.

4. Ellis Conklin, "Stayin' Alive: 7–4 Victory Guarantees Saturday Night Fever," *Seattle Post-Intelligencer*, 10/7/95, A1.
5. Barbara A. Serrano, "M's Take a Stand," *Seattle Times*, 10/7/95, A1.
6. Jim Caple, "Mariners' Broadcaster No DiMaggio," *Saint Paul Pioneer Press*, 10/7/95, 5G.
7. Jack Curry, "Johnson Humbles Yankees to Give Mariners Hope," *New York Times*, 10/7/95, sec. 1, p. 29.
8. Phone interview with Stanley, 2/24/07.
9. Conklin, "Stayin' Alive," A1.
10. Phone interview with Leyritz, 2/28/07.
11. Caple, "Mariners' Broadcaster," 5G.
12. Art Thiel, "Mariners' 'Crazy' Lefties, Fans Show Yankees a Little Attitude," *Seattle Post-Intelligencer*, 10/7/95, C1.
13. Phone interview with Boggs, 5/15/07.
14. Leyritz interview.
15. Whiteside, "Duo Left Out," 77.
16. Jim Street, "Coleman's Speed Comes into Play in 7th Inning," *Seattle Post-Intelligencer*, 10/7/95, C4.
17. Ian O'Connor, "Leaders a Big Zero Johnson Smokes Mattingly, Velarde," *New York Daily News*, 10/7/95, 38.
18. Stanley interview.
19. Dave Van Dyck, "Chicago White Sox," *Sporting News*, 1/23/95.
20. Jon Heyman, "McDowell: Deep Limbo," *New York Newsday*, 3/22/95, A62.
21. Ibid.
22. Joe Donnelly, "Key Sore; Cortisone Next," *New York Newsday*, 6/4/95, sports sec., p. 2.
23. Jeff Bradley, *New York Daily News*, 5/25/95, 96.
24. Phone interview with Showalter, 2/24/07.
25. Phone interview with McDowell, 11/20/06.
26. Ibid.
27. Steve Jacobson, "Shining Moment," *New York Newsday*, 10/6/95, 100.
28. Ibid.
29. Kathy George, "School Board Learns New Superintendent Is Full of Surprises," *Seattle Post-Intelligencer*, 10/6/95, A1.
30. David Schaefer, "10 Percent Boost in Bus Fares Sought," *Seattle Times*, 10/7/95, A1.
31. Tom Paulson, "Groups Protest GOP Spending Plan," *Seattle Post-Intelligencer*, 10/6/95, C4.
32. Phone interview with Davis, 3/16/07.
33. Bob Sherwin, "Martinez Slows in Trek to Win First-Base Job," *Seattle Times*, 3/28/90, D2.

34. Phone interview with Belcher, 3/14/07.

35. Steve Kelley, "Martinez Believes He's Ready for M's," *Seattle Times*, 8/10/95, C1.

36. Buster Olney, "Seattle's 9-run 8th Sends O's, Benitez Packing, 10–2," *Baltimore Sun*, 6/8/95, 1D.

37. Referenced during ABC's broadcast of Game 3.

38. Laura Vecsey, "It's Great to Be Back in Seattle, Especially after the Bronx Zoo," *Seattle Post-Intelligencer*, 10/7/95, C1.

39. Jim Moore, "Clamor in Kingdome Nearly Buries Needle," *Seattle Post-Intelligencer*, 10/7/95, C3.

40. Jeff Bradley, " 'Fan' Makes Change on Gerald's Head," *New York Daily News*, 10/7/95, 39.

41. Serrano, "M's Take a Stand," A1.

42. Bud Withers, "Williams Struck, Cut by Quarter," *Seattle Post-Intelligencer*, 10/7/95, C4.

43. Steve Jacobson, "McDowell Gritty in His Matchup," *New York Newsday*, 10/7/95, A49.

44. "Piniella Upset over Umpire's Warning," *Seattle Times*, 10/8/95, D4.

45. "Head-Ups Play Shifted Game in Mariners' Favor," *Seattle Post-Intelligencer*, 10/7/95, C5.

46. Whiteside, "Duo Left Out," 77.

47. Bud Withers, "Velarde Unravels as the Mariners Erupt," *Seattle Post-Intelligencer*, 10/7/95, C4.

48. Referenced during ABC's broadcast of Game 3.

49. Withers, "Williams Struck," C4.

50. Phone interview with Charlton, 2/6/07.

51. Gordon Edes and Ross Newhan, "Grounded Coleman Sits and Waits," *Los Angeles Times*, 10/21/85, part 3, p. 20.

52. Marty Noble, "Oh, Is He Explosive!" *New York Newsday*, 7/26/93, 91.

53. Steve Jacobson, "Enough Blame to Go Around," *New York Newsday*, 7/30/93, 175.

54. Joe Sexton, "Coleman Expresses Regret over Incident," *New York Times*, 7/30/93, B9.

55. Steve Marantz, "Royal Reckoning," *Sporting News*, 2/14/94, 16.

56. Ibid.

57. Laura Vecsey, "Coleman Sparks 'Em, Charlton Stops 'Em in Historic M's Ride," *Seattle Post-Intelligencer*, 8/22/95, B1.

58. Ibid.

59. Jim Street, "Seattle Acquires Coleman from K.C. to Fill Leadoff Spot," *Seattle Post-Intelligencer*, 8/16/95, D1.

60. Bob Sherwin, "Coleman Brings M's Up to Speed," *Seattle Times*, 8/17/95, C1.

61. Bob Finnigan, "M's Cling to Life: Sixth-Inning Explosion Forces Game 4 Today," *Seattle Times*, 10/7/95, B1.
62. Referenced during ABC's broadcast of Game 3.
63. Jeff Bradley, "Yank Order Is Too Tall, Randy Cuts Sweep Short," *New York Daily News*, 10/7/95, 37.
64. McDowell interview.
65. Jim Street, "Play It Again M's: Tino, Randy Come Up Big, Seattle Beats Yanks 7–4," *Seattle Post-Intelligencer*, 10/7/95, C1.
66. Ibid.
67. Jack O'Connell, "In the Field, at Plate, It's Getting Rough Out There," *Hartford Courant*, 10/8/95, E7.
68. Withers, "Velarde Unravels," C4.
69. Joel Sherman, *Birth of a Dynasty: Behind the Pinstripes with the 1996 Yankees* (Holtzbrinck Publishers, 2006), 221.
70. Buster Olney, *The Last Night of the Yankee Dynasty: The Game, the Team, and the Cost of Greatness* (New York: HarperCollins, 2004) 136.
71. Sherman, *Birth of a Dynasty*, 199.
72. Olney, *The Last Night*, 137.
73. Ibid., 138.
74. Sherman, *Birth of a Dynasty*, 242.
75. Bob Sherwin, "Mariner Bullpen Key to Series," *Seattle Times*, 10/7/95, B5.
76. Withers, "Velarde Unravels," C4.
77. Bob Ryan, "Johnson Saves Season Again," *Boston Globe*, 10/7/95, 77.
78. Murray Chass, "Division Series Schedule Calls for Sweeping Change," *New York Times*, 10/7/95, sec. 1, p. 30.
79. Steve Kelley, "Randy and Donnie: One Magic Moment," *Seattle Times*, 10/7/95, B1.
80. Jennifer Frey, "Mariners Hold Off Yankees, 7–4," *Washington Post*, 10/7/95, D08.
81. Kelley, "Randy and Donnie," B1.
82. Ryan, "Johnson Saves Season," 77.

9. Game 4: Saint Edgar

1. Bob Sherwin, "Mariner Bullpen Key to Series," *Seattle Times*, 10/7/95, B5.
2. Adam Berkowitz, "Tonight's Matchup," *Daily News*, 10/7/95, 46.
3. Mike Sullivan, "Kamieniecki Likes the Surroundings in Cleveland," *Columbus Dispatch*, 3/22/00, 4F.
4. John Harper, *New York Daily News*, 5/6/95, 36.
5. Jon Heyman, "Green Fans, and It Shows," *New York Newsday*, 10/7/95, A51.
6. Jeff Bradley, "Yanks Order Is Too Tall, Randy Cuts Sweep Short," *New York Daily News*, 10/7/95, 37.

7. Referenced during ABC's Broadcast of Game 4.

8. Ken Wheeler, " Mariners, Yankees Set Record," *Portland Oregonian*, 10/8/95, C06.

9. Referenced during ABC's broadcast of Game 4.

10. Ibid.

11. Ibid.

12. Ibid.

13. Phone interview with Bosio, 10/3/07.

14. Bob Finnigan, "Lou Piniella: Clubhouse Leader," *Seattle Times*, 10/10/95, C1.

15. "Piniella Upset over Umpires' Warning," *Seattle Times*, 10/8/95, D14.

16. Referenced during ABC's broadcast of Game 4.

17. Ibid

18. Bosio interview, 10/3/07.

19. Ibid.

20. Ibid.

21. Bob Sherwin, "M's Finally Get Some Relief," *Seattle Times*, 10/8/95, D14.

22. Burt Graeff, "Mariners Rally, Force Game 5," Cleveland *Plain Dealer*, 10/8/95, 14D.

23. Larry Whiteside, "Mariners Roar Back, Tie Series with NY," *Boston Globe*, 10/8/95, 72.

24. John Harper, "Martinez the Grand Mariner," *New York Daily News*, 10/8/95, 67.

25. Phone interview with Belcher, 3/14/07.

26. Jack O'Connell, "See Ya . . . in Game 5," *Hartford Courant*, 10/8/95, E1.

27. Phone interview with Boggs, 5/15/07.

28. Phone interview with Charlton, 2/6/07.

29. Bob Finnigan, "Who's on Third for Mariners? Not Edgar," *Seattle Times*, 4/5/93, B6.

30. Referenced during ABC's broadcast of Game 4.

31. Ibid.

32. Joe Gergen, "Martinezes: Deadly Double," *New York Newsday*, 10/8/95, 4.

33. Harper, "Martinez the Grand Mariner," 67.

34. Jeff Bradley, "To Yanks, Edgar Slam Is Force 5," *New York Daily News*, 10/8/95, 65.

35. Phone interview with Butterfield, 2/25/07.

36. Murray Chass, "The Mariners' 10th Man May Be the Kingdome," *New York Times*, 10/8/95, sec. 8, p. 9.

37. Mike Lupica, "Yankee Daze Turns into Wasted Nite," *New York Daily News*, 10/8/95, 64.

38. Andrew Gross, "Quantum Leap," *Yankees Magazine* 16, no. 6 (8/22/95), 20.

39. Phone interview with Showalter, 2/24/07.
40. Referenced during ABC's broadcast of Game 4.
41. Sherwin, "M's Finally Get Some Relief," D14.
42. Charlton interview.
43. Ibid.
44. Ibid.
45. Ibid.
46. Art Thiel, "Mariners' 'Crazy' Lefties, Fans Show Yankees a Little Attitude," *Seattle Post-Intelligencer*, 10/7/95, C1.
47. Charlton interview.
48. Jack O'Connell, "Wetteland Goes Along for the Ride," *Hartford Courant*, 4/28/95, C1.
49. Joel Sherman, *Birth of a Dynasty: Behind the Pinstripes with the 1996 Yankees* (Holtzbrinck Publishers, 2006), 292.
50. Showalter interview.
51. Referenced during ABC's broadcast of Game 4.
52. Bill Madden, "Wette's Pretty 'Ugly,'" *New York Daily News*, 10/8/95, 66.
53. Tyrone Beason, "Mariners' Voice Niehaus Floating on Air," *Seattle Times*, 10/8/95, A23.
54. Bob Finnigan, "Take It to the Limit: Edgar's 2 Homers, 7 RBI's Drive M's into Series Finale," *Seattle Times*, 10/8/95, D1.
55. Madden, "Wette's Pretty 'Ugly,'" 66.
56. Referenced during ABC's broadcast of Game 4.
57. Sherwin, "M's Finally Get Some Relief," D14.
58. Ibid.
59. Jennifer Frey, "E. Martinez Powers Mariners to Game 5," *Washington Post*, 10/8/95, D01.
60. Ibid.
61. Madden, "Wette's Pretty 'Ugly,'" 66.
62. Bradley, "To Yanks," 65.
63. O'Connell, "See Ya," E1.
64. Jack Curry, "For the Yankees, the Unthinkable Is Here: Game 5," *New York Times*, 10/8/95, sec. 8, p. 1.

10. Game 5: Warriors, Heroes, and Heartbreak

1. Phone interview with Showalter, 2/24/07.
2. Phone interview with Piniella, 2/23/07.
3. Ian O'Connor, "Captain Leads Yanks on the Field and through Battle," *New York Daily News*, 10/9/95, 47.
4. Bob Ryan, "Sky Is the Limit under Kingdome: Encore May Blow the Roof Off Playoffs," *Boston Globe*, 10/10/95, 61.
5. Phone interview with McDowell, 11/20/06.

6. Phone interview with Leyritz, 2/28/07.
7. Phone interview with Stanley, 2/24/07.
8. Referenced during ABC's broadcast of Game 5.
9. Phone interview with Bosio, 10/3/07.
10. In-person interview with Griffin, 11/8/07.
11. Art Thiel, "Game's Final Play Puts Finishing Touch on Sprawling Series," *Seattle Post-Intelligencer*, 10/9/95, D2.
12. In-person interview with Cora, 2/18/08.
13. Mike Lupica, "A Night of Drama, Don, Junior in Starring Roles," *New York Daily News*, 10/9/95, 22.
14. Showalter interview.
15. In-person interview with Sherlock, 5/5/07.
16. Referenced during NBC's broadcast of Game 1.
17. Referenced during ABC's broadcast of Game 5.
18. "Johnson May Start on Friday: Relief Job in Game 5 Only Second as a Mariner," *Seattle Post-Intelligencer*, 10/9/95, D2.
19. Murray Chass, "Yanks Can't Recapture the Magic from 1976," *New York Times*, 10/9/95, C9.
20. Jack O'Connell, "Striking Out with The Boss," *Hartford Courant*, 10/9/95, C4.
21. Phone interview with Strange, 12/18/06.
22. Showalter interview.
23. Strange interview.
24. Jim Street, "Yankees Go Home: Edgar's Two Run Double in 11th Saves Mariners," *Seattle Post-Intelligencer*, 10/9/95, D1.
25. Ibid.
26. Strange interview.
27. Chass, "Yanks Can't Recapture the Magic," 9.
28. Mike Blowers, "Mariners Were Just Like Their Fans: They Never Quit Believing," *Seattle Post-Intelligencer*, 10/9/95, D3.
29. Phone interview with David Sussman, 9/5/07.
30. McDowell interview.
31. Phone interview with Down, 6/5/08.
32. Phone interview with Charlton, 2/6/07.
33. Phone interview with Boggs, 5/15/07.
34. Bob Finnigan, "Miracle Mariners: Pair of Aces, Edgar's Clutch Hit Ends Series for the Ages in 11th," *Seattle Times*, 10/9/95, E1.
35. Ibid.
36. Sherlock interview.
37. Bud Withers, "Surprise: NY Owner Upbeat," *Seattle Post-Intelligencer*, 10/9/95, D4.

38. David Lennon, "Yankees Left Domestruck: Lose after Taking Lead in 11th," *Newsday*, 10/9/95, A54.

39. Nick Daschel, "Martinez Speaks Loudly with Big Stick," Clark County (WA) *Columbian*, 10/9/95, B3.

40. Referenced during ABC's broadcast of Game 5.

41. Ibid.

42. Phone interview with Velarde, 7/23/08.

43. Bob Ryan, "The Miracles Never Ceased," *Boston Globe*, 10/9/95, 39.

44. Ed Barmakian, "Cora Stood Tall for the Mariners," *Trenton Times*, 10/9/95, B1.

45. Joel Sherman, *Birth of a Dynasty: Behind the Pinstripes with the 1996 Yankees* (Holtzbrinck Publishers, 2006), 23.

46. McDowell interview.

47. Ibid.

48. Joe Gergen, "Victory Makes Seattle Perk Up," *New York Newsday*, 10/10/95, A58.

49. Bosio interview.

50. Sussman interview.

51. Phone interview with Martinez, 1/30/08.

52. Boggs interview.

53. Street, "Yankees Go Home," D1.

54. In-person interview with Perlozzo, 2/16/08.

55. Finnigan, "Miracle Mariners," E1.

56. Piniella interview.

57. Leyritz interview.

58. Velarde interview.

11. Deconstructing the Yankees

1. Bill Madden, "A Permanent End for Some," *New York Daily News*, 10/9/95, 46.

2. Jeff Bradley, "Yanks Get Last Looks," *New York Daily News*, 10/10/95, 47.

3. Joe Gergen, "Starters Made Final Decision," *New York Newsday*, 10/9/95, A53.

4. Phone interview with Leyritz, 2/28/07.

5. Phone interview with Butterfield, 2/25/07.

6. Steve Jacobson, "For Mattingly, a Job Well Done," *New York Newsday*, 10/9/95, A55.

7. Phone interview with Sussman, 9/5/07.

8. Madden, "A Permanent End," 46.

9. Jack Curry, "Yanks Awaken to the Dim Light of the Off Season," *New York Times*, 10/10/95, B9.

10. Leyritz interview.

11. Ian O'Connor, "Captain Leads Yanks on Field and through Battle," *New York Daily News*, 10/9/95, 47.

12. Mike Lupica, "Don Gives Everything and Maybe That's All," *New York Daily News*, 10/10/95, 46.

13. Bradley, "Yanks Get Last Looks," 47.

14. Lupica, "Don Gives Everything," 46.

15. Ian O'Connor, "File Under 'Classic' Yanks–Mariners: One for the Ages," *New York Daily News*, 10/10/95.

16. David Lennon, "Yankees Left Domestruck: Lose after Taking Lead in 11th," *New York Newsday*, 10/9/95, A54.

17. Bill Madden, "Lou Finds Route to Make Bronx Seem Far Away," *New York Daily News*, 10/10/95, 53.

18. Mike Lupica, "Dive Bombers Take Last Fall: Yanks, Buck Cry, Cry Again," *New York Daily News*, 10/9/95, 44.

19. Ibid.

20. Phone interview with O'Neill, 3/7/07.

21. Bob Raissman, "Yankee Voices Feel Pain, Loss Hurts Waldman, Kay," *New York Daily News*, 10/10/95, 48.

22. "Steinbrenner Won't Talk about Future," *Portland Oregonian*, 10/9/95, C04.

23. Phone interview with Sterling, 2/13/08.

24. Phone interview with Down, 6/5/08.

25. Sussman interview.

26. Phone interview with McDowell, 11/20/06.

27. Phone interview with Stanley, 2/24/07.

28. Roger Angell, *A Pitcher's Story: Innings with David Cone* (New York: Warner Books, 2001), 12.

29. Phone interview with Mattingly, 4/2/08.

30. Phone interview with Boggs, 5/15/07.

31. Raissman, "Yankee Voices Feel Pain," 48.

32. Butterfield interview.

33. Showalter interview.

34. Raissman, "Yankee Voices Feel Pain," 48.

35. Angell, *A Pitcher's Story*, 12.

36. Mattingly interview.

37. Jack Curry, "Showalter Return in '96 Is Hinted by Michael," *New York Times*, 10/19/95, B17.

38. Jon Heyman, "A Stick Shift? Yanks GM to Become Top Scout," *New York Newsday*, 10/16/95, A54.

39. John Harper, "Stick with Buck, Michael Sees Offer Coming," *New York Daily News*, 10/19/95, 76.

40. Joel Sherman, *Birth of a Dynasty: Behind the Pinstripes with the 1996 Yankees* (Holtzbrinck Publishers, 2006), 34.

41. Heyman, "A Stick Shift?" A54.

42. Jack O'Connell, "Showalter Won't Return," *Hartford Courant*, 10/27/95, C1.

43. Jeff Bradley, "Boss to Toss Odd Bouquet Buck to End, One of the Guys," *New York Daily News*, 10/28/95, 40.

44. Mike Lupica, "Crawl Back? Buck Passes He's No Quitter, But Boss Qualifies," *New York Daily News*, 10/27/95, 88.

45. Murray Chass, "No Yankee Jacket Required: Is Showalter In or Out?" *New York Times*, 10/27/95, B13.

46. Ibid.

47. O'Connell, "Showalter Won't Return," C1.

48. Lupica, "Crawl Back?" 88.

49. Sherman, *Birth of a Dynasty*, 34.

50. Jeff Bradley, "Buck Bashers Aim to Sleaze Connors: Showalter Portrait of Paranoia," *New York Daily News*, 10/29/95, 46.

51. Joe Gergen, "As the Yankees Turn, George Stomps All Over Sport," *New York Newsday*, 10/28/95, A47.

52. Ibid.

53. Lupica, "Crawl Back?" 88.

54. Dave Anderson, "Showalter Too Classy for George," *New York Times*, 10/28/95, sec. 1, p. 27.

55. Mike Lupica, "Below Average Joe," *New York Daily News*, 10/31/95, 49.

56. Sherman, *Birth of a Dynasty*, 32.

57. Jon Heyman, "Girardi's In, Stanley's Out," *New York Newsday*, 11/21/95, A58.

58. John Harper, "Yanks Get Rockie, Throw Out Stanley," *New York Daily News*, 11/21/95, 50.

59. Sherman, *Birth of a Dynasty*, 302.

60. Jack Curry, "Mattingly Makes Speech, but Not Quite a Farewell," *New York Times*, 11/22/95, B11.

61. Jack O'Connell, "Yanks: Opening at First?" *Hartford Courant*, 11/22/95, C1.

62. John Harper, "Randy Leaves with Last of Yank Class of '95," *New York Daily News*, 11/23/95, 88.

63. Jack Curry, "Velarde Becomes Latest Yank to Hit the Road," *New York Times*, 11/23/95, B21.

64. Harper, "Randy Leaves," 88.

65. John Giannone, "A Confused Straw Axed," *New York Daily News*, 12/1/95, 103.

66. Jack Curry, "Yankees Won't Be Giving Strawberry a Second Chance," *New York Times*, 12/1/95, B19.

67. Jack Curry, "Yanks Get Martinez for Davis, Hitchcock," *New York Times*, 12/8/95, B19.
68. Jack O'Connell, "It's Martinez's Job: Yankees Sign First Baseman for Five Years," *Hartford Courant*, 12/8/95, C1.
69. Murray Chass, "In a Flurry of Activity, Free Agents Choose Their Teams," *New York Times*, 12/15/95, B9.
70. John Giannone, "Yankees Get the Big Chill, Top Names Give Cold Shoulder," *New York Daily News*, 12/15/95, 118.
71. Sherman, *Birth of a Dynasty*, 51.
72. Ibid., 198.

12. Safeco Is Born

1. Phone interview with Piniella, 2/23/07.
2. Phone interview with Belcher, 3/14/07.
3. Phone interview with Bosio, 10/3/07.
4. Ellis E. Conklin and Steve Miletech, "M's Do It: Fans Give M's Wild Ovation," *Seattle Post-Intelligencer*, 10/9/95, A1.
5. Steve Kelley, "Seattle Holds Nothing Back as Storybook Run Continues," *Seattle Times*, 10/9/95, E1.
6. Mike Blowers, "Mariners Were Just Like Their Fans: They Never Quit Believing," *Seattle Post-Intelligencer*, 10/9/95, D3.
7. Ian O'Connor, "File under 'Classic' Yanks-Mariners: One for the Ages," *New York Daily News*, 10/10/95.
8. Tom Pedulla, "Seattle Lives Up to Slogan: 'Refuse to Lose,'" *USA Today*, 10/9/95, 1C.
9. Phone interview with Buhner, 11/8/07.
10. Nick Daschel, "Martinez Speaks Loudly with Big Stick," *Clark County (WA) Columbian*, 10/9/95, B3.
11. Bob Finnigan, "Miracle Mariners: Pair of Aces, Edgar's Clutch Hit End Series for the Ages in 11th," *Seattle Times*, 10/9/95, E1.
12. Seattle Post-Intelligencer, *A Magic Season: The Year the Mariners Made Seattle a Baseball Town* (Seattle: P-I Books, 1995), 93.
13. Conklin, "M's Do It," A1.
14. Jennifer Bjorhus, Eric Pryne, and Sarah Lopez Williams, "M's Tide Rolls On," *Seattle Times*, 10/9/95, A1.
15. Rudy Martzke, "Markets Switch to Follow Mariners," *USA Today*, 10/10/95, 2C.
16. Steven Goldsmith, "Mariners Earn Record TV Ratings," *Seattle Post-Intelligencer*, 10/10/95, C1.
17. Ellis E. Conklin, "Niehaus Leads Cheers at Rally for Mariners," *Seattle Post-Intelligencer*, 10/10/95, C4.

18. Ibid.
19. Bjorhus, "M's Tide Rolls On," A1.
20. Ibid.
21. Conklin, "M's Do It," A1.
22. Angelo Bruscas, "Blowers Rediscovers Aggressiveness at Bat," *Seattle Post-Intelligencer*, 10/11/95, D3.
23. David Postman, "Republicans Say Stadium Plan Needs Major Fixes," *Seattle Times*, 10/12/95, A1.
24. Ibid.
25. "Legislators Ignoring Economic Reality in Argument against M's," *Seattle Post Intelligencer*, 10/15/95, E2.
26. Michael Paulson, "Pressure Put Stadium over the Top: Lobbying and Fan Support Unprecedented," *Seattle Post-Intelligencer*, 10/16/95, B1.
27. "Legislators," *Seattle Post Intelligencer*, E2.
28. Larry Lange, "Baseball Fans Rally at Capitol for Stadium Financing," *Seattle Post-Intelligencer*, 10/13/95, A12.
29. "Legislators," *Seattle Post-Intelligencer*, E2.
30. David Postman, "House Passes Bill to Fund Stadium, But Not Dome Upgrades," *Seattle Times*, 10/14/95, A1.
31. Ibid.
32. Michael Paulson and Ed Penhale, "Stadium Deal One Step Closer: House Votes Yes, Senate No; Legislators to Return Today," *Seattle Post-Intelligencer*, 10/14/95, A1.
33. Interview with Armstrong, 11/8/07
34. David Postman, "Legislature OK's Plan for Stadium: But County Must Pass Taxes; Dome Repairs Not Covered," *Seattle Times*, 10/15/95, A1.
35. Ibid.
36. Ed Penhale, "It's Thumbs Up for Baseball Stadium," *Seattle Post-Intelligencer*, 10/24/95, A1.
37. "County Council Must Just Say 'Yes,'" *Seattle Post-Intelligencer*, 10/16/95, A7.
38. Ed Penhale, "Stadium Deal Puts Council in Hot Seat: Members Are Keen on Team But Wary on Plan," *Seattle Post-Intelligencer*, 10/16/95, A1.
39. Ibid.
40. Ed Penhale, "County Council Hammered on Stadium Package Laments," *Seattle Post-Intelligencer*, 10/18/95, A1.
41. David Schaefer and David Postman, "Stadium Gets OK: Next Issue Is Site," *Seattle Times*, 10/24/95, A1.
42. Ellis E. Conklin, "Jay Saves the Day: Buhner's Blast Gives M's 5-2 Win," *Seattle Post-Intelligencer*, 10/14/95, A1.
43. Bob Finnigan, "Benes, M's Hitter Flop: Piniella Shakes Up Lineup," *Seattle Post-Intelligencer*, 10/15/95, D1.

44. Jim Street, "Down to the Dome: Thome's HR Puts M's Down 3-2 in Series," *Seattle Post-Intelligencer*, 10/16/95, C1.

45. Ibid.

46. Ellis E. Conklin, "Thanks for the Ride M's: The Party's Over as Indians Go to the Series," *Seattle Post-Intelligencer*, 10/18/95, A1.

47. Steve Kelley, "Kingdome Fans Laud M's, Demand Encore for Baseball," *Seattle Times*, 10/18/95, D1.

48. Angelo Bruscas, "Fans' Show of Support after Loss Moves Piniella," *Seattle Post-Intelligencer*, 10/18/95, D5.

49. Conklin, "Thanks for the Ride," A1.

50. Art Thiel, *Out of Leftfield: How the Mariners Made Baseball Fly in Seattle* (Seattle: Sasquatch Books, 2003), 144.

51. "Mariners Fans Gather for Groundbreaking," *Portland Oregonian*, 3/9/97, C07.

52. Ed Penhale, "A Big Signing for the M's: Safeco Field," *Seattle Post-Intelligencer*, 6/5/98, A1.

53. Ibid.

54. Thiel, *Out of Leftfield*, 163.

55. "Mariners Fans," *Portland Oregonian*, C07.

56. Alan Snel and Ellis E. Conklin, "Fans Give New Ballyard High-Fives: Opening Night's Crowd Agog—It Loves the Place," *Seattle Post-Intelligencer*, 7/16/99, A8.

57. Ibid.

58. Blaine Newnham, "The Eye's the Limit as Outdoor Palaces Graces City Lineup," *Seattle Times*, 7/16/95, D1.

59. Ronald Tillery, "Players Unsure How Park Will Affect Them: M's Not Yet Settled in New Home," *Seattle Post-Intelligencer*, 7/16/99, E1.

60. Holly Cain, "Safeco Impresses Visitors: Padres Say Atmosphere Similar to Classic Parks in Phoenix and Denver," *Seattle Post-Intelligencer*, 7/16/96, E7.

61. Angelo Bruscas, "Owners Use Opener to Focus on Baseball: Politics Set Aside for Celebration," *Seattle Post-Intelligencer*, 7/16/99, E2.

62. Ibid.

63. Robert L. Jamieson, "Gone in 16.8 Seconds: Perfect Demolition Leaves Dome a Fallen Souffle," *Seattle Post-Intelligencer*, 3/27/00, E1; Lisa Stiffler, "The Big Tumble Makes a Rumble," *Seattle Post-Intelligencer*, 3/27/00, A13.

64. Vanessa Ho, "The Crowds: They Came, They Saw and They Were Conquered," *Seattle Post-Intelligencer*, 3/27/00.

65. Jamieson, "Gone in 16.8 Seconds," E1.

66. Ibid.

67. Ho, "The Crowds," 3/27/00.

INDEX

ABOUT THE AUTHOR

Chris Donnelly is a graduate of the College of New Jersey and a life-long baseball fan. He resides in the Trenton-Princeton, New Jersey, area with his wife, Jamie.